AF413171

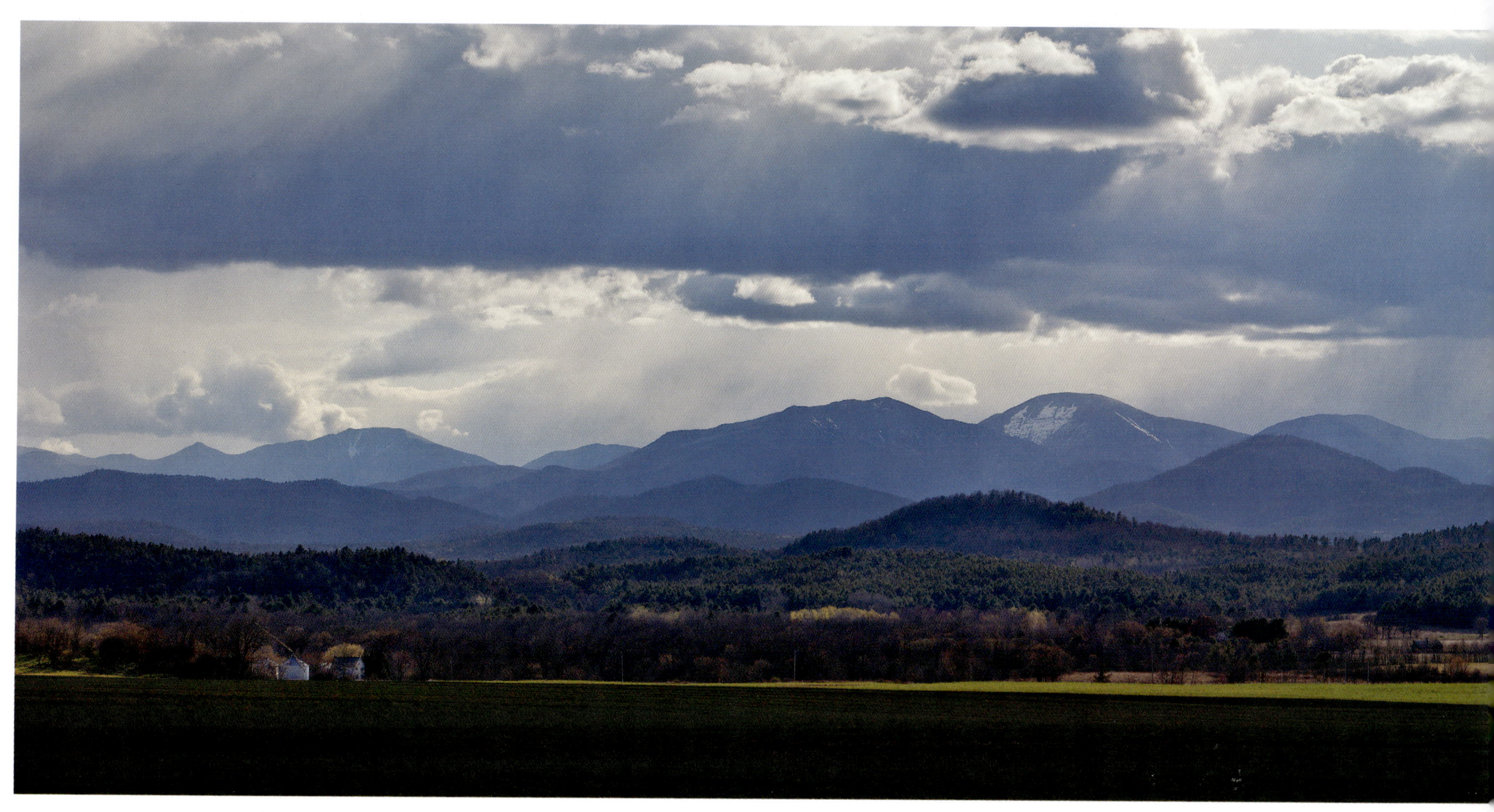

Looking west toward the High Peaks over farmland in the eastern foothills of the Adirondacks.

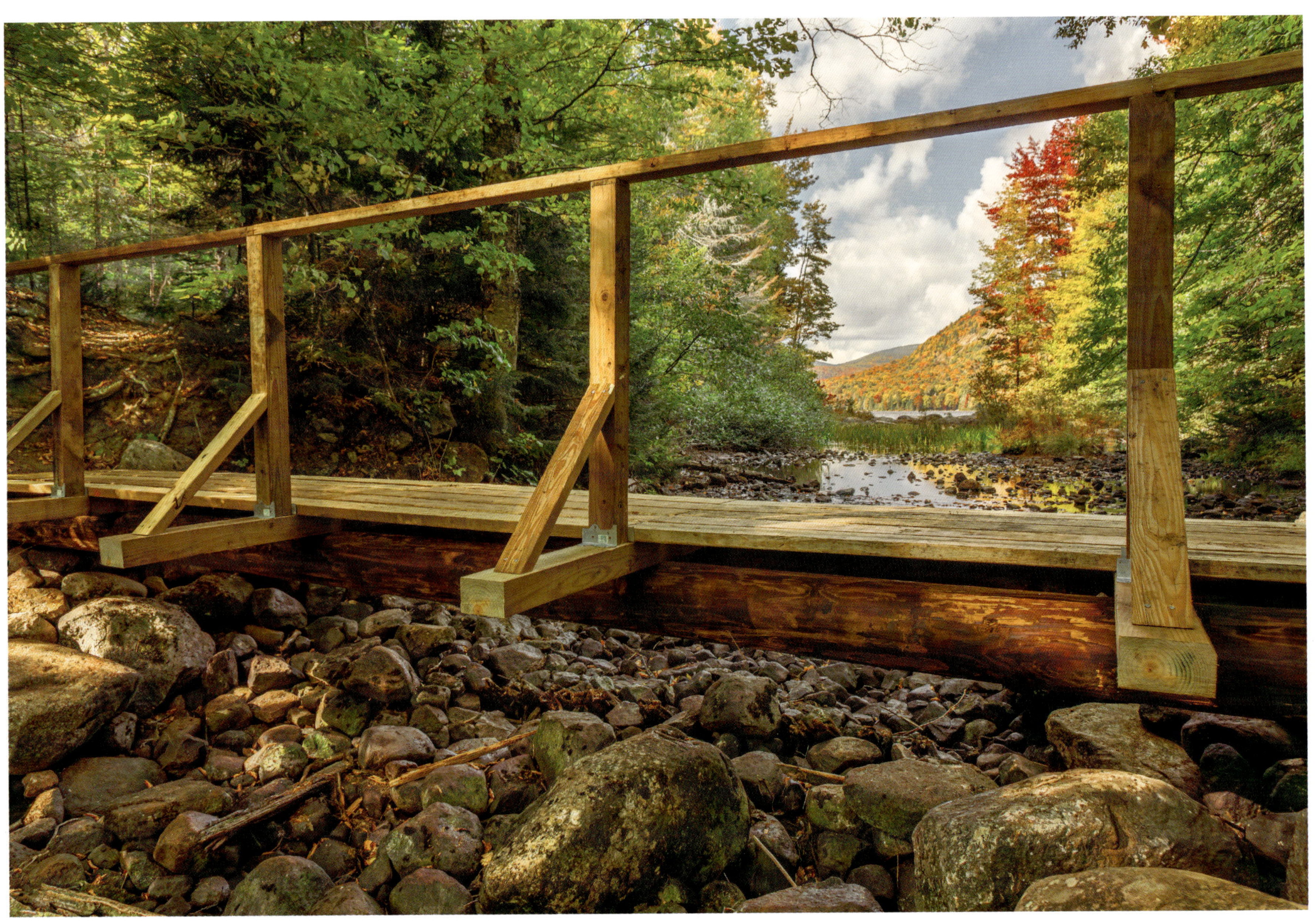

Bridge over Tirrel Pond outflow along the Northville-Placid trail.

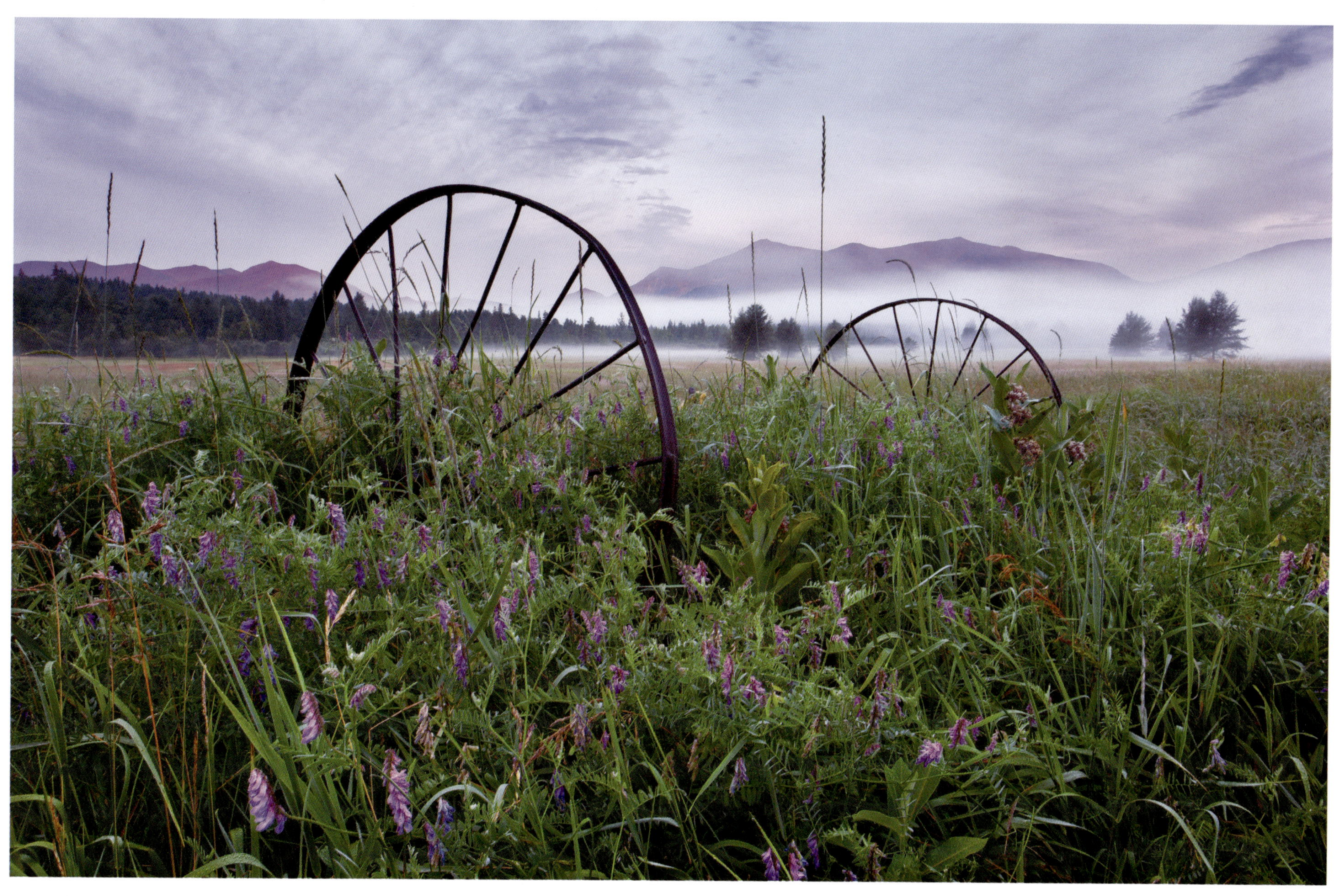

A rusted old farm implement in an abandoned farm meadow in Wilmington at sunrise. The Sentinel Range is in the background. The purple of the sunrise nearly perfectly matched the purple wildflowers in the foreground.

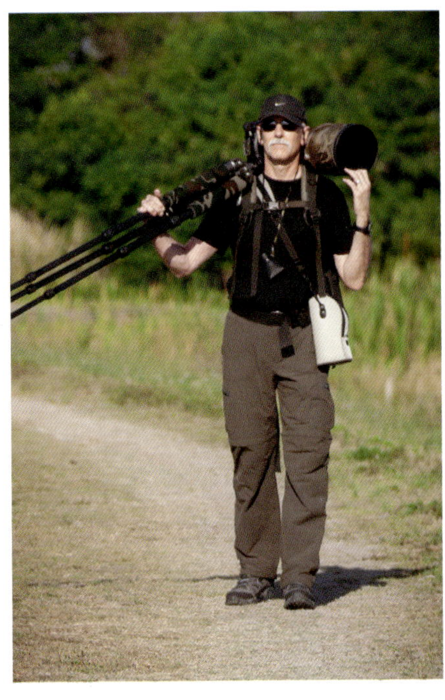

It was around this time that I got even more serious about photography. I spent fifteen years as a cooperative member of a couple of different Adirondack art galleries, and I found success entering juried art shows. Getting accepted into these shows, sharing my prints with gallery customers, and getting published in various Adirondack magazines pushed me toward constant improvement. Now, since I've retired, I've continued this quest and find I have a portfolio of photos that I'm excited to share with others.

In this book I've tried to balance between the big and the small; the grand view and the hidden details. I love the mountains at dawn. My favorite moments are when the stars are still visible and the slightest pink appears in the eastern sky. I'm just sitting on a ledge, waiting for the early light to sweep across the valleys. It's a profoundly spiritual moment before I have to think about exposure or shutter speed or other technical adjustments. I feel like I'm just a small part of the larger world, and I don't have a thought in my head except the sounds around me and the feel of the wind on my face.

But as much as I'm drawn to the mountaintops with their grand views, I find a similar feeling while watching a loon fish under the still waters of a wilderness pond or seeing an eagle dive for breakfast from its perch on a dead tree along the shore. Sometimes the same feeling comes from just watching the morning mist drift like an apparition across a still lake. I love the quality of light in the early morning.

Capturing images of wildlife often requires setting up my tripod and camera the night before, then quietly crawling up to it in the dark before sunrise so I'm not noticed. Or it requires paddling to a point upstream and then drifting silently with the current as the forest grows accustomed to my presence.

You can't rush. It takes hours. But the time isn't wasted. It's a stealth born of reverence as my own thoughts settle like the silt in a lake bottom. Things that were previously hidden are revealed, and the wilderness carries on as if I'm not there. The prize is seeing a fox trot through the undergrowth, witnessing the early sunlight illuminating a deer drinking at the lake edge, or capturing the narrow slip of moon before it's overtaken by the brightness of the sun.

When I go exploring I often have a particular image in mind, but frequently my favorite images emerge in moments of serendipity when I least expect them. So I've learned that, no matter what my expectations are, I need to leave myself open. So I'll paddle or hike to a favorite spot and just see what happens.

I process my digital negatives with the intent of creating a photo that looks just the way the scene appeared when I shot it. I will often combine three exposures, taken in rapid succession (using luminance masking) so that there is good, noise-free detail in the highlights, mid-tones, and shadows. And I continue to explore and hunt for those images that capture a fleeting moment in time, or a scene that might otherwise be missed.

But the most important ingredient for me, when capturing that elusive quality of landscape and light, is the centeredness and resonance I feel when I can just sit and empty myself of everything and find the balance that comes from stillness and solitude. That's when my mental chatter dissipates and my vision seems to expand.

I hope I have succeeded in capturing these scenes in such a way that they strike the same chord when you see them as I felt when I shot them.

The photos in this book are available as prints. Please visit RussHartung Photography.com for contact information and details.

—Russ Hartung

INTRODUCTION

Solitude is the word I used for the title of this book because it captures the feeling I seek when I'm traveling the trails, waterways, and roads of the Adirondack Park.

Solitude is hard to find these days—and harder still to capture in an image. But there's no better place to discover it than the Adirondacks. It's the feeling of being on top of a mountain before sunrise and watching the light change over landscapes of unbroken wilderness that can stretch as far as vision allows. It's the serenity of drifting across a misty lake in my kayak and hearing a loon's echoing call in the distance. It's even the chorus of enveloping rain striking the forest leaves during a sudden thunderstorm—

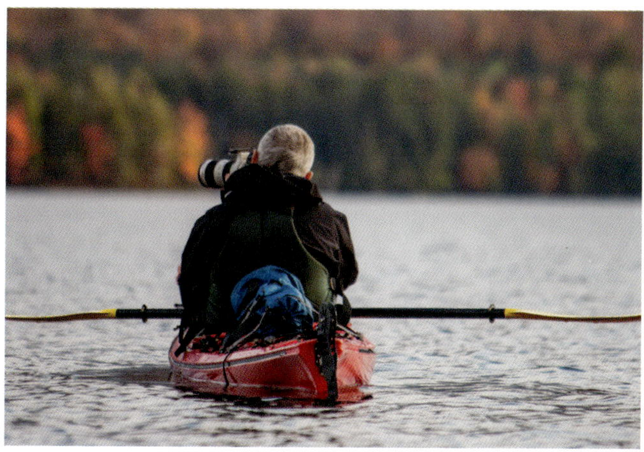

and the symphony of peepers along the shore as I lie in my tent later that evening. And it's the vicarious pleasure I share when I see someone pushing off from a weathered dock to fish a hidden cove; or when I see someone slowly paddling across a shrouded lake in the fog; or when I see a lone figure staring off toward a horizon of overlapping peaks from a rocky outcrop at the end of a hard climb.

I first became fascinated with trying to capture the Adirondacks in photographs when I was around seven years old. My family was coming home from my grandfather's camp on Lake Champlain, and my parents bought me a book of Adirondack postcards. I spent much of the drive reliving our time in the Adirondacks through those images. When I got my first Kodak Brownie camera, I started trying to capture some of those scenes myself.

As I grew up in proximity to the Adirondacks, I came back as often as I could. In addition to our trips to my grandfather's place, I spent two weeks each year at a wilderness-oriented summer camp near Tupper Lake. Then, when applying to medical school, my first choice was Albany, New York, because of its proximity to the Adirondacks. After residency I came back to the Adirondack region for the rest of my career.

During more than thirty years working in the chaos and stress of a busy emergency department, I often sought the solitude of the mountains and waterways to ease the lingering tension. As my career was winding down, I spent more time honing my photographic technique and exploring the park—paddling and backpacking every secluded sanctuary I could find.

To my wife and soulmate Cathy, who put up with many early morning alarms and often worried about me when I was alone in the wilderness. And to my daughter Genna, my fellow photographer and companion who understood and appreciated the hours of waiting and searching for the best images.

Also a big thank-you to Jake Bonar from North Country Books/Globe Pequot, who first recognized the potential for a collection of my Adirondack photographs and was willing to take a chance and advocate for me.

North Country Books
An imprint of The Globe Pequot Publishing Group, Inc.
64 South Main Street
Essex, CT 06426
www.globepequot.com

Distributed by NATIONAL BOOK NETWORK

British Library Cataloguing in Publication Information available

Library of Congress Cataloging-in-Publication Data

Names: Hartung, Russ, 1958– author, photographer.
Title: Adirondack solitude : Peace and stillness in the Adirondack
    wilderness / Russ Hartung.
Description: Essex, CT : North Country Books, [2025] | Summary: "Adirondack
    Solitude will give readers the key to peaceful and meditative presence
    among the Adirondacks no matter where they are"—Provided by publisher.
Identifiers: LCCN 2024061272 (print) | LCCN 2024061273 (ebook) | ISBN
    9781493089819 (cloth ; acid-free paper) | ISBN 9781493089826 (epub)
Subjects: LCSH: Adirondack Mountains (N.Y.)—Pictorial works.
Classification: LCC F127.A2 H435 2025 (print) | LCC F127.A2 (ebook) | DDC
    917.47/500222—dc23/eng/20250226
LC record available at https://lccn.loc.gov/2024061272
LC ebook record available at https://lccn.loc.gov/2024061273

Printed in India

ADIRONDACK SOLITUDE

Peace and Stillness in the Adirondack Wilderness

Photography of
RUSS HARTUNG

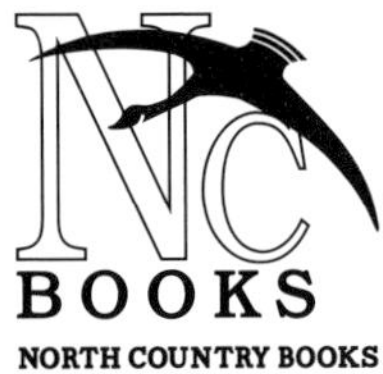

NC BOOKS

NORTH COUNTRY BOOKS

ADIRONDACK SOLITUDE

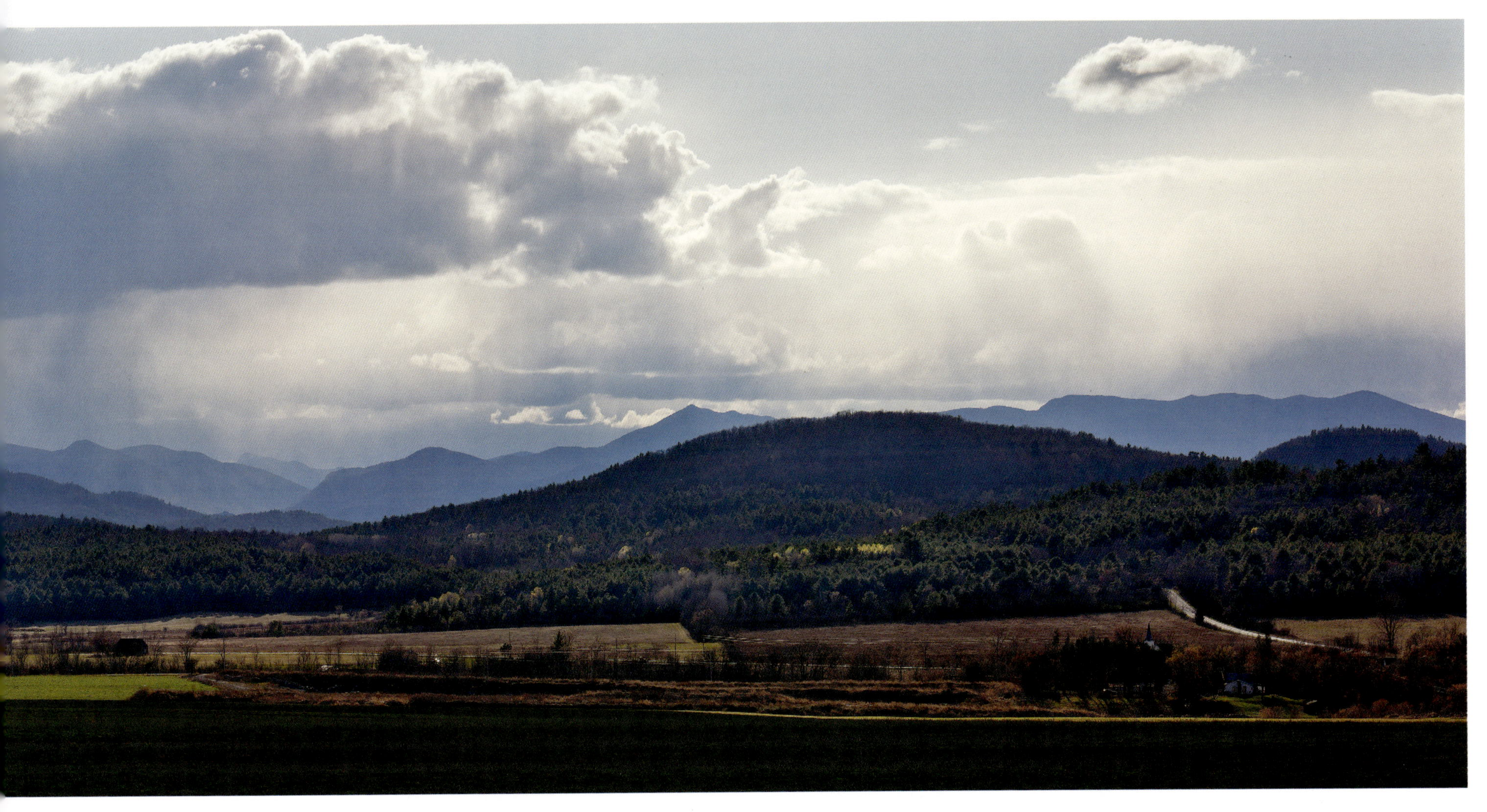

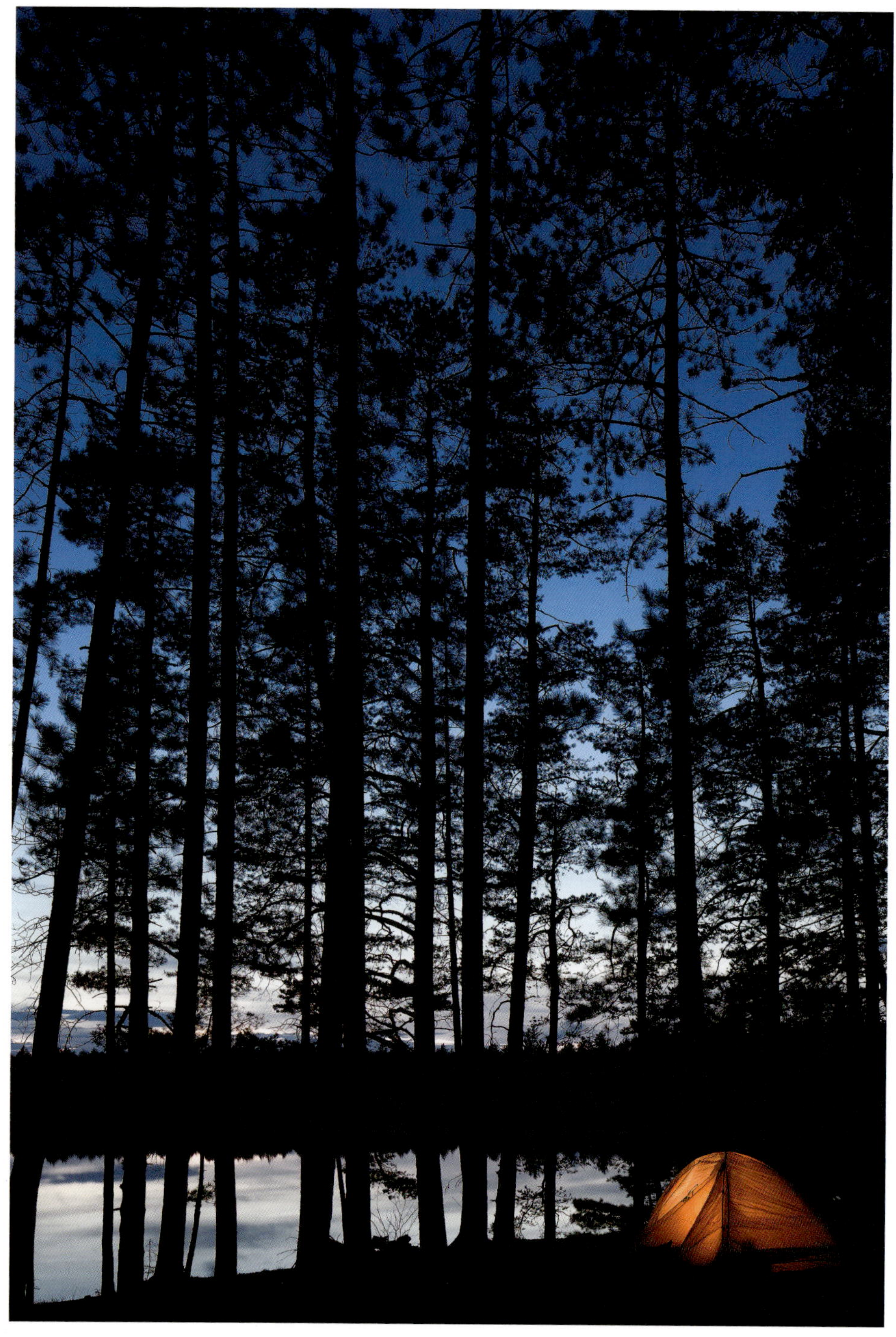

Dusk at a campsite on Little Green Pond.

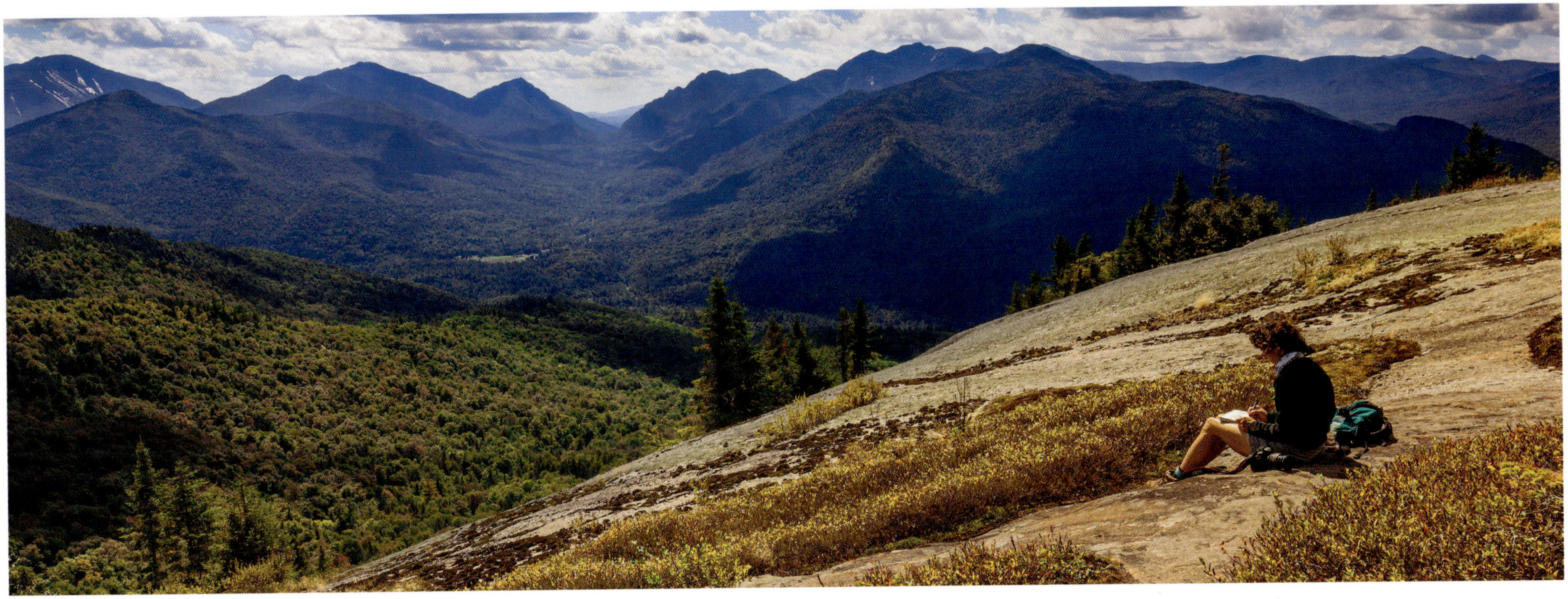

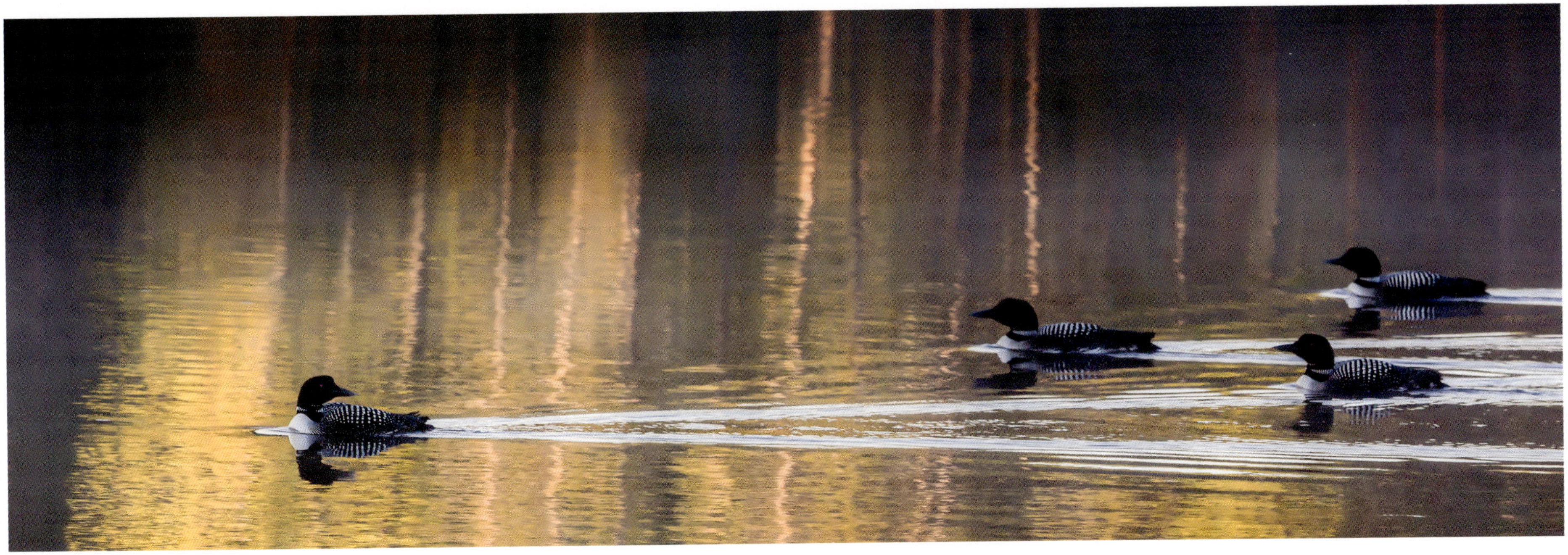

Top: Sketching on top of Hopkins Mountain. *Bottom:* Leader of the pack looks back to check on the rest.

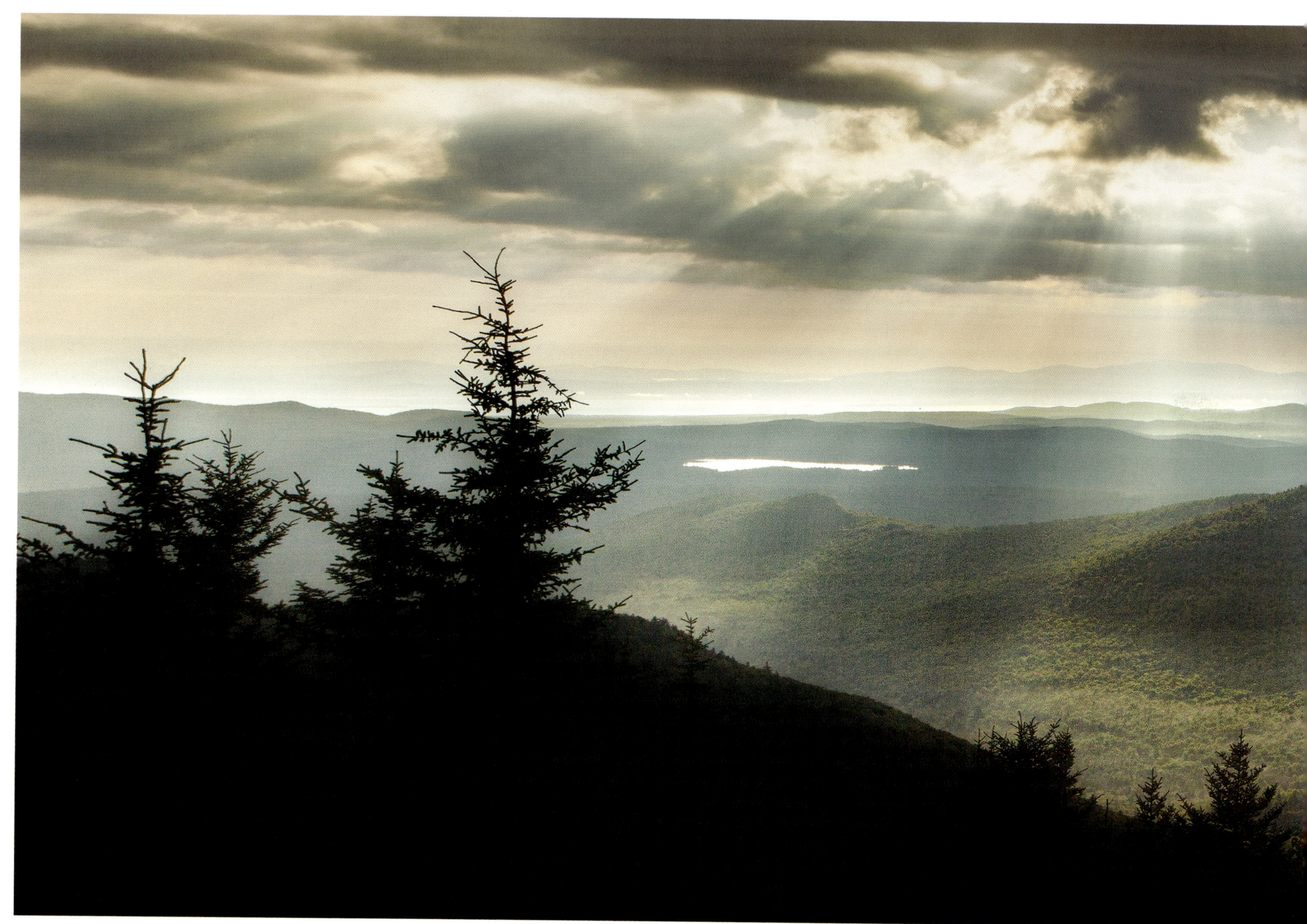

God rays from the top of Catamount Mountain.

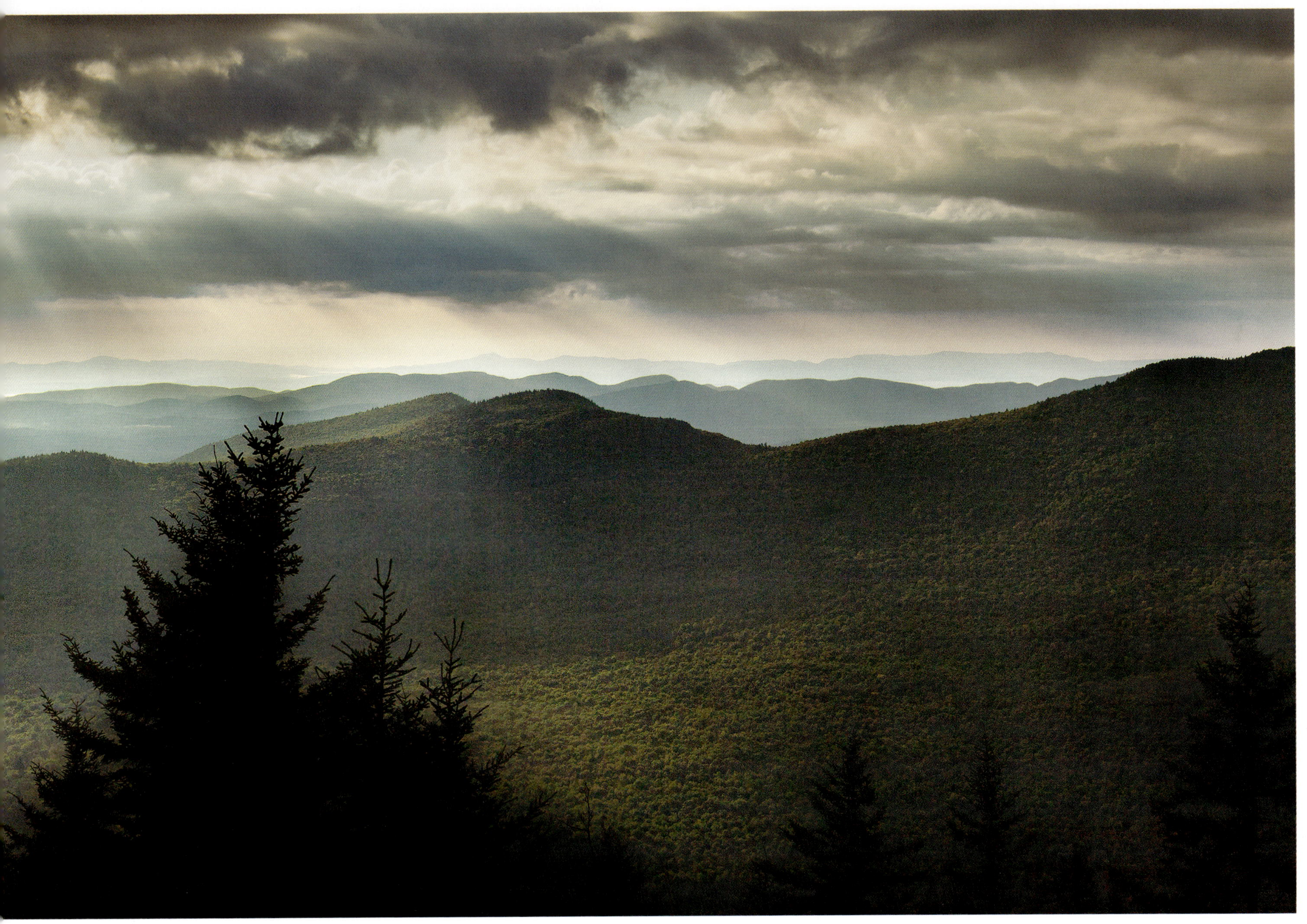

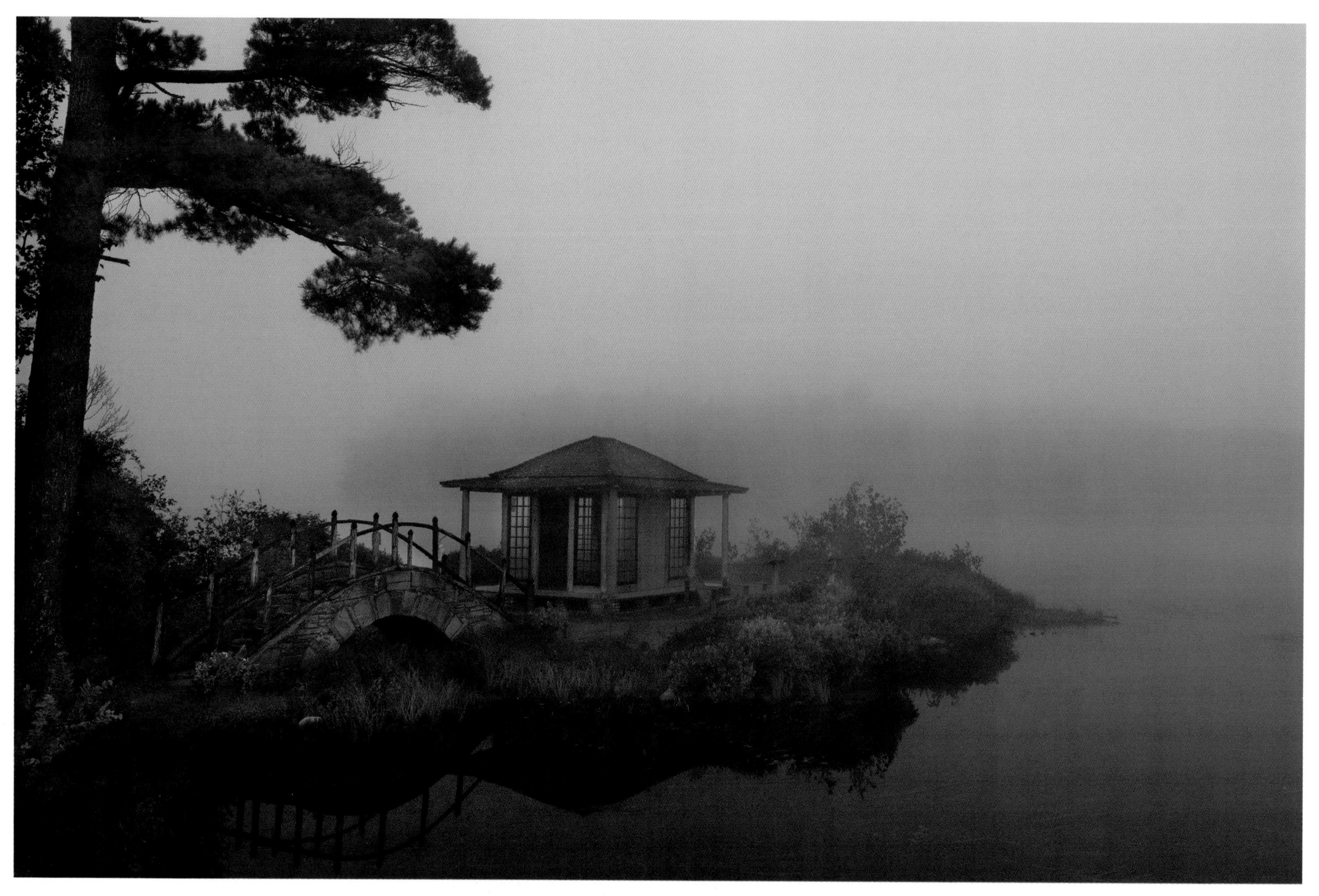

The Tea House at White Pine Camp. This Adirondack "Great Camp" served as the summer White House
(the Camp David of its day) for President Calvin Coolidge in 1926. Among his guests was future president Herbert Hoover.

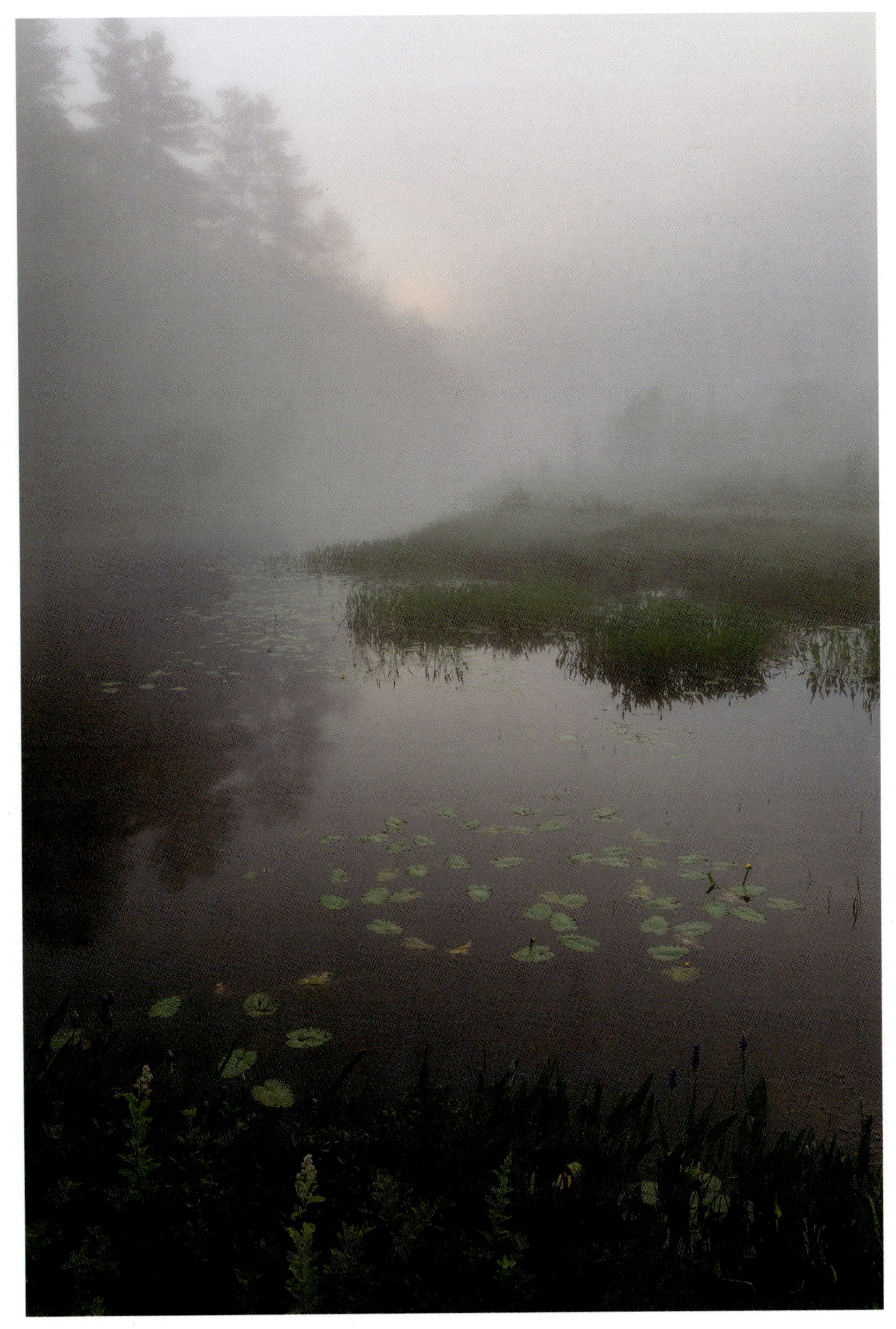

Misty pond and lily pads near Speculator.

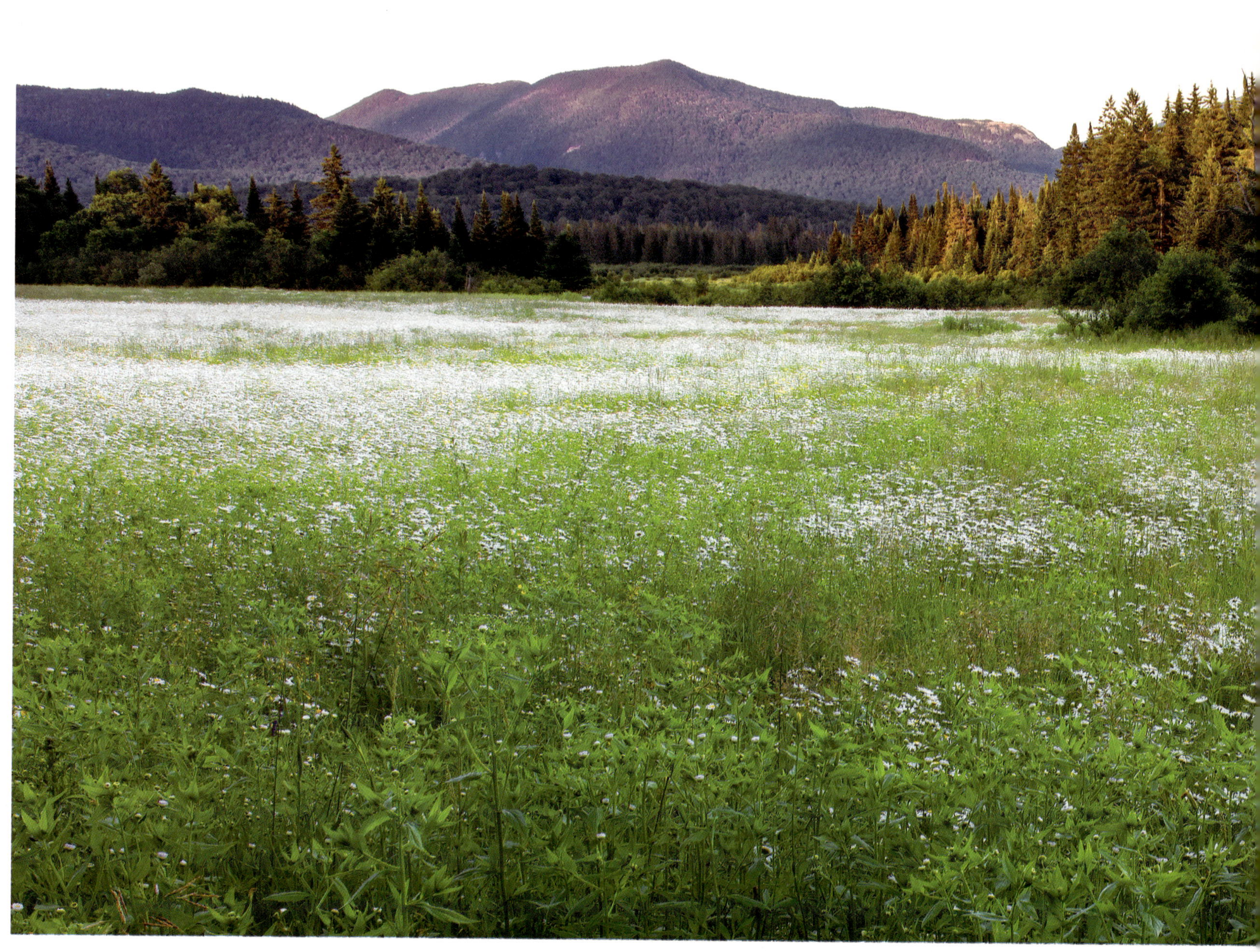

Meadow and distant mountains along the Adirondack Loj Road.

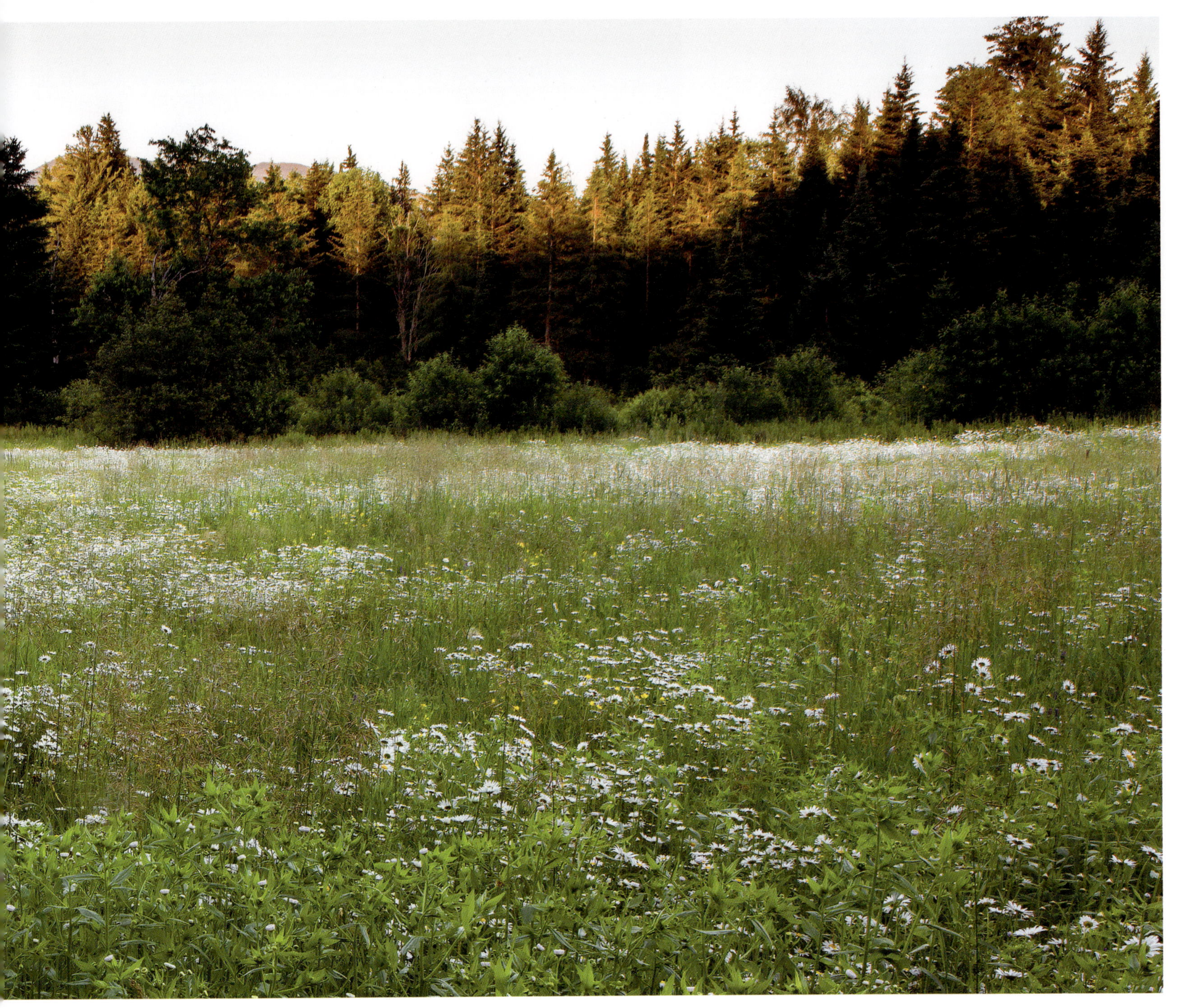

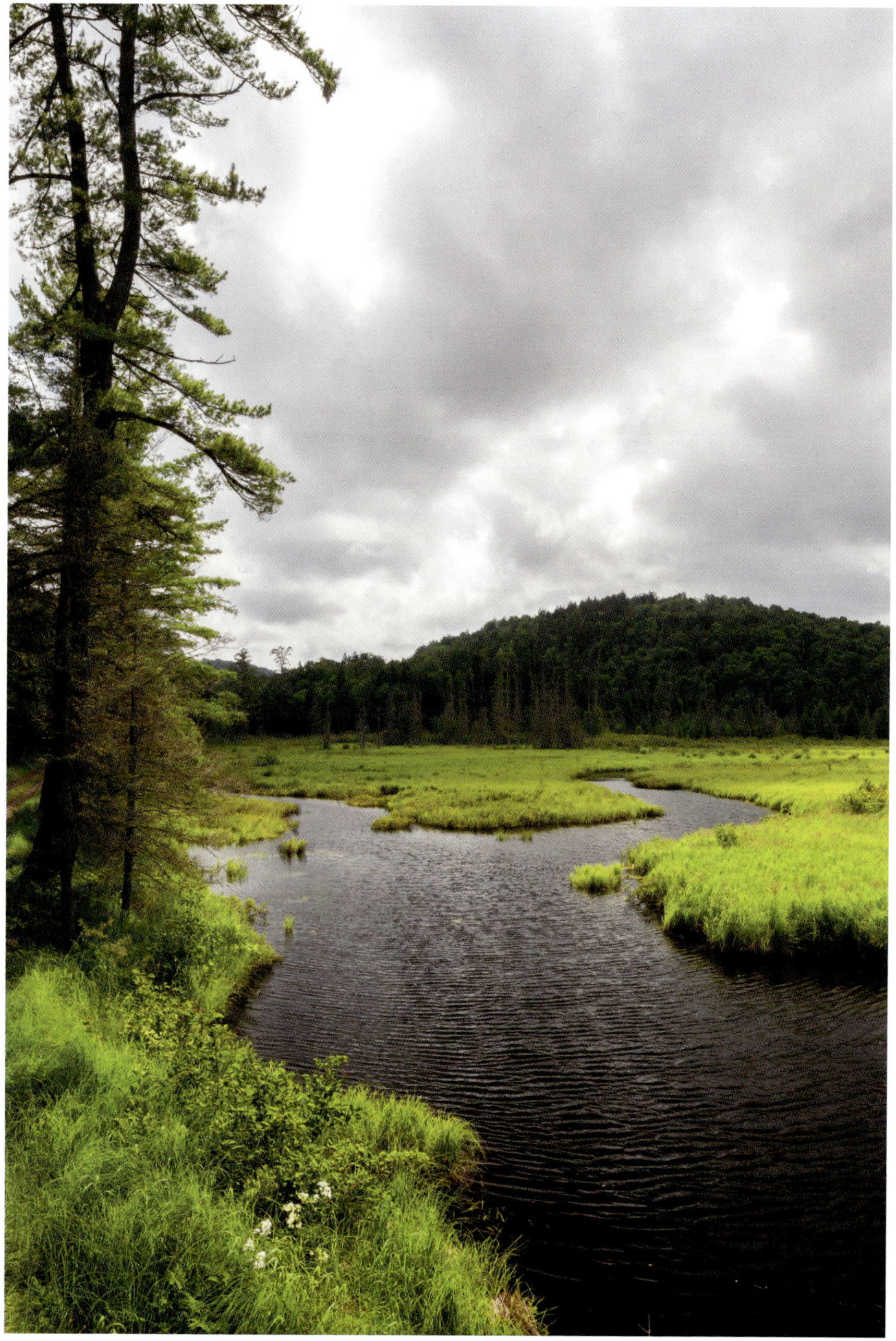

The jungle green of the Adirondacks in July west of Tupper Lake.

Spotlighted section of shoreline opposite Low's Ridge.

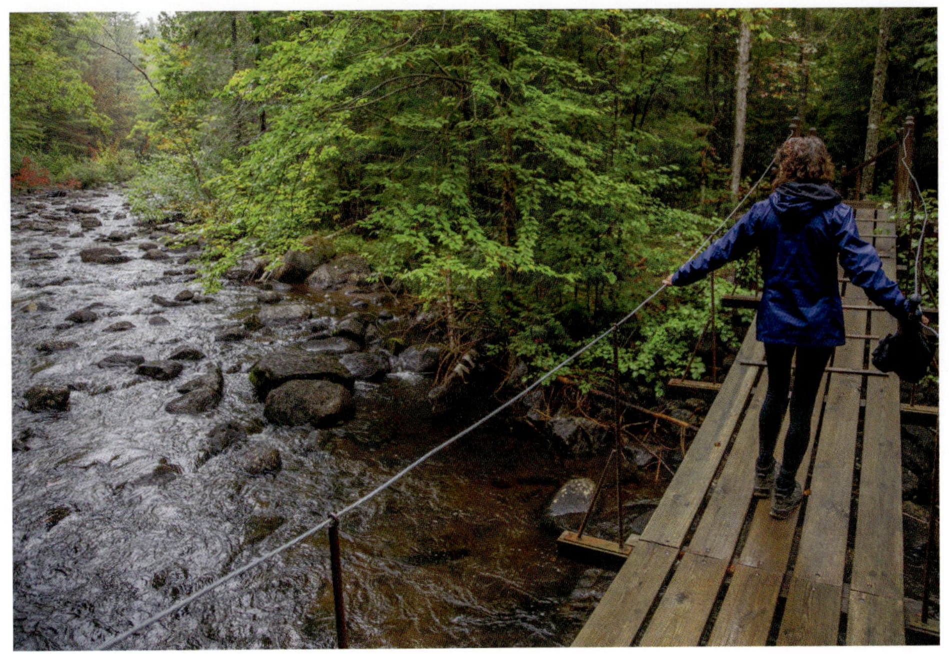

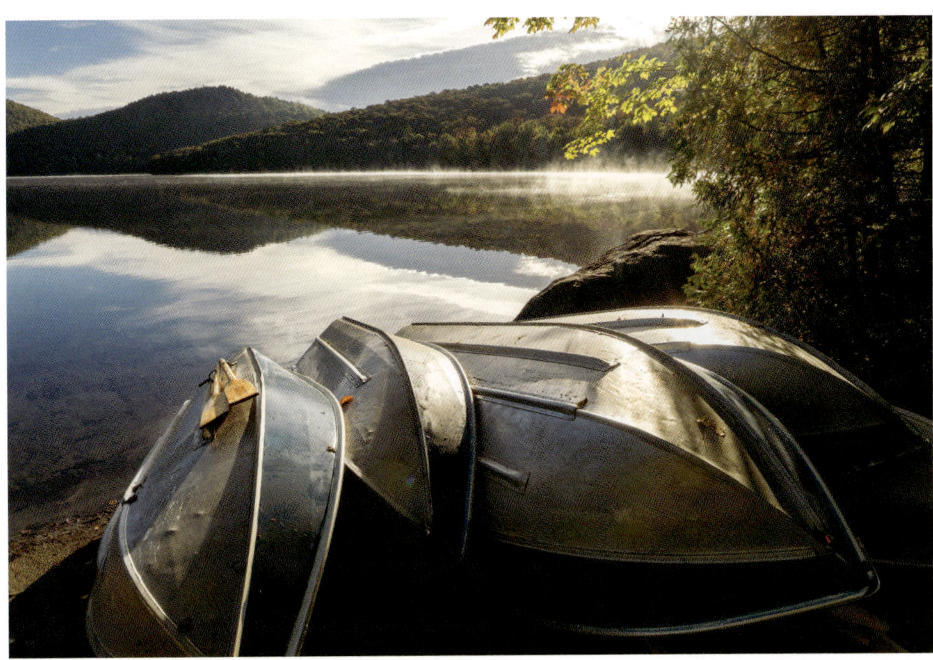

Top: Traversing a stream on a wilderness suspension bridge.
Bottom: Rowboats stacked on the shore at Elk Lake Lodge.

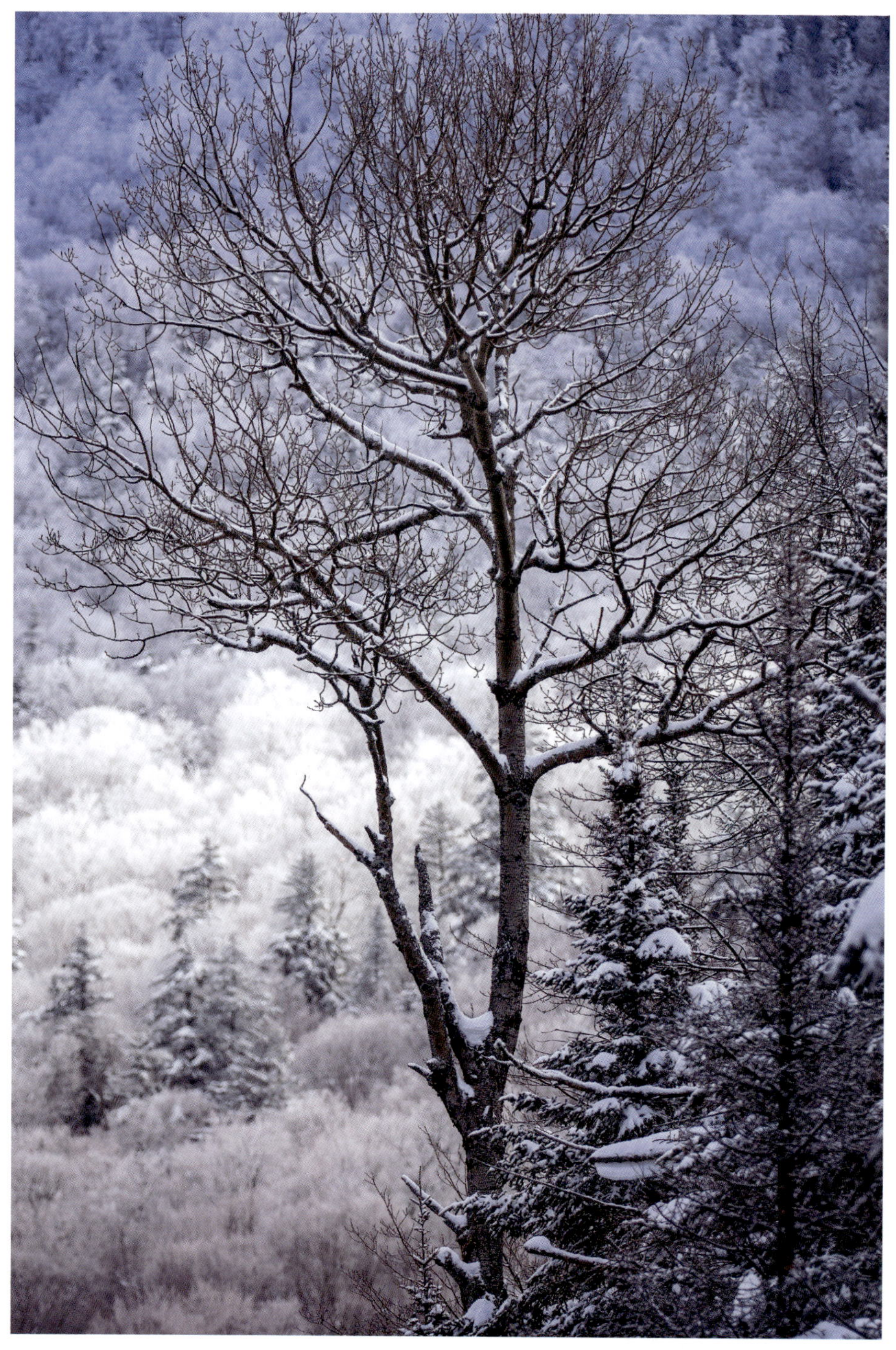

Tree dusted with new snow.

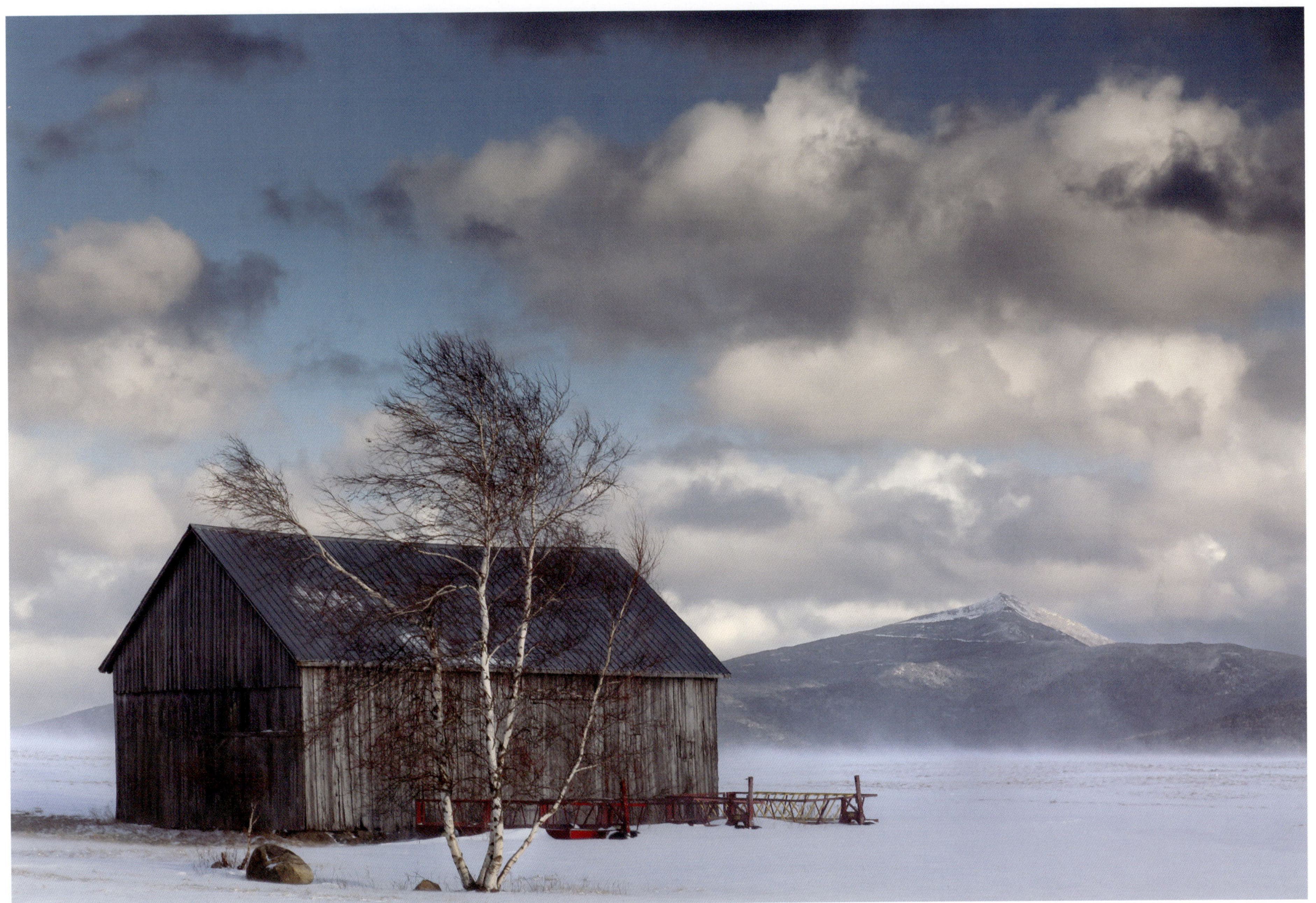

Barn buffeted by wind on a high plateau with Whiteface Mountain in the background.

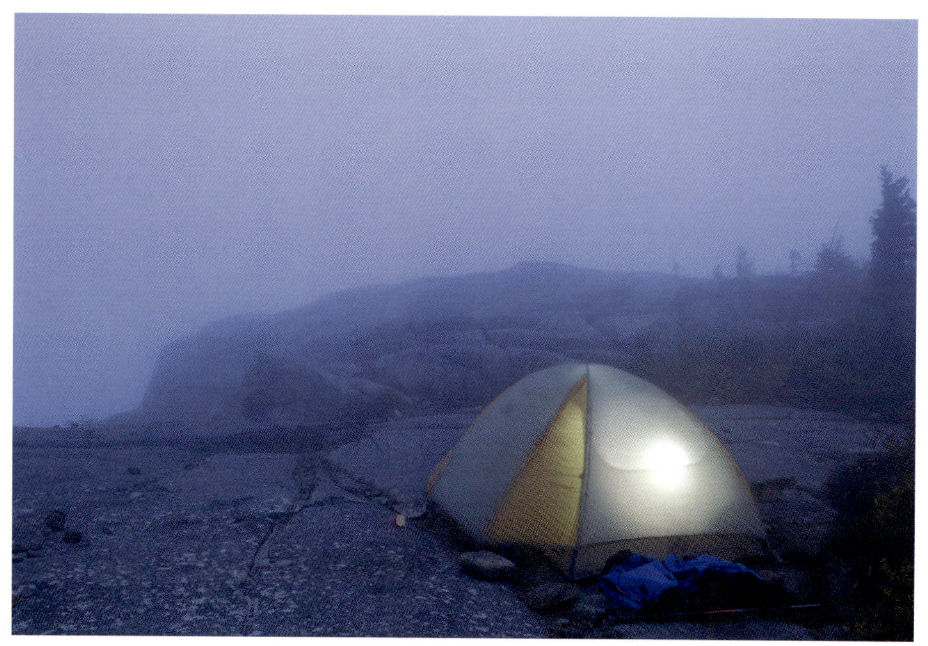

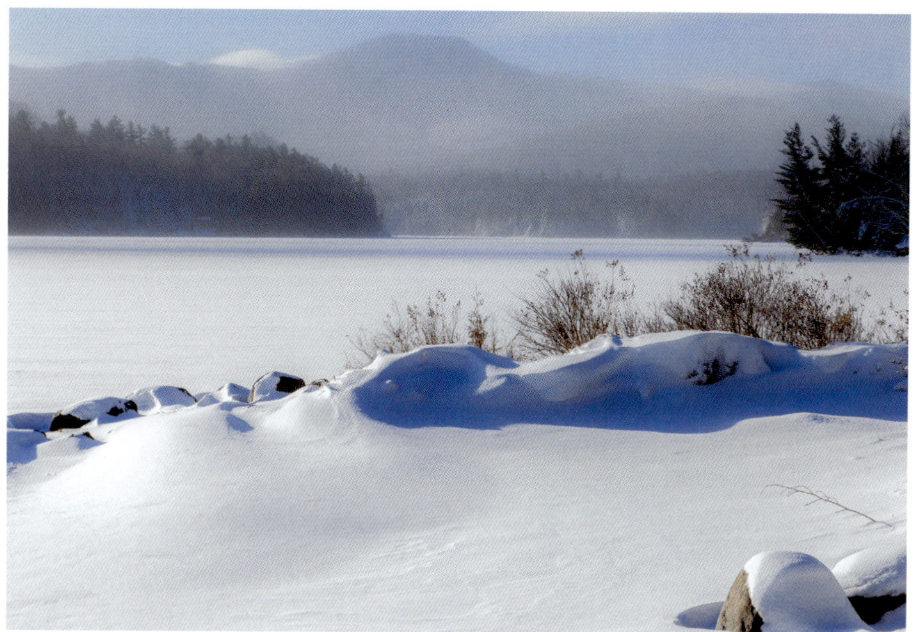

Top: I spent the night on a ridge off the trail so I could do some sunrise photography.
Instead I woke up to wind and thick fog.
Bottom: Twenty below in February on Moose Pond.

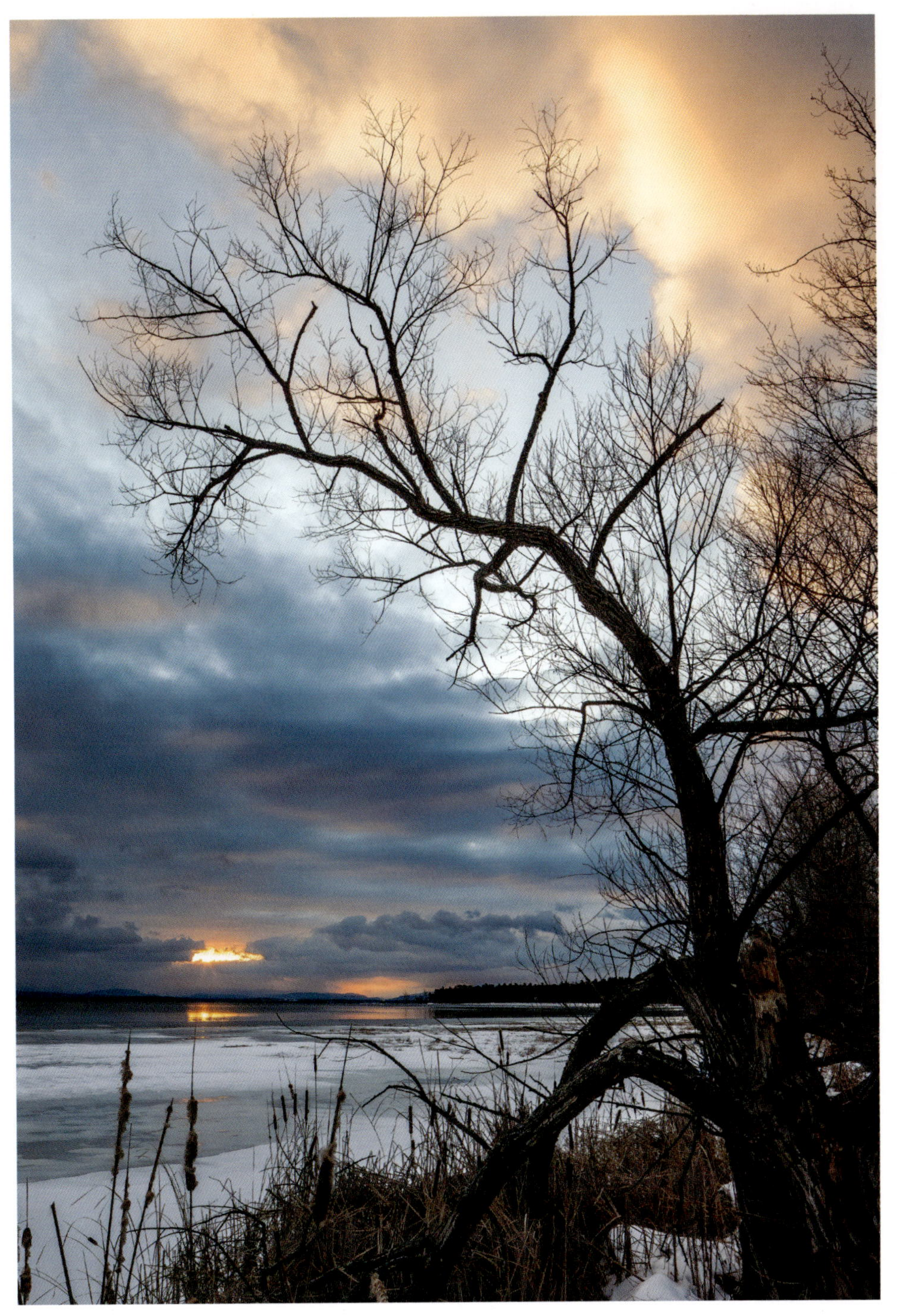

Late winter at Ausable Point as the sun was rising.

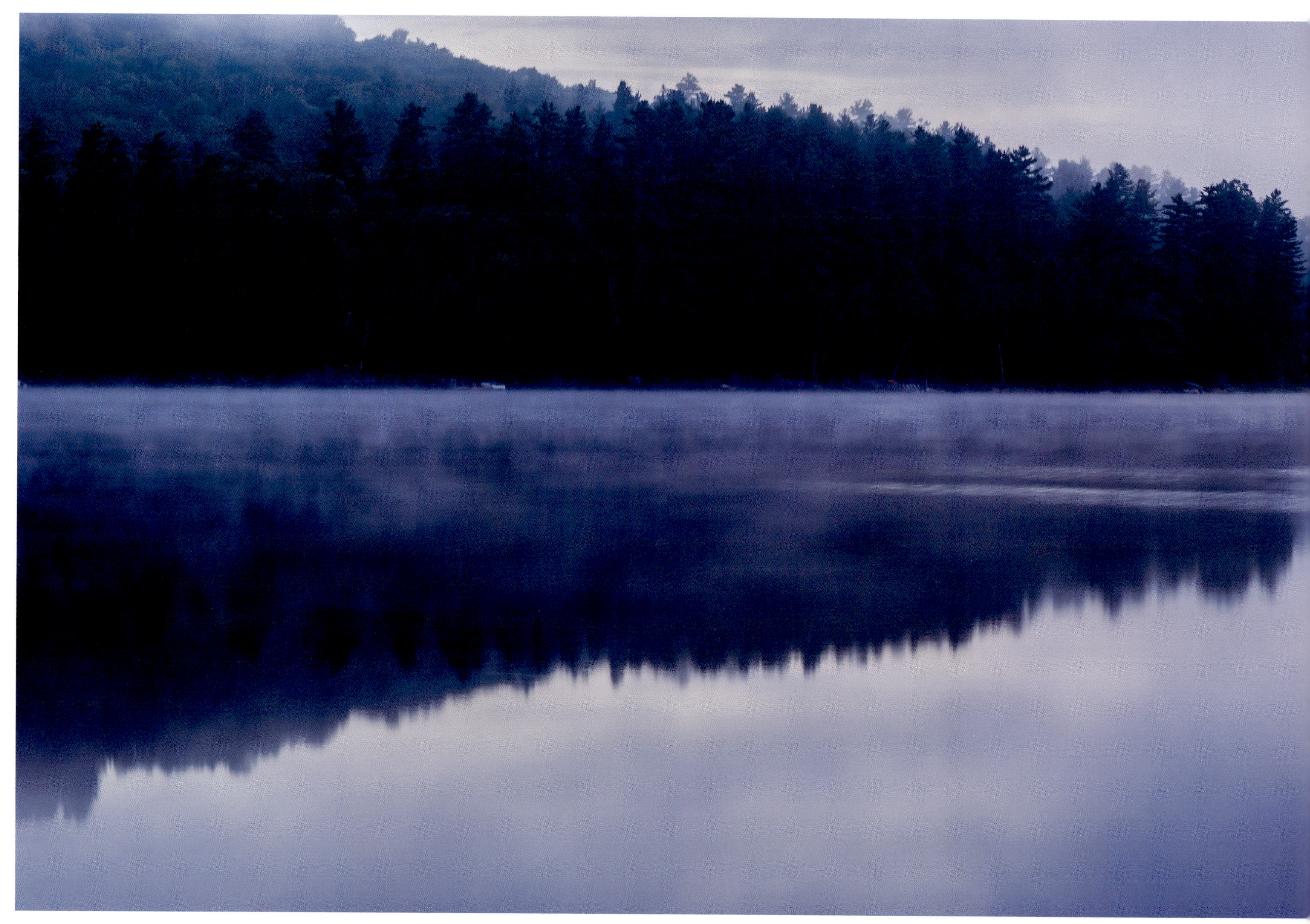

Long Lake at dawn.

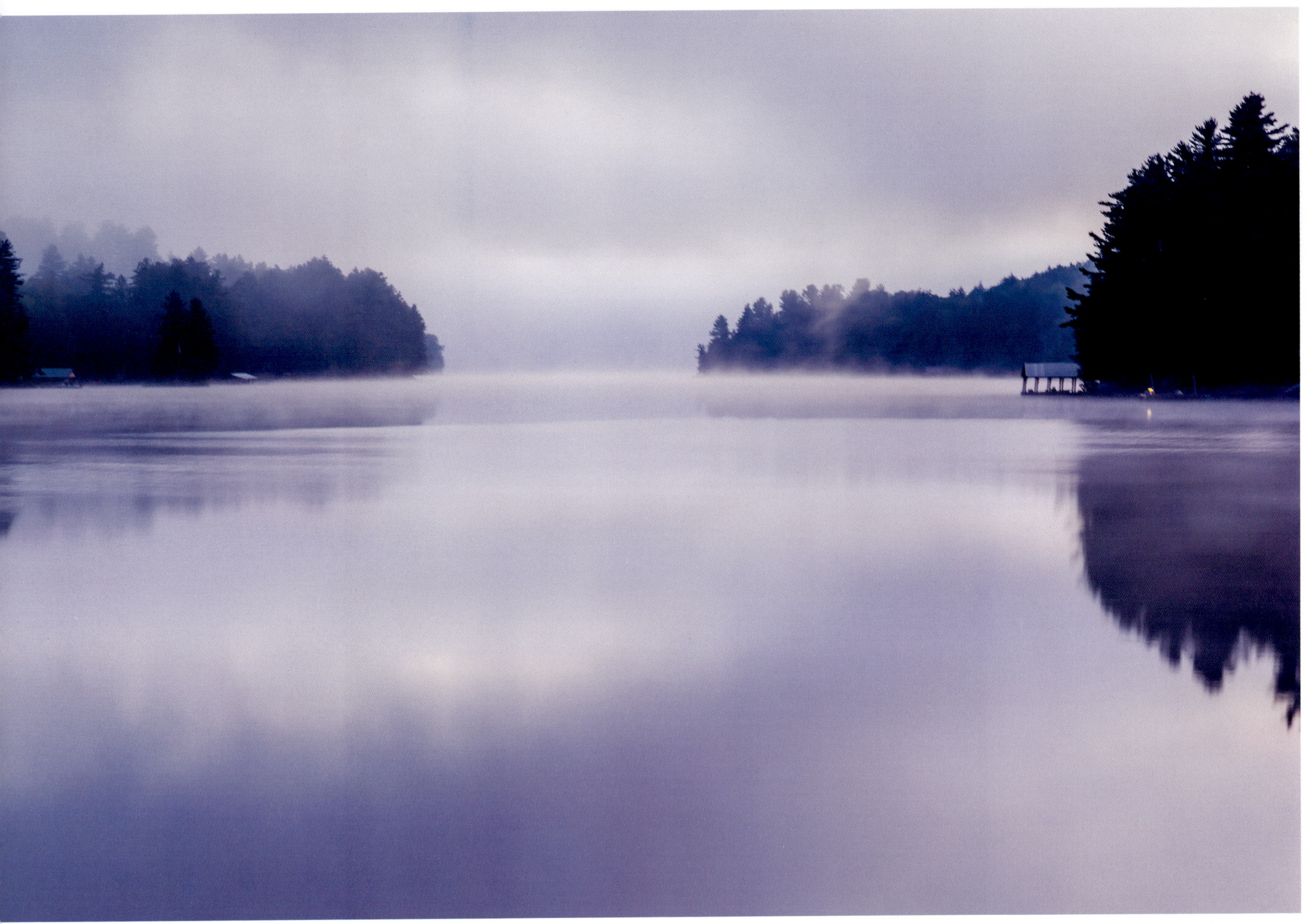

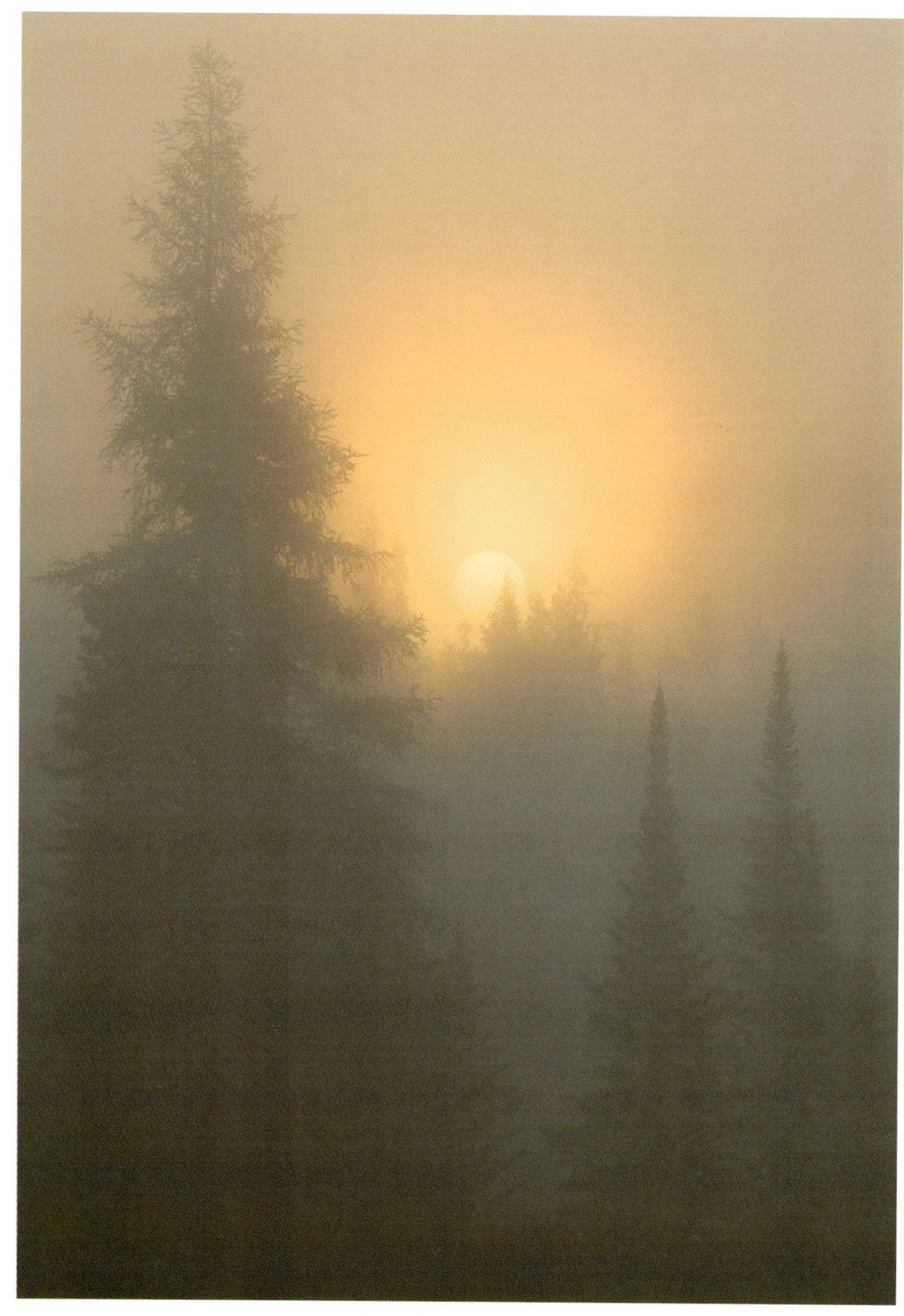

Foggy sunrise on the Bloomingdale Bog Trail.

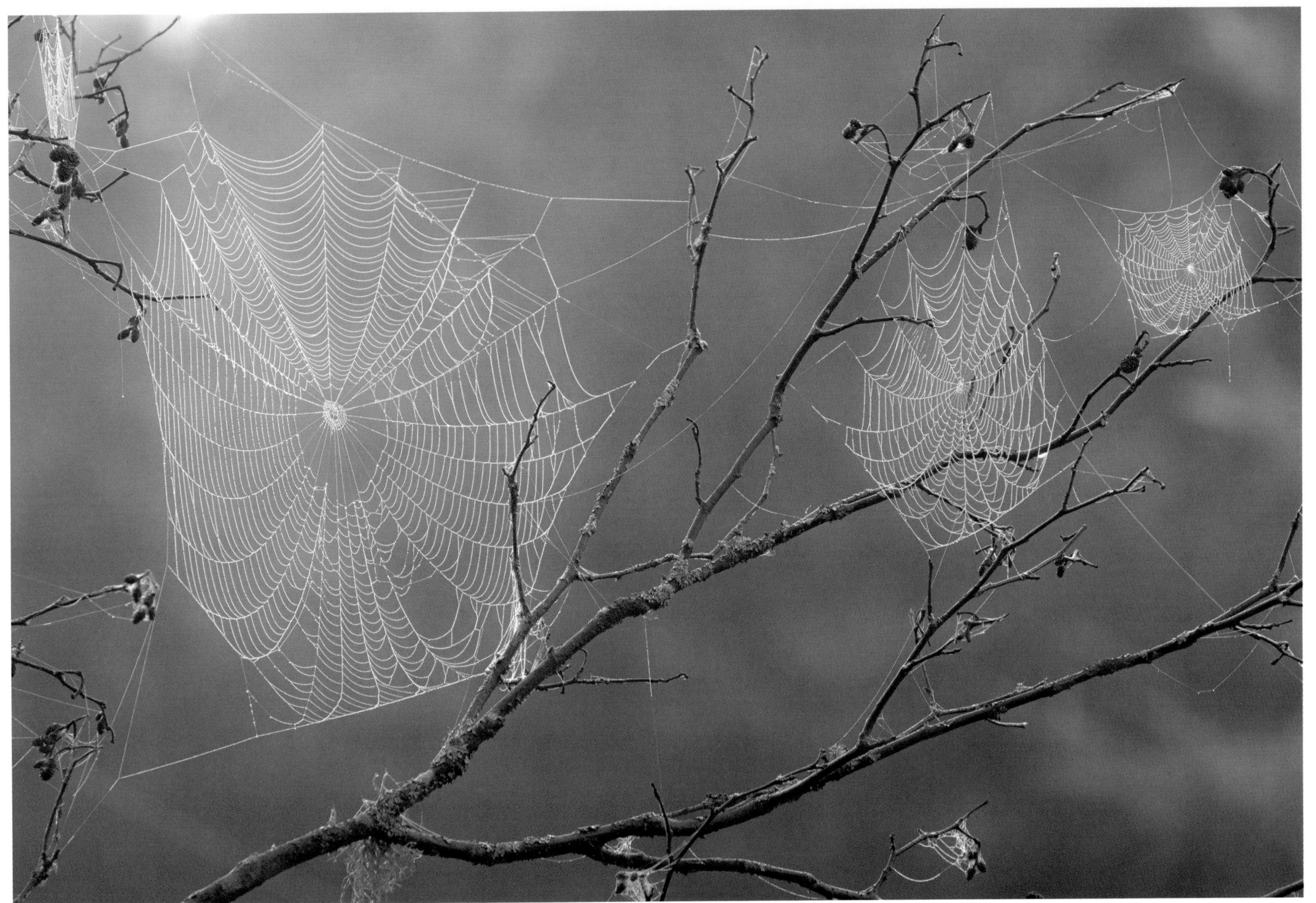

Spiderwebs covered in morning dew on the Bloomingdale Bog Trail.

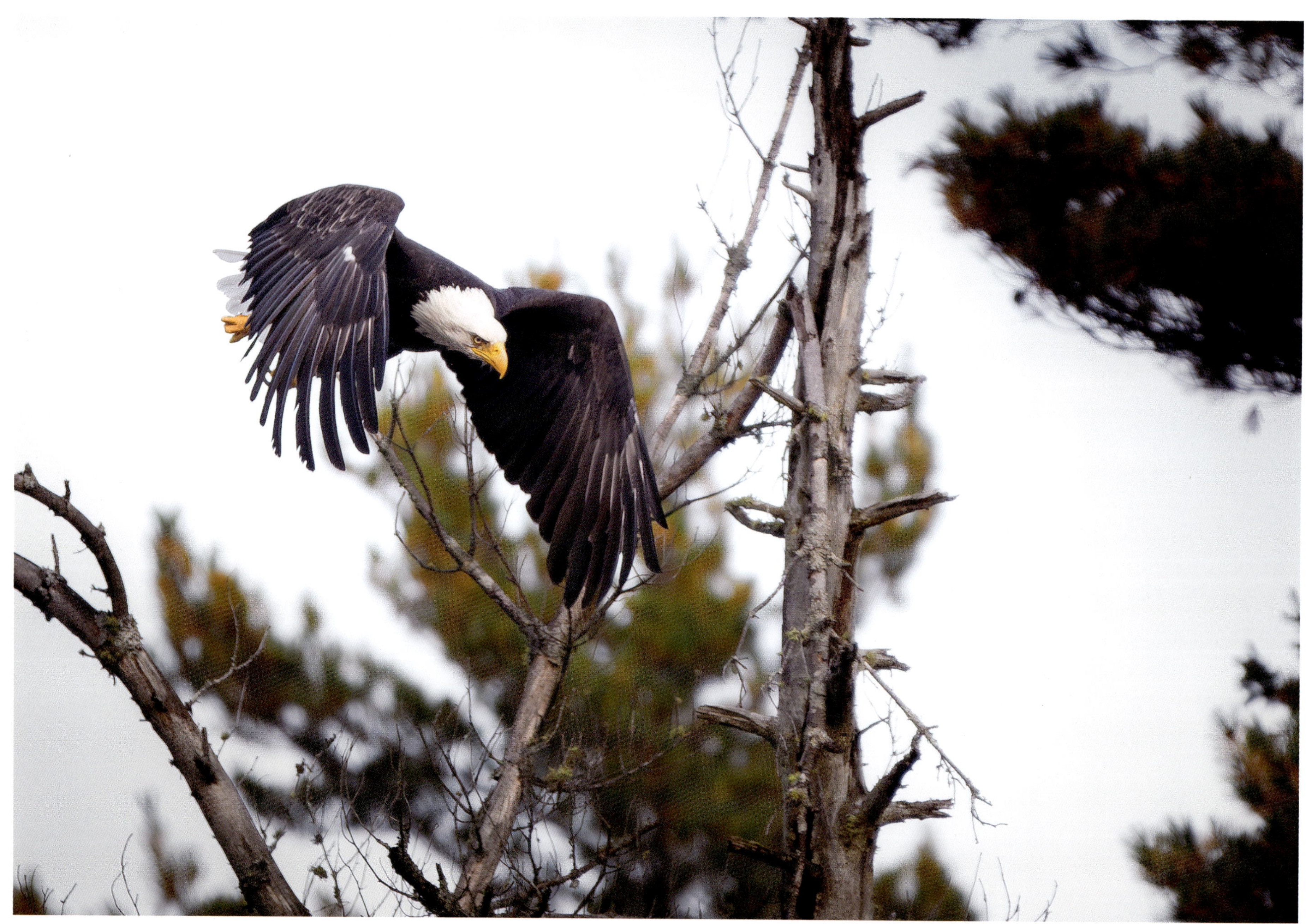

Mature bald eagle in flight at Middle Saranac Lake.

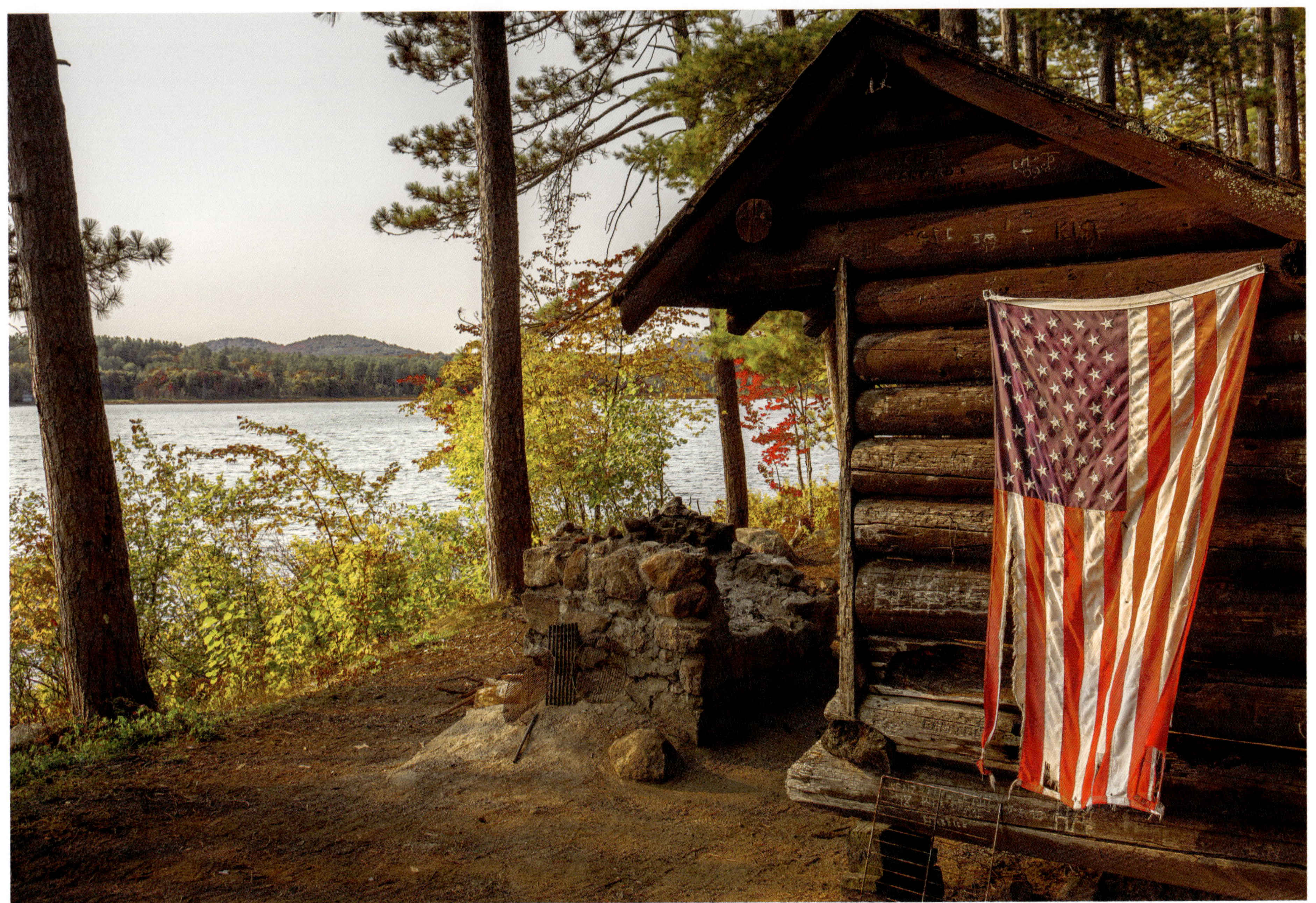

Tattered American flag at wilderness lean-to on Long Lake.

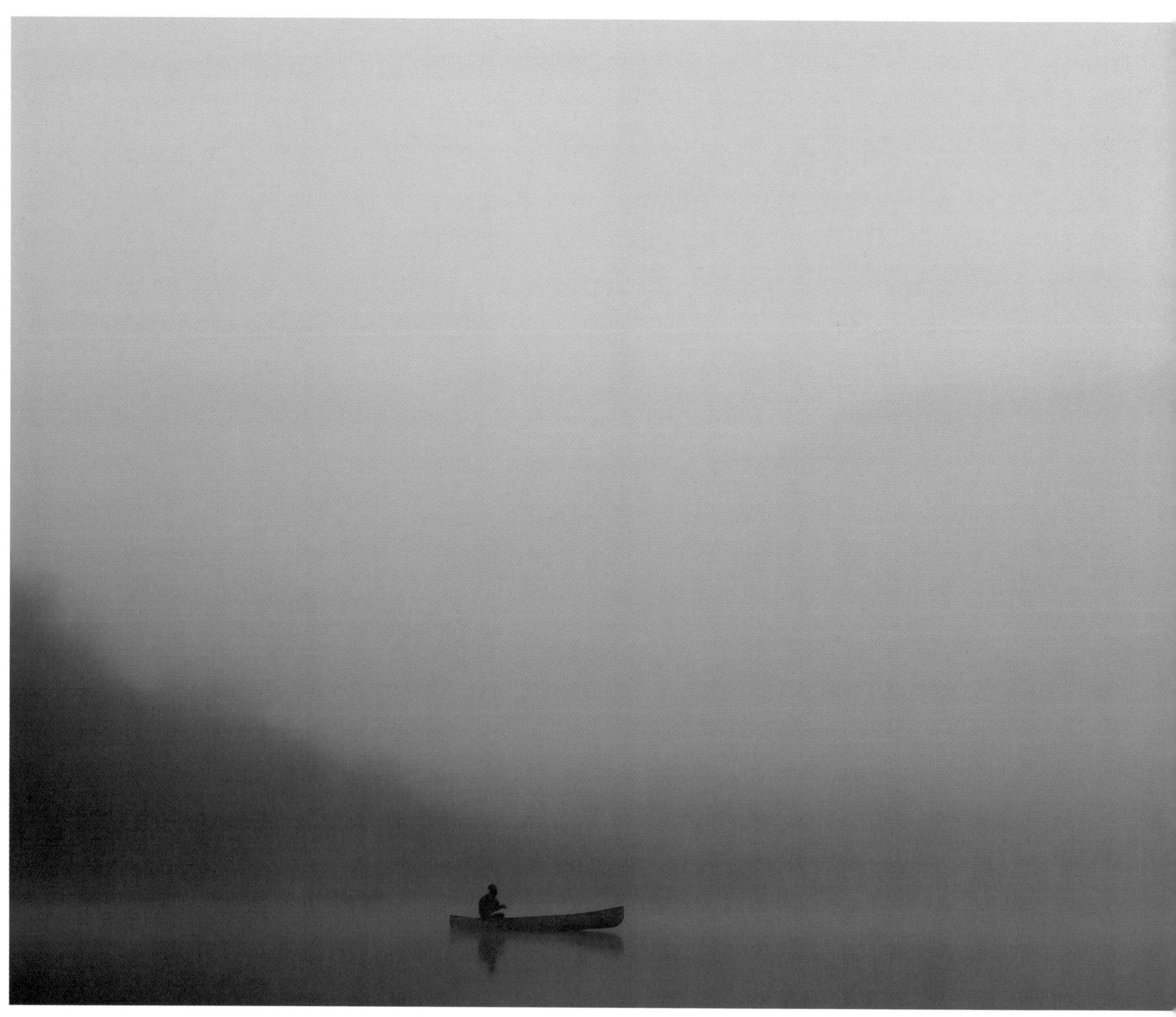

Solitude. Before sunrise a lone canoeist glides through the mist across Heart Lake in the High Peaks region. He was moving so slowly that he didn't even create a wake.

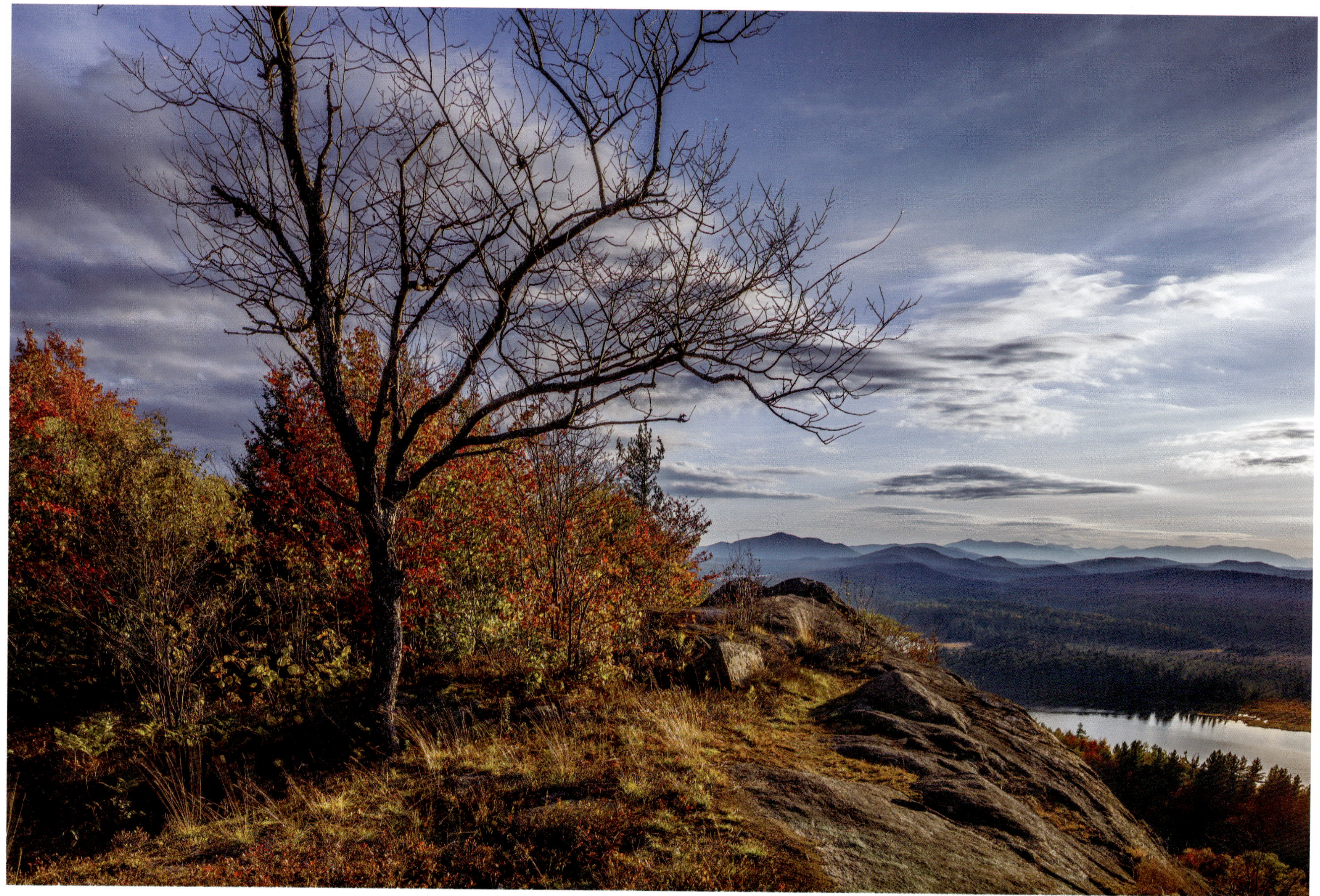

Just past peak foliage season on Low's Ridge.

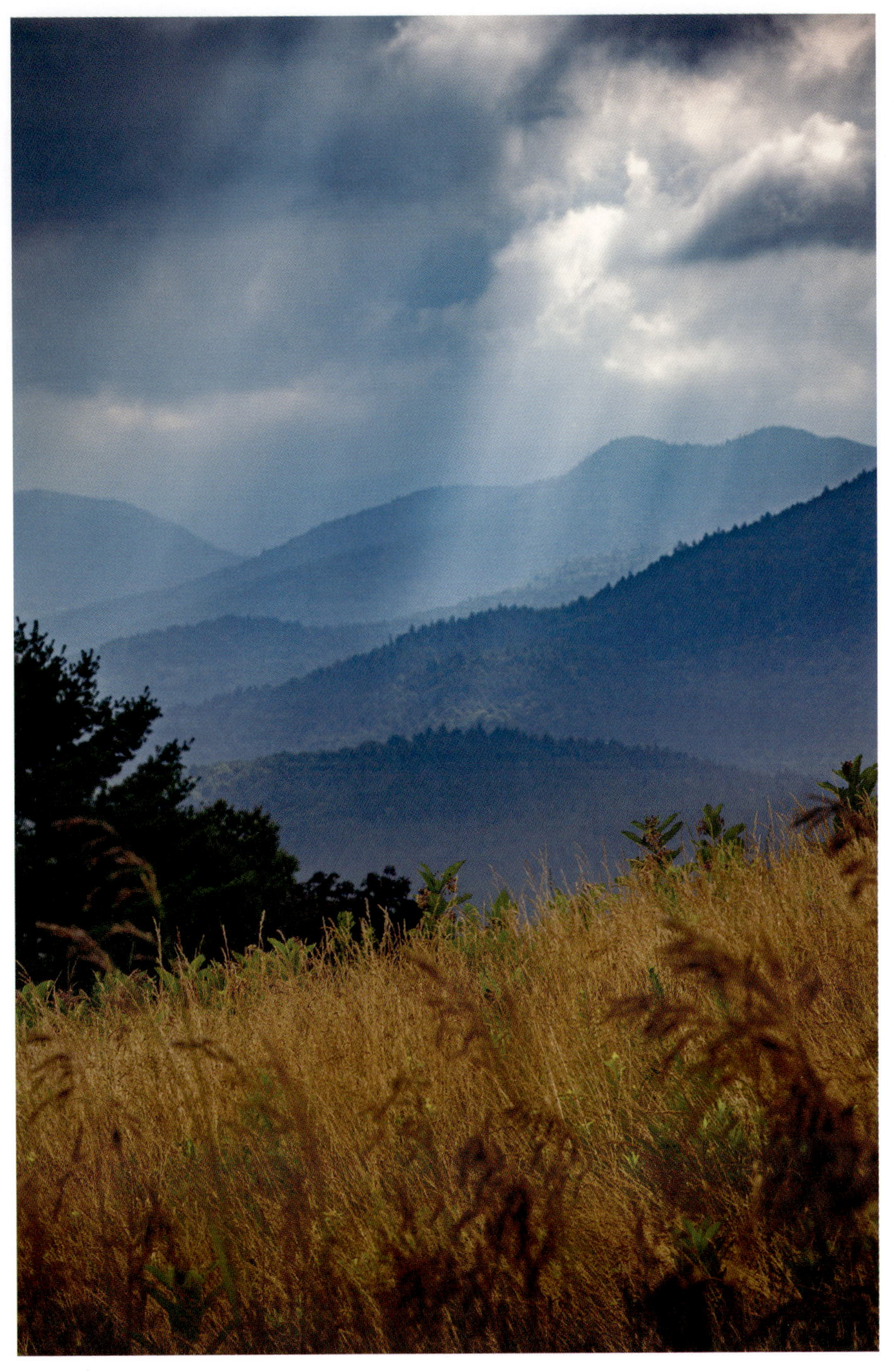

Late-afternoon rays breaking through the clouds in late summer.

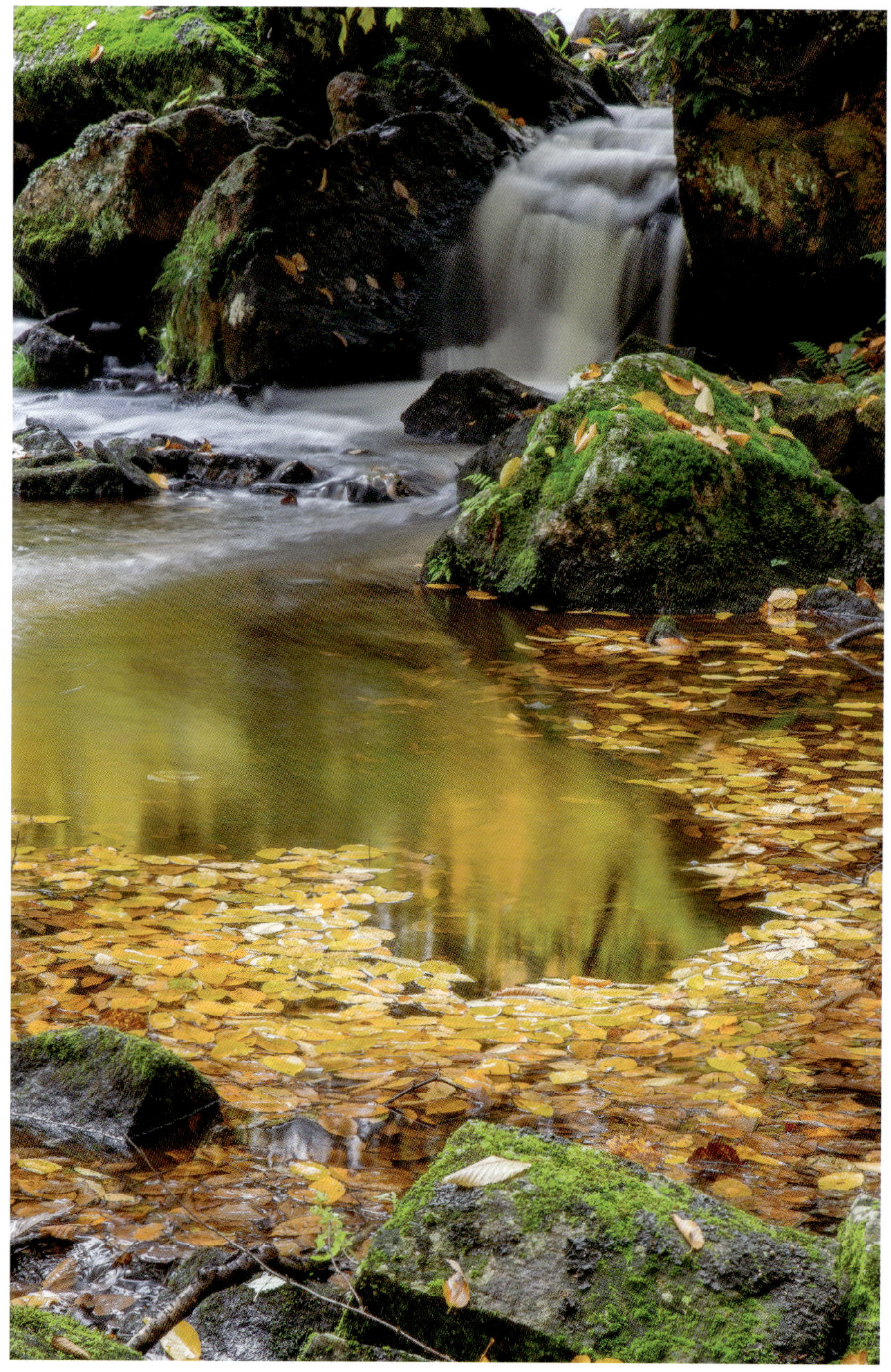

Fallen leaves in still backwater of a cascade on the Meacham Lake outflow.

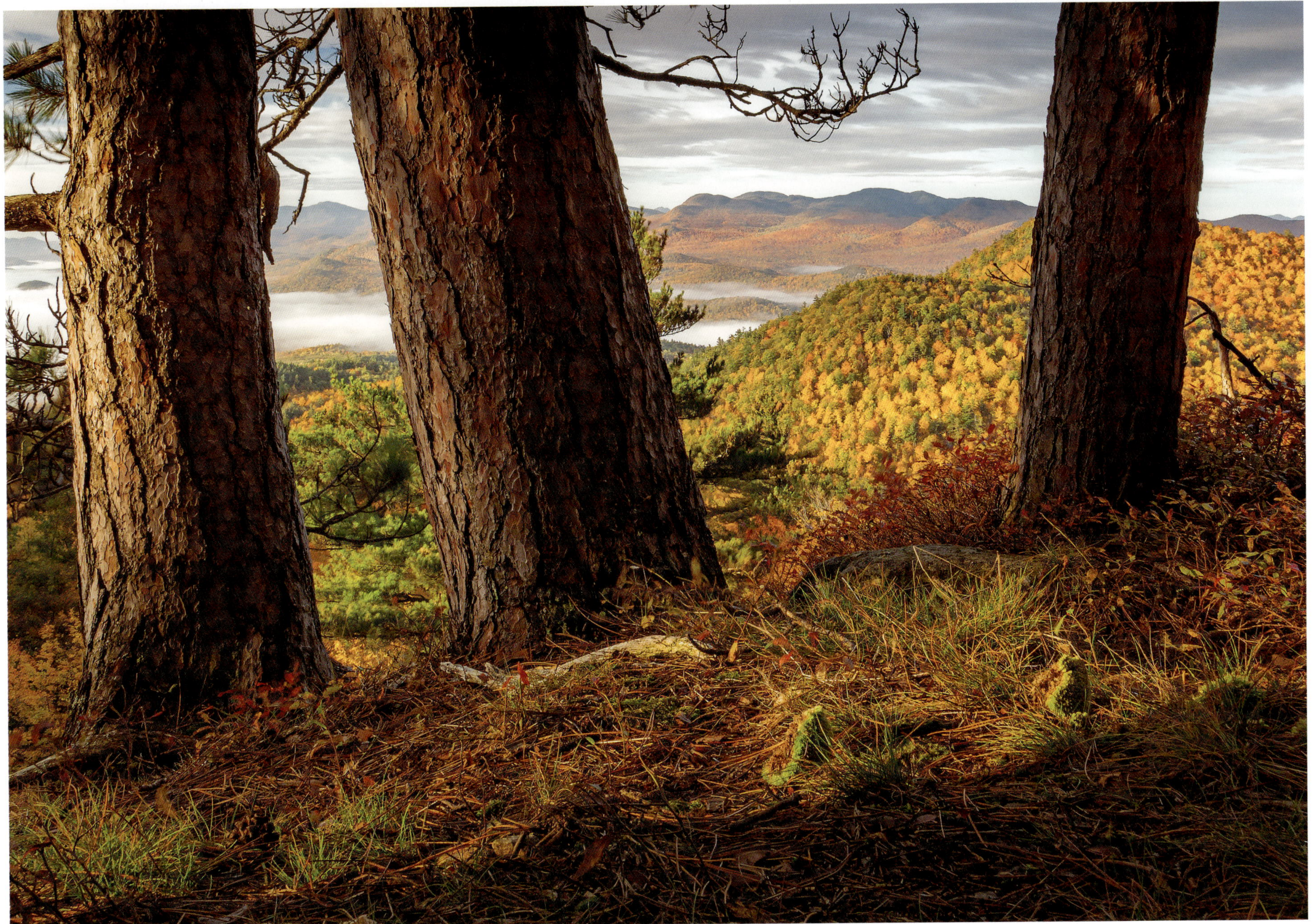

Sunrise cloud inversion on Poke-O-Moonshine Mountain.

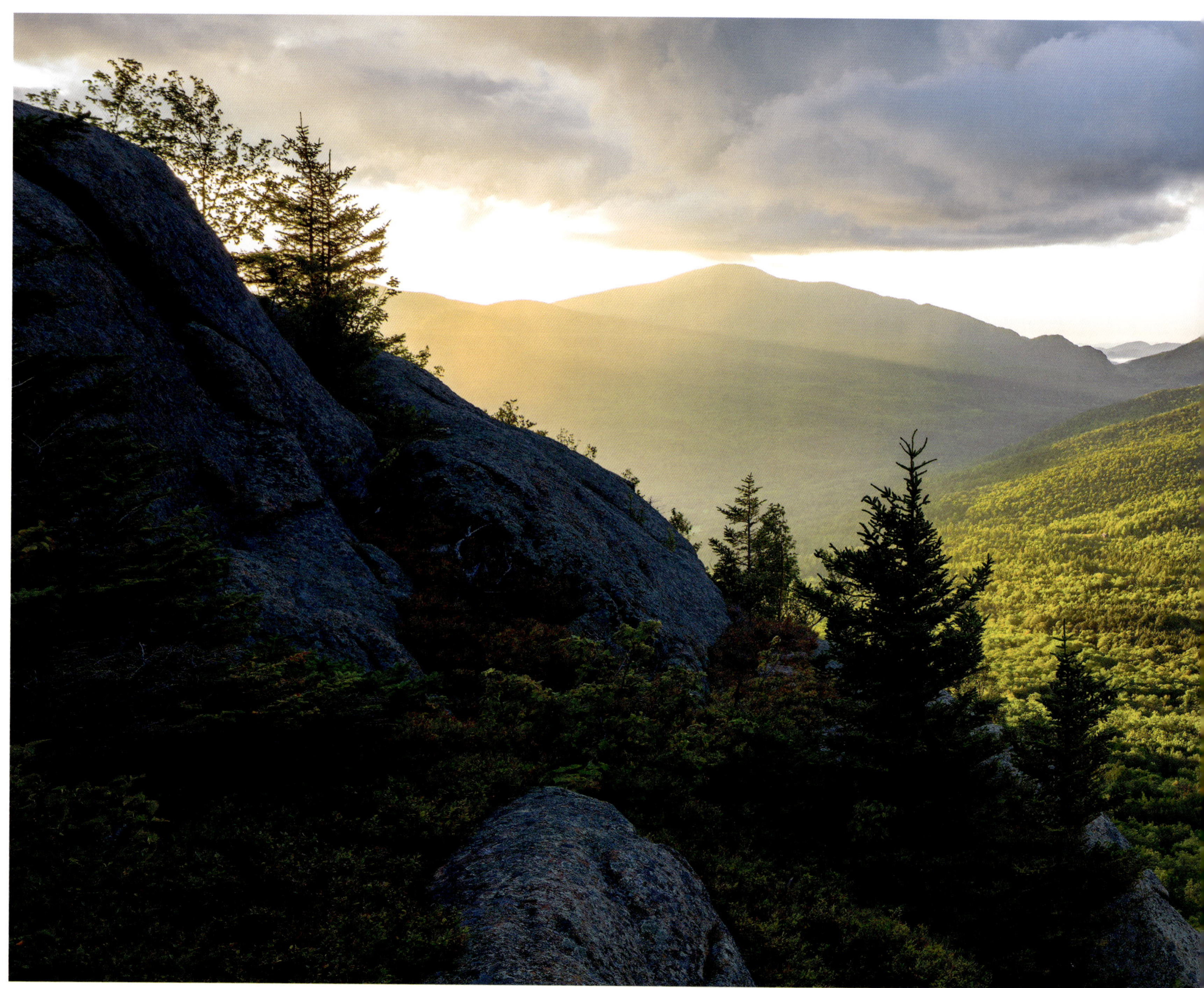

Sunrise from Little Porter Mountain.

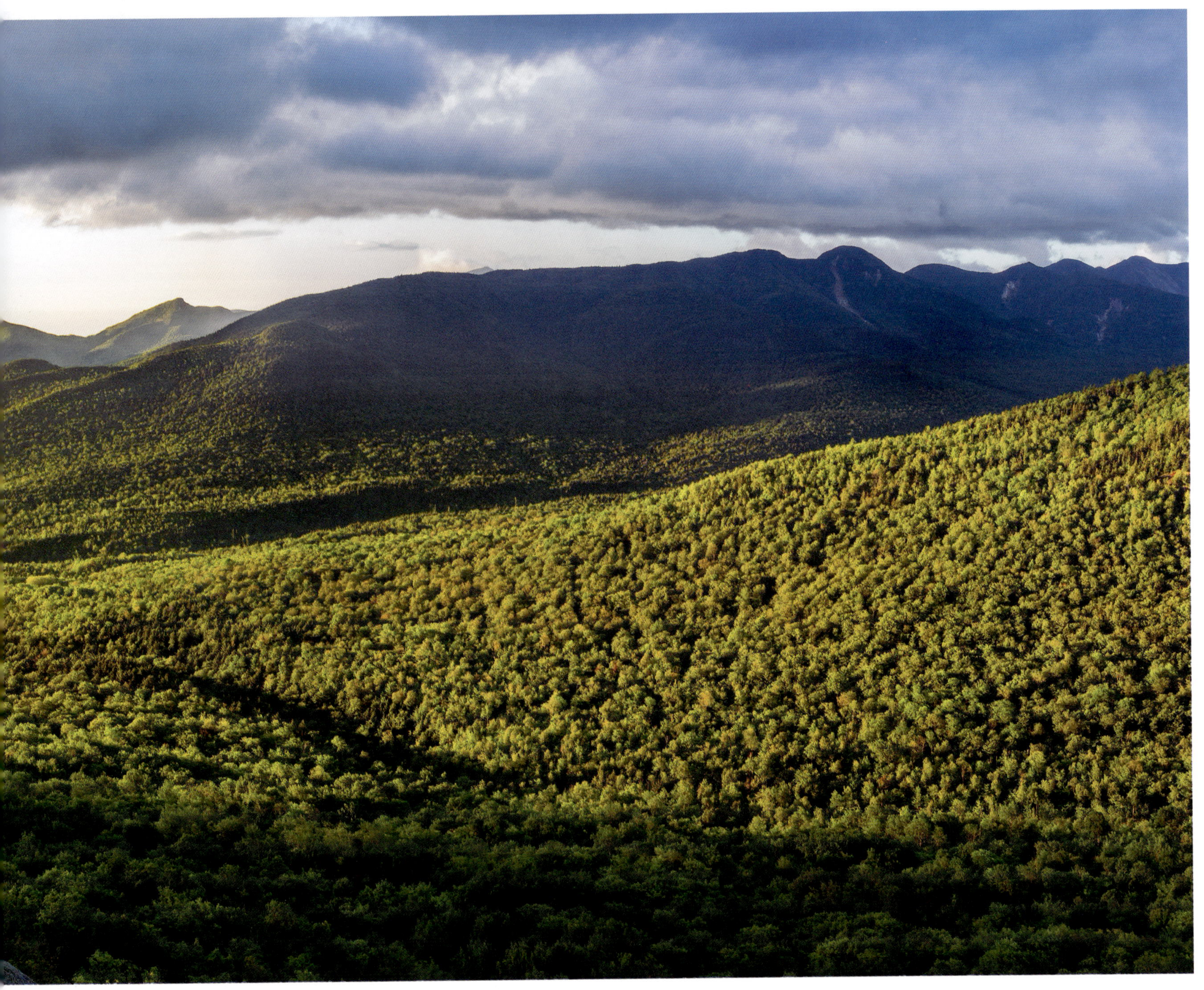

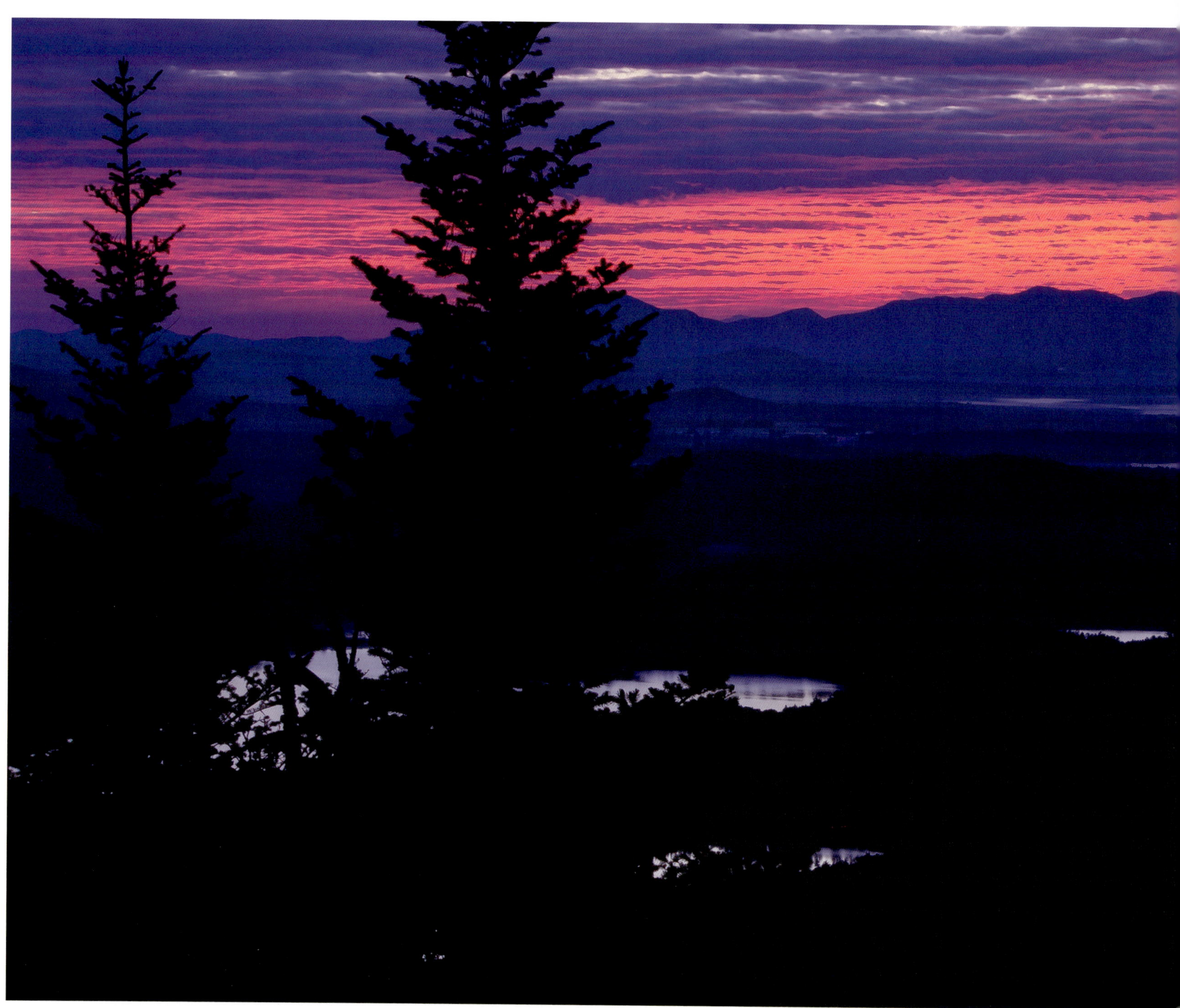

View over the Saint Regis Canoe Area from the top of Saint Regis Mountain at sunrise.

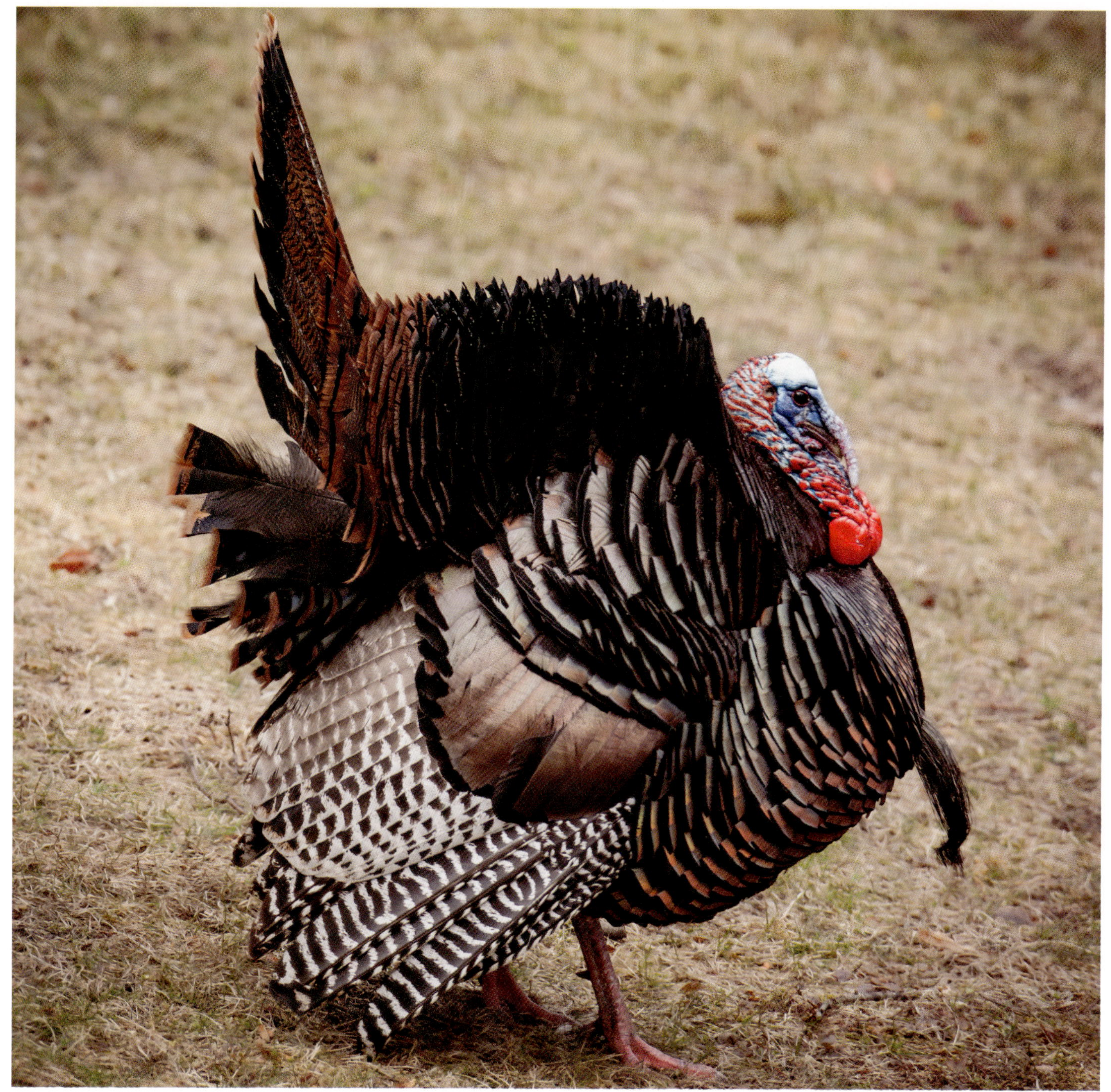

Male wild turkey in full plumage.

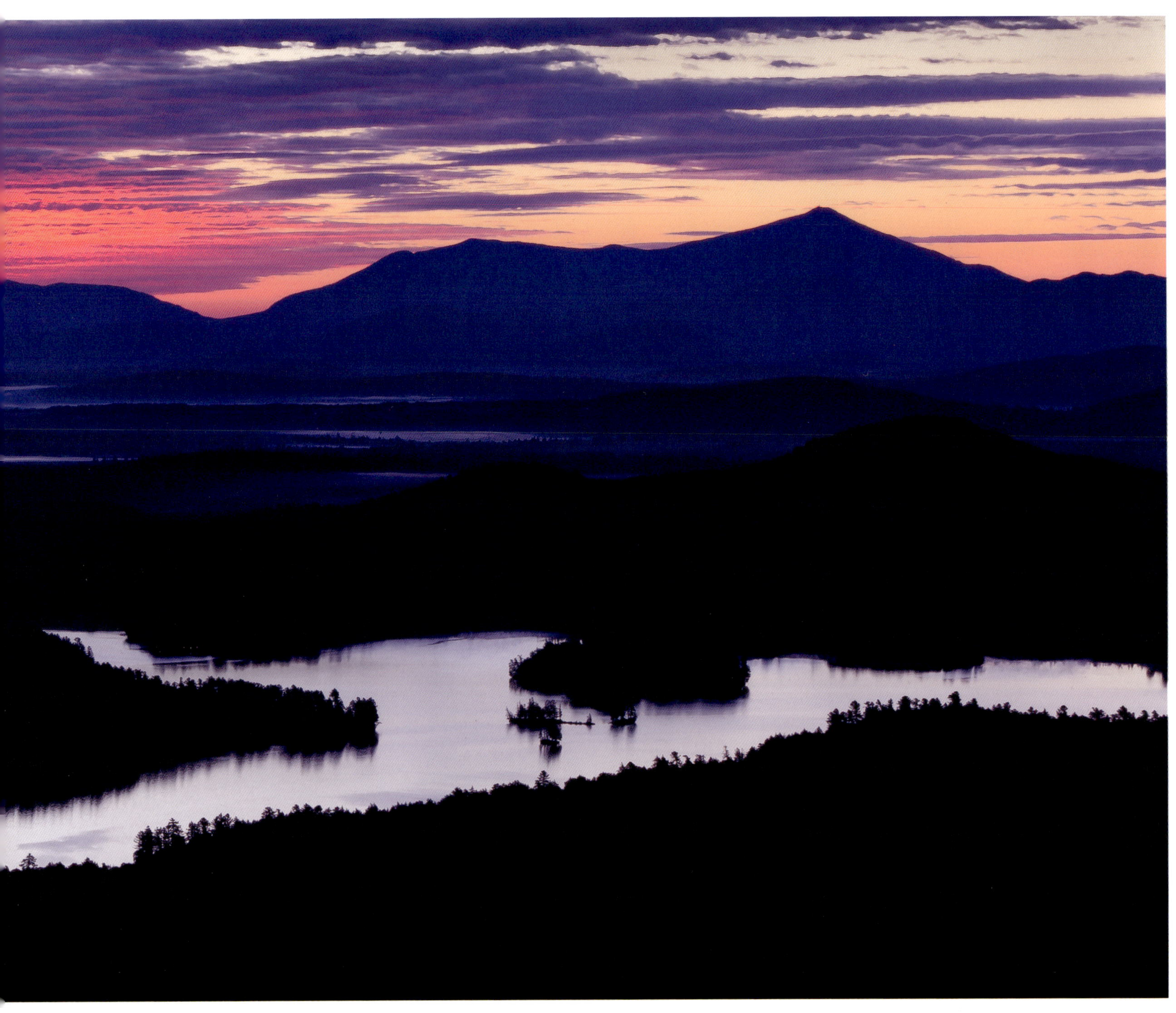

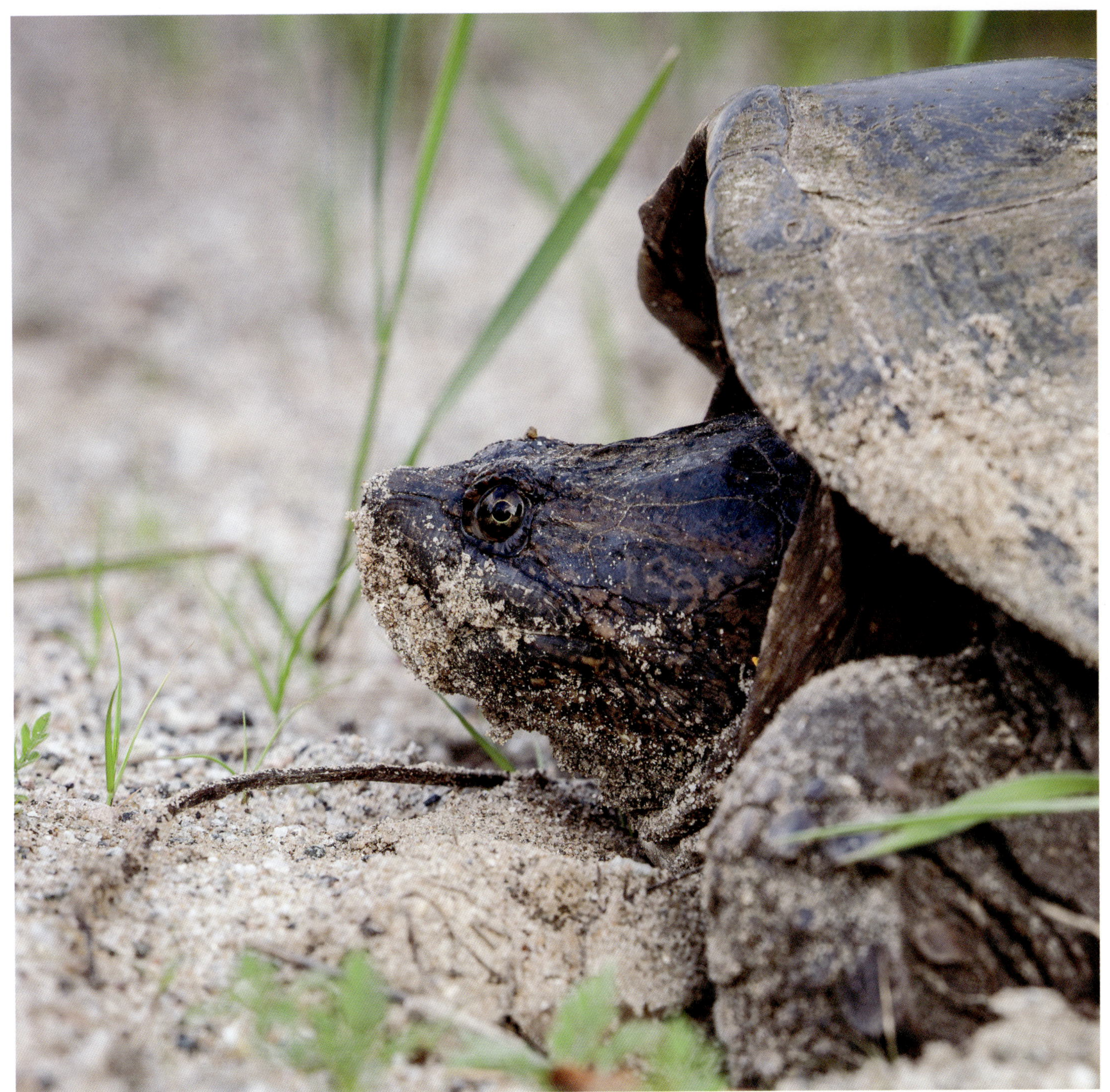

Snapping turtle laying eggs in the sand.

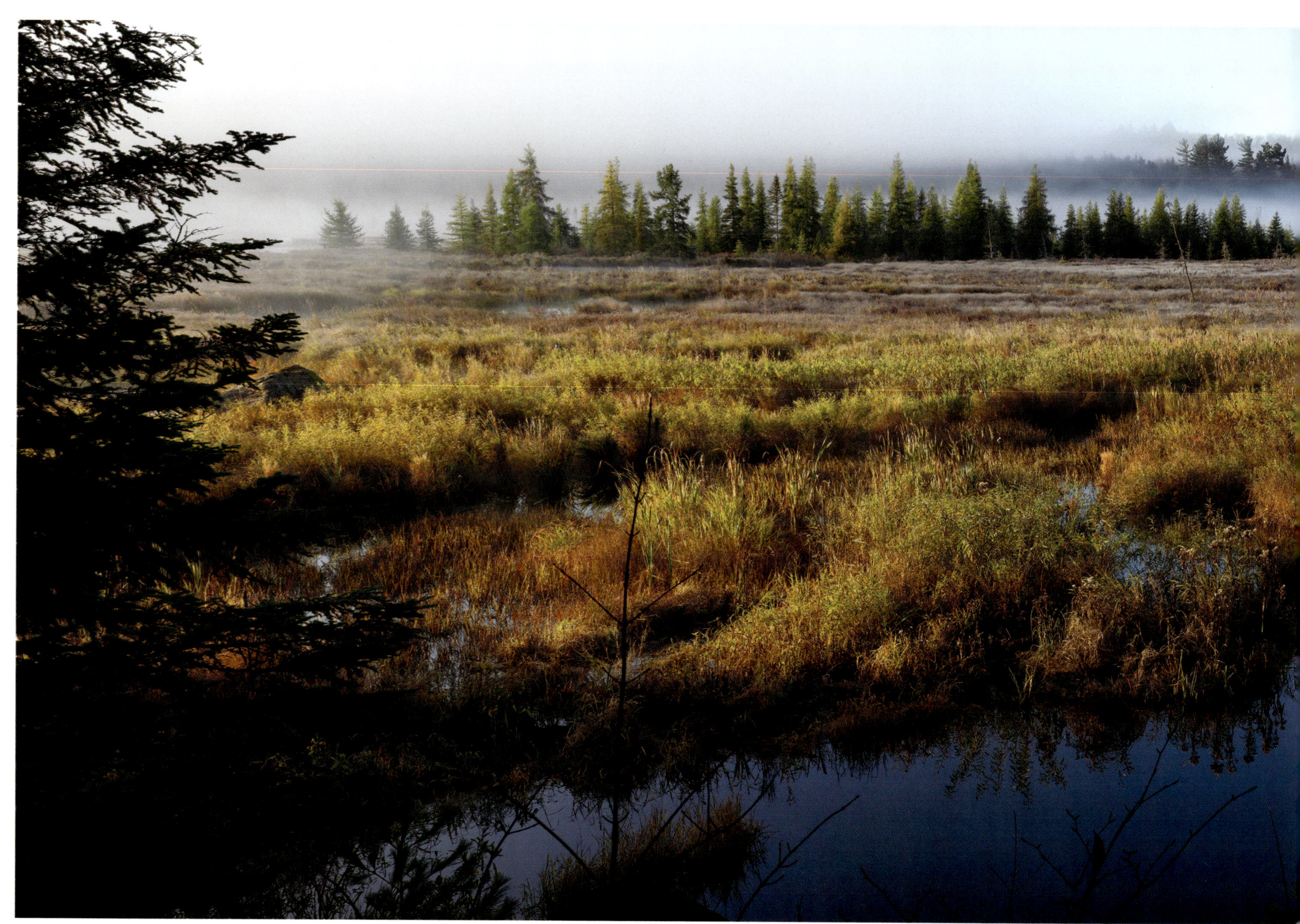

Sunrise on the trail at the Paul Smith's College Visitor Interpretive Center.

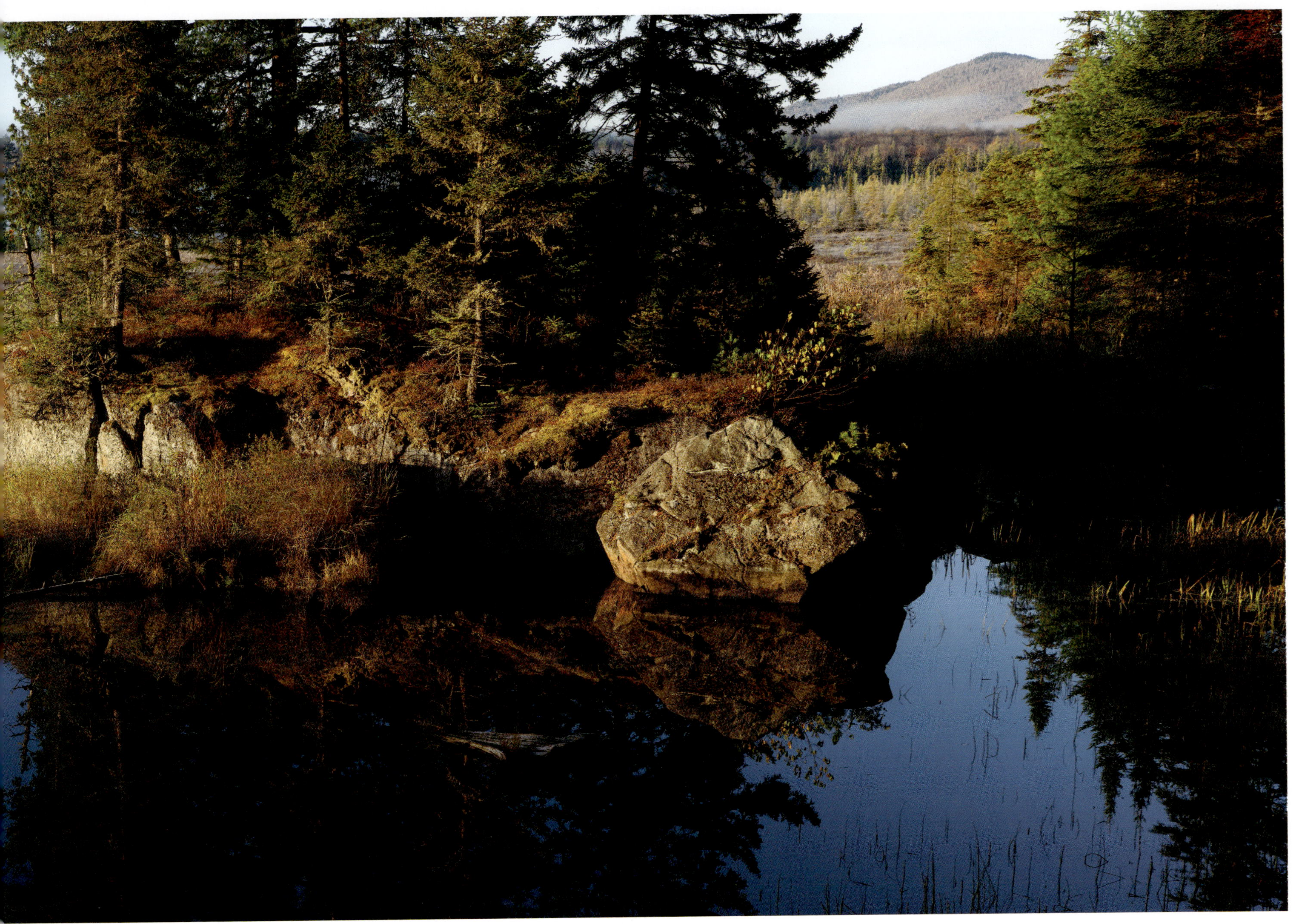

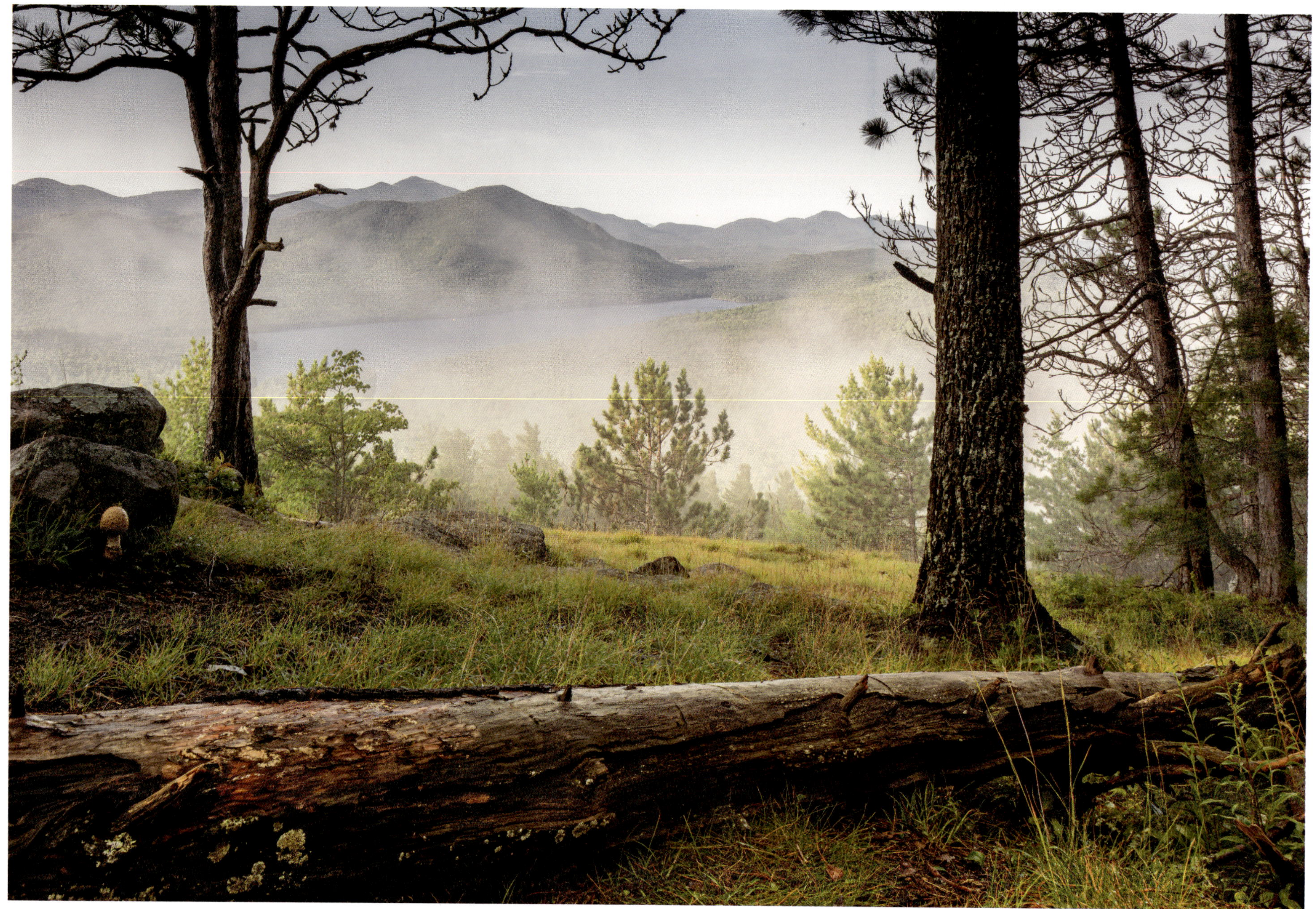

Mushroom and mist on Silver Lake Mountain.

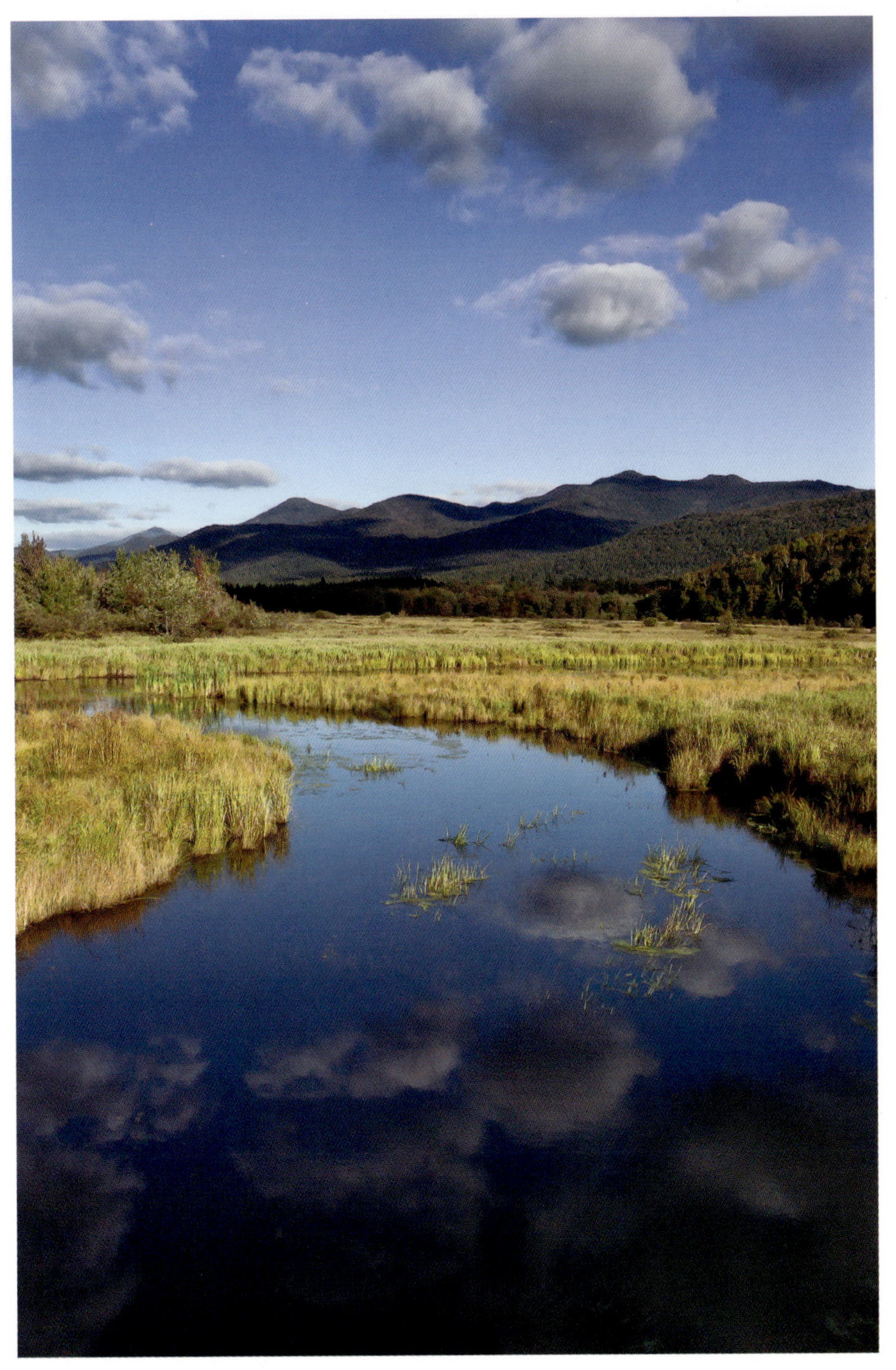

Late-summer afternoon near Saranac Lake—looking toward the
McKenzie Mountain Wilderness and Whiteface Mountain.

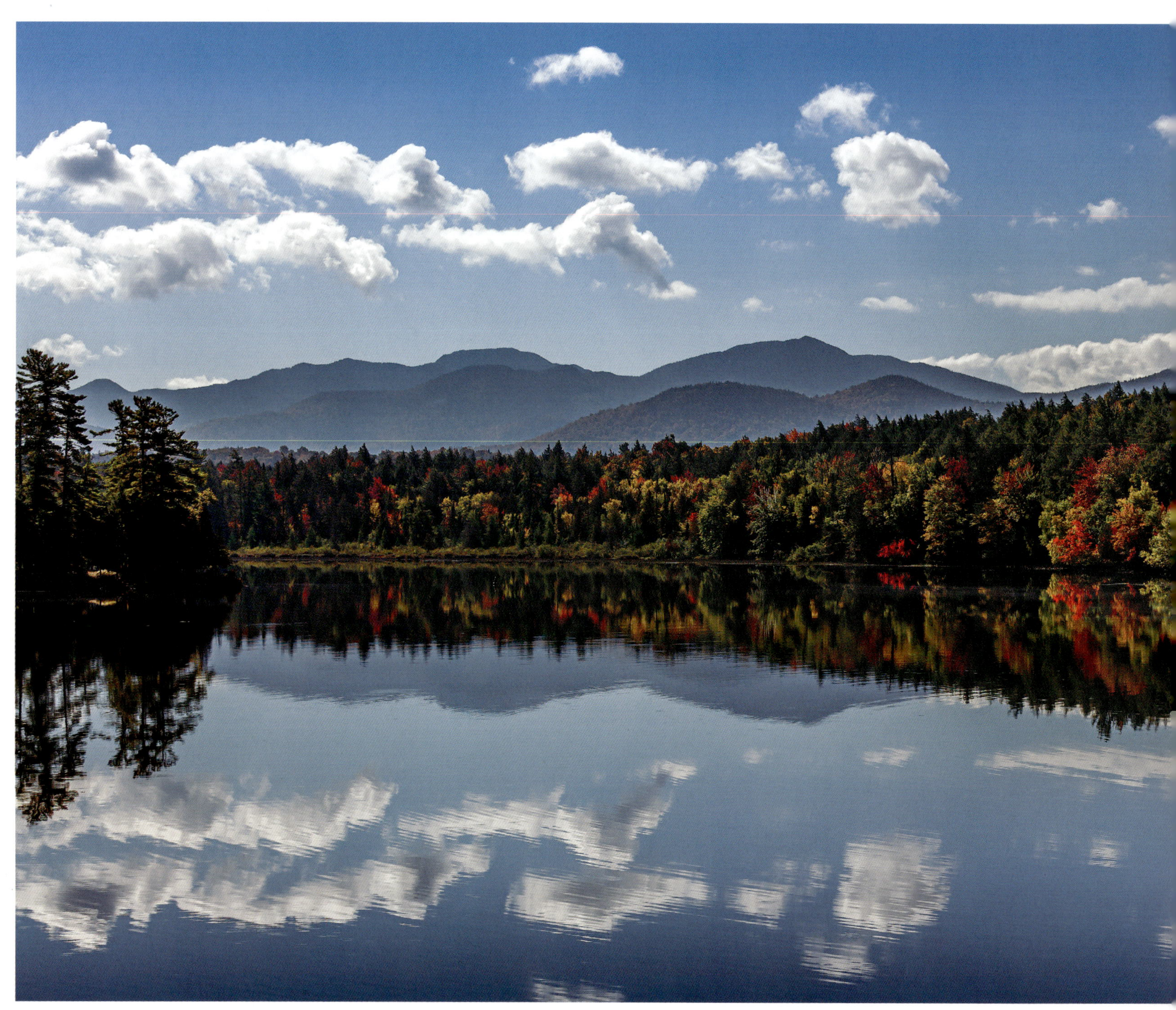

A boat sets out from a dock on Kiwassa Lake.

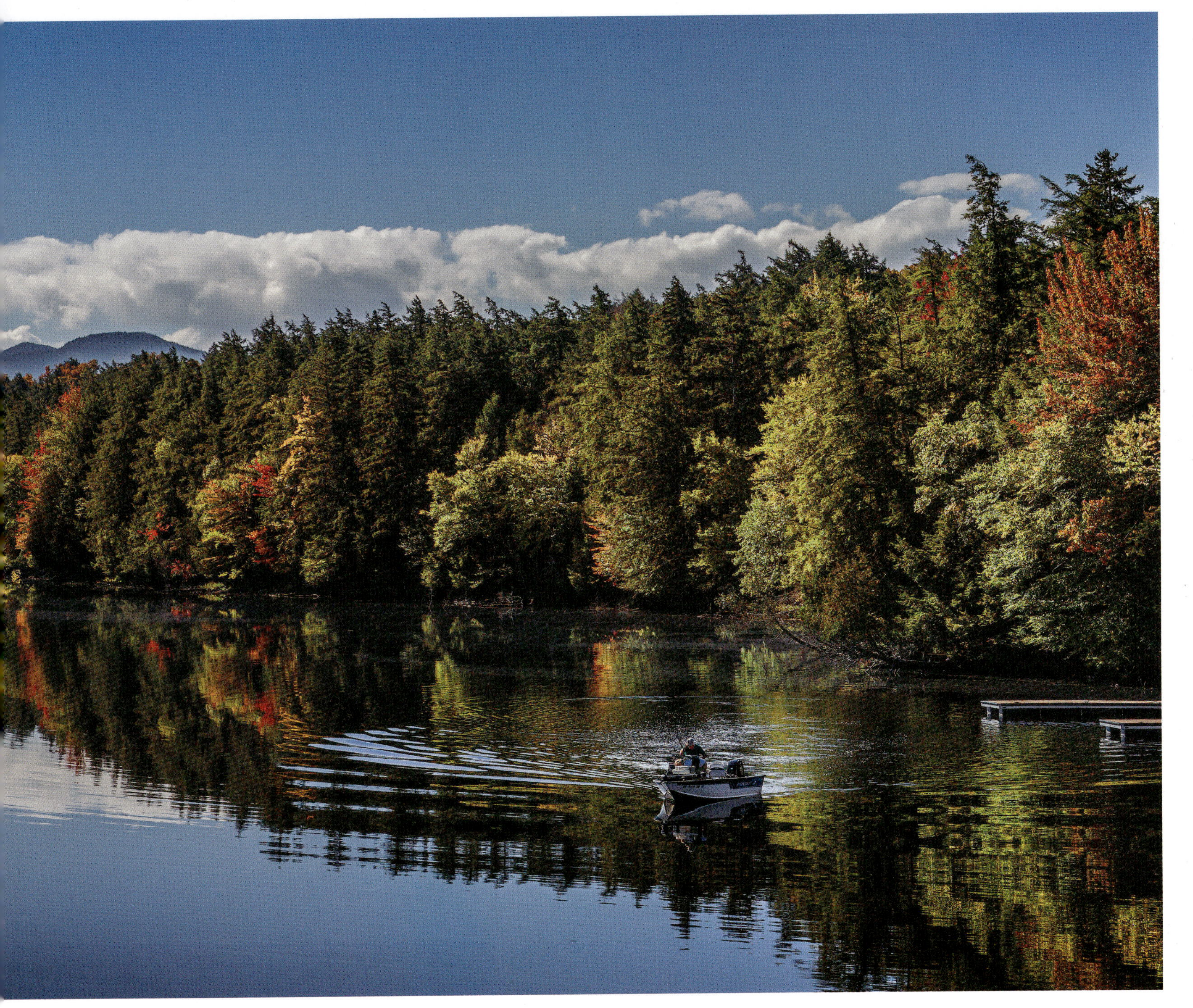

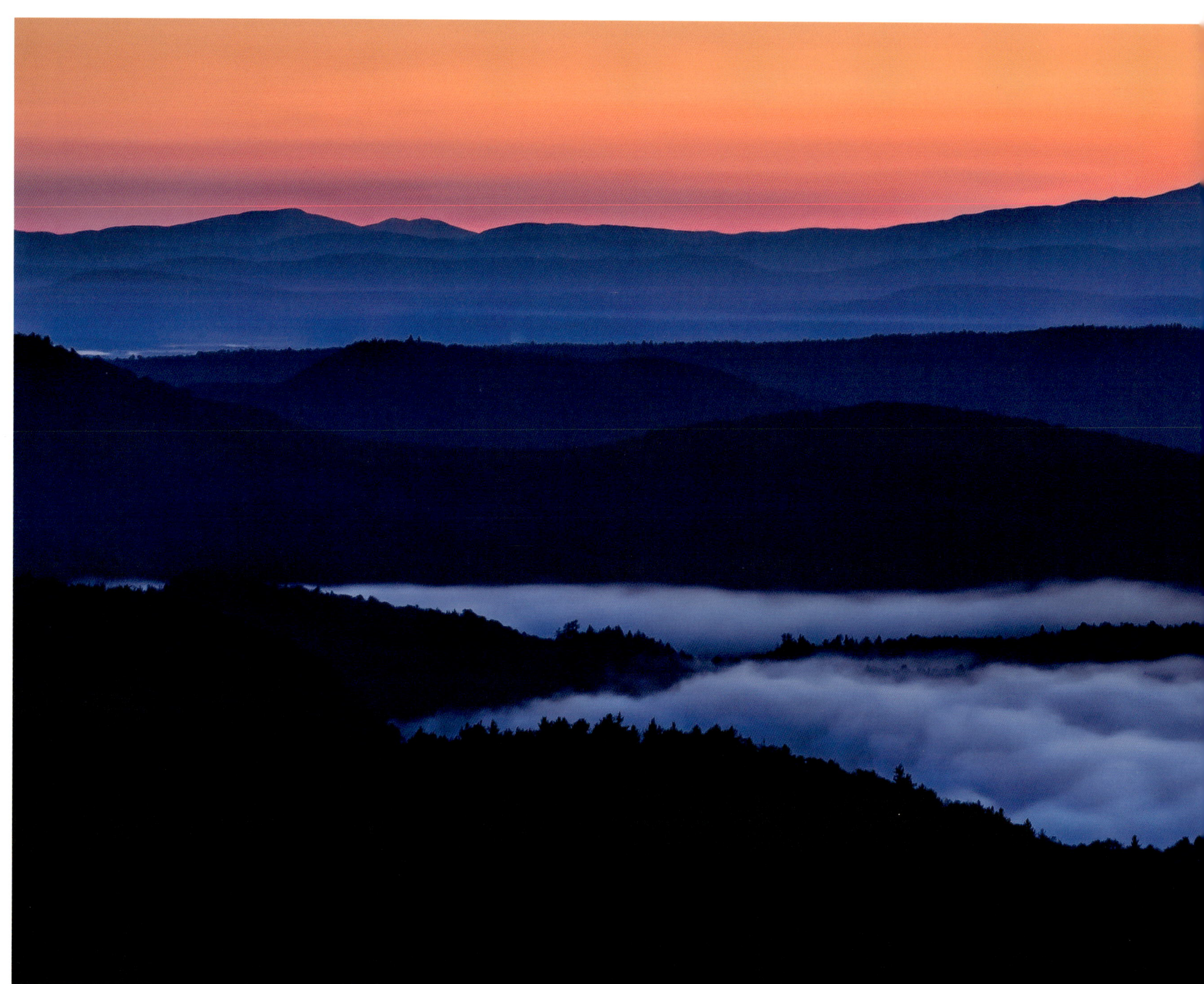

Fog in the valleys at dawn looking east from Pharaoh Mountain.

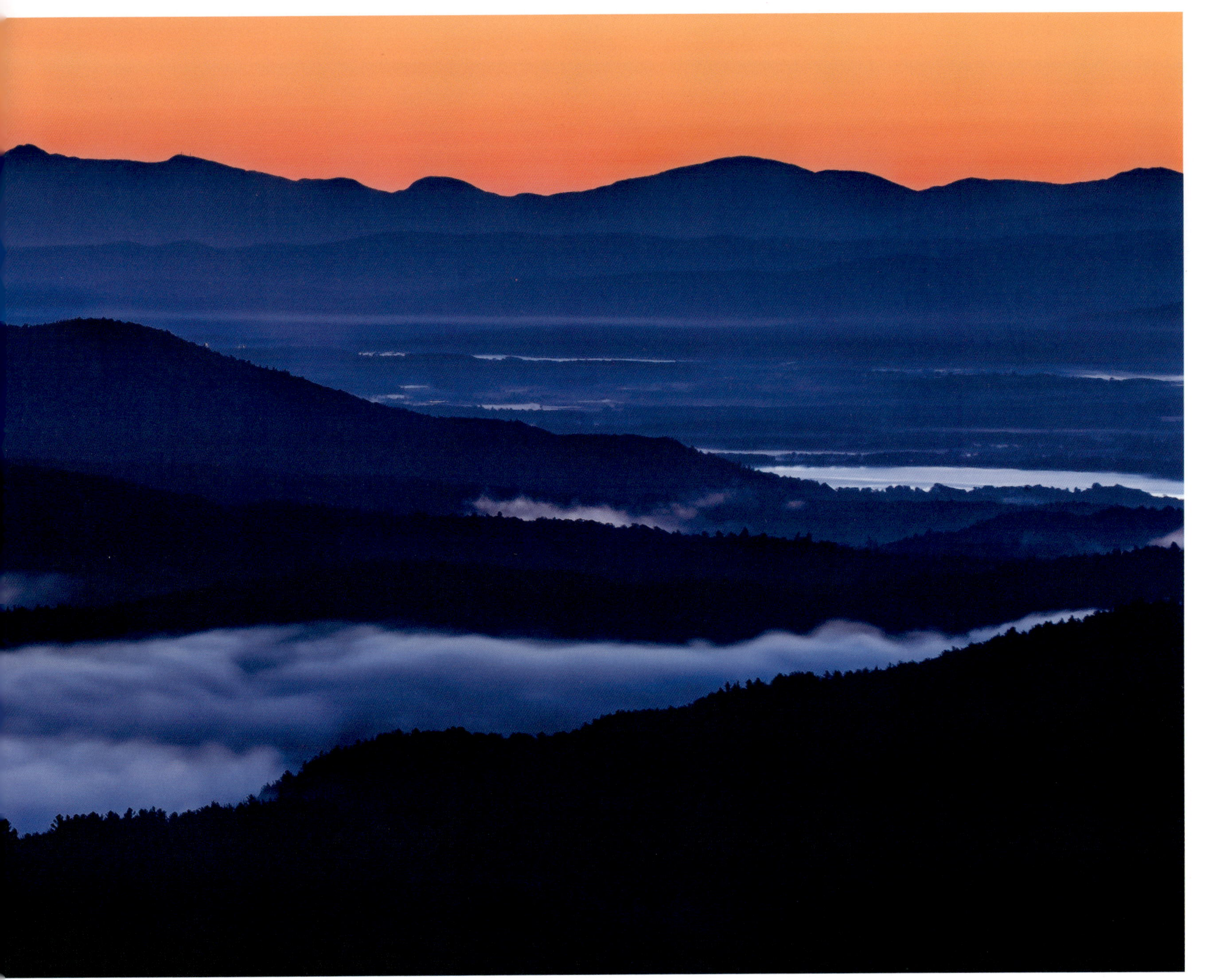

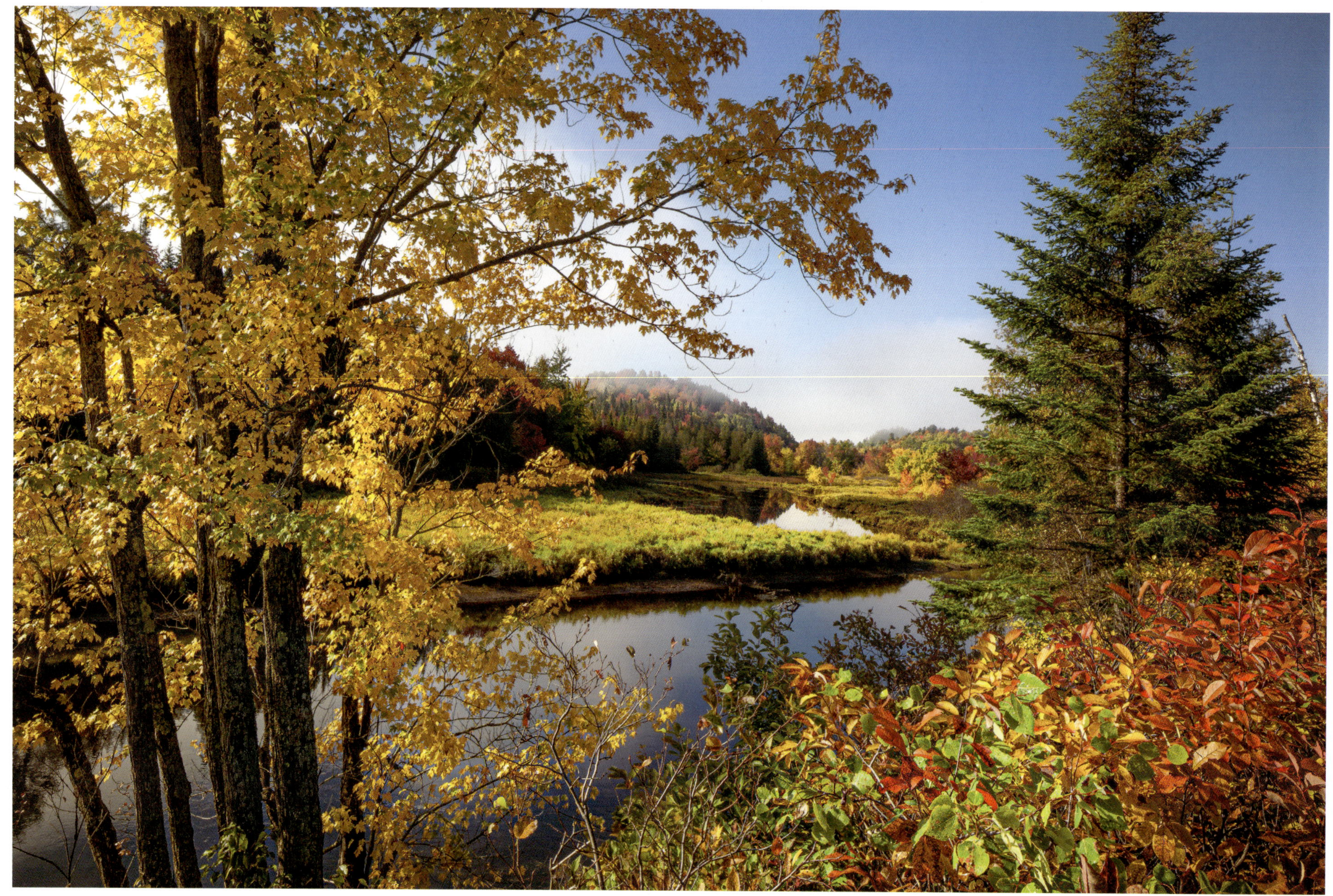

Peak fall colors along Route 3 on the way to Saranac Lake.

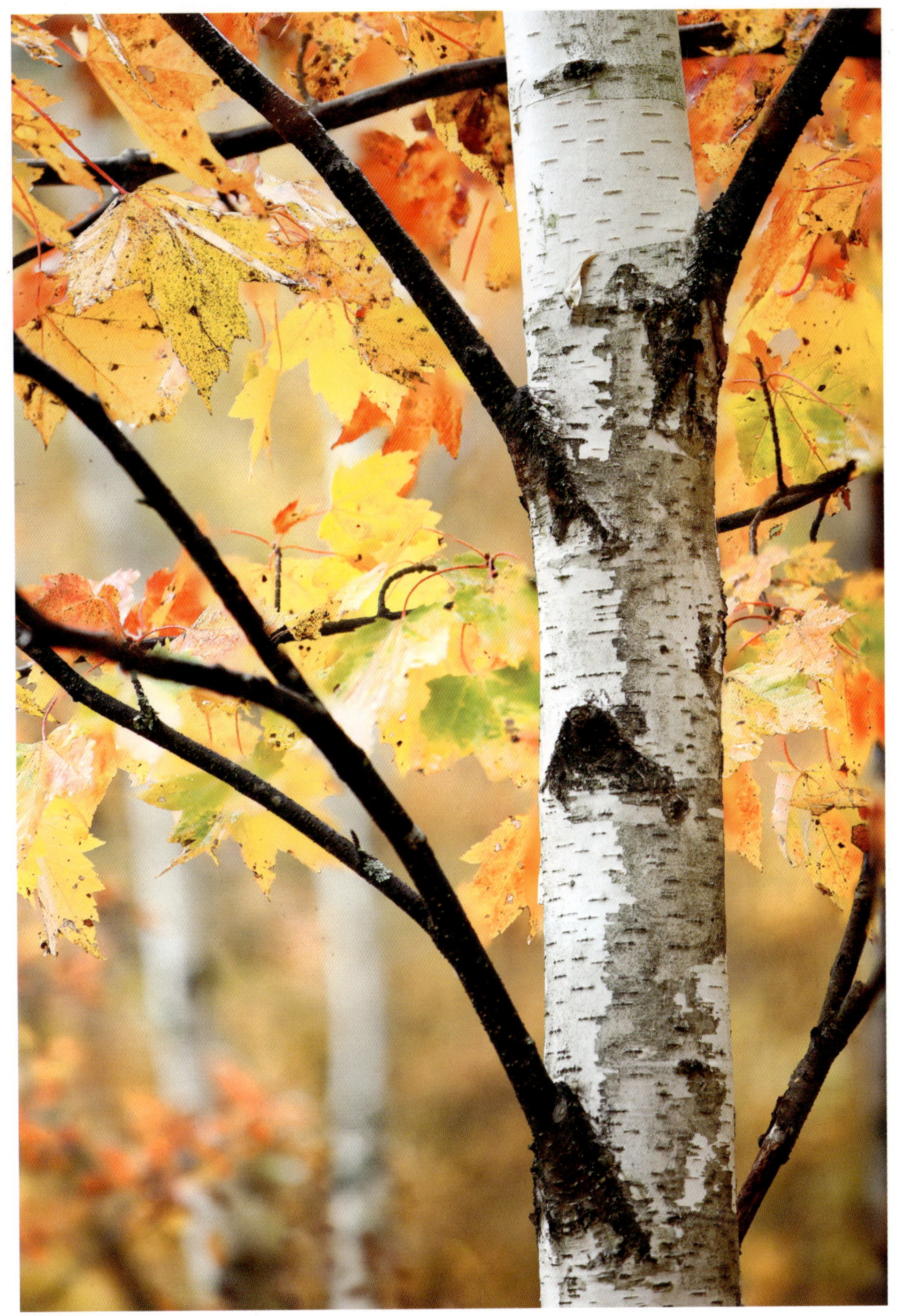

The colors shimmer on three birches at Duck Pond just after a light rain.

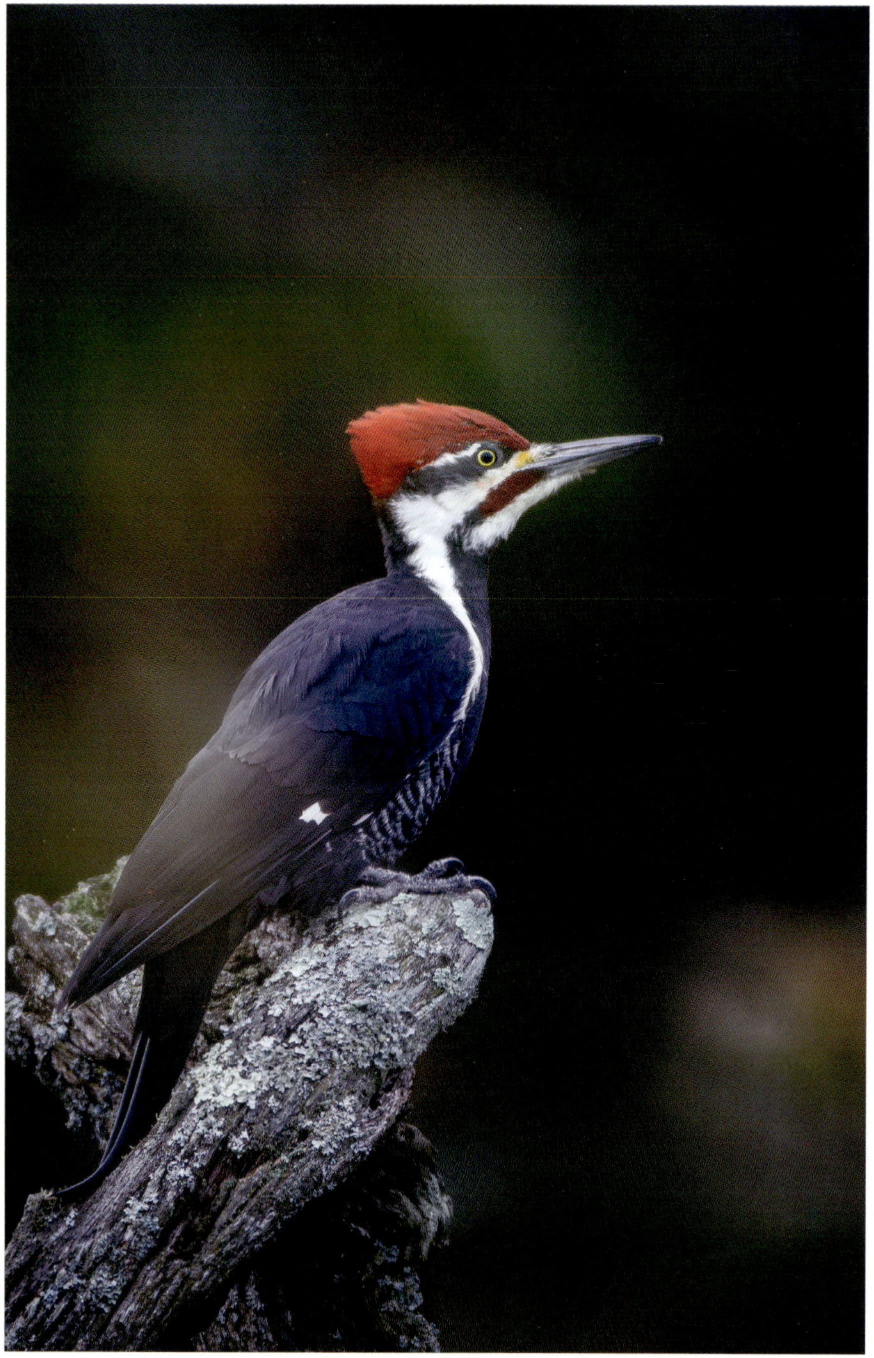

Pileated woodpecker at Ausable Point. You know they've been at work when you see large chunks of wood at the base of a tree.

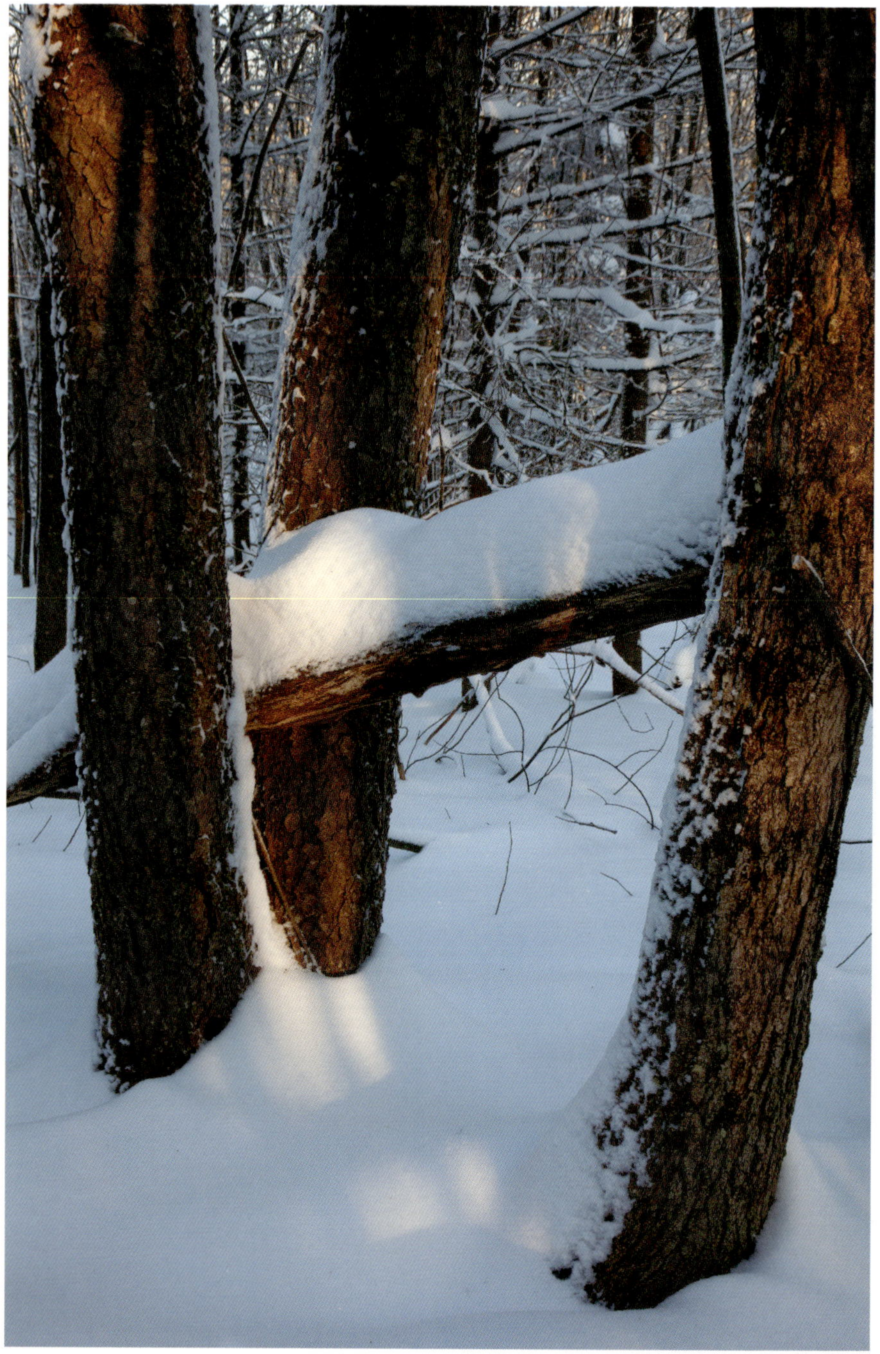

New snow in the late-afternoon light.

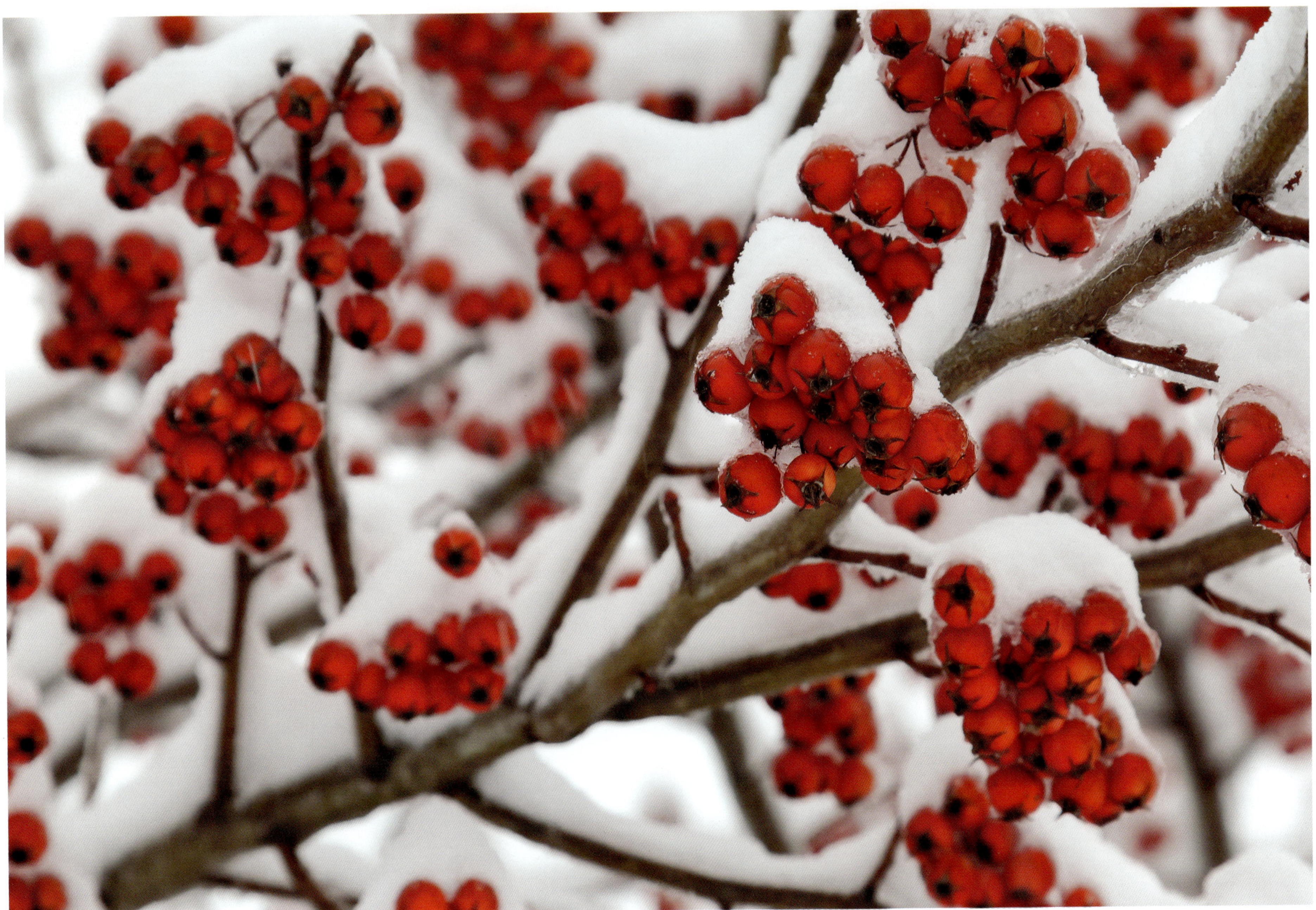

Red berries during a snowstorm in January.

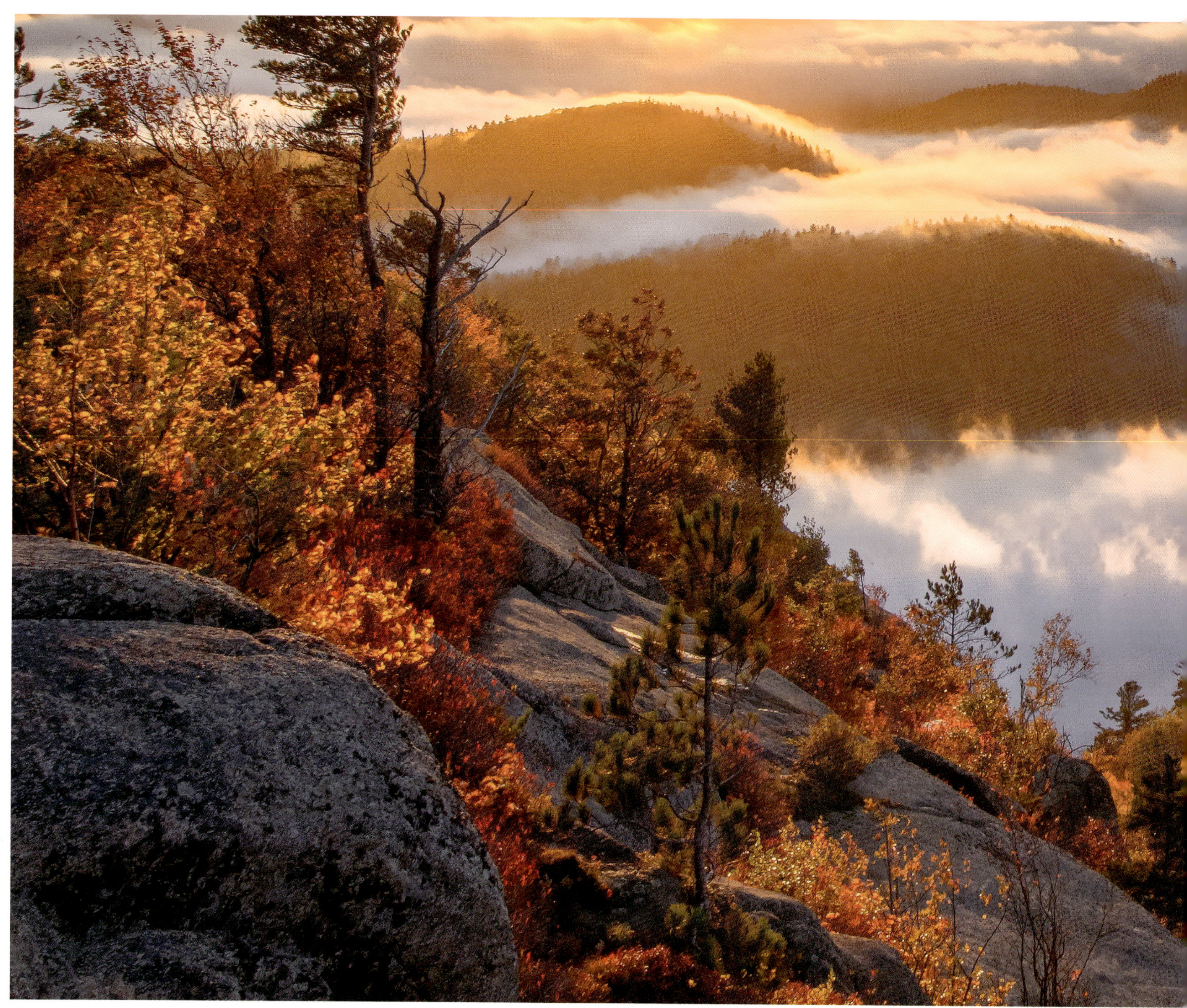

Cloud inversion at sunrise on Poke-O-Moonshine Mountain in the fall.

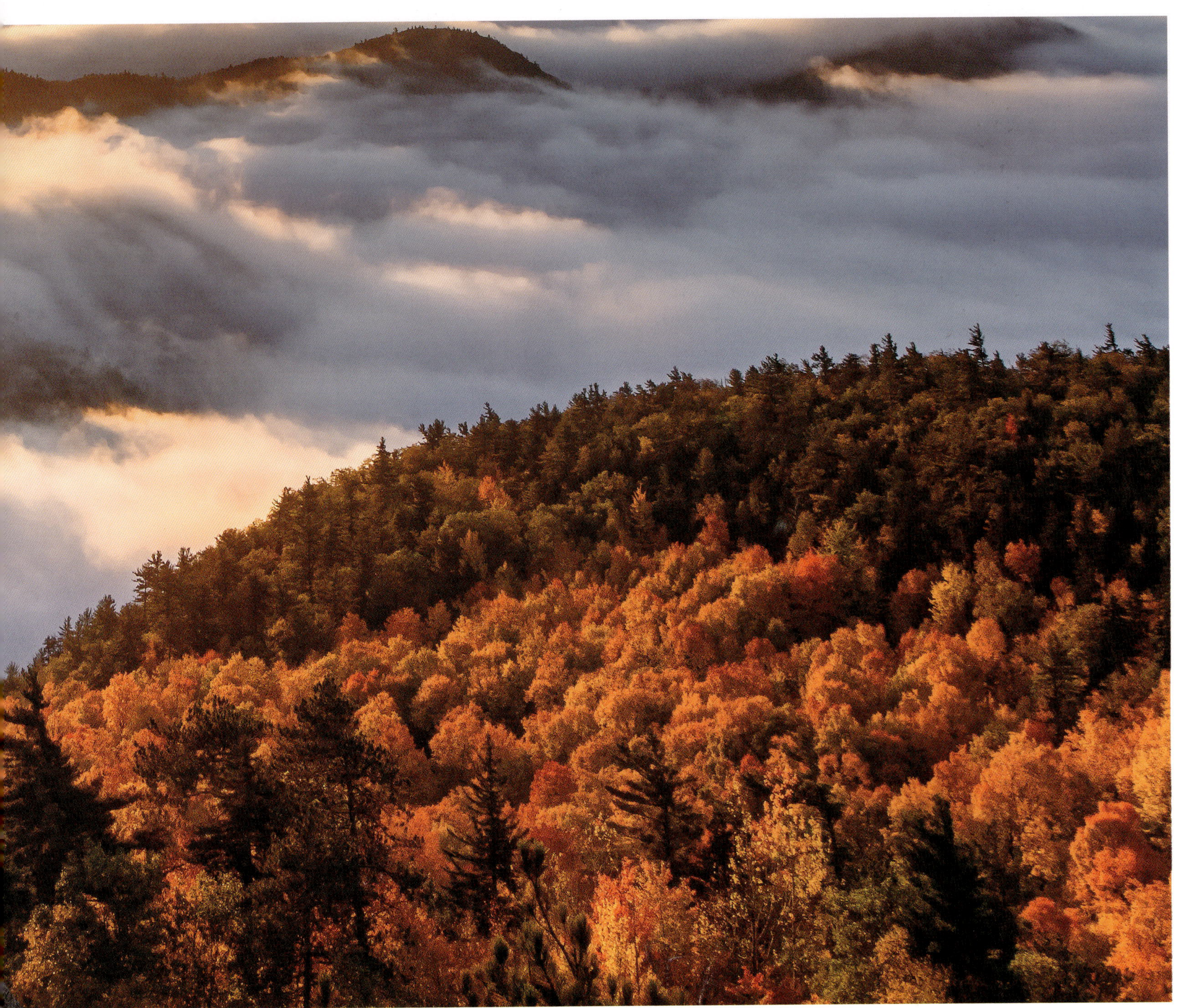

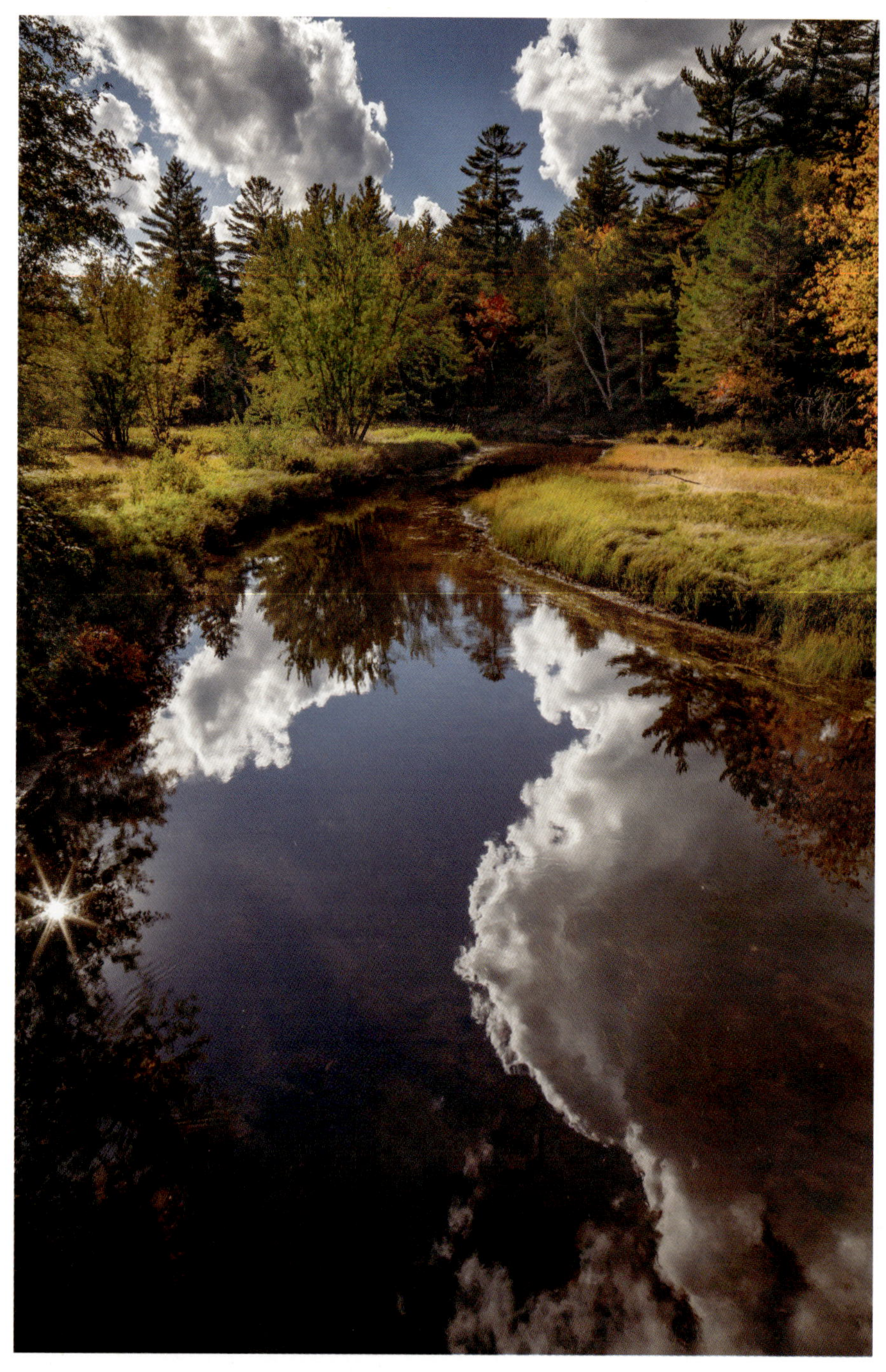

The clouds frame a reflection in this creek near Lower
Saranac Lake. The sun provides an exclamation point.

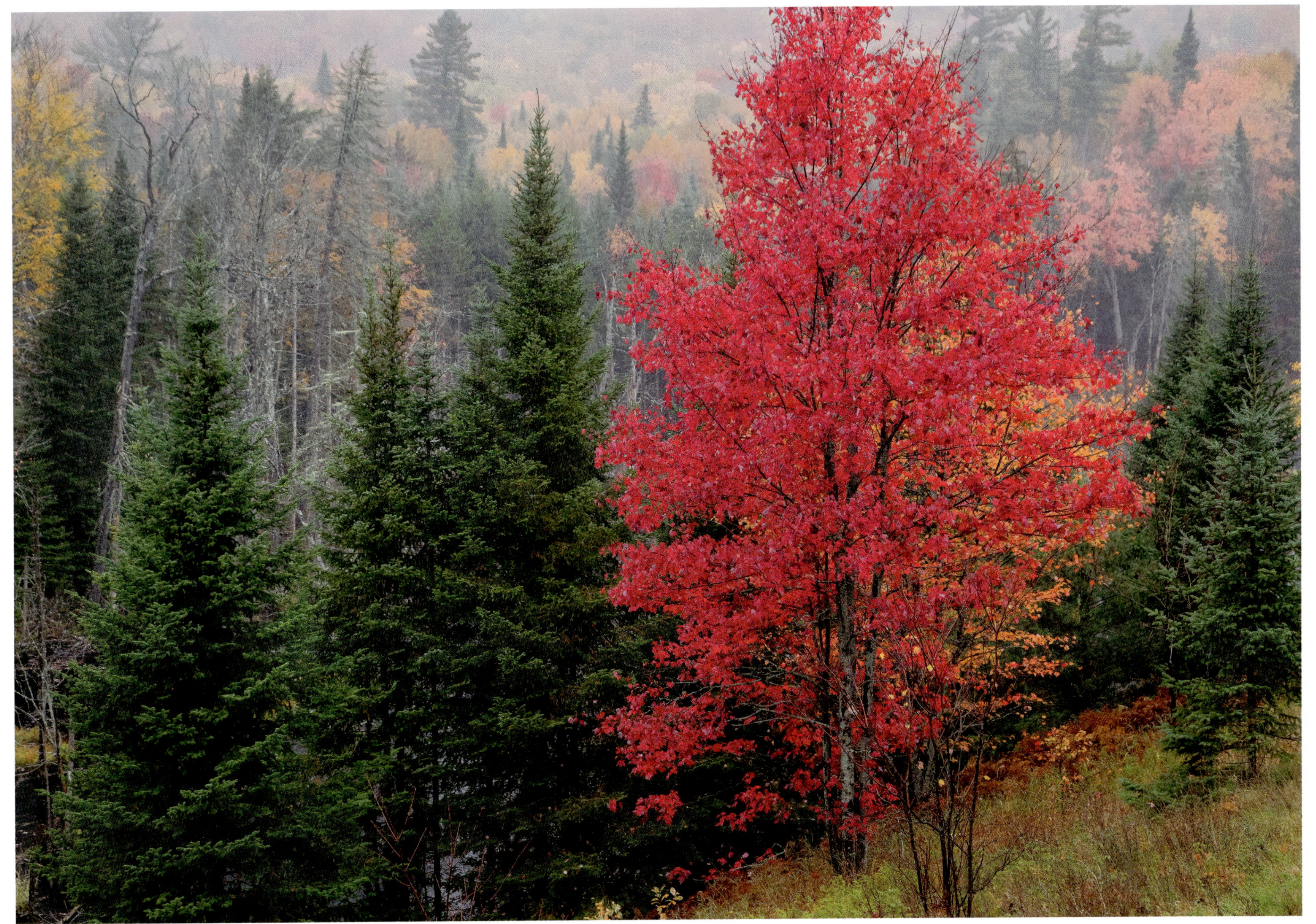

Red maple in the rain.

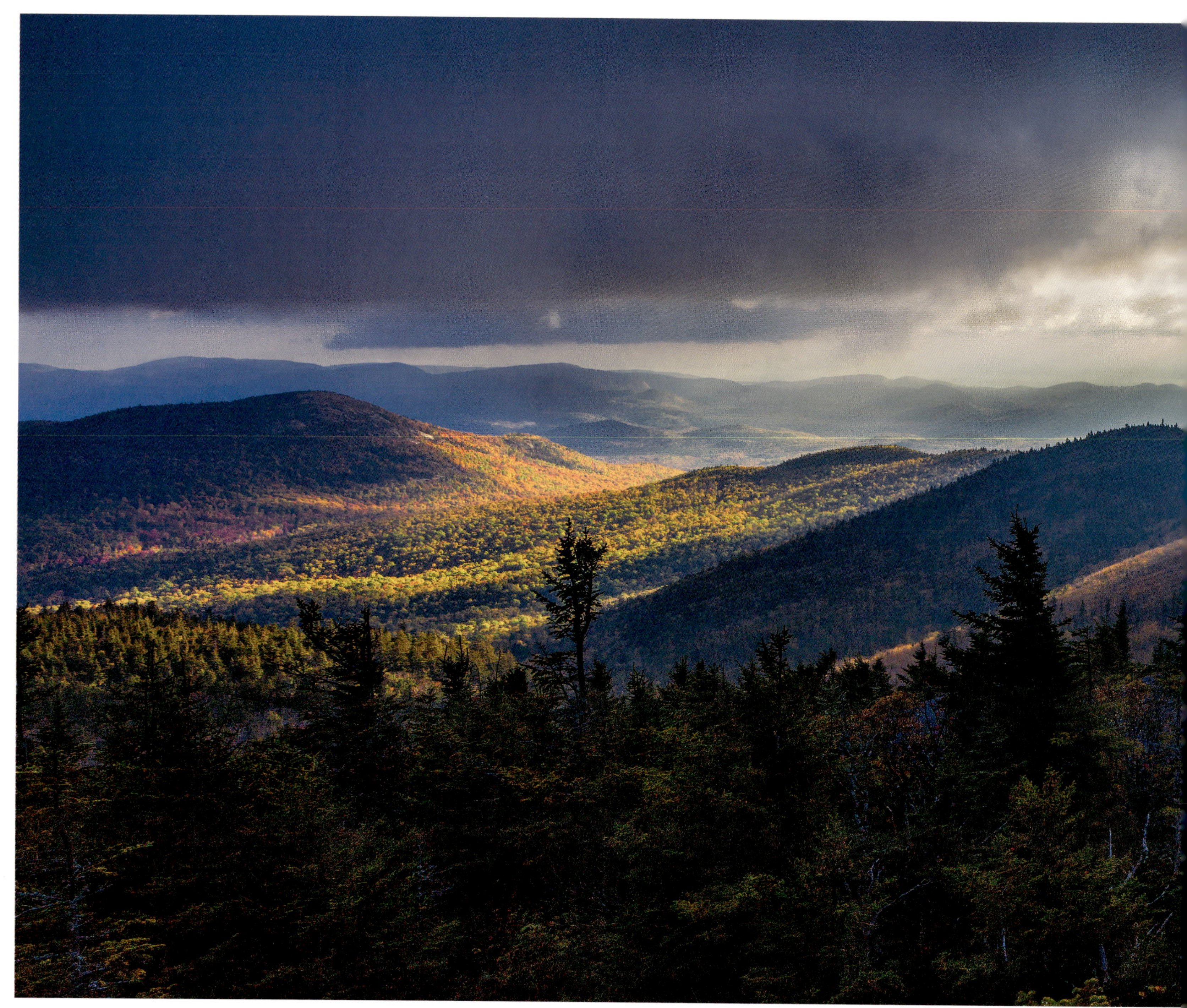

After a long morning of thick fog, the sun finally started to break through in patches on Jay Mountain.

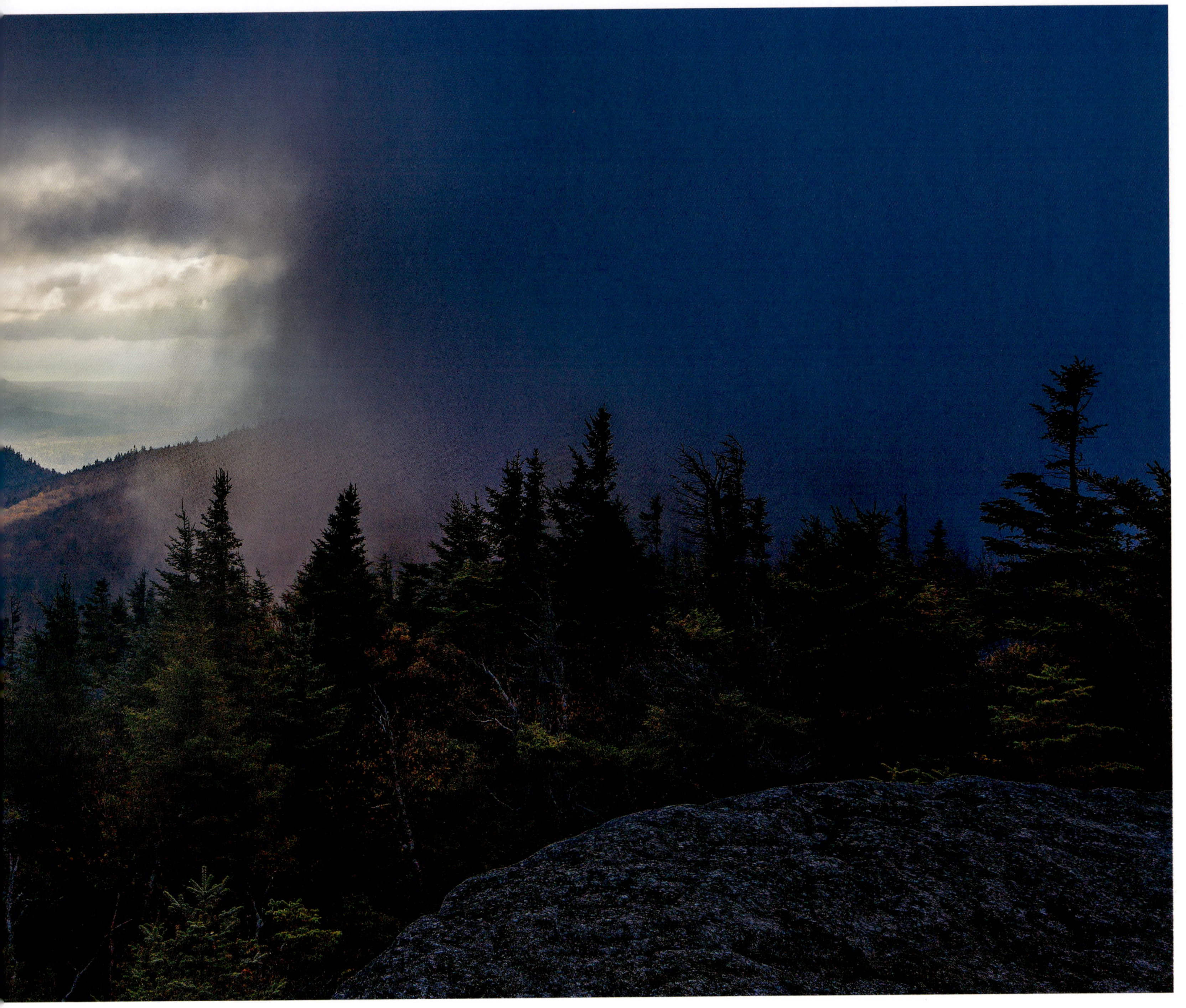

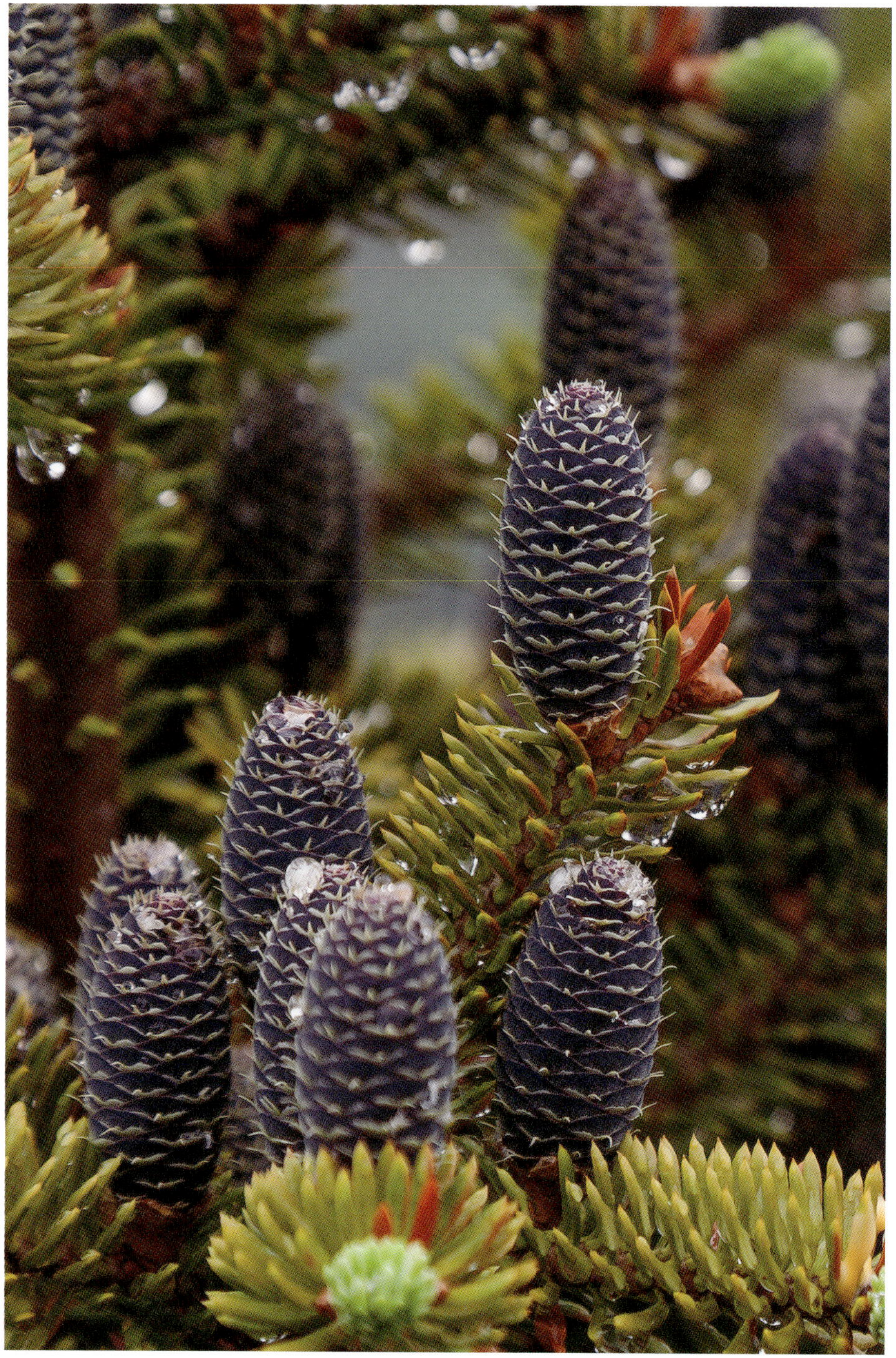

Balsam fir seed cones on Mount Jo.

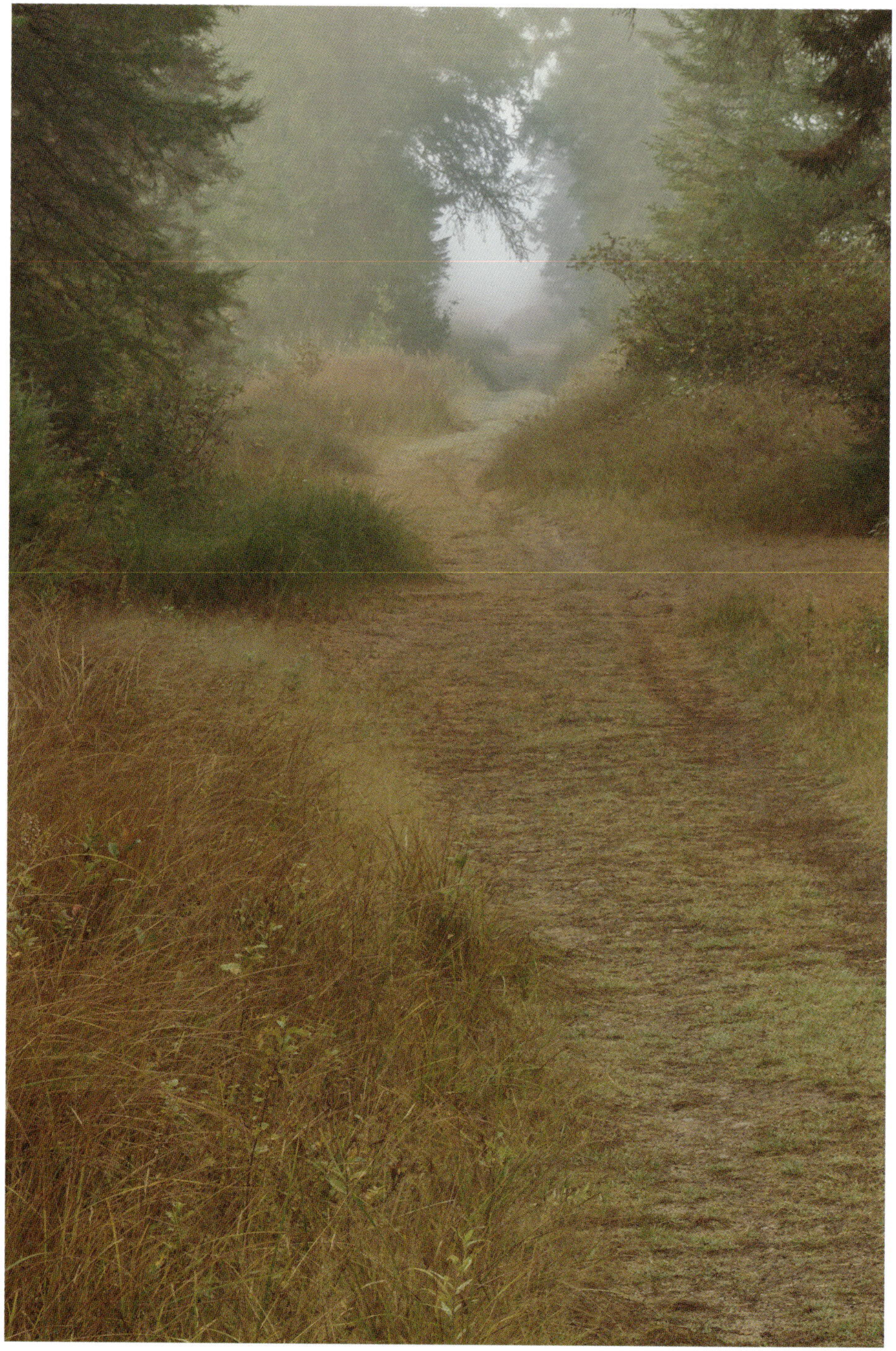

Bloomingdale Bog Trail in the early morning fog.

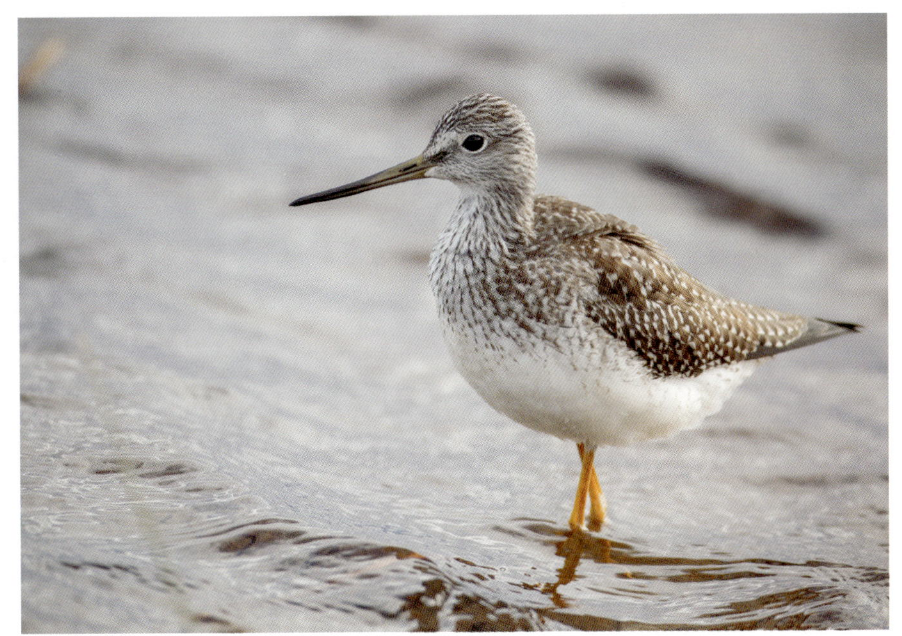

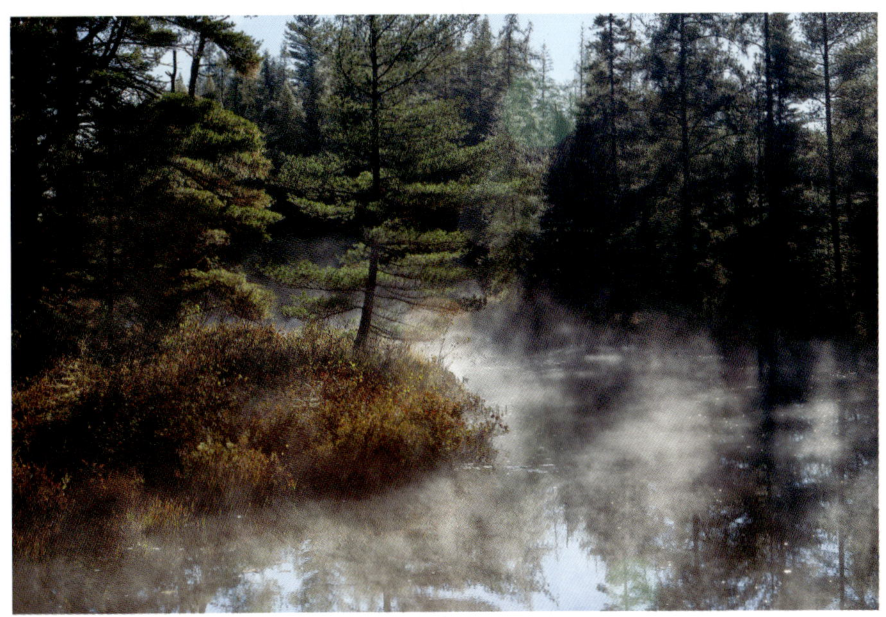

Top: Greater yellowlegs feeding at Ausable Point.
Bottom: Misty inlet near Bloomingdale.

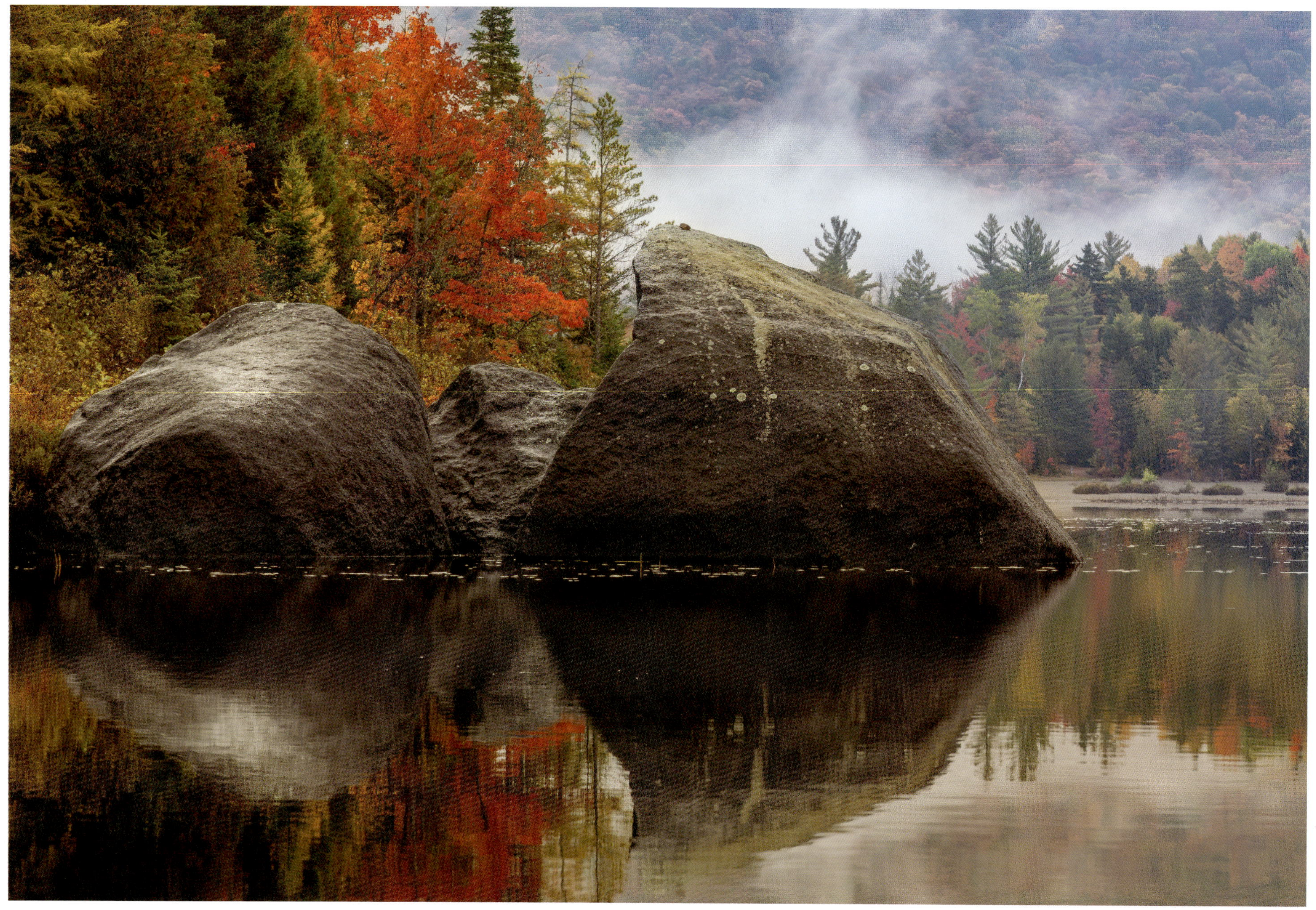

Boulders on Cheney Pond on a misty fall morning.

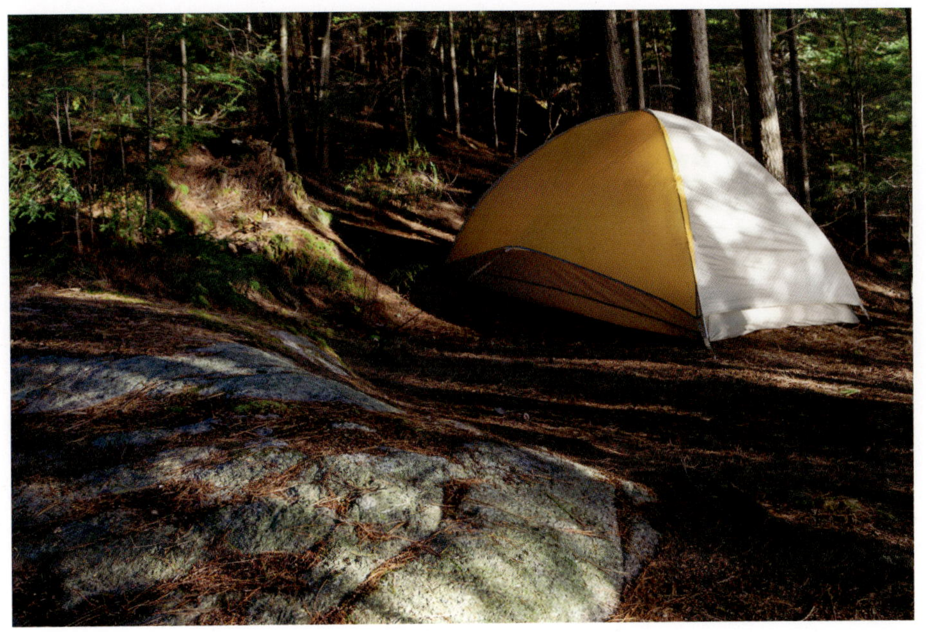

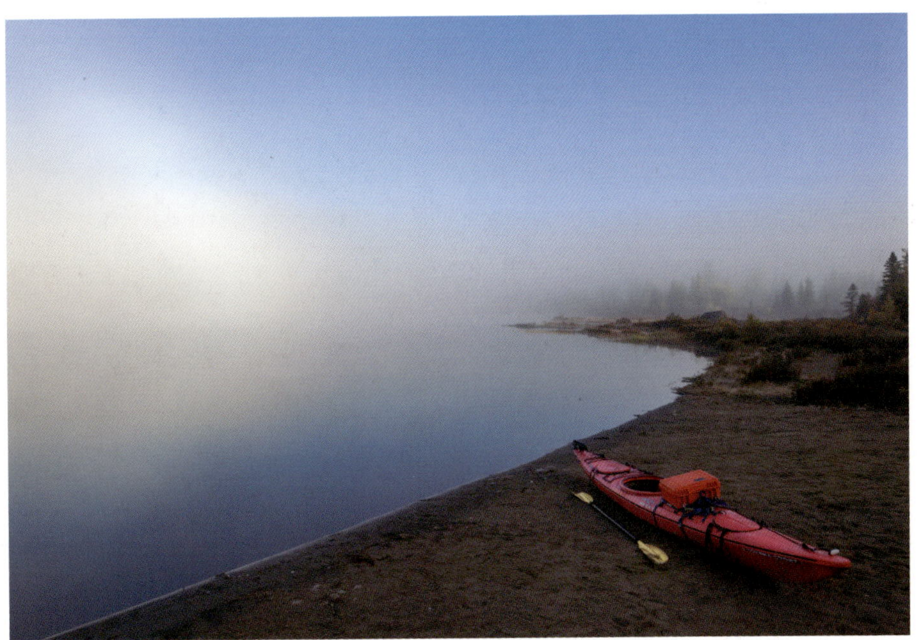

Top: Dappled light at a campsite on Upper Saranac Lake.
Bottom: As the sun burned away the cold morning fog, an apparitional scene (a "fogbow")
appeared as the sun's low rays lit up the receding fog at a campsite near Newcomb.

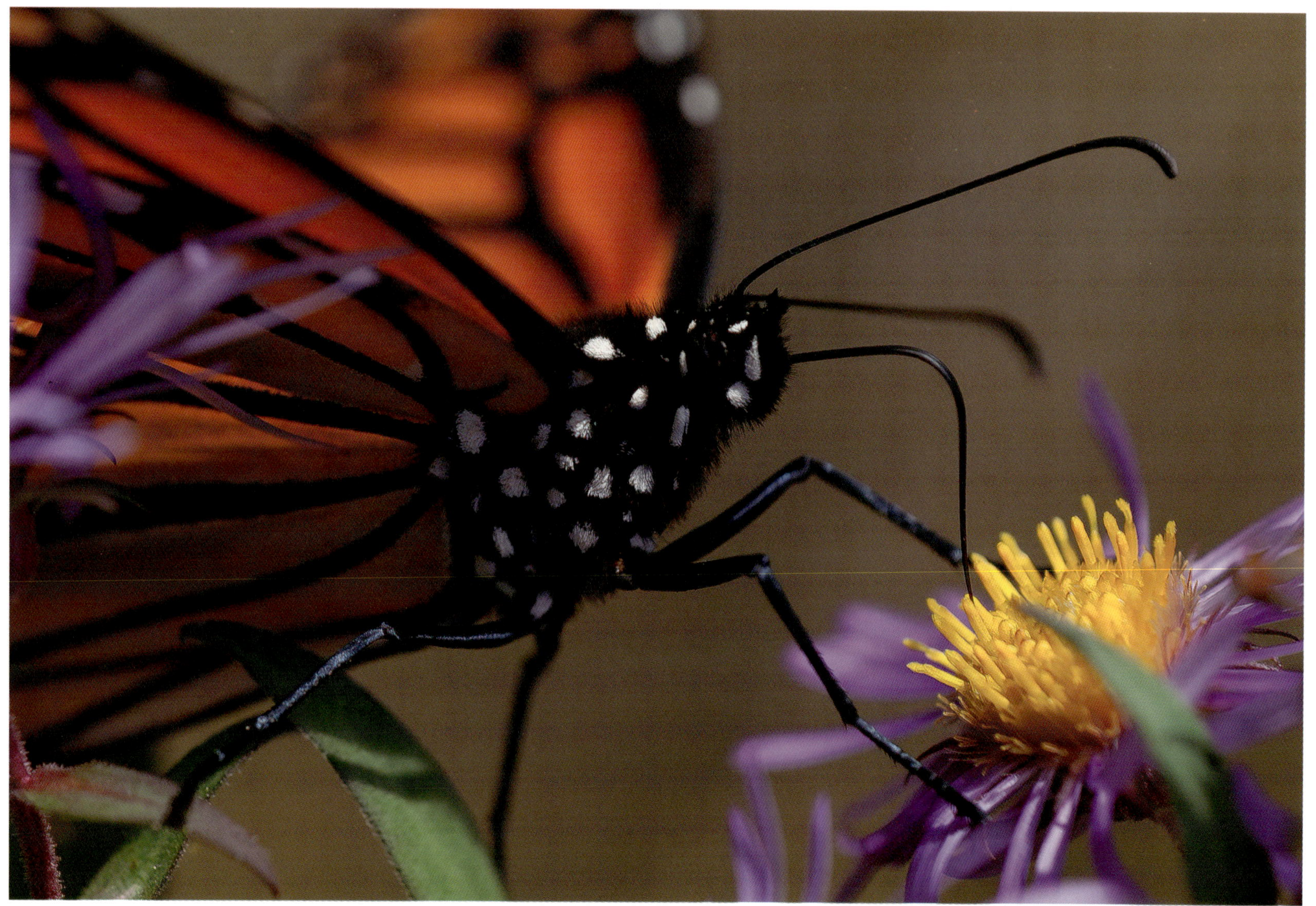

Monarch butterfly sipping nectar through its proboscis.

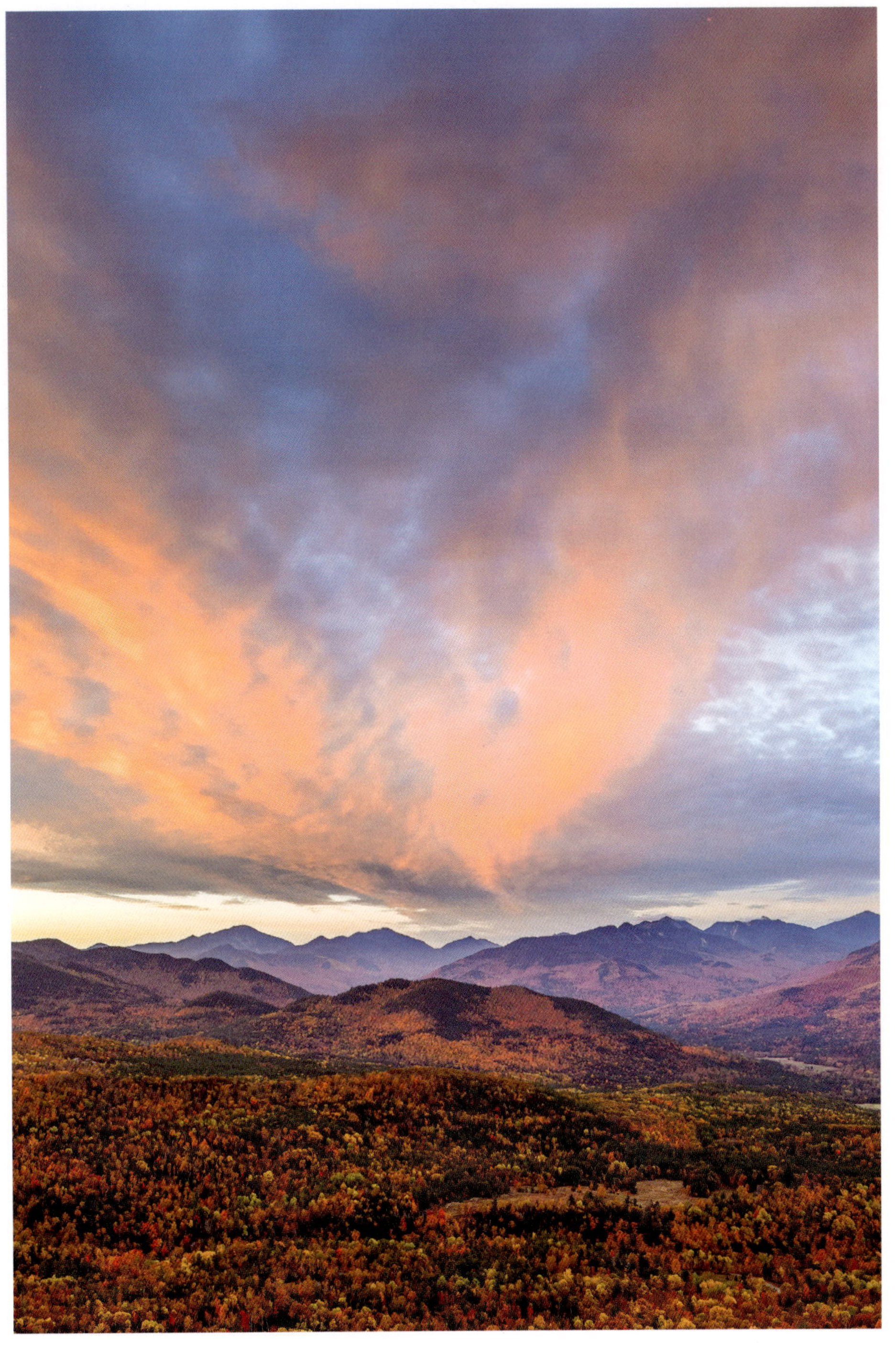

Sunrise from Big Crow Mountain in the fall.

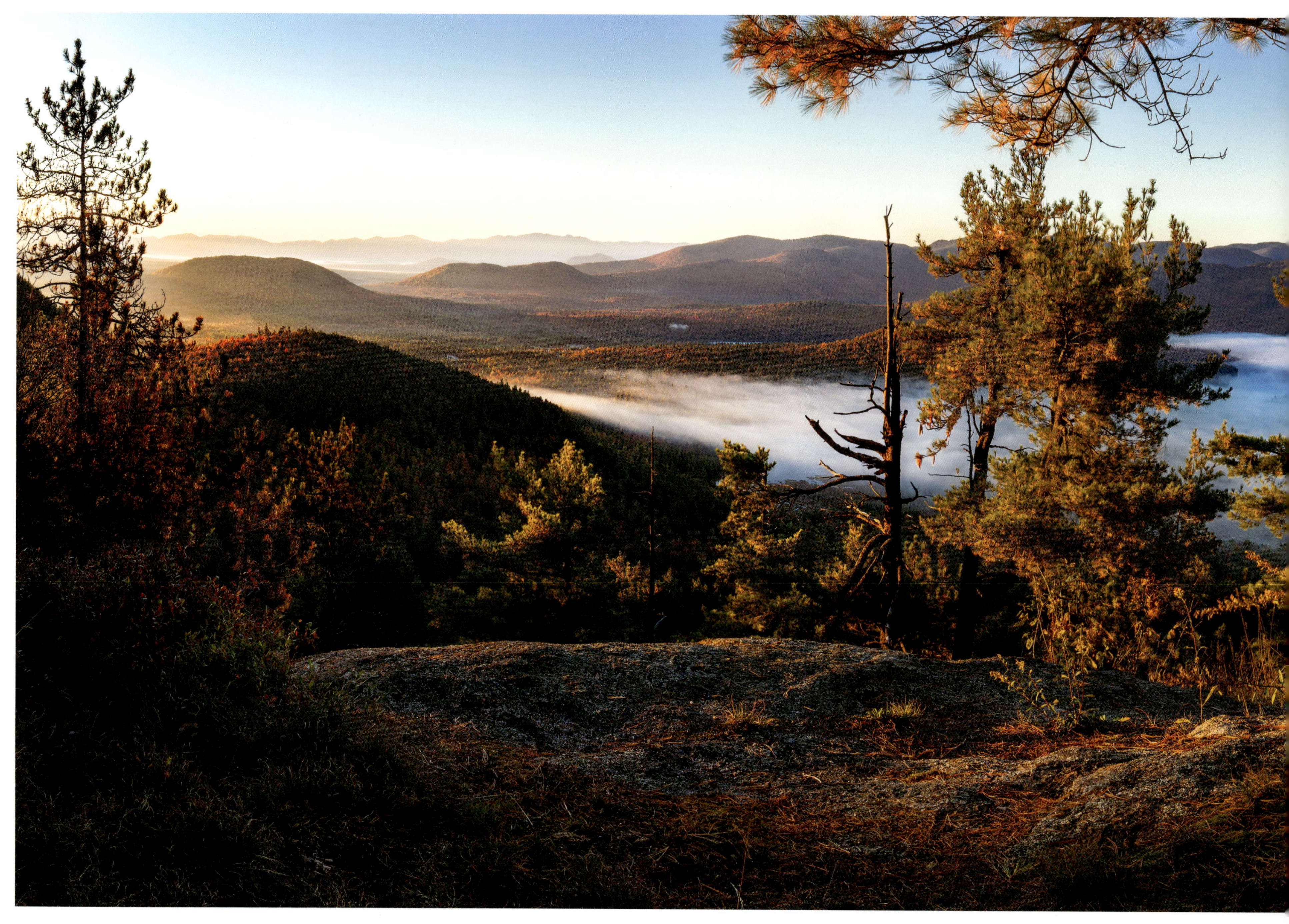

The first rays of the sun from the top of Silver Lake Mountain. The warm water from the lakes condensed in the cool air to create fog in the valley.

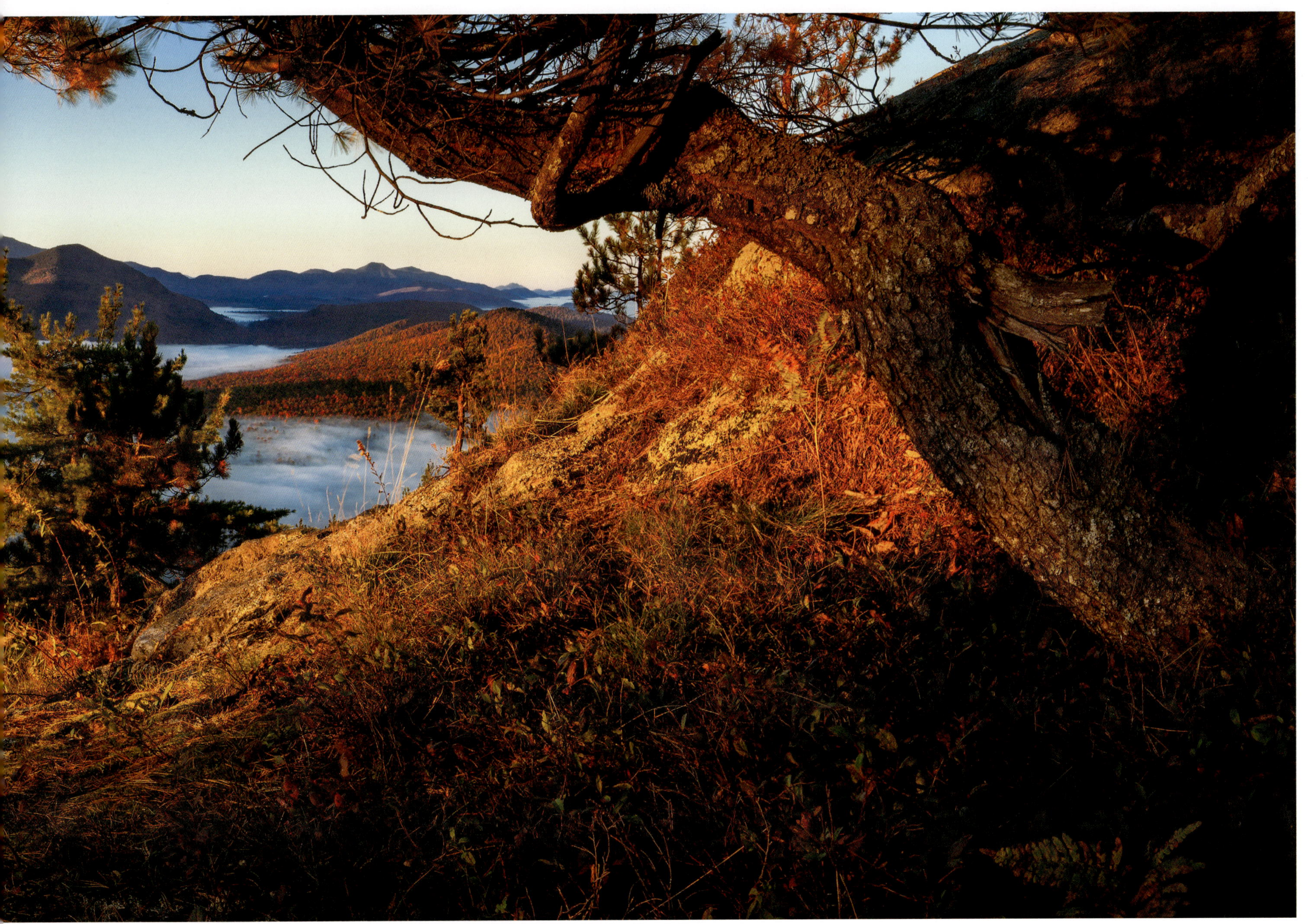

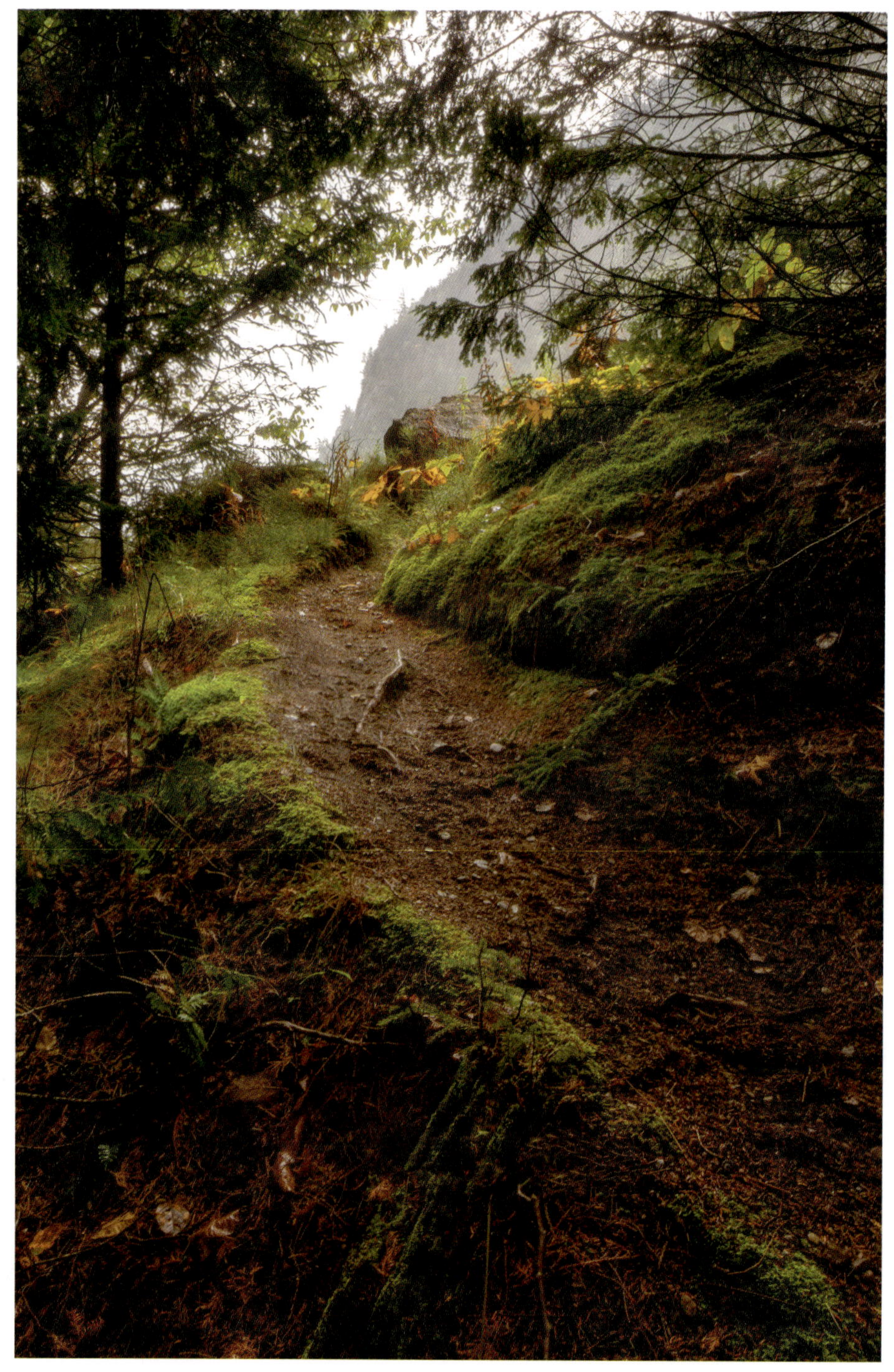

Steep climb up the bank from a fishing spot on the Ausable River.

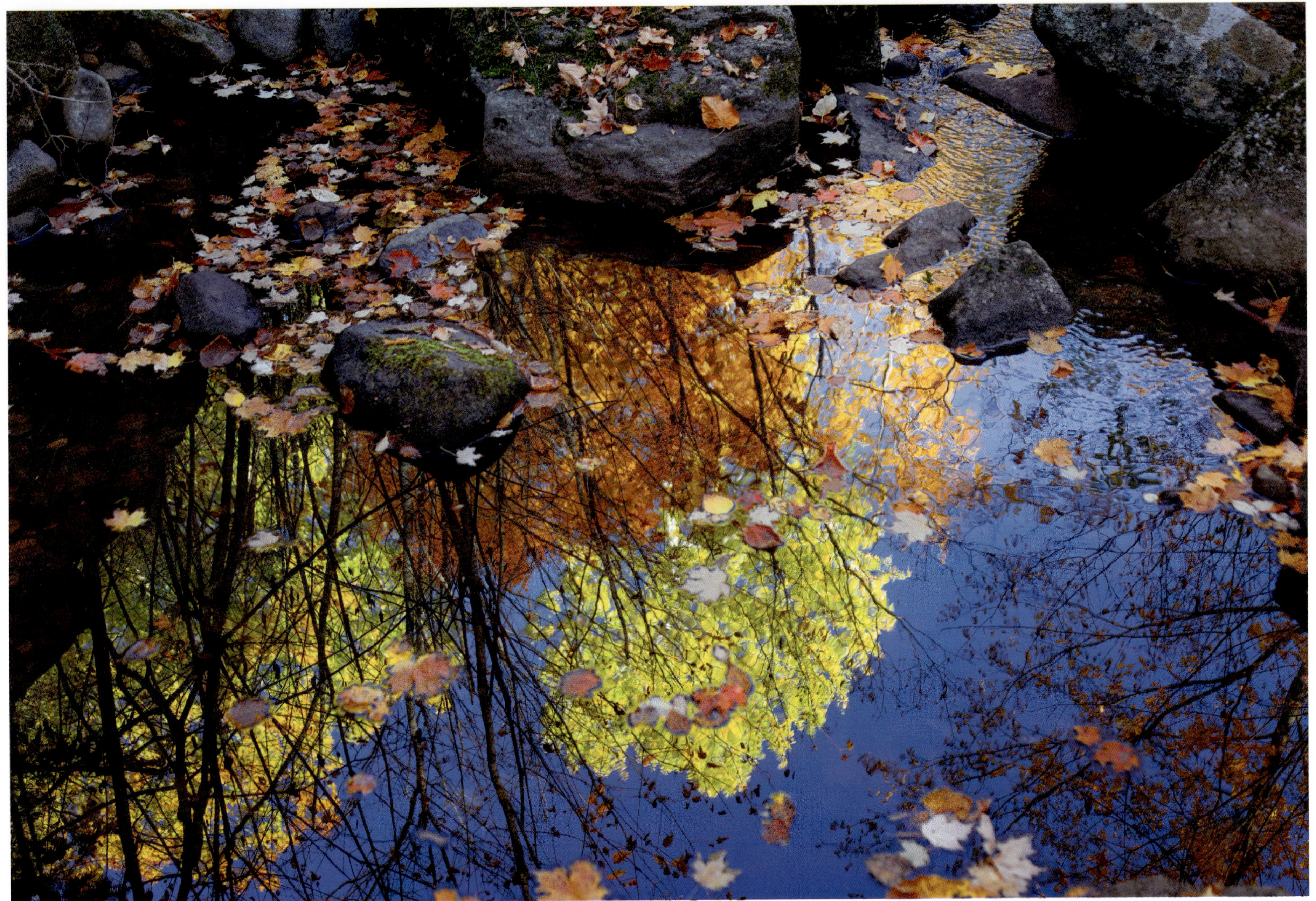

Reflections in a stream on the trail to Hurricane Mountain.

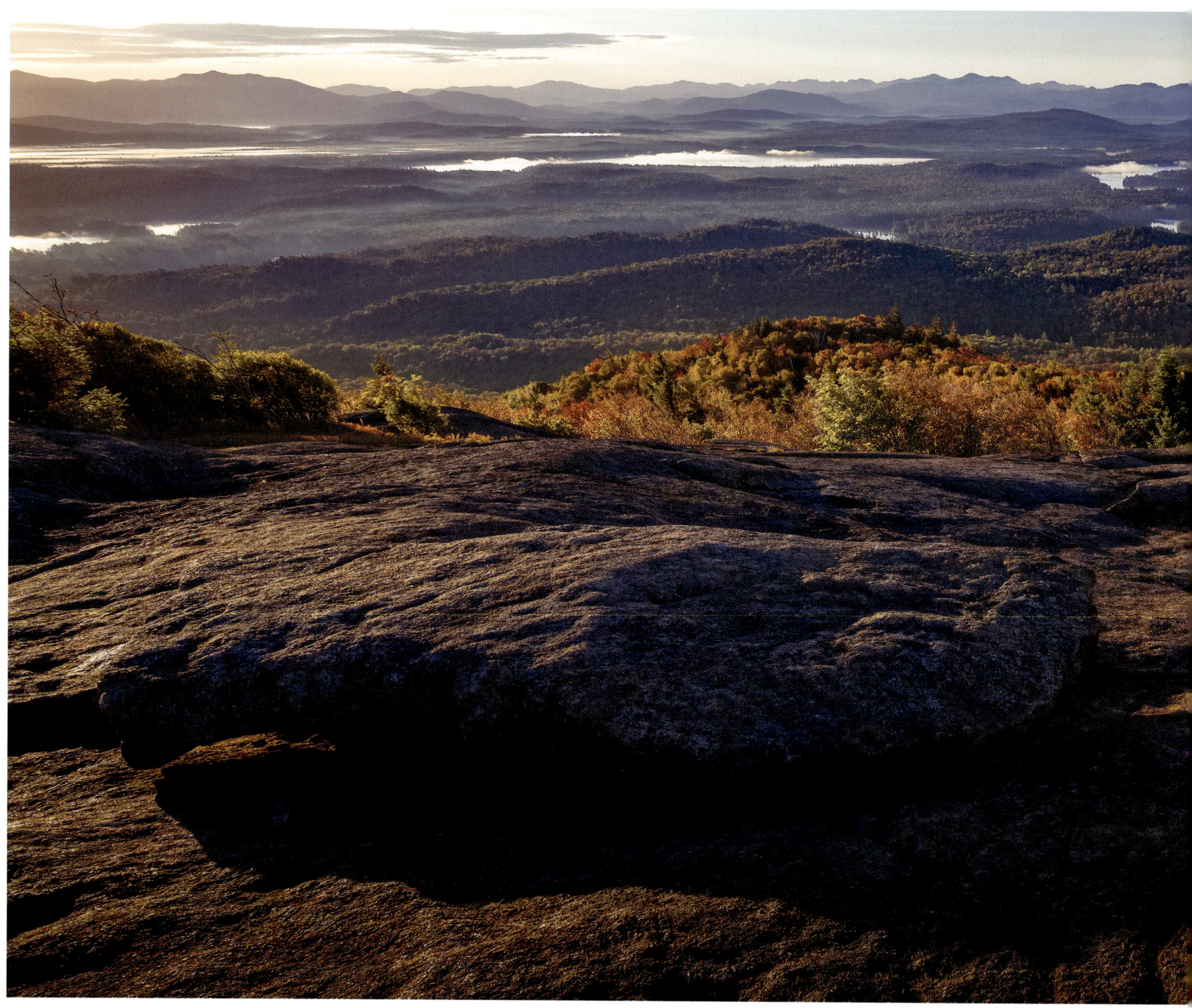

Early light over the Saint Regis Canoe Area from the top of Saint Regis Mountain.

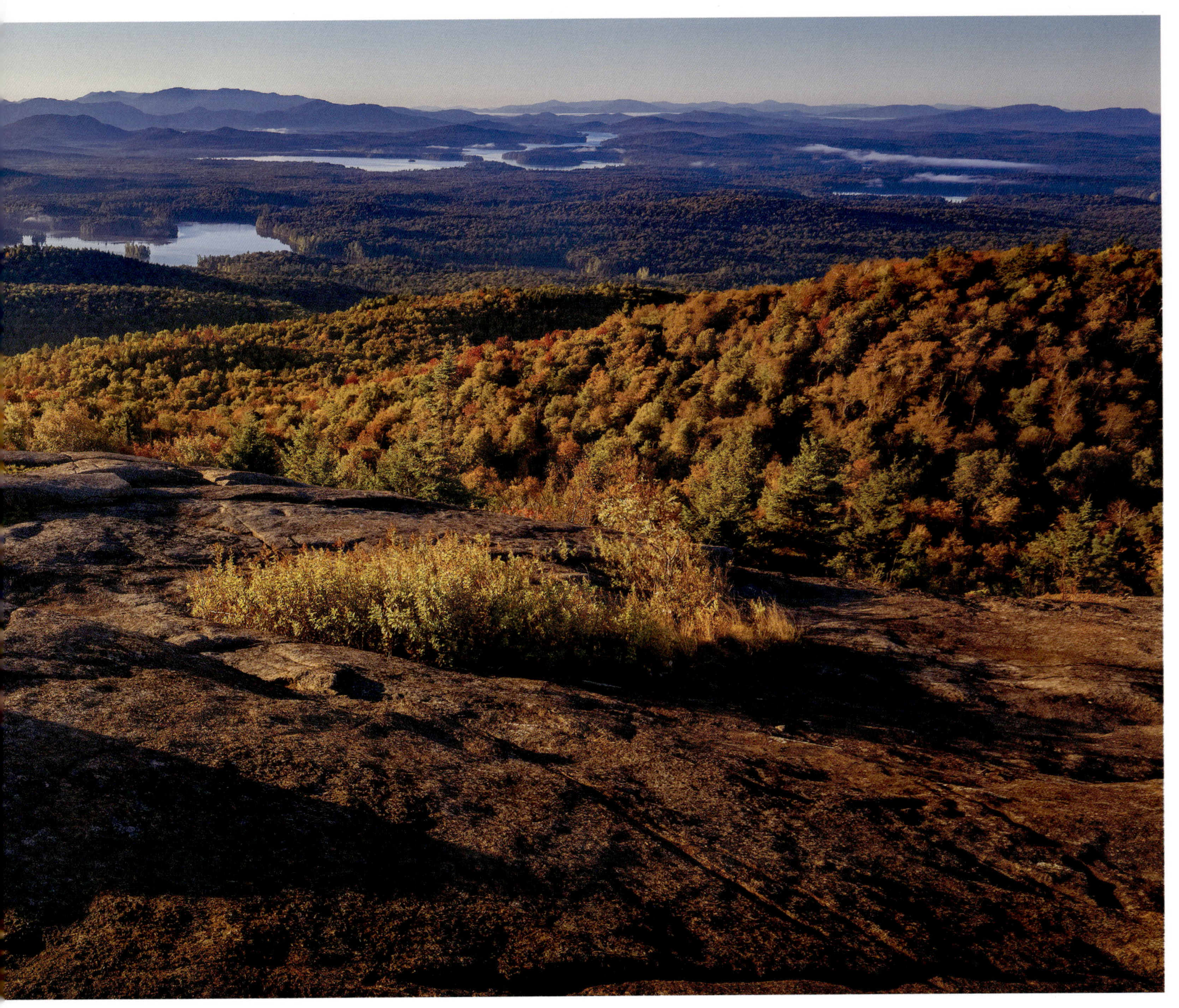

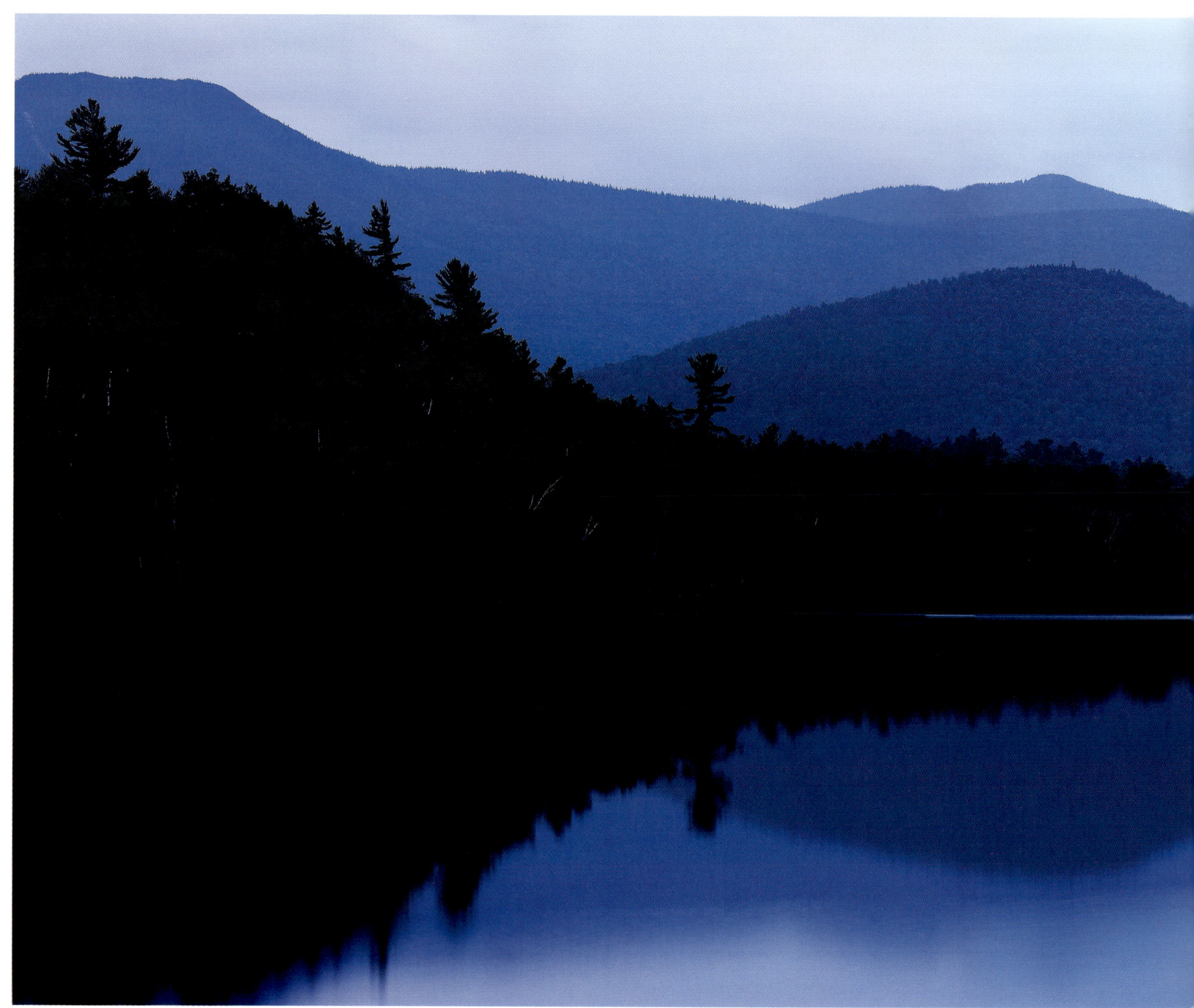

View from the canoe/kayak launch at Franklin Falls at dusk.

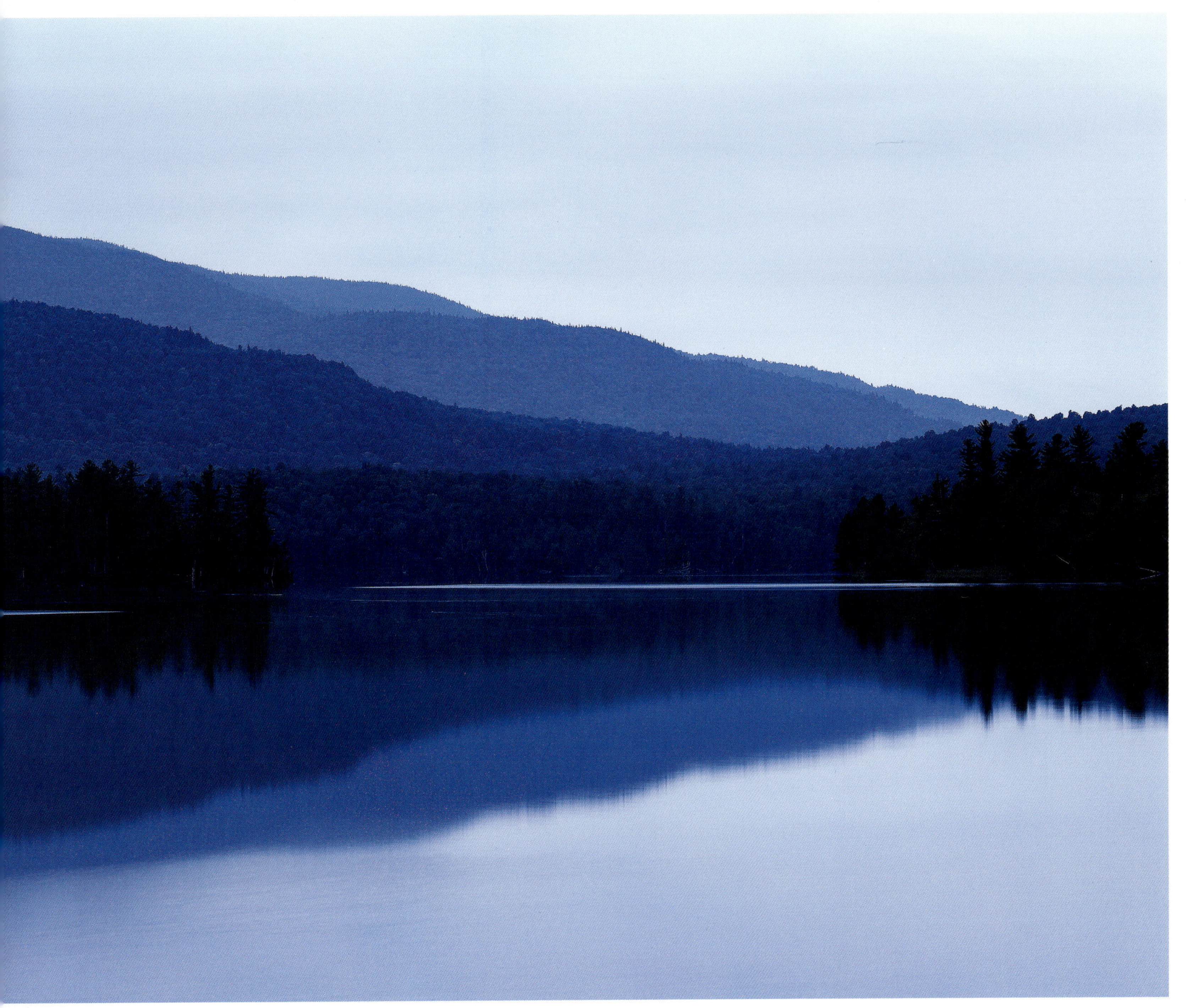

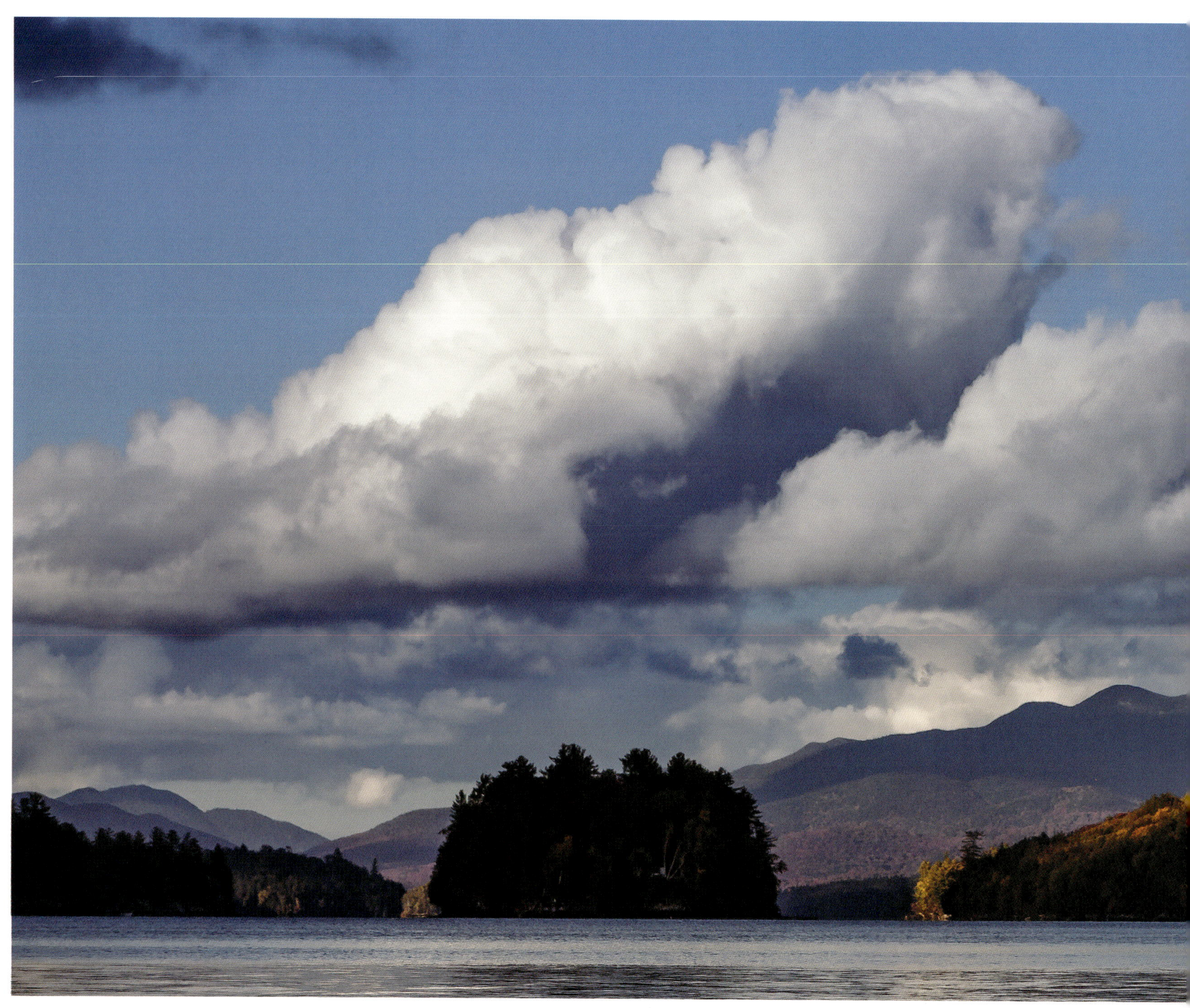

View from my kayak on Long Lake in early October.

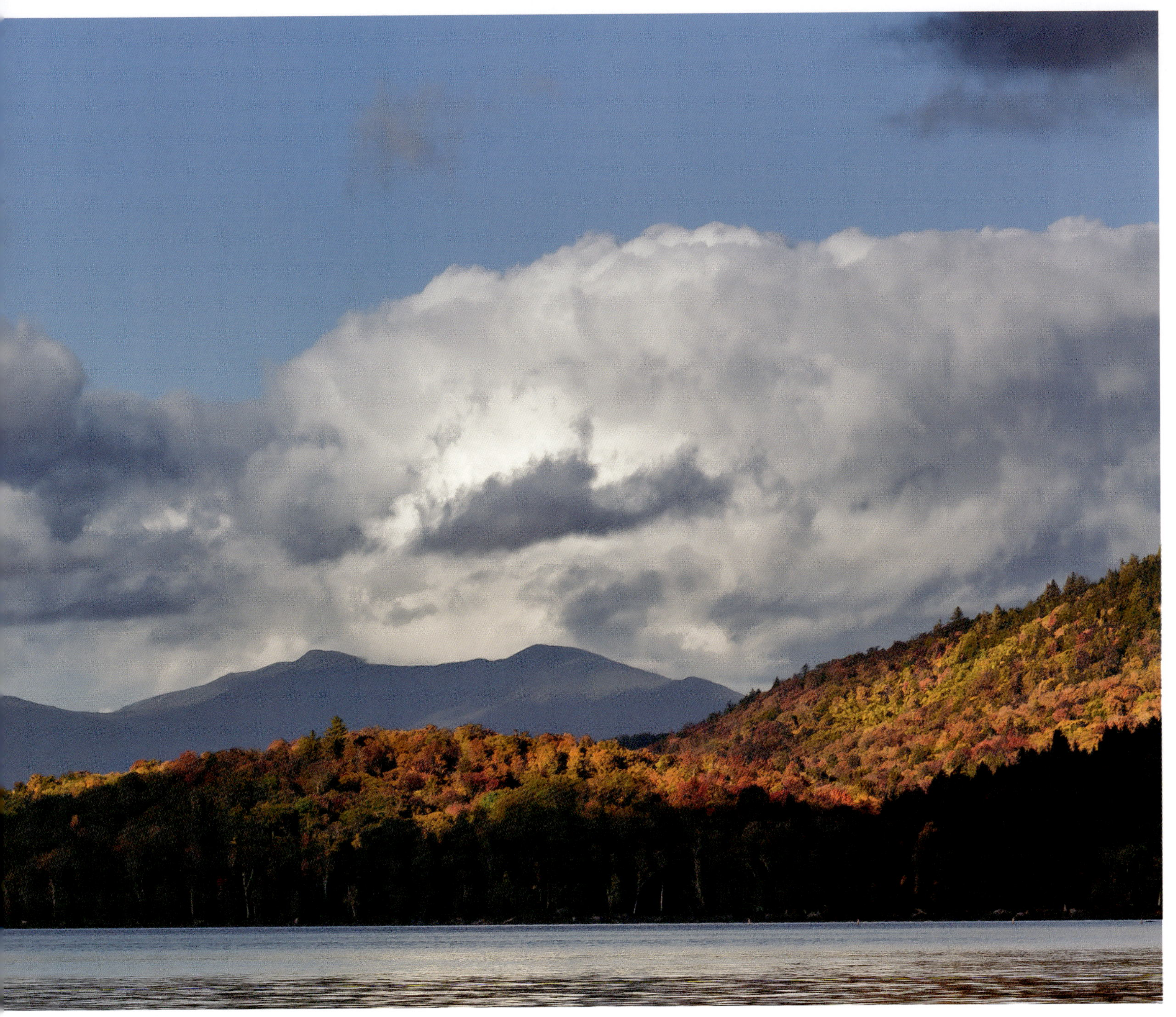

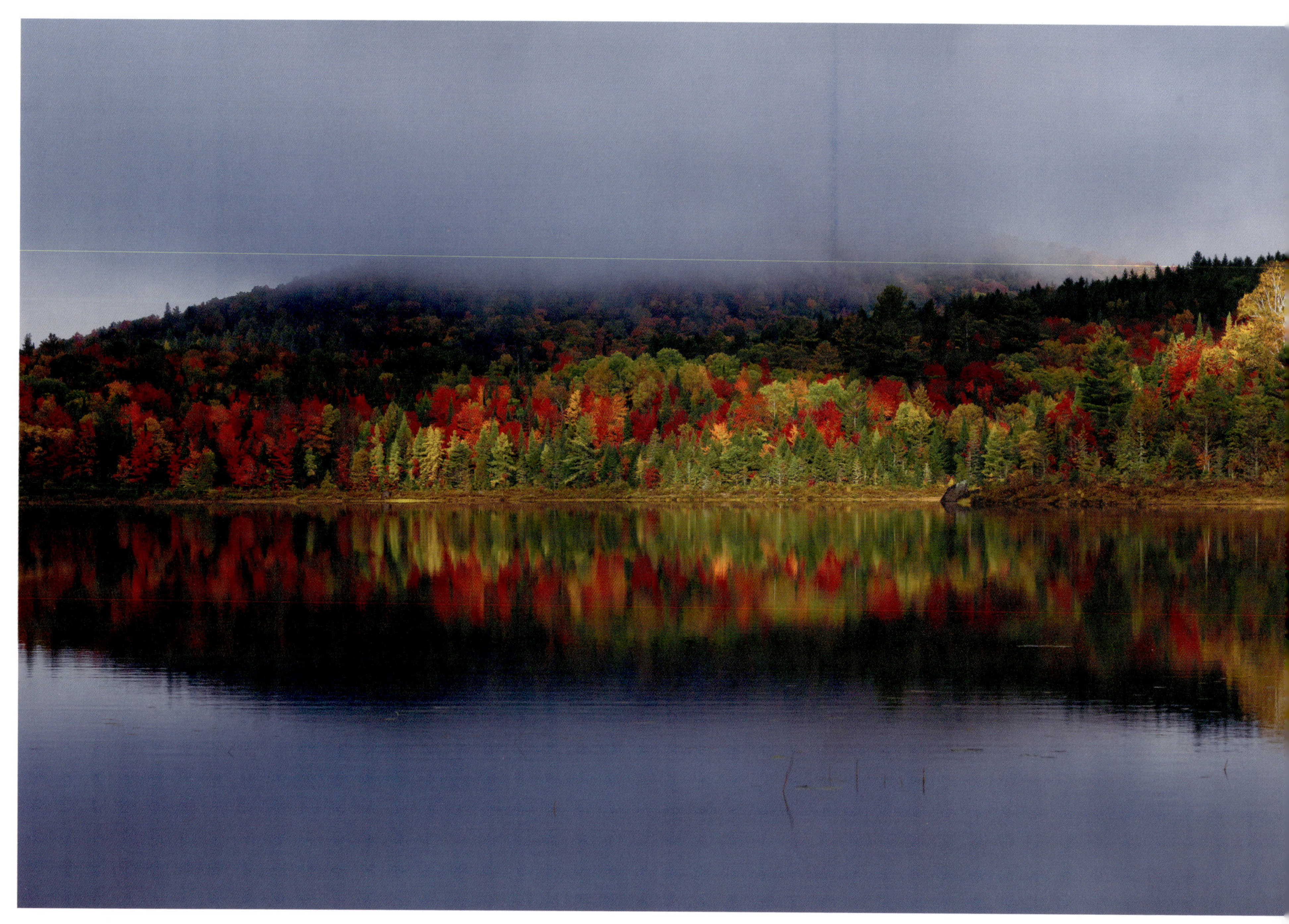

As the fog started to burn off, the sun's rays lit up the opposite shore on Cheney Pond. We heard coyotes there the previous night.

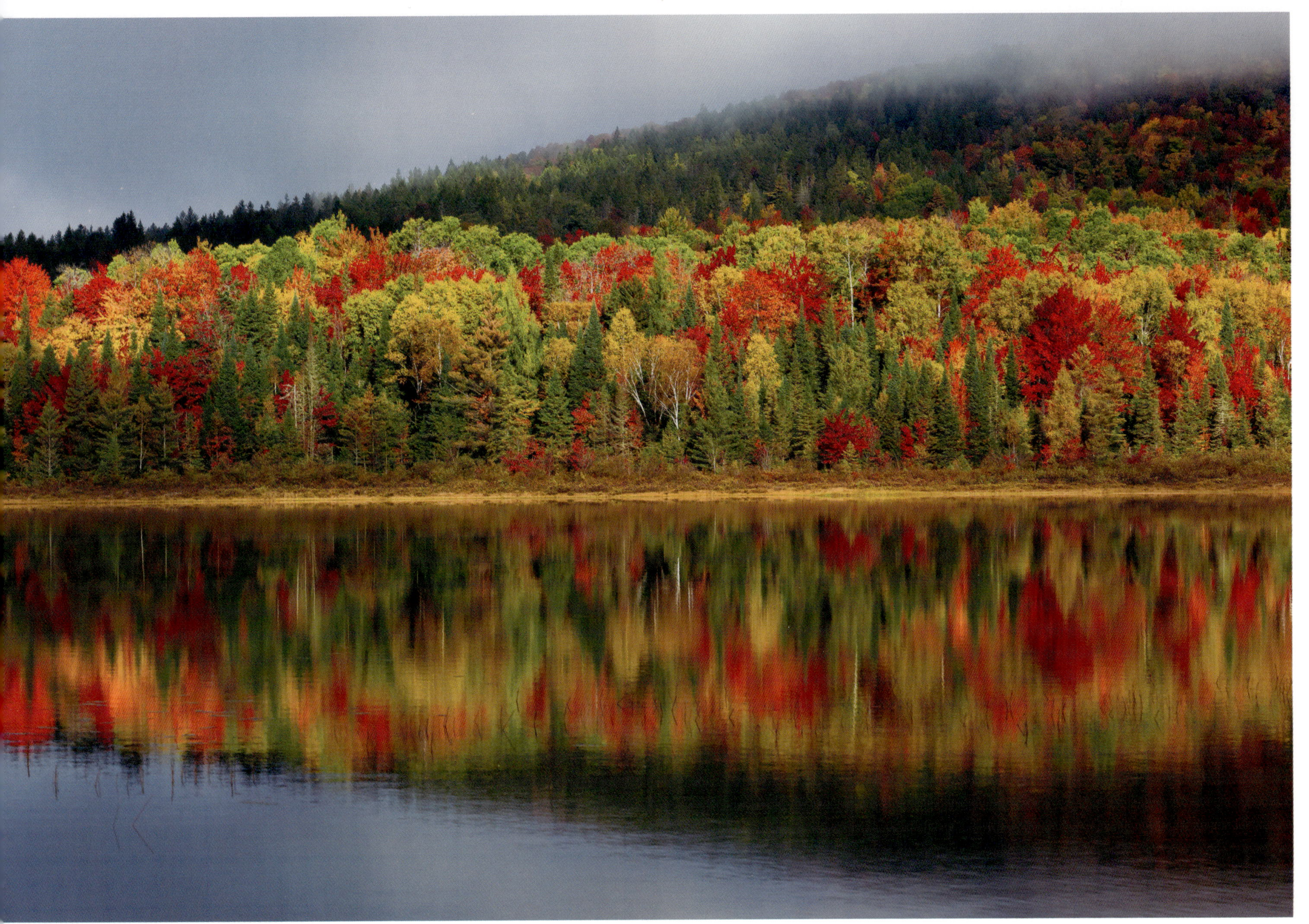

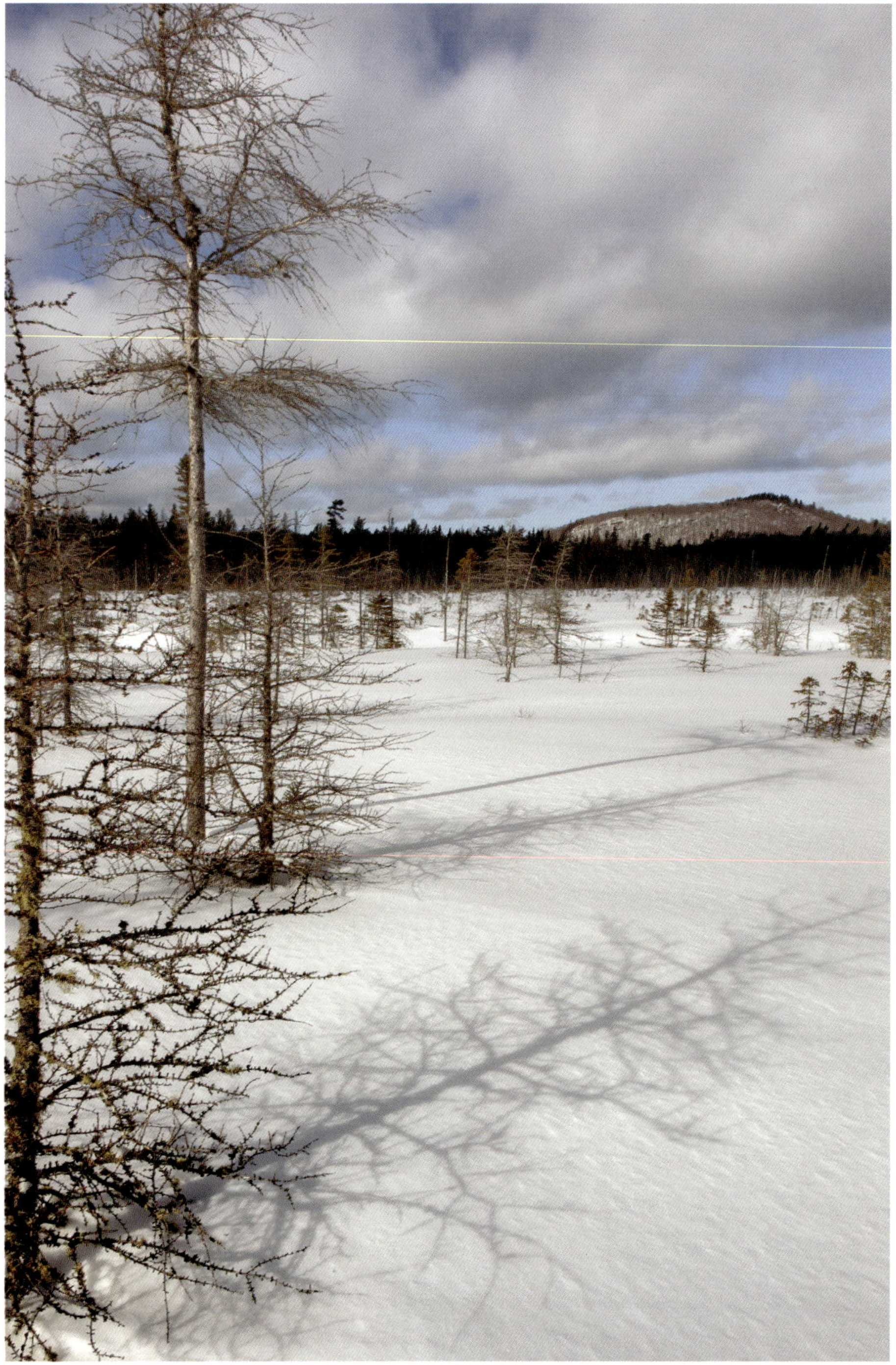

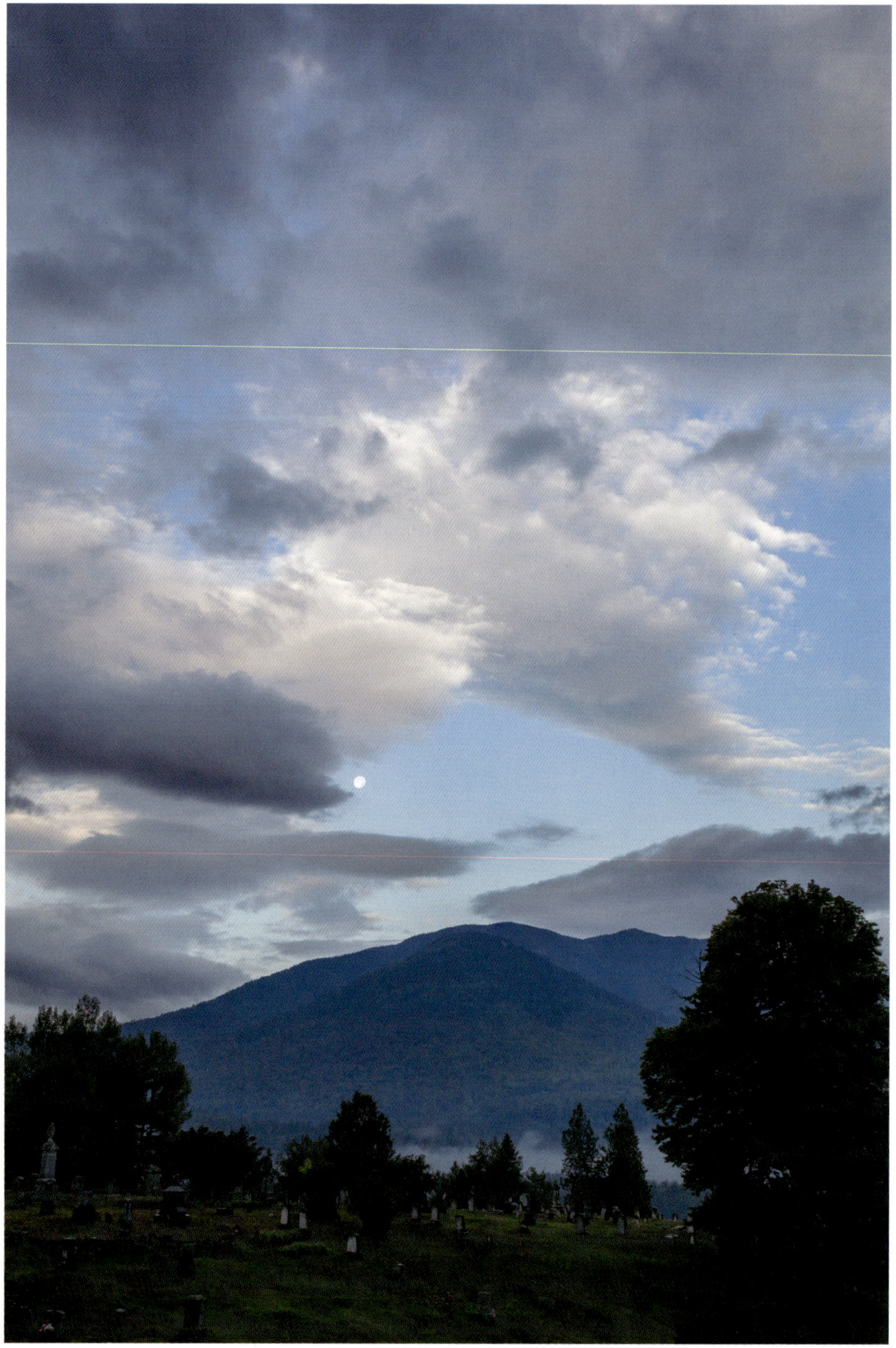

   Winter on the trails at Paul Smith College's Visitor Interpretive Center.

Moonset over Porter and Cascade Mountains from the cemetery in Keene.

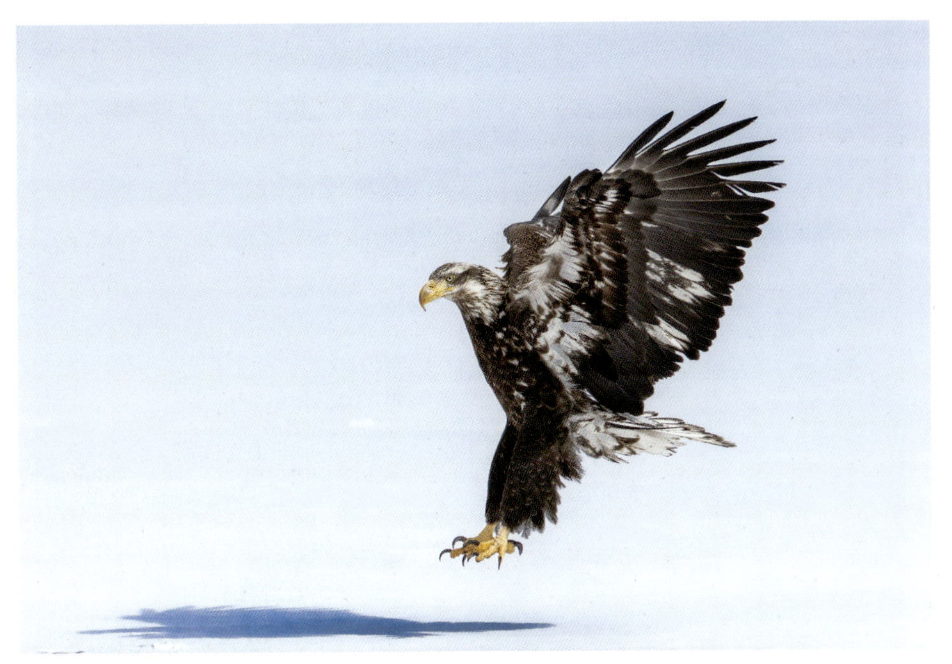

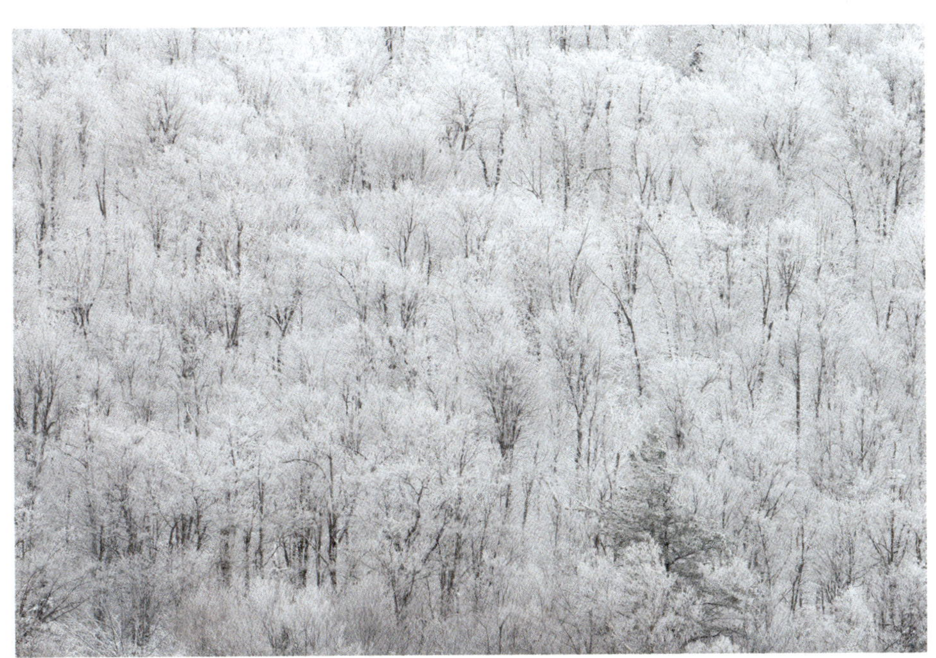

Top: Juvenile bald eagle landing on the snow at Ausable Point.
Bottom: Patterns made by trees and recent snowfall.

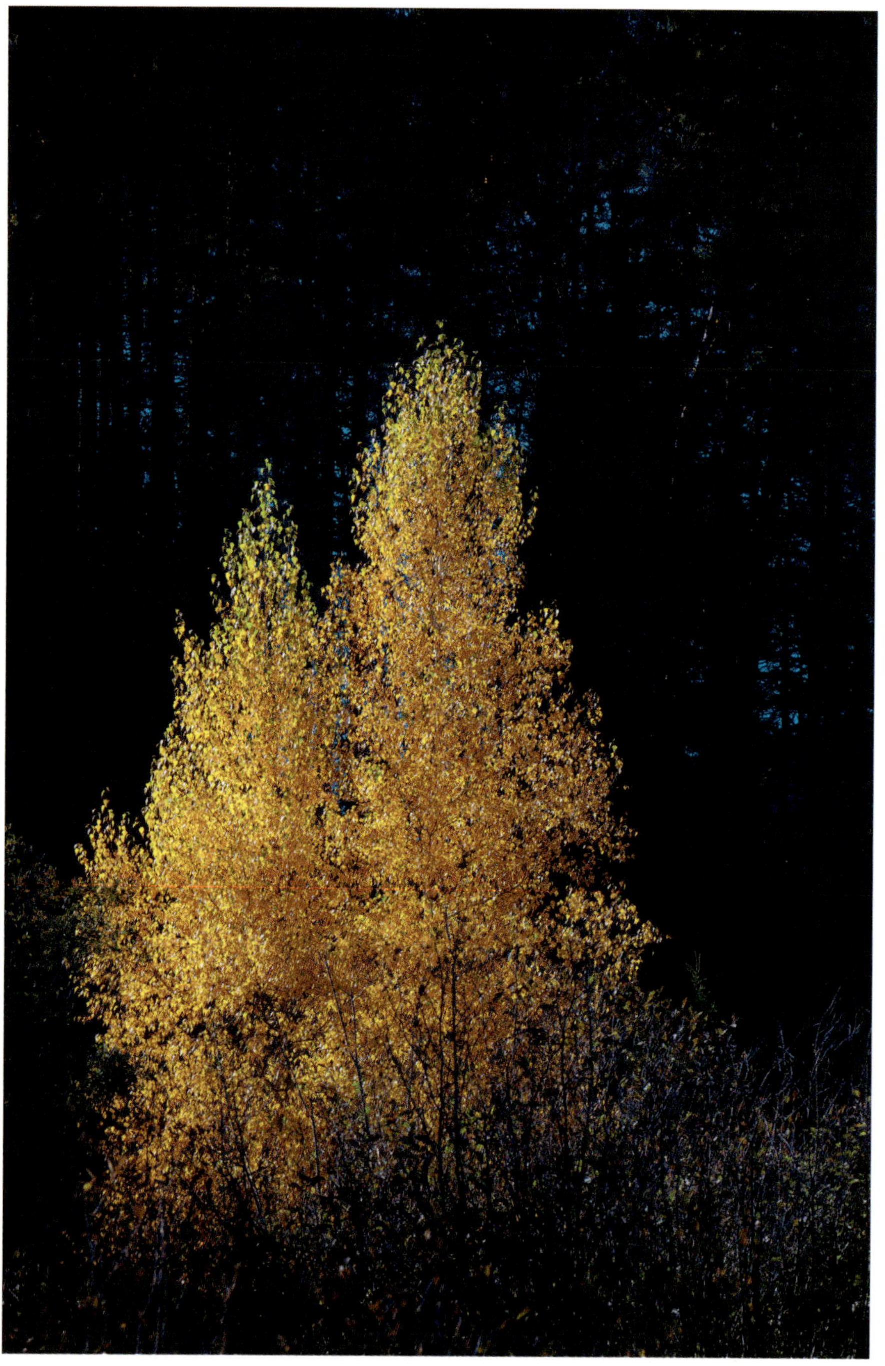

The low angle of the sun lit up this tree near Duck Pond while leaving the background dark.

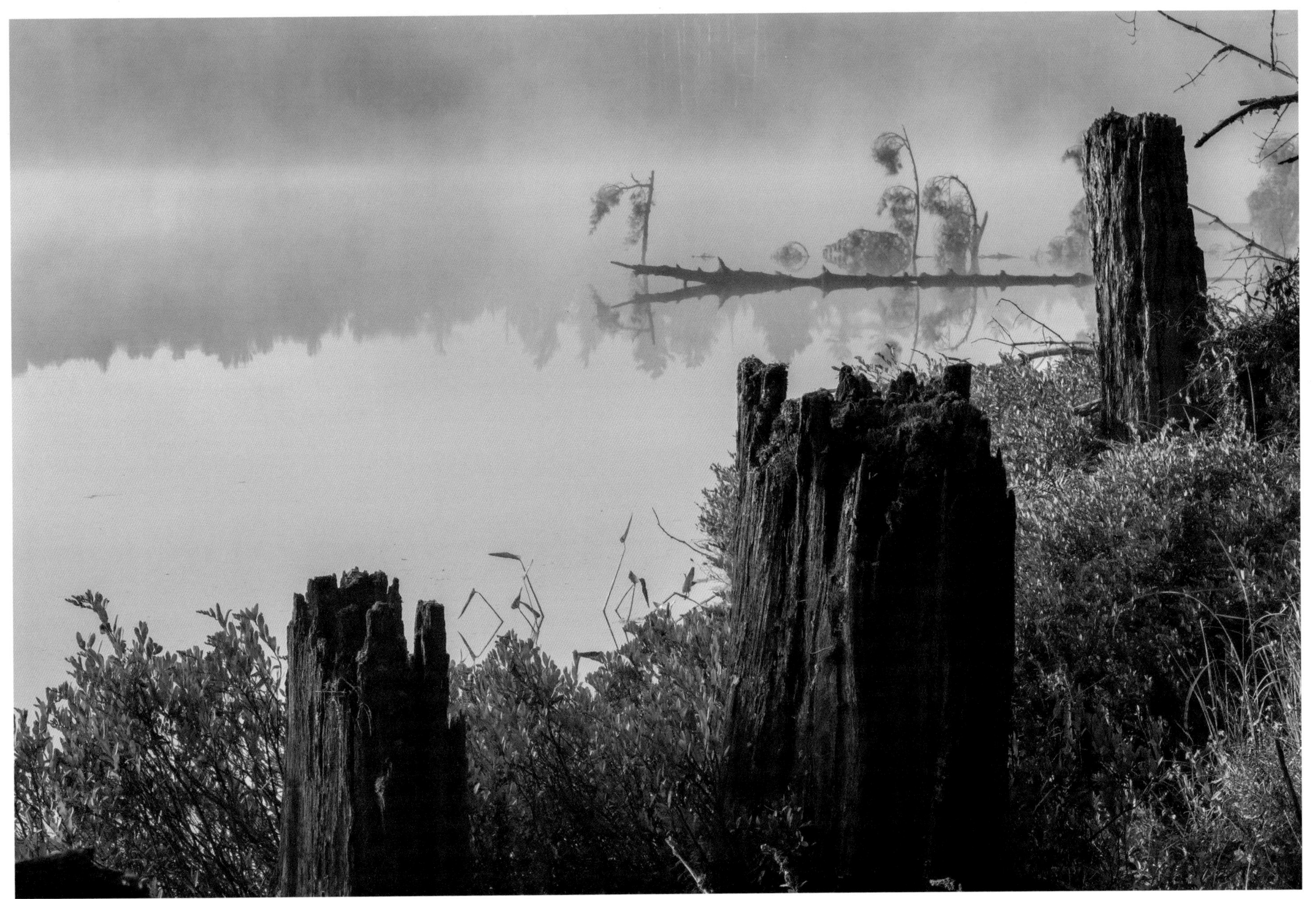

Lakeshore at Massawepie Scout Camp.

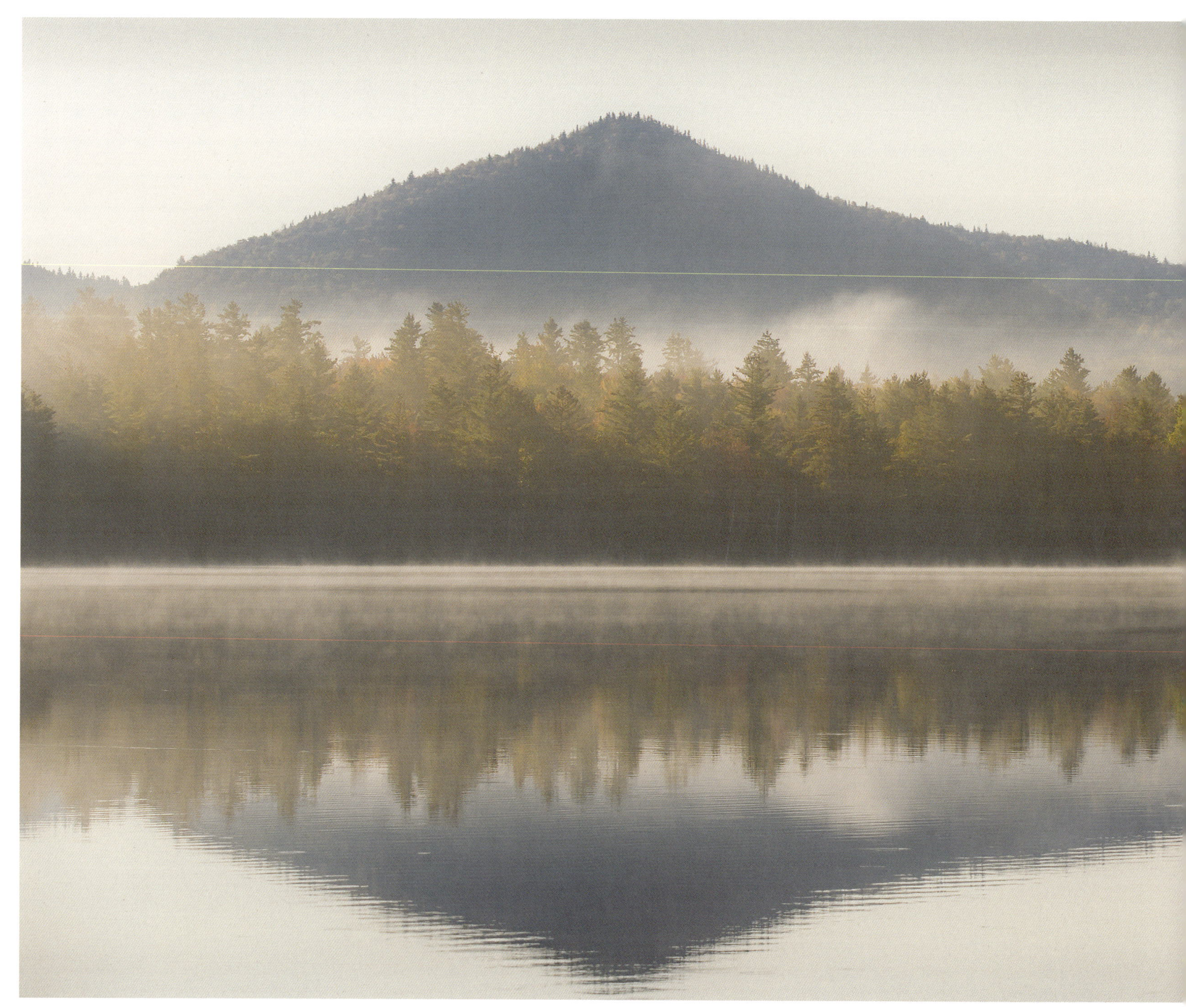

Morning on Lake Kushaqua.

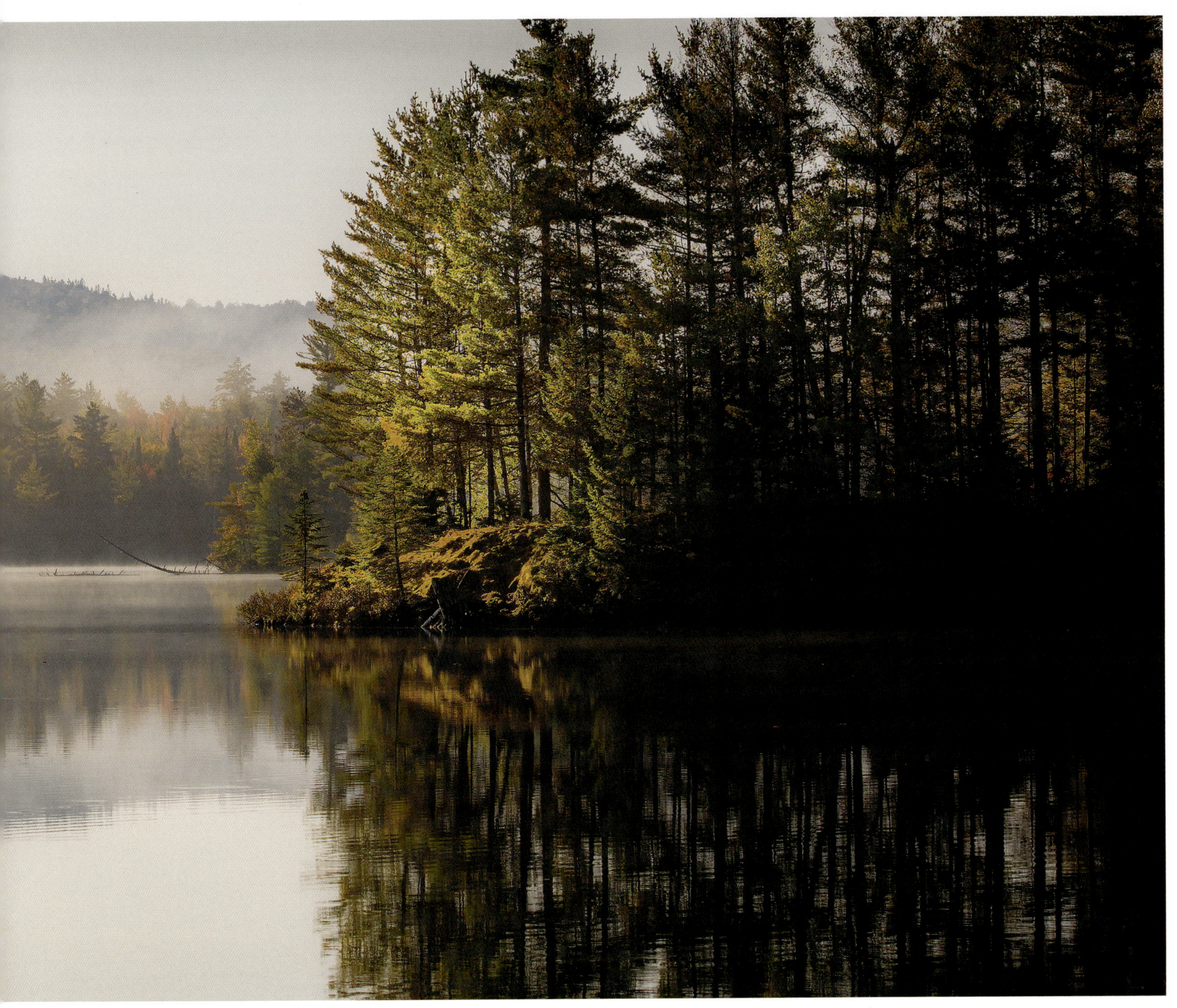

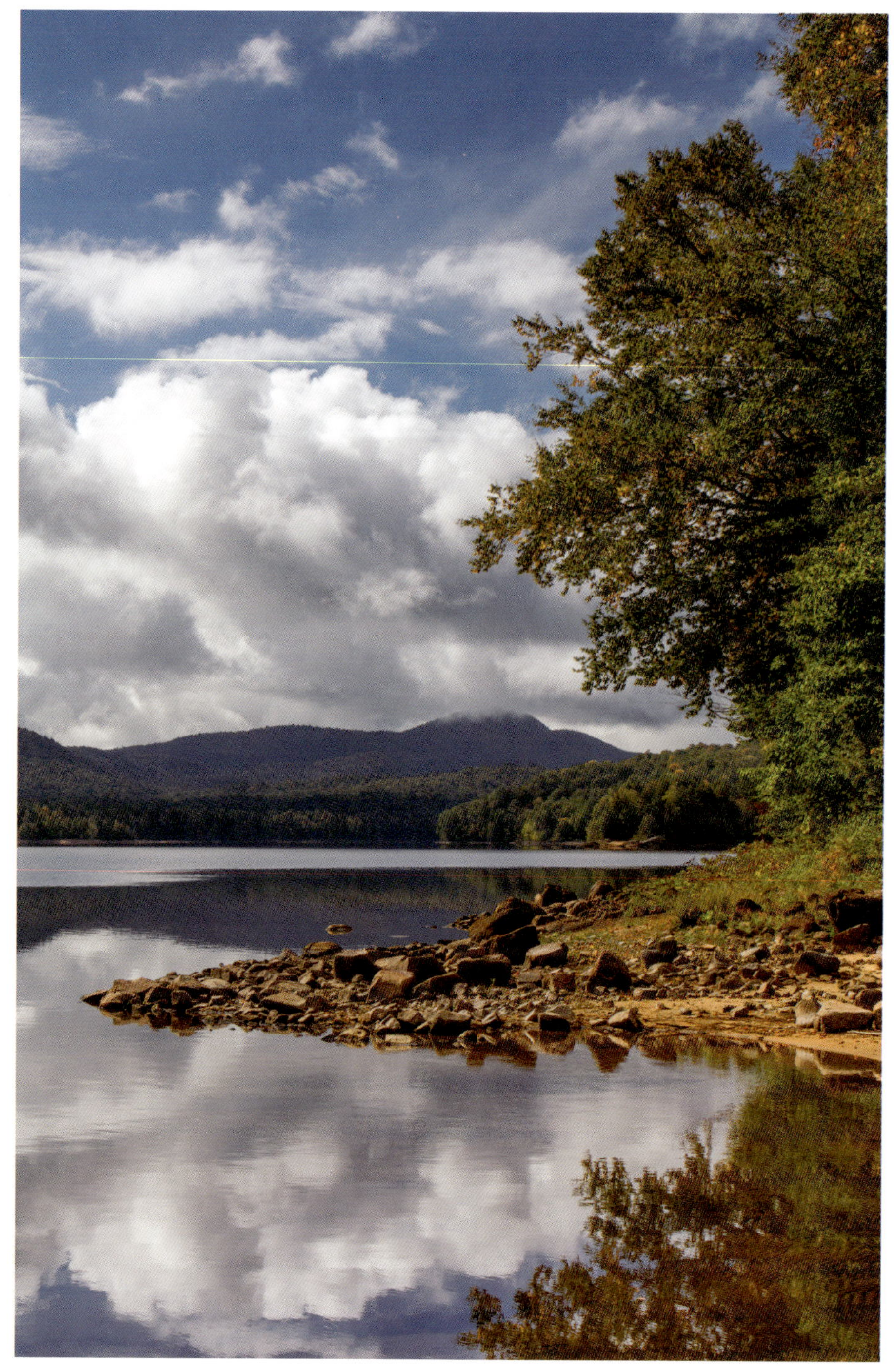

View from our campsite on Indian Lake.

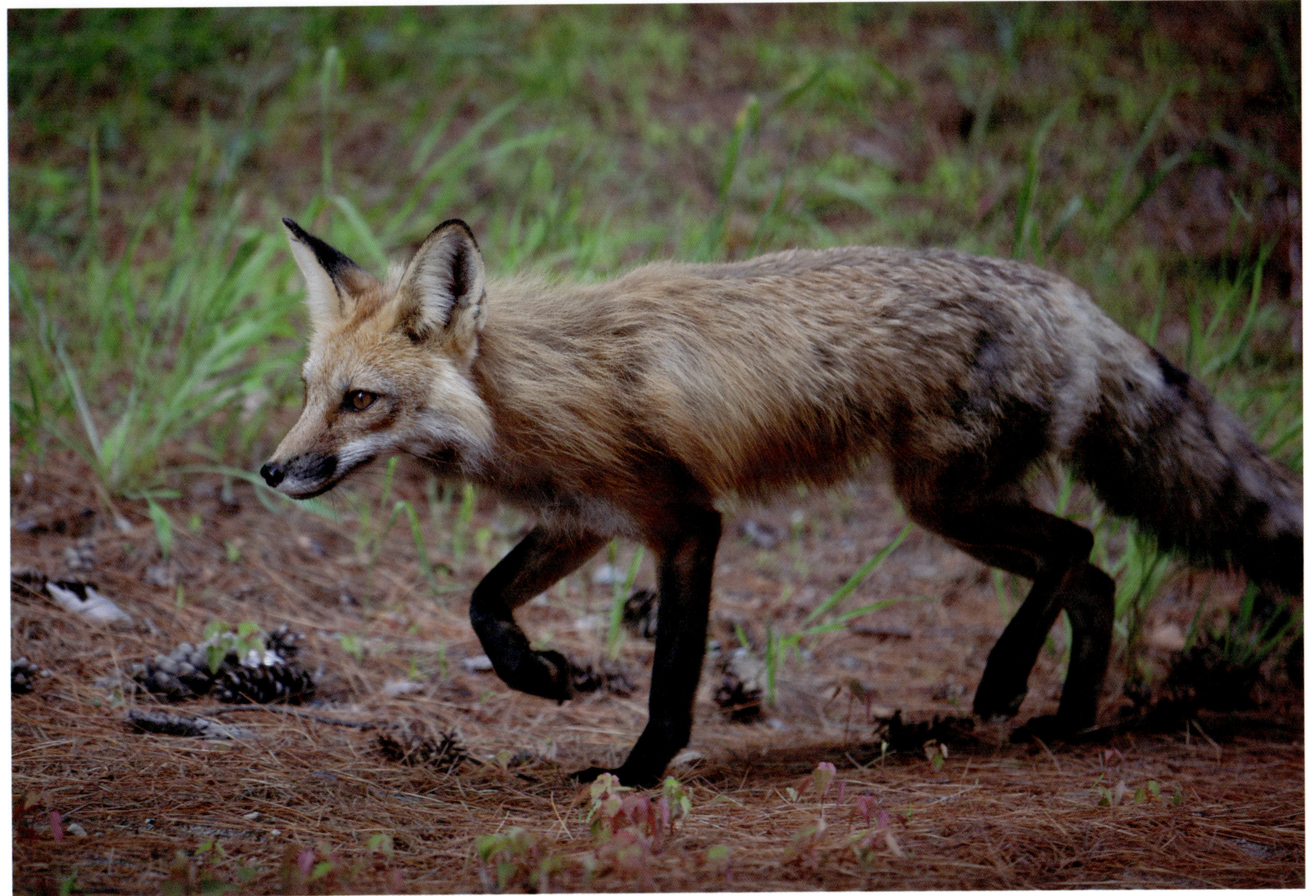

Red fox passing through the woods near Lake Placid.

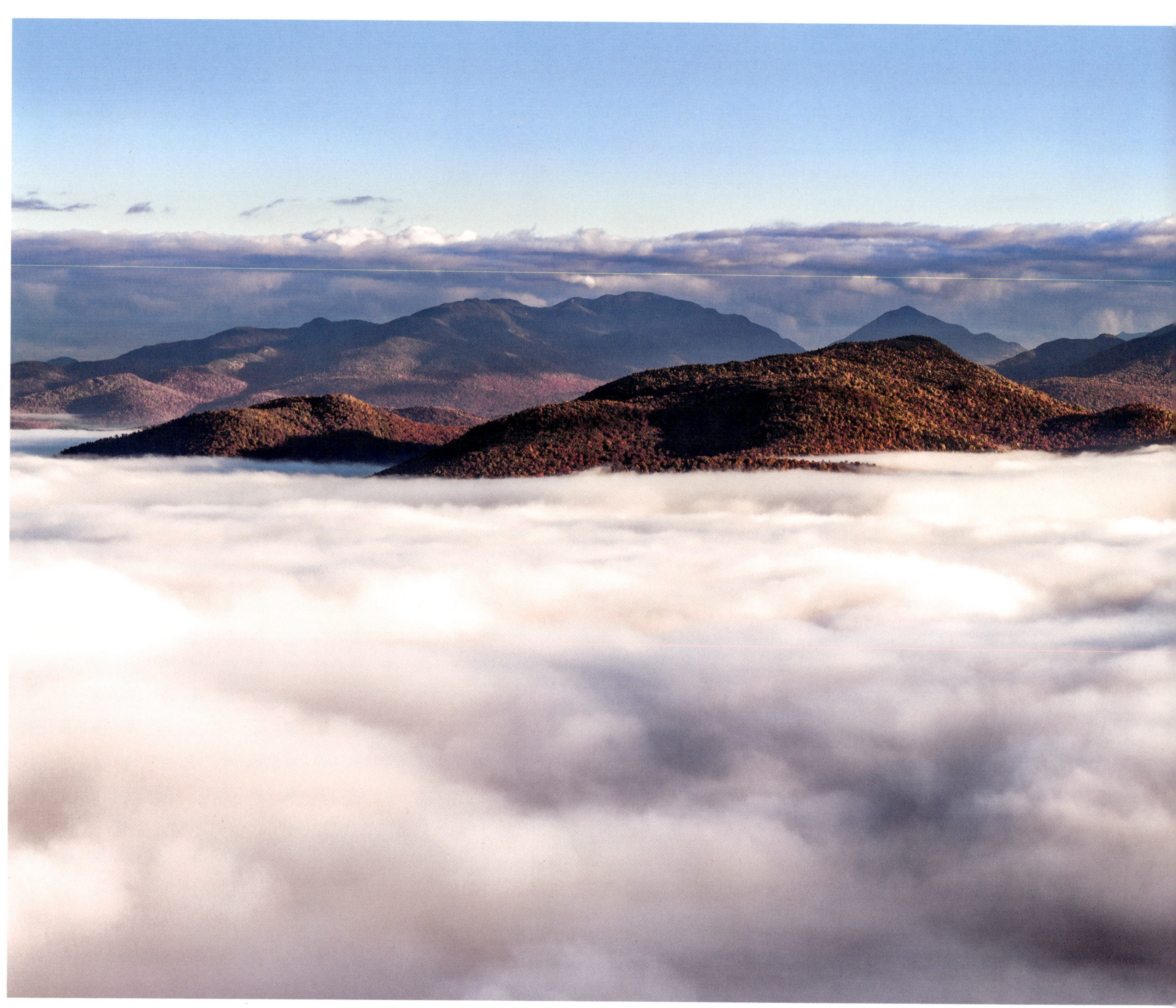

A cloud inversion settles between the mountains in the High Peaks Wilderness. View from the south.

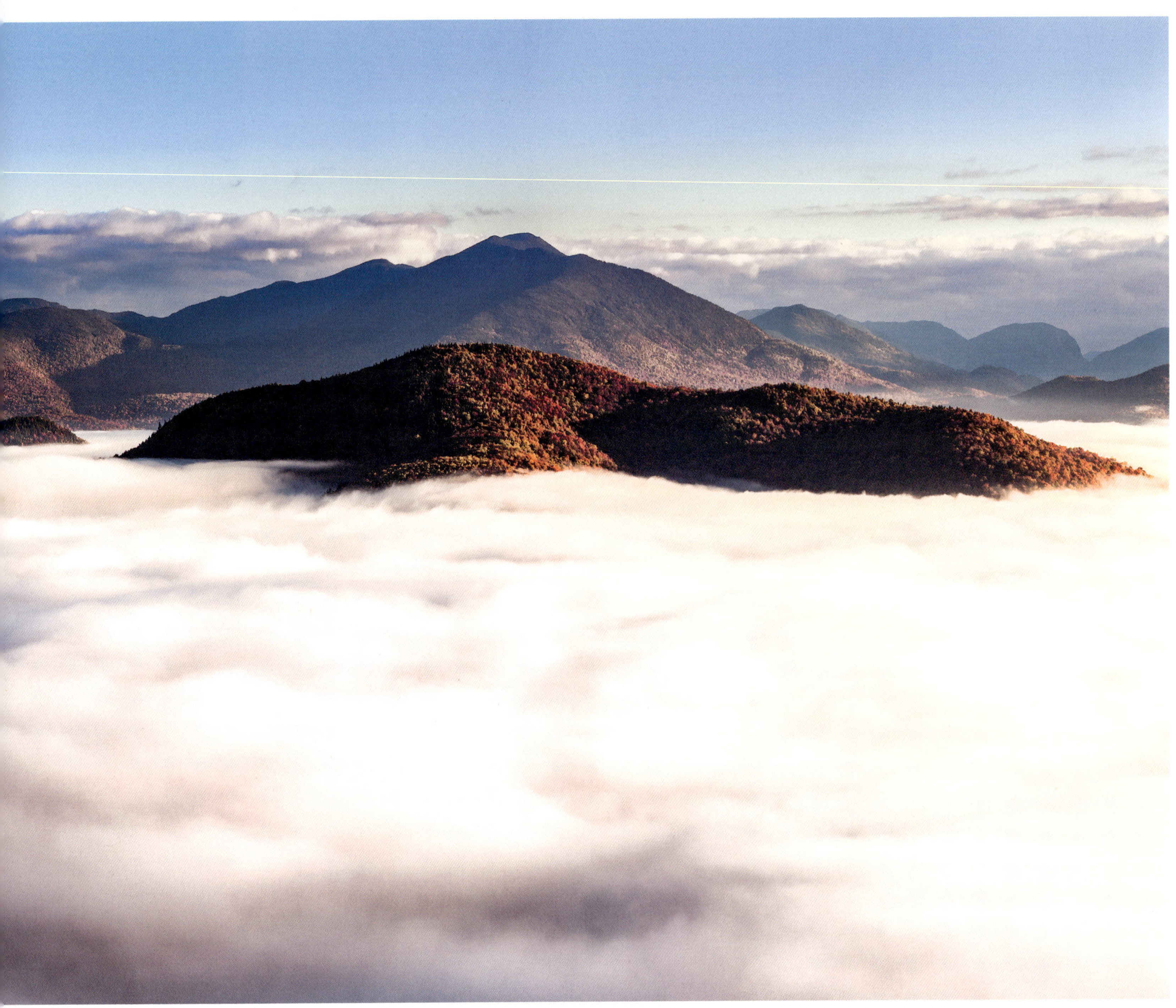

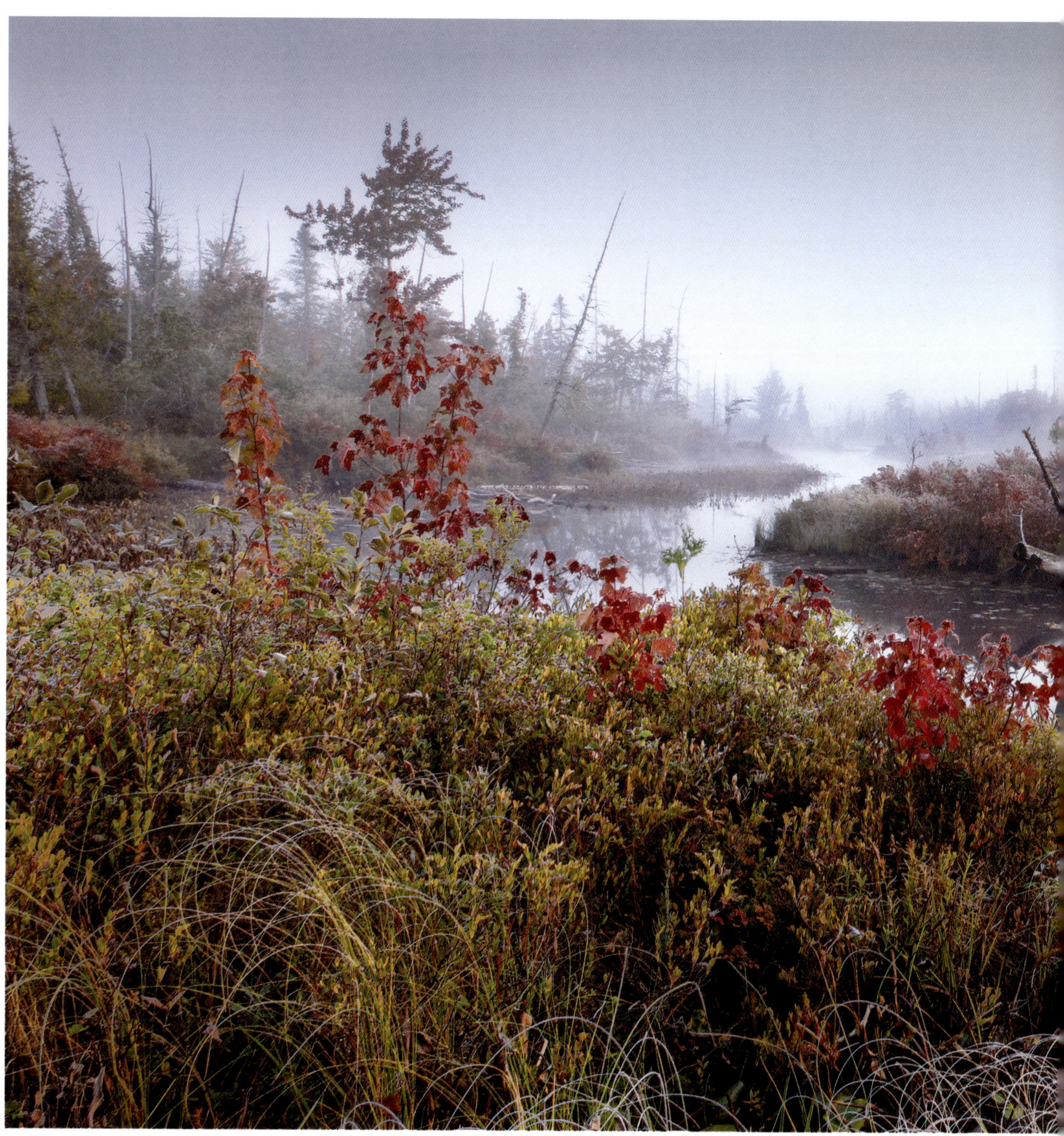

Early frost at the inlet to Middle Saranac Lake.

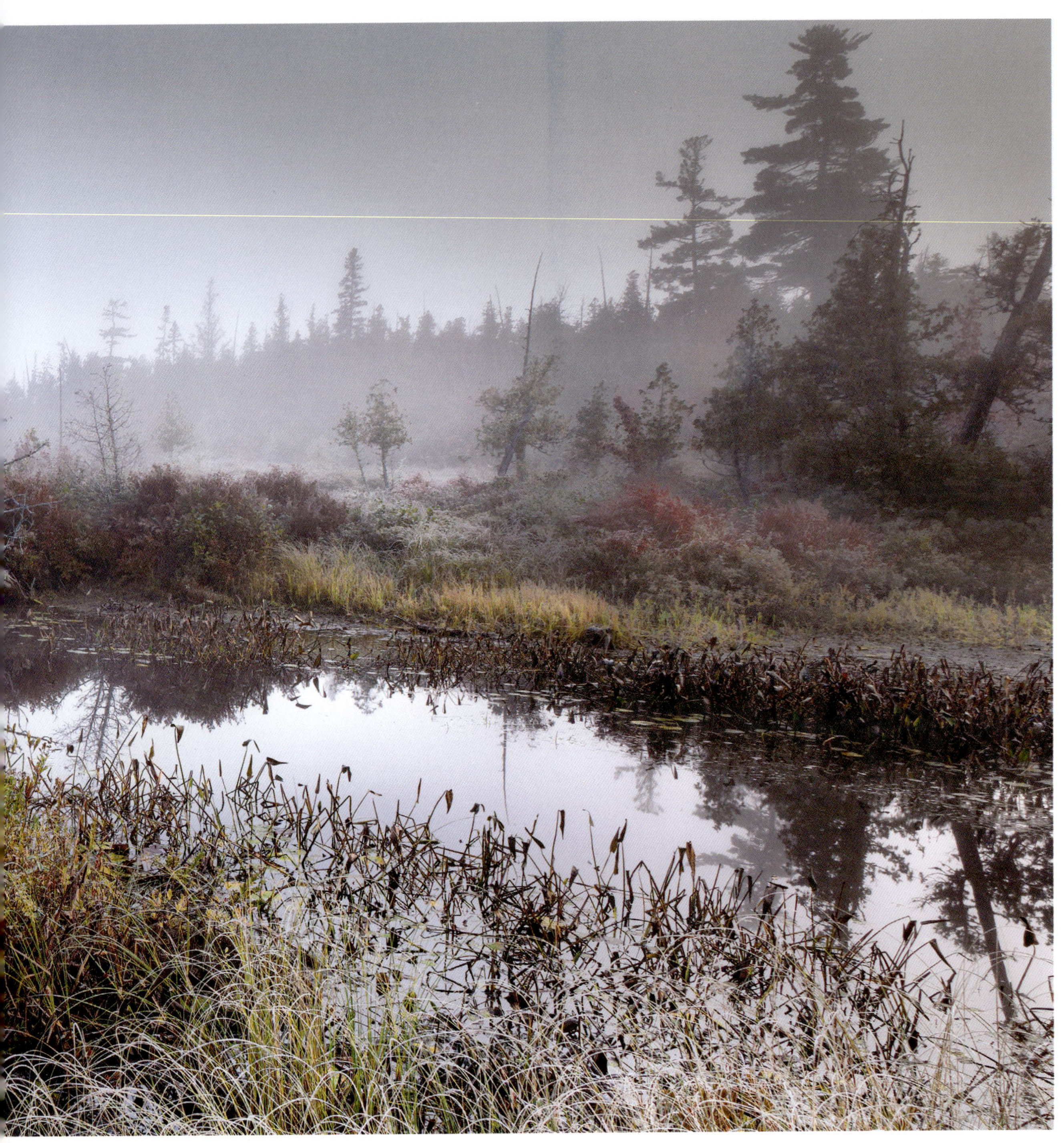

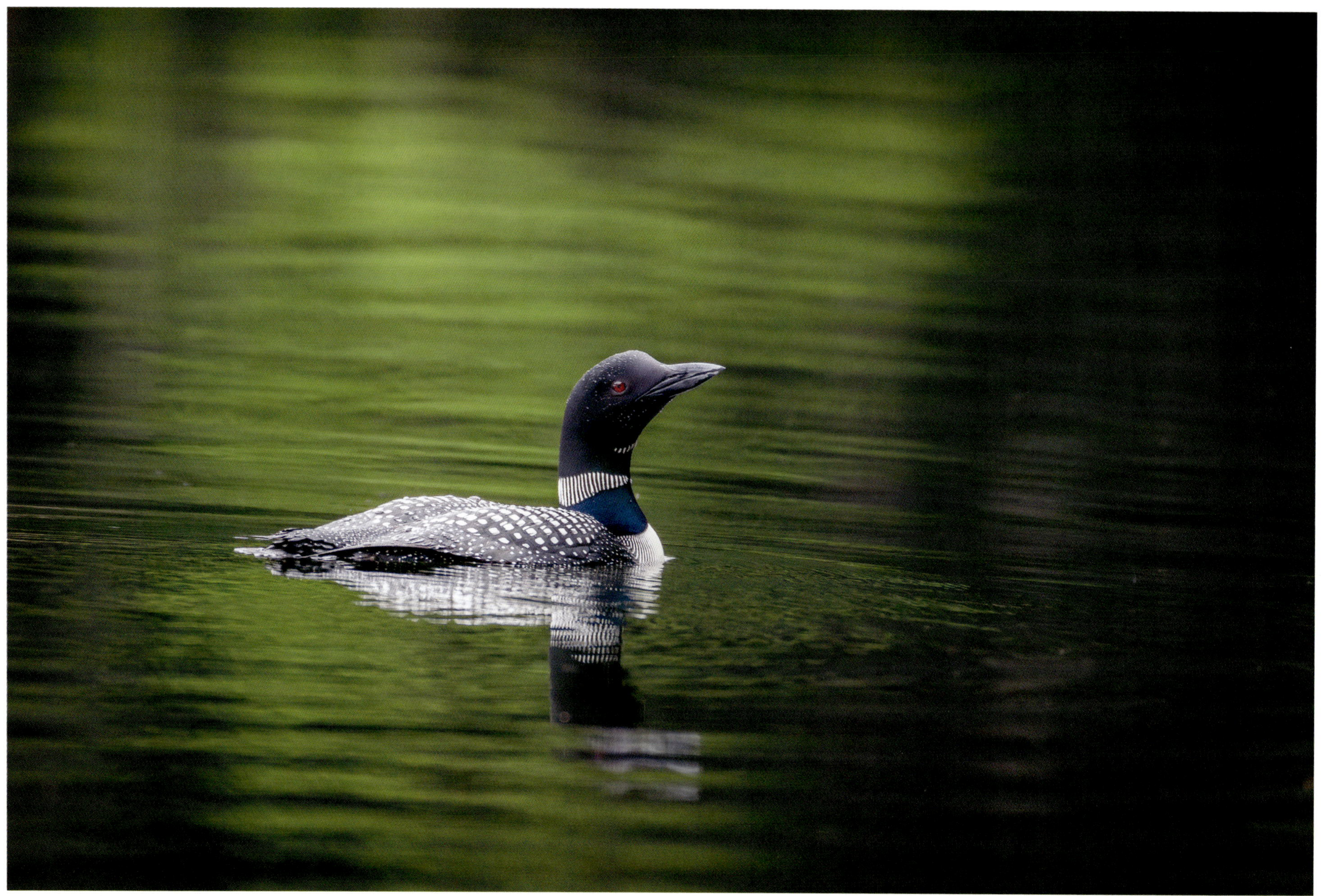

Loon fishing on Little Green Pond.

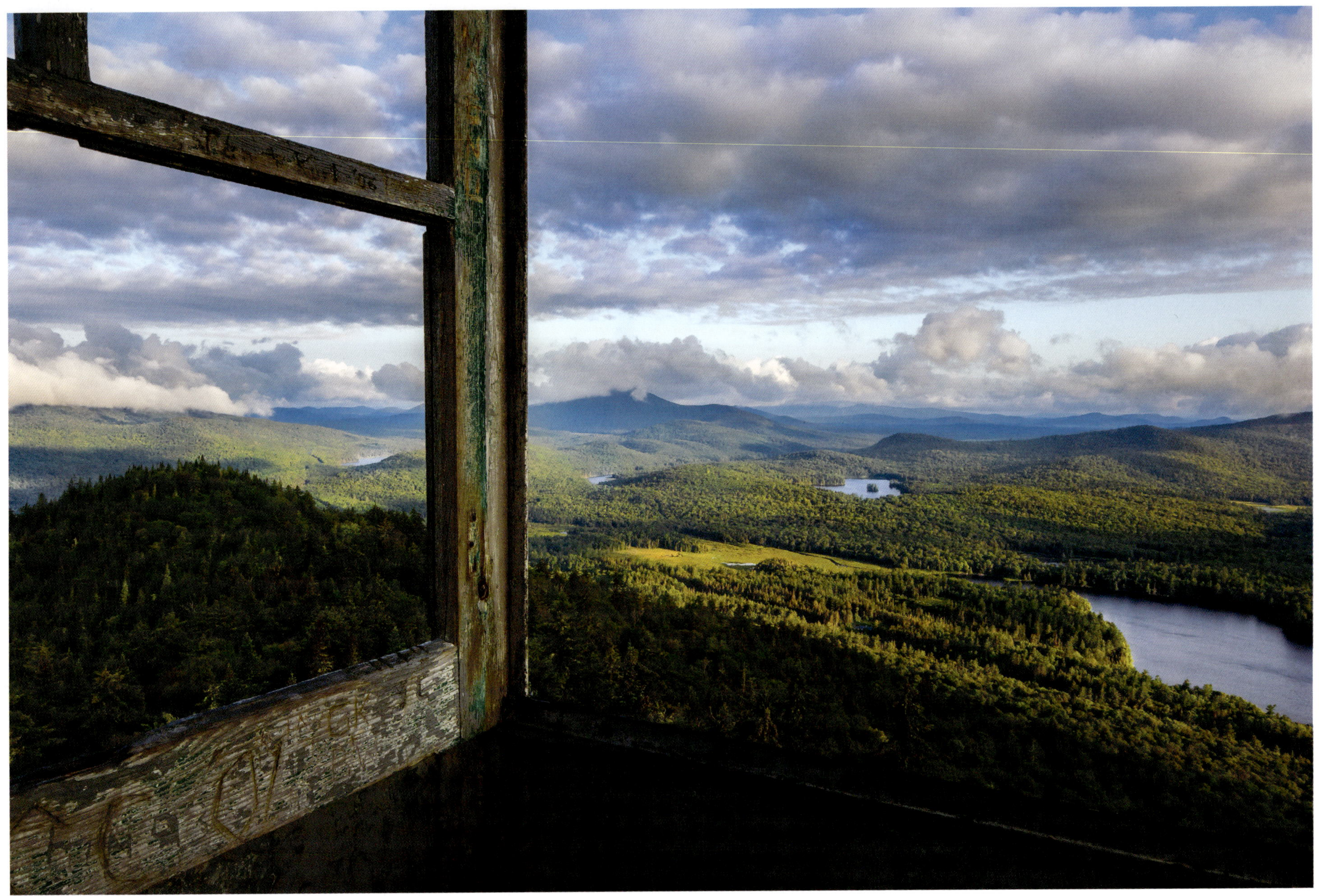

View toward the northwest from the abandoned fire tower on Goodnow Mountain.

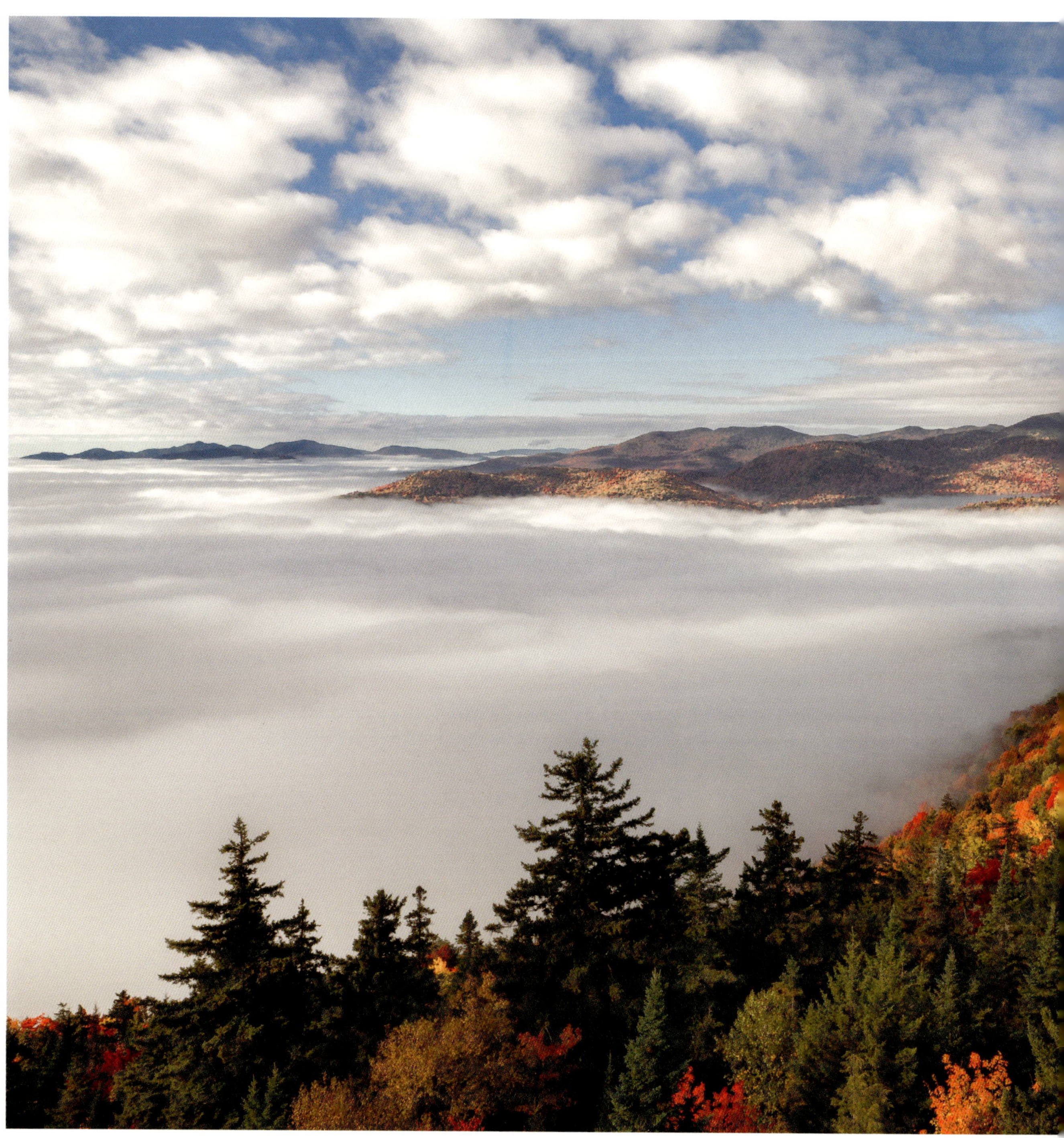

View from the Goodnow Mountain fire tower during peak foliage season.

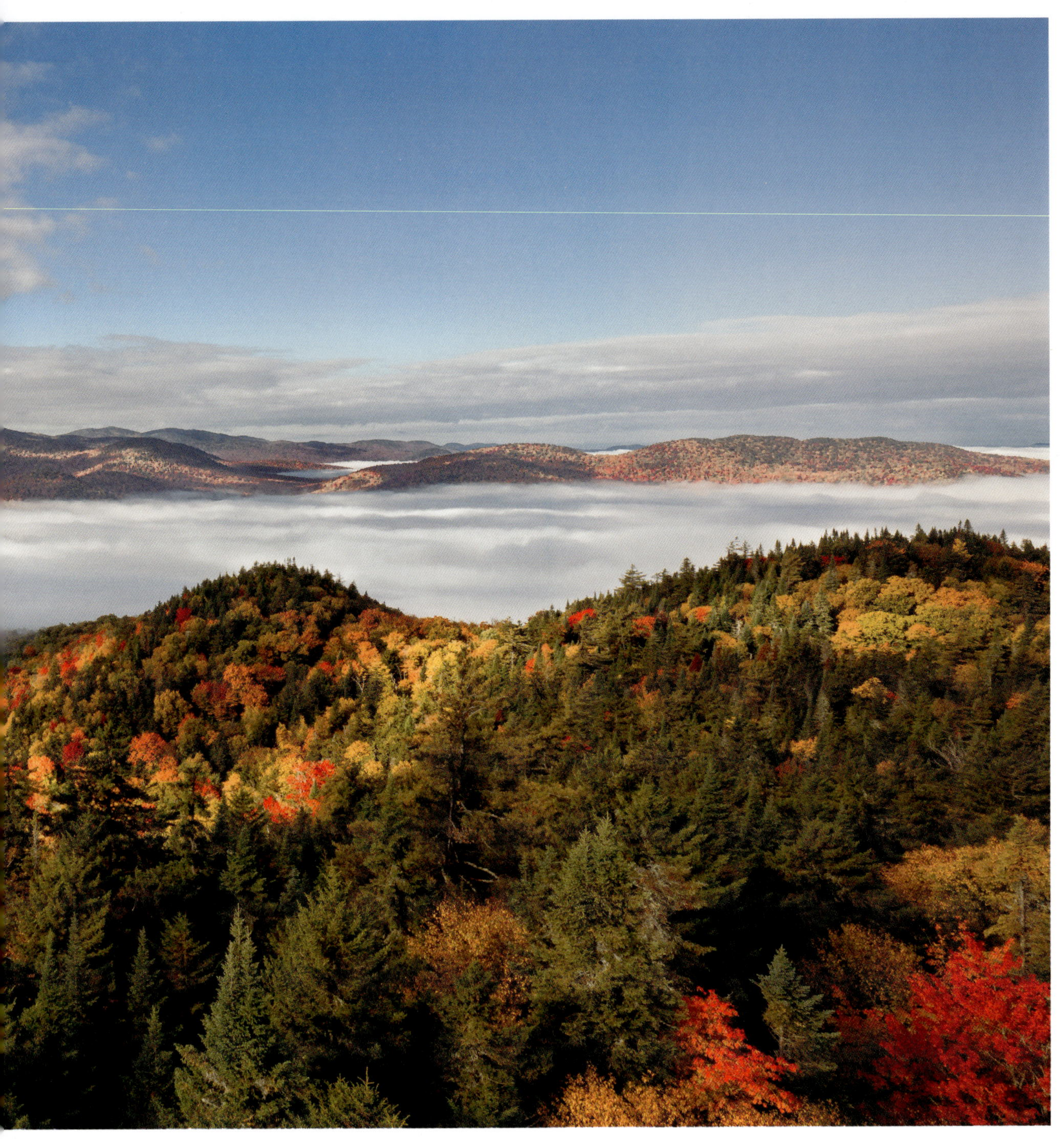

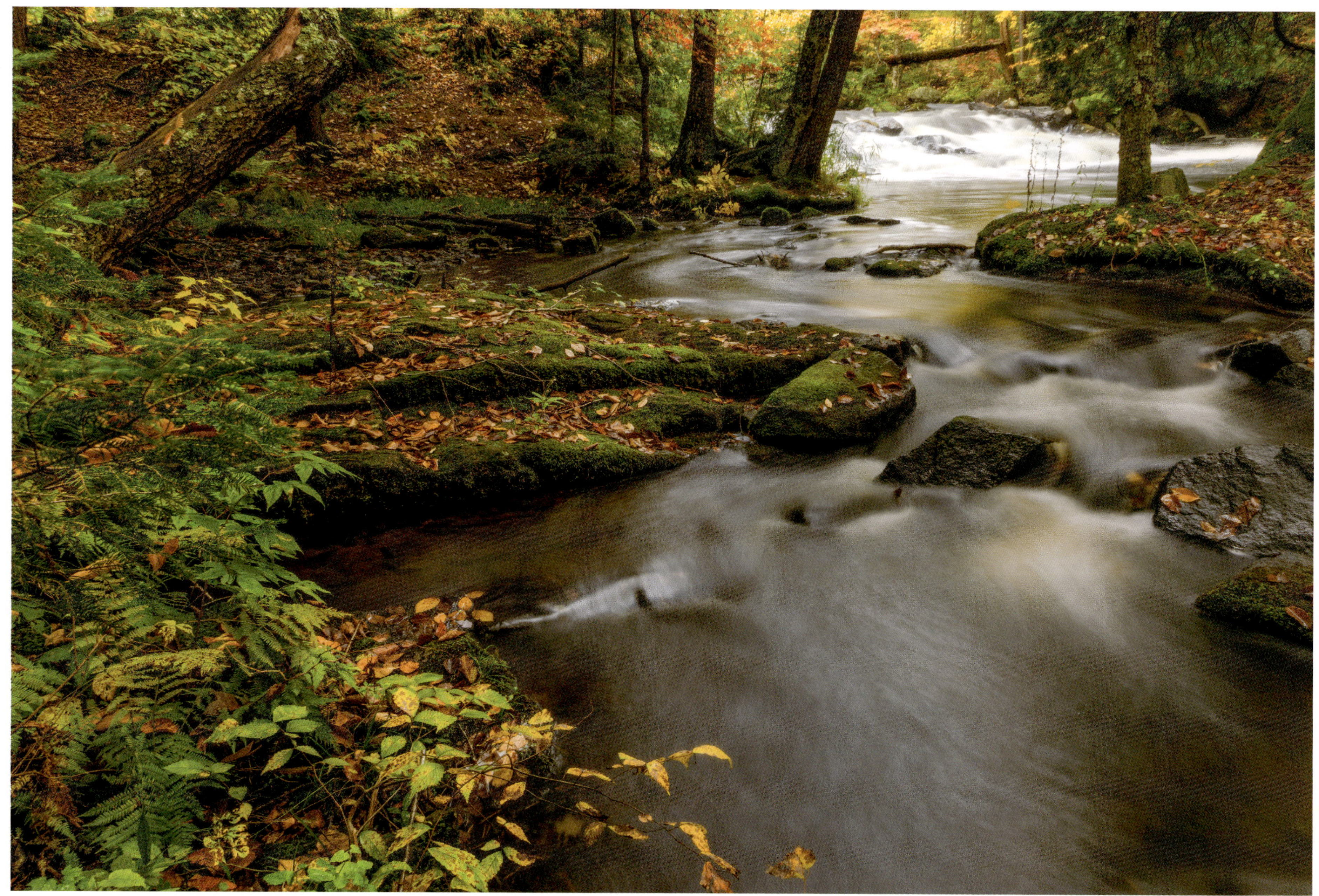

Along the shore of the Meacham Lake outflow.

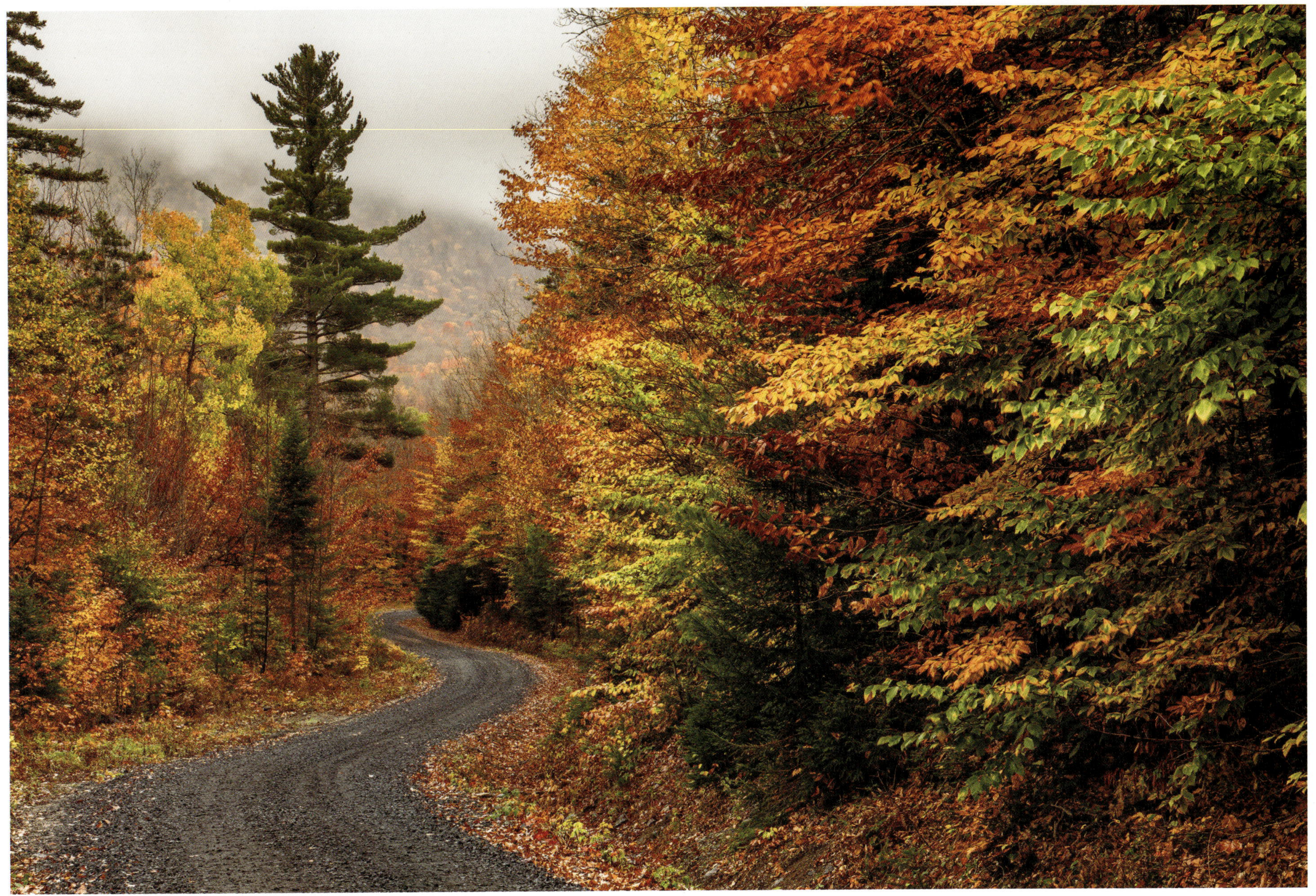

A winding gravel road through the Boreas Ponds Tract.

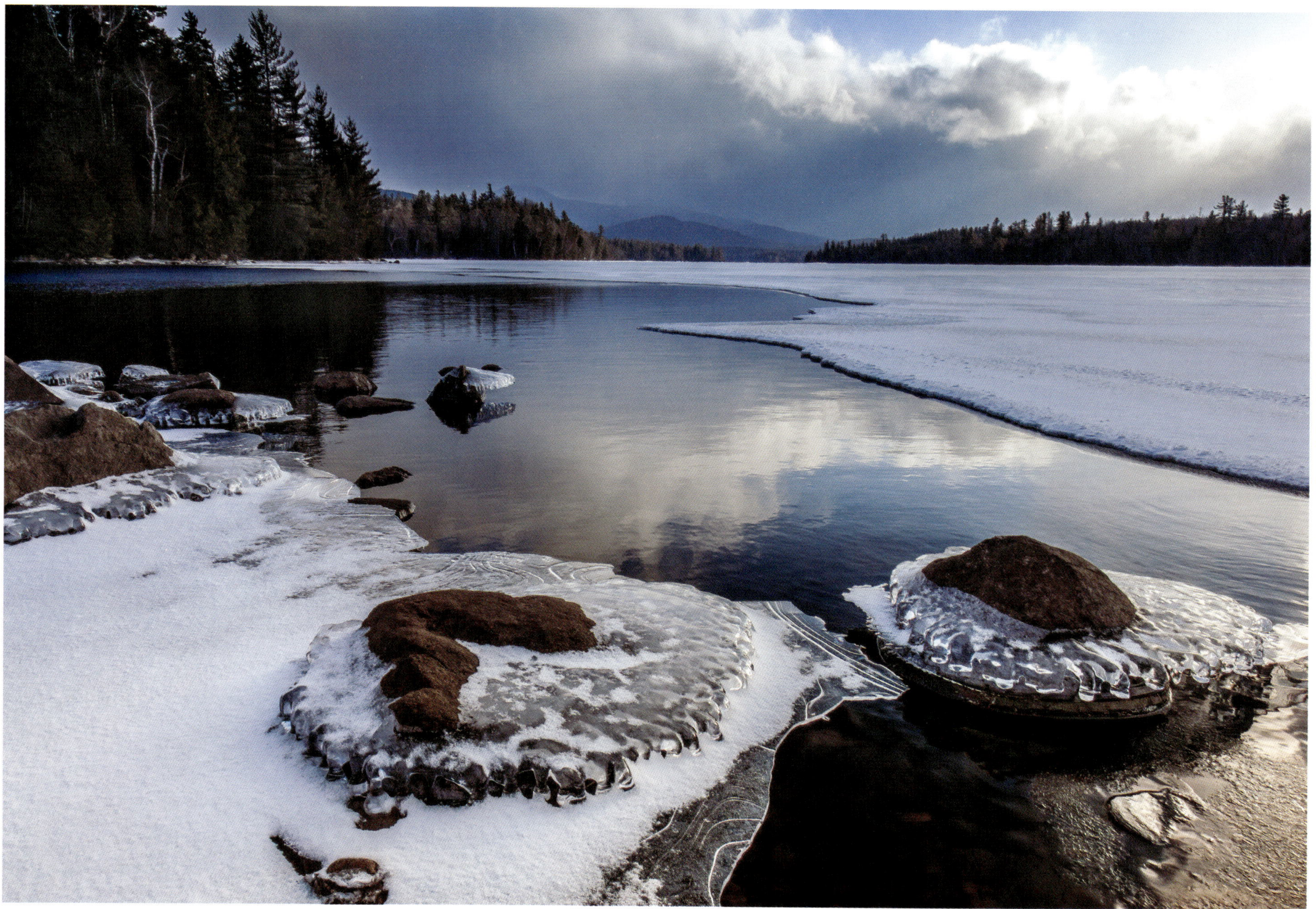

Early spring "ice-out" at Franklin Falls.

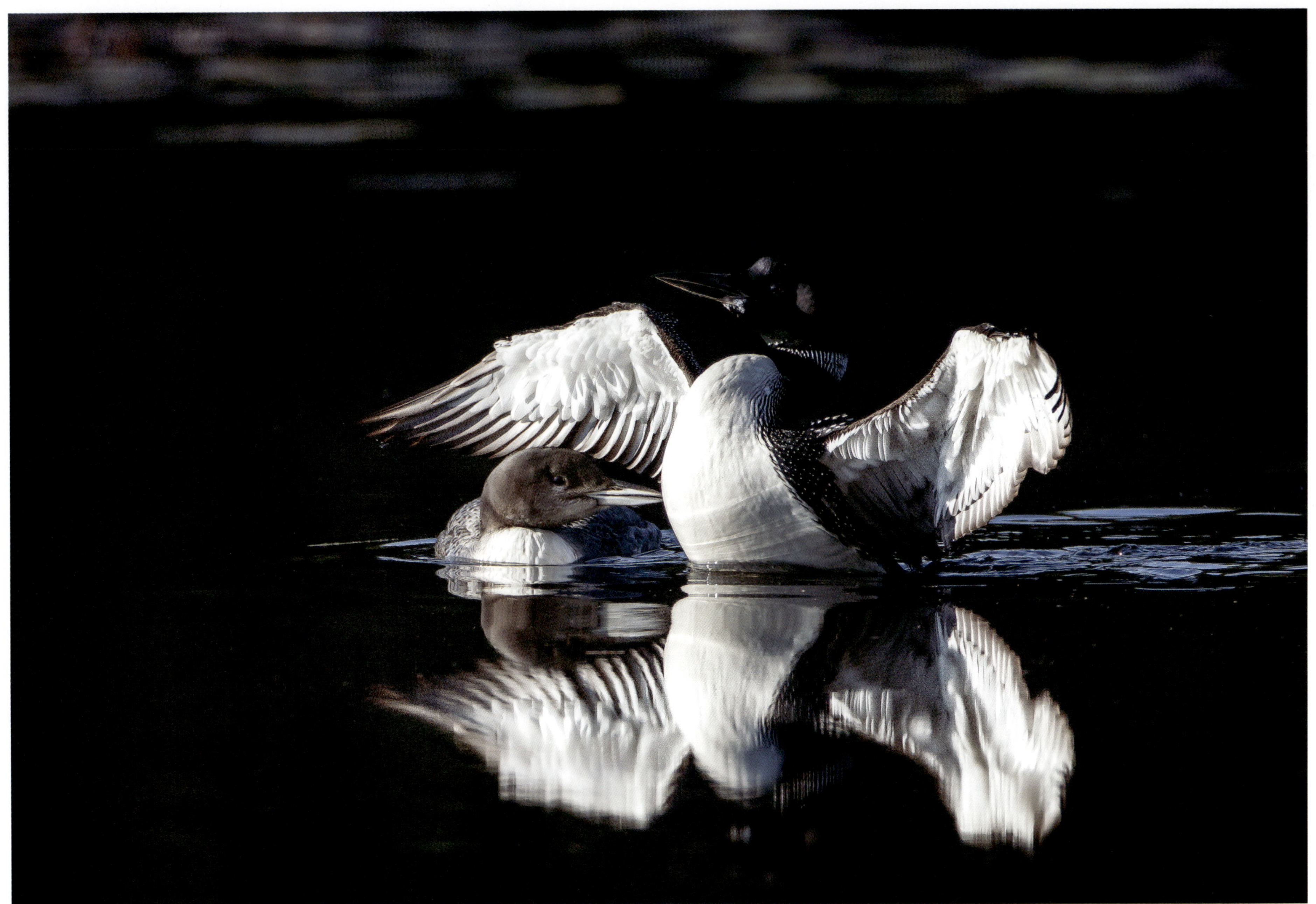

Momma loon trying to teach her uncooperative chick to fish.

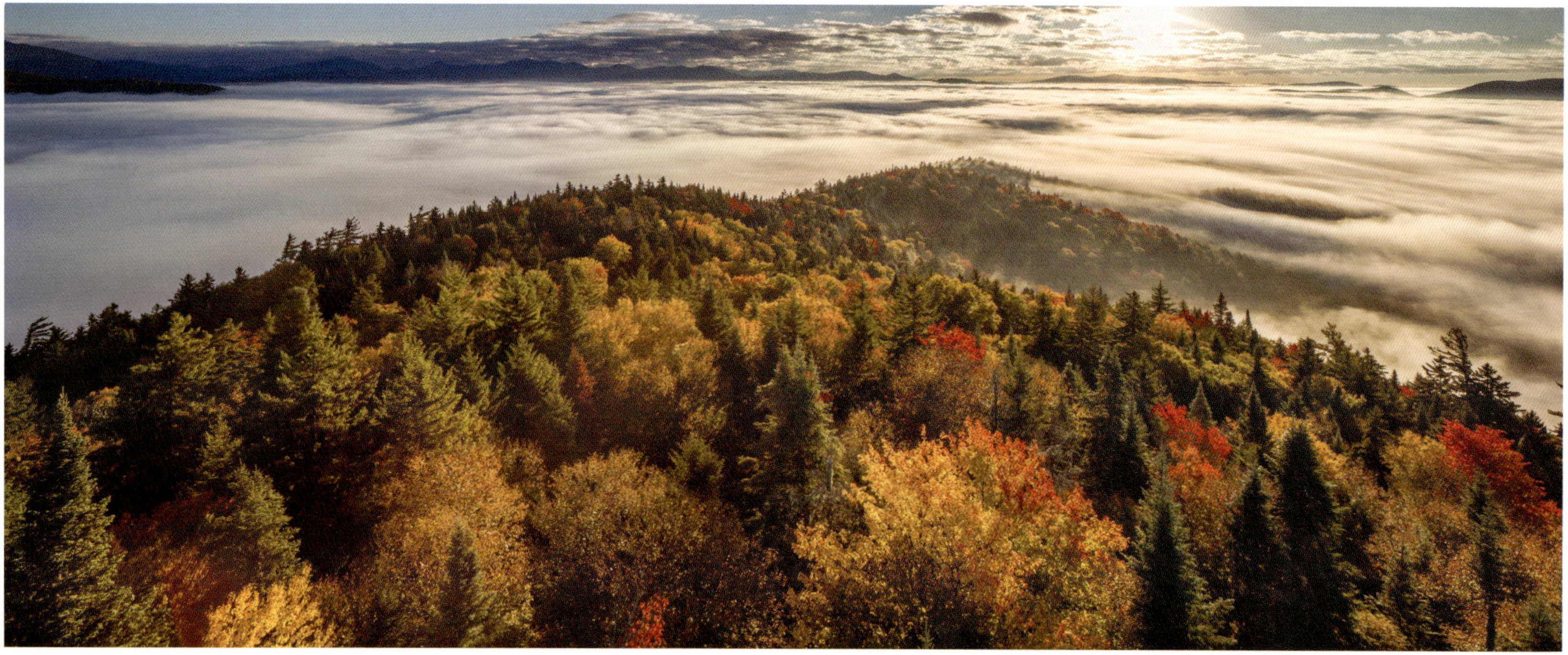

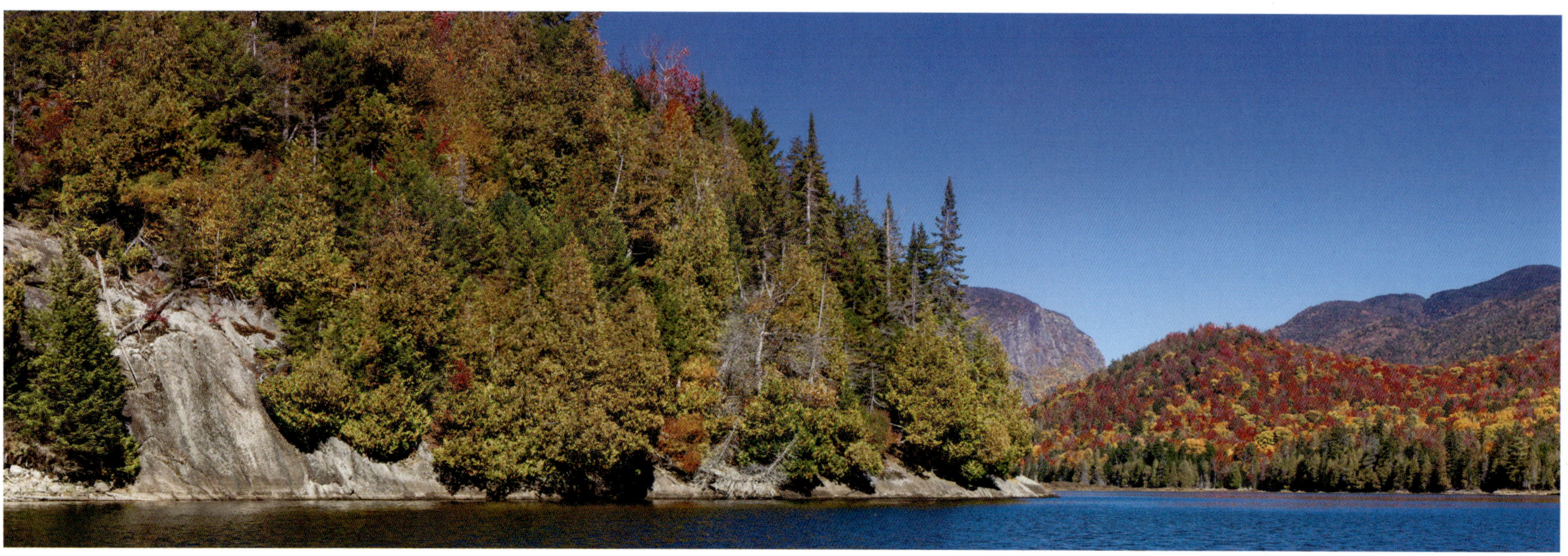

Top: Looking east from the Goodnow Mountain fire tower over an early morning cloud inversion.
Bottom: Henderson Lake is a man-made lake where the old Iron Works was located at the town of Tahawus. Teddy Roosevelt was hunting here in 1901 when he received word that President William McKinley had been shot. Henderson Lake is also one of the points of origin of the Hudson River.

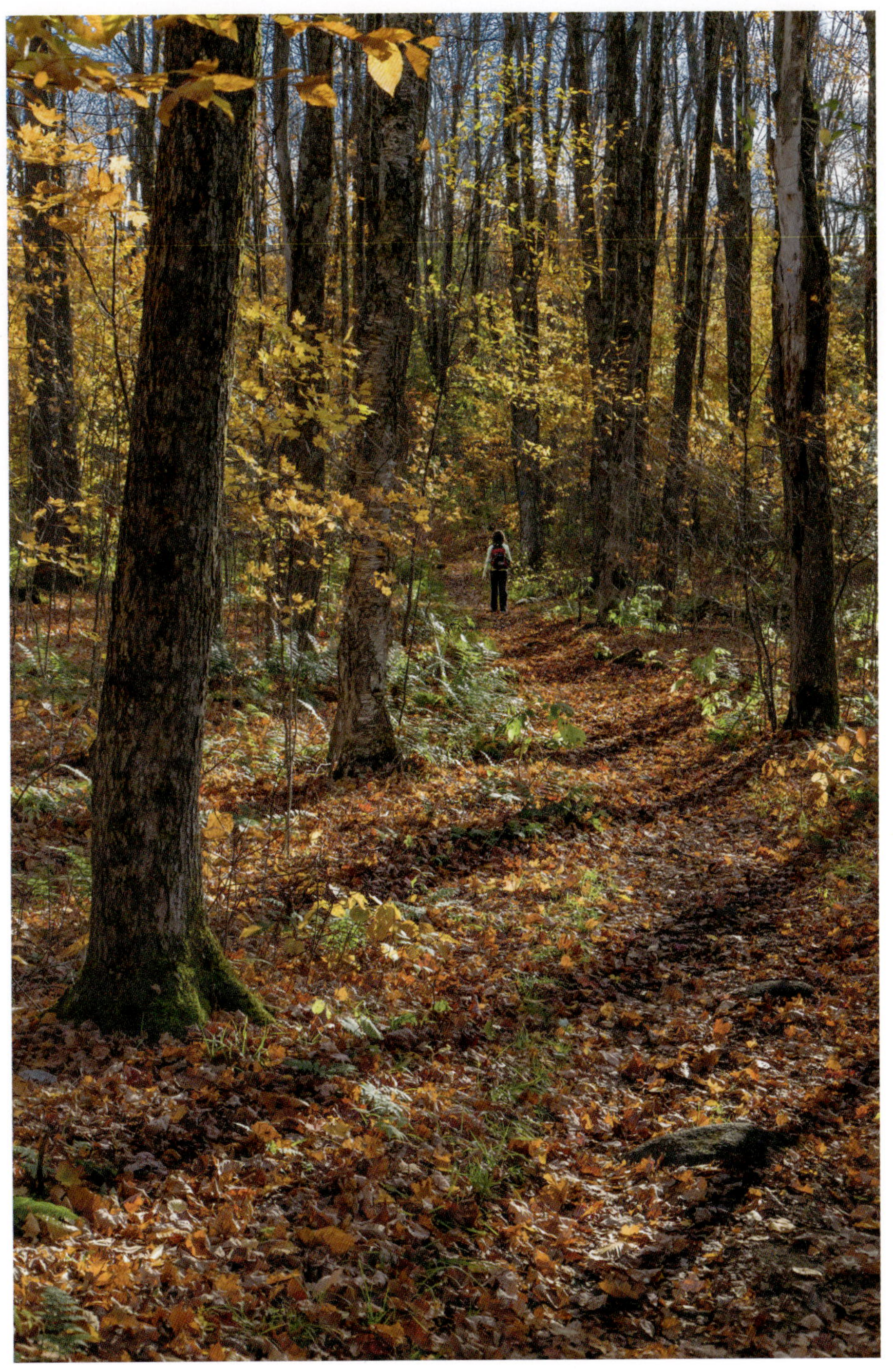

Hiking on the old trail to Mount Van Hoevenberg during the late fall.

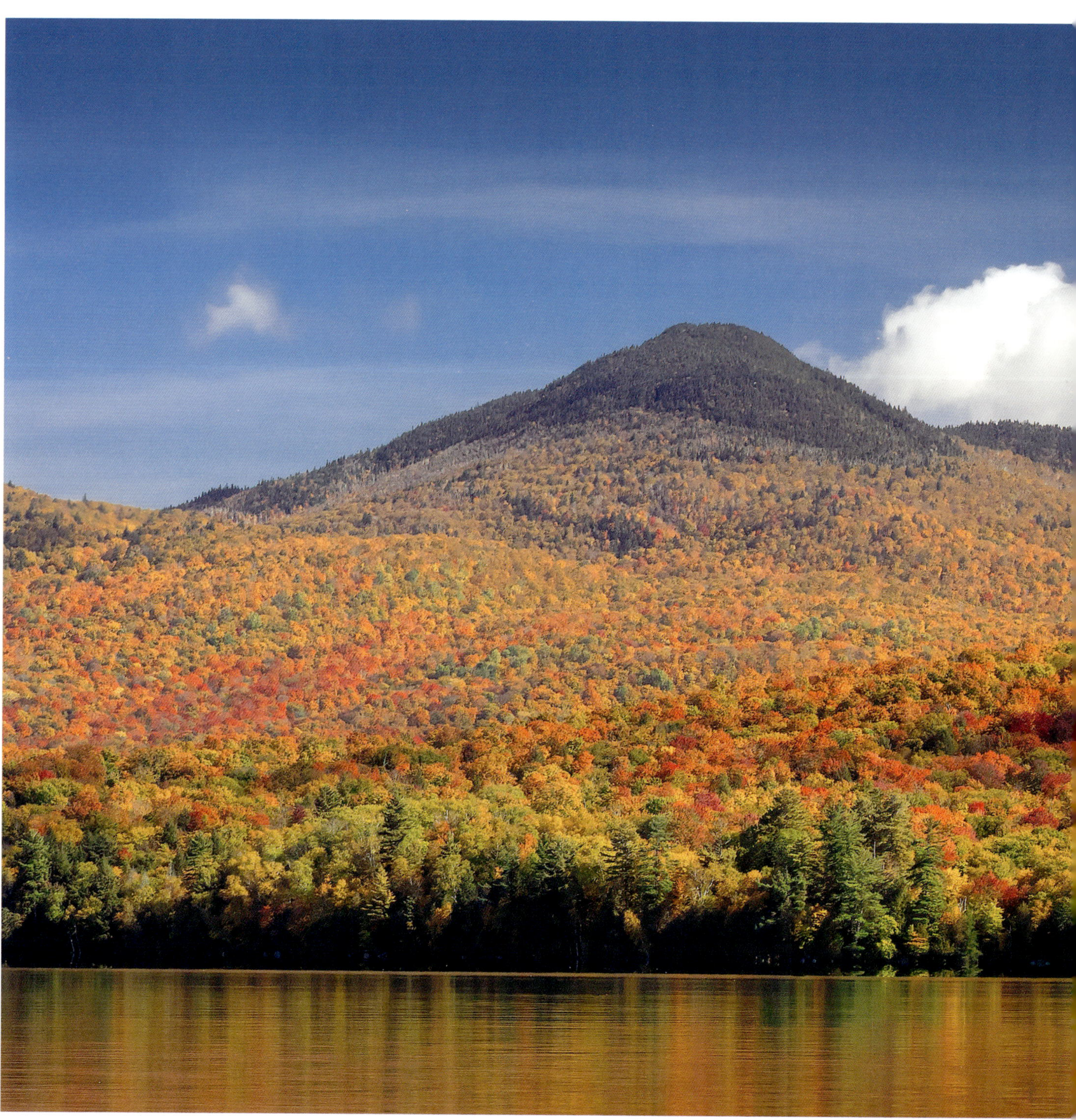

A kayaker paddles to a campsite on Meacham Lake during peak foliage season.

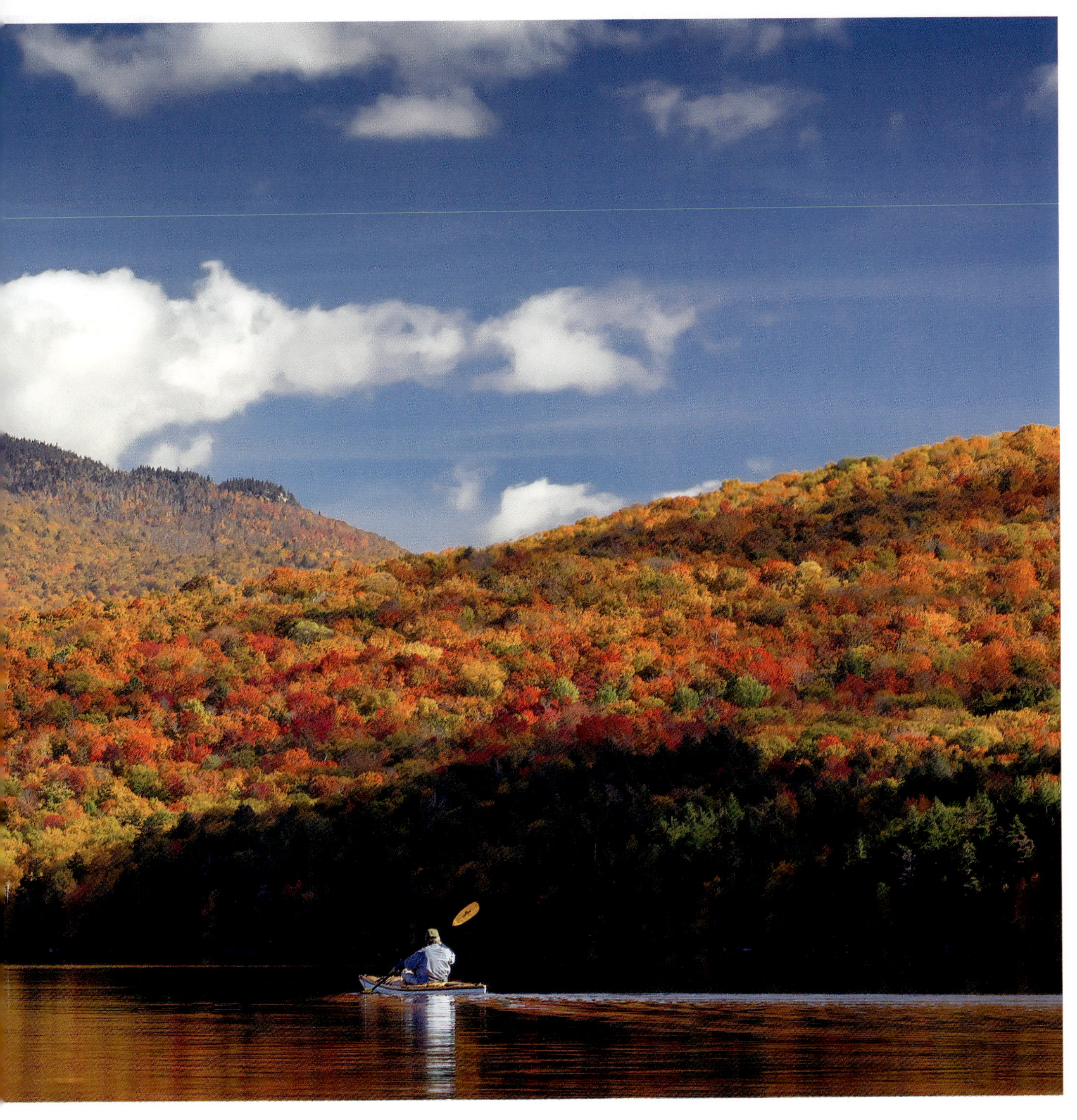

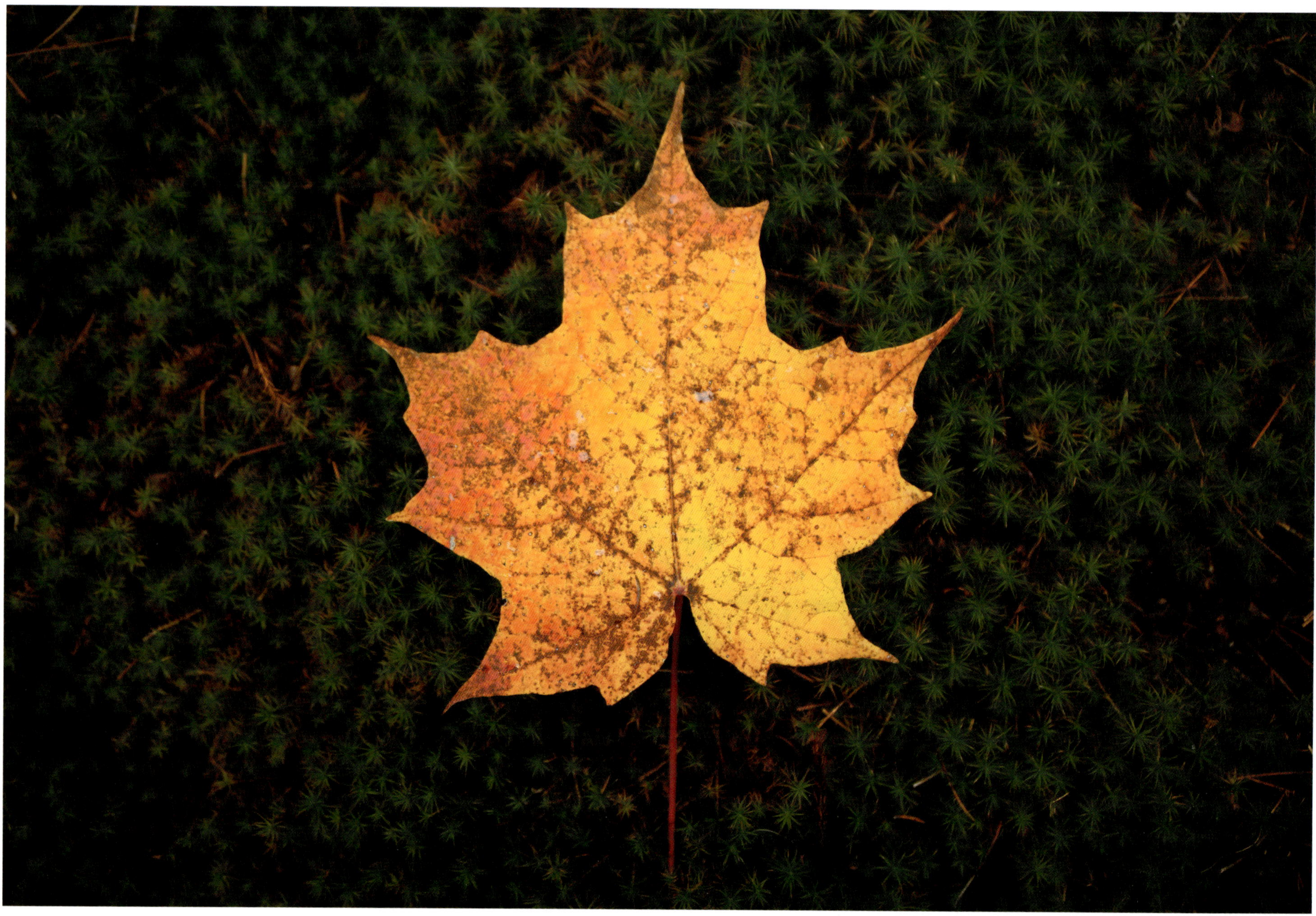

Single maple leaf on a bed of green ground cover.

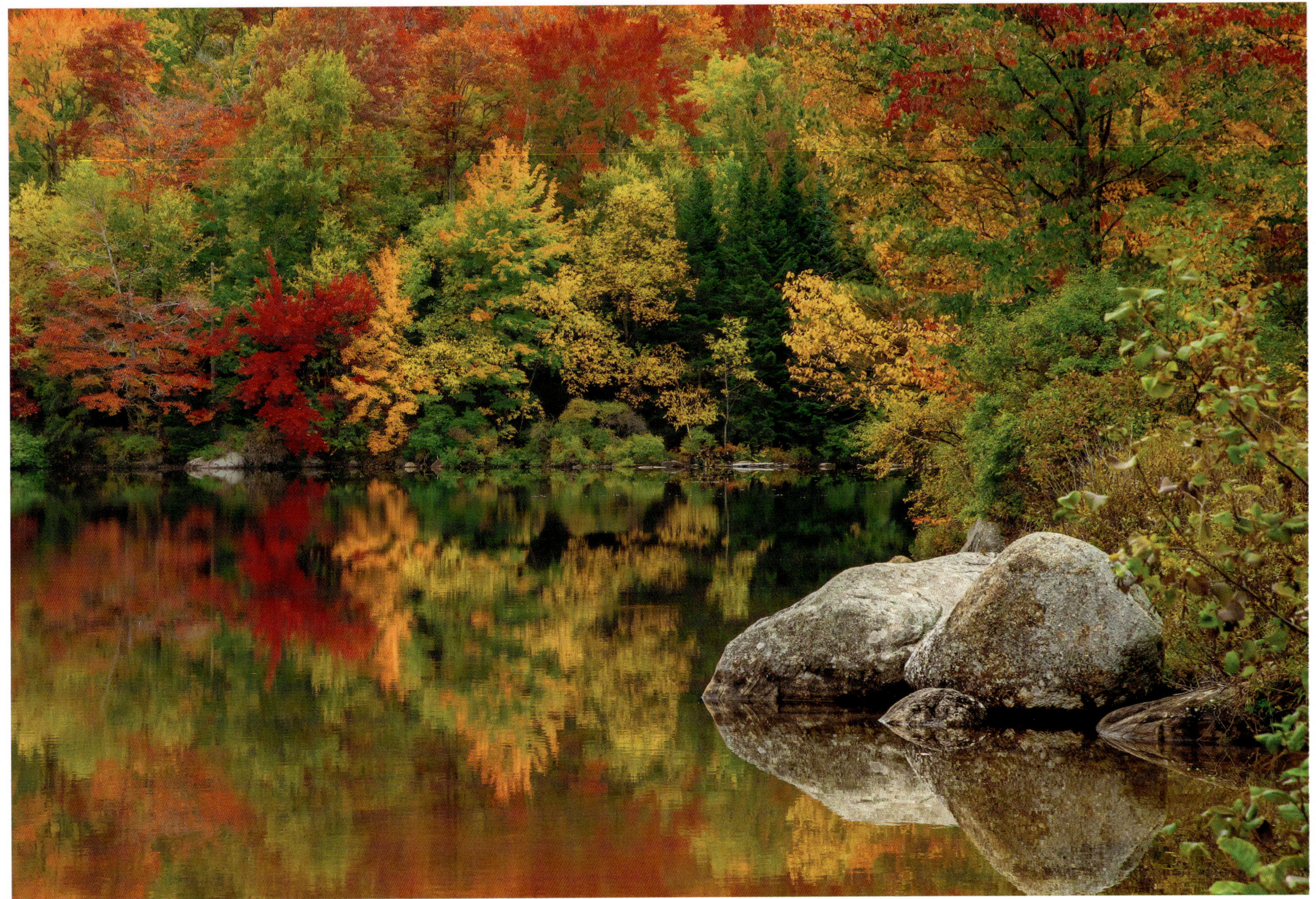

Kayak put-in on the shore of Debar Pond in the fall.

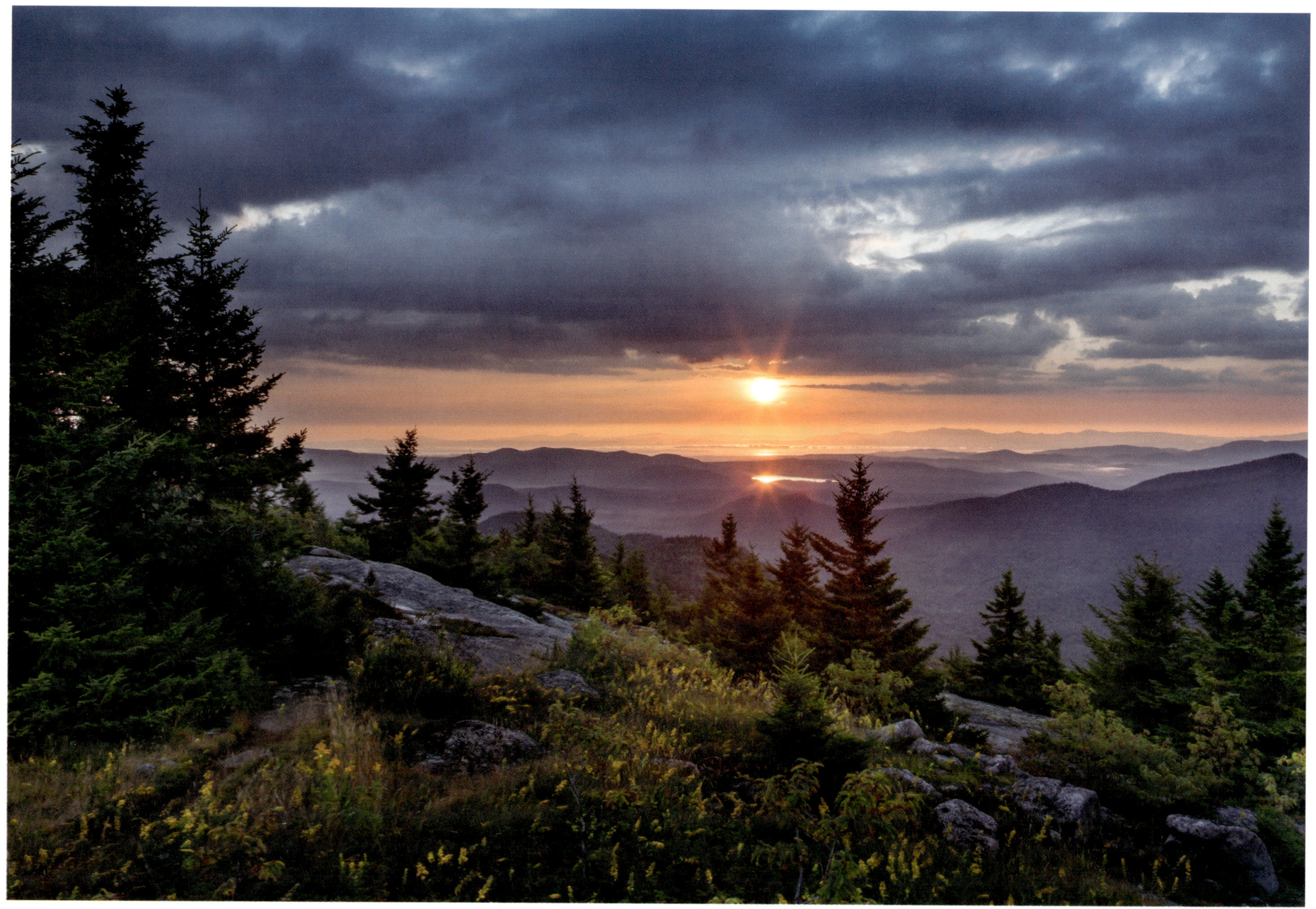

Sunrise over Lake Champlain from the top of Catamount Mountain.

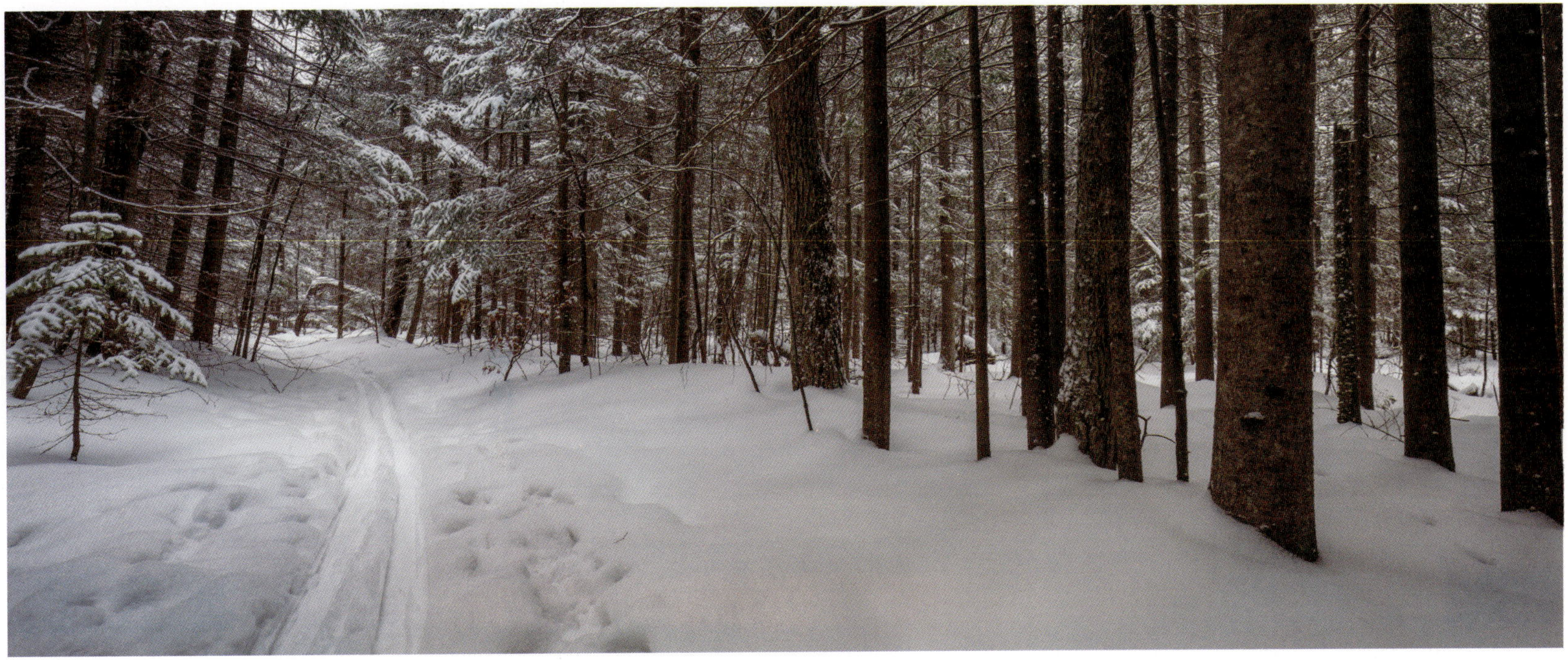

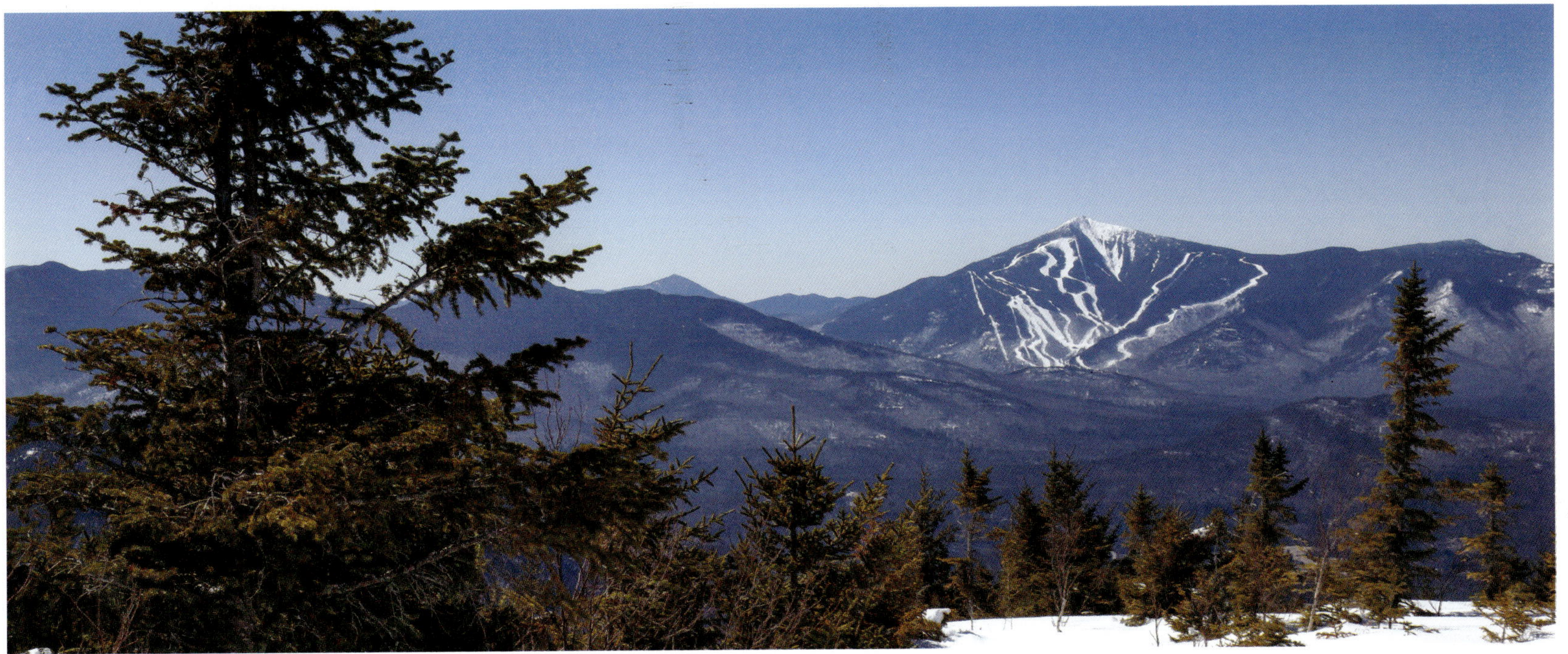

Top: Backcountry ski trail on Rand Hill.
Bottom: The Whiteface Mountain ski area was one of the venues for the 1980 Winter Olympics.

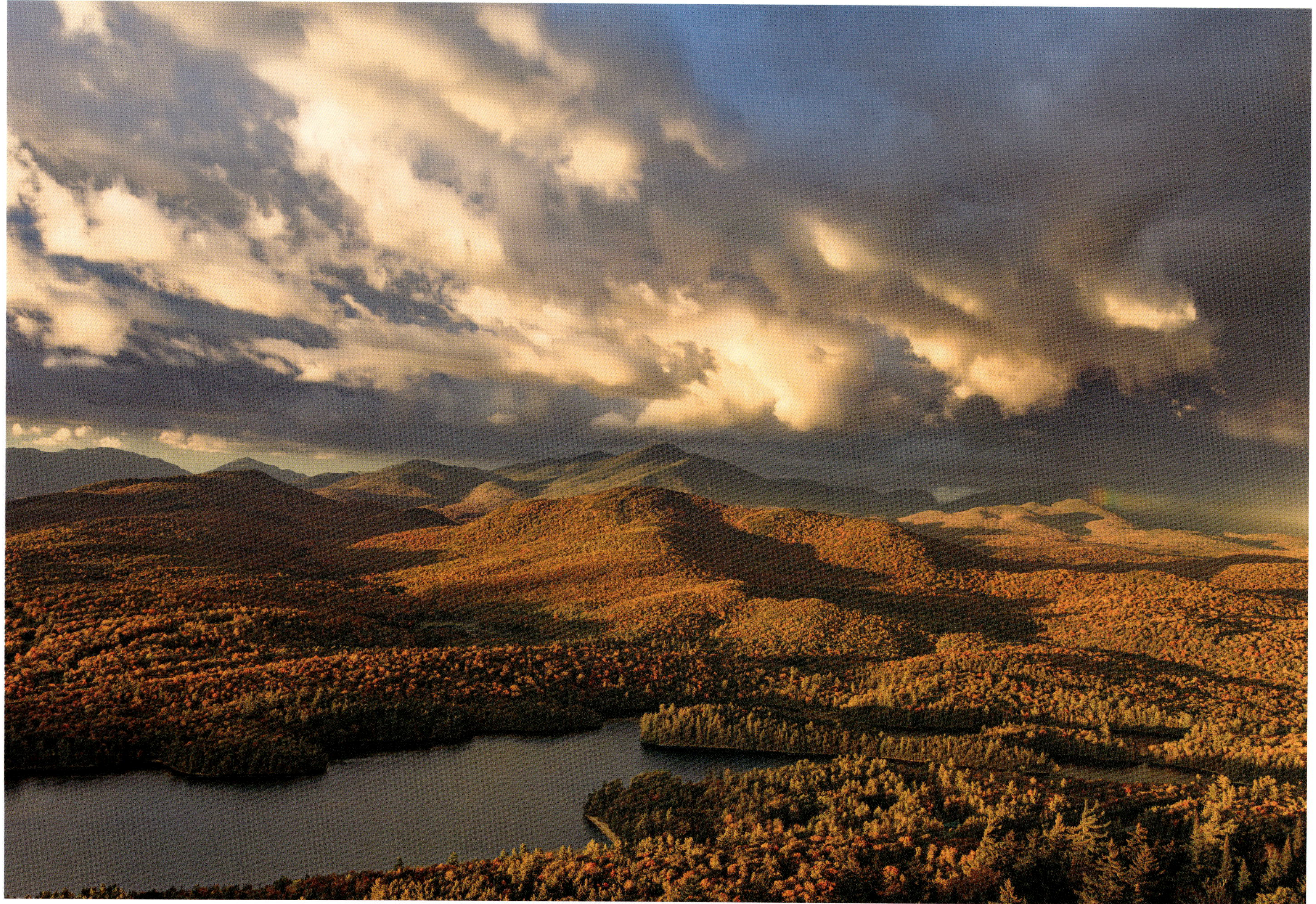

Sunset and rainbow over the southern High Peaks from the Goodnow Mountain fire tower.

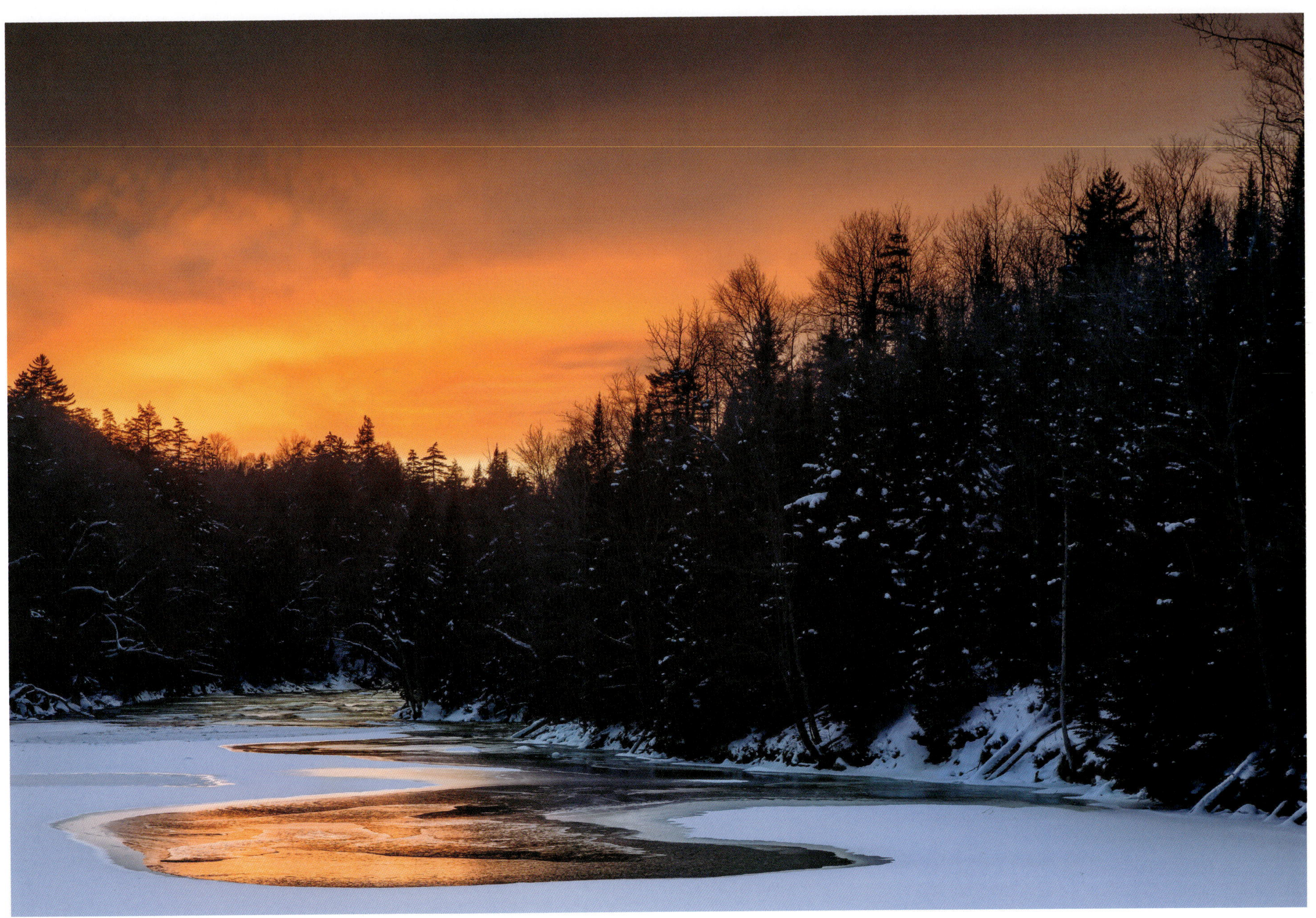

Sunset highlights an approaching storm over the rapids at the Franklin Falls Pond inflow.

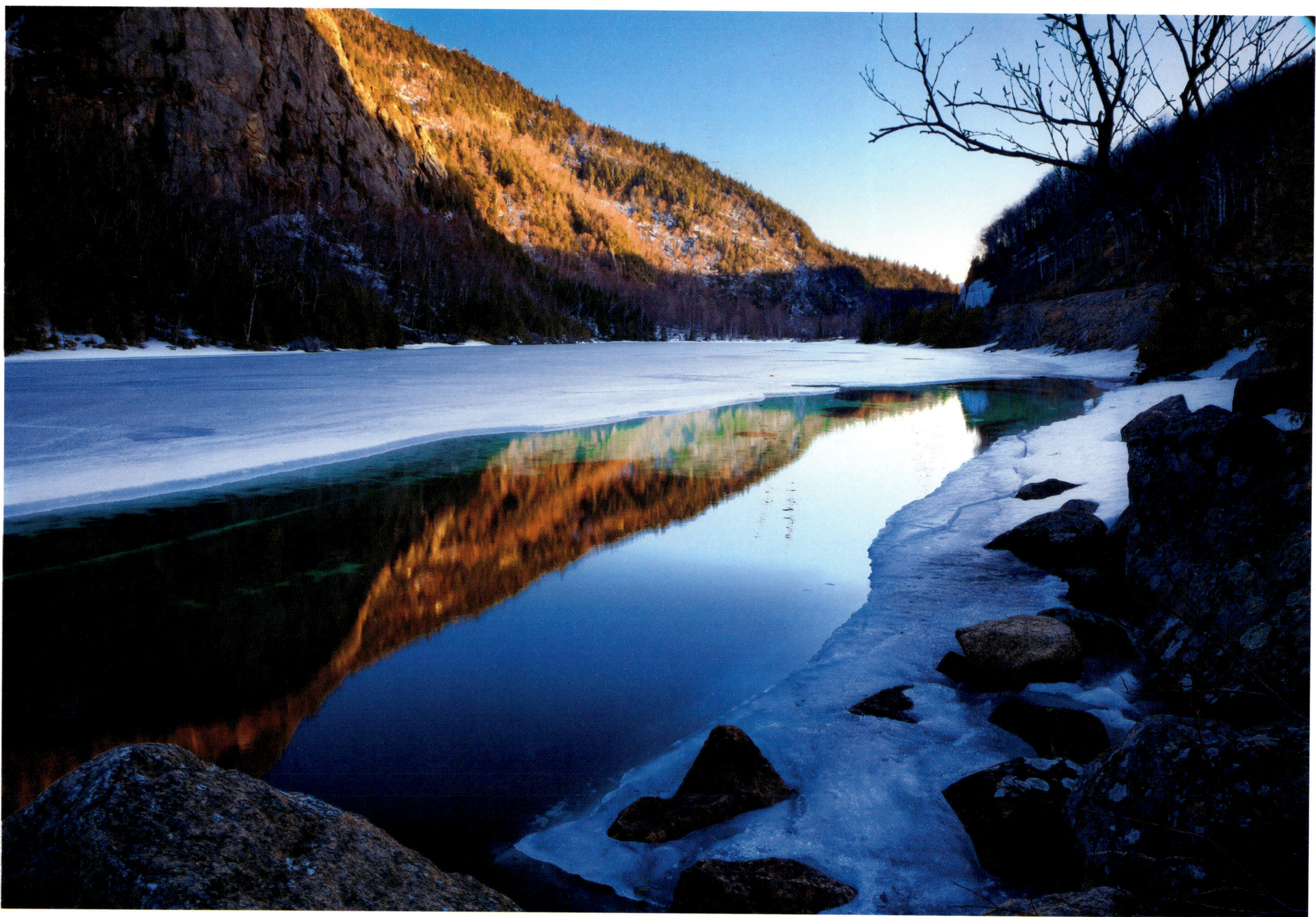

   As Cascade Lake melted in the spring, the ice under the surface took on a turquoise-green hue that contrasted with the warm glow on the mountains.

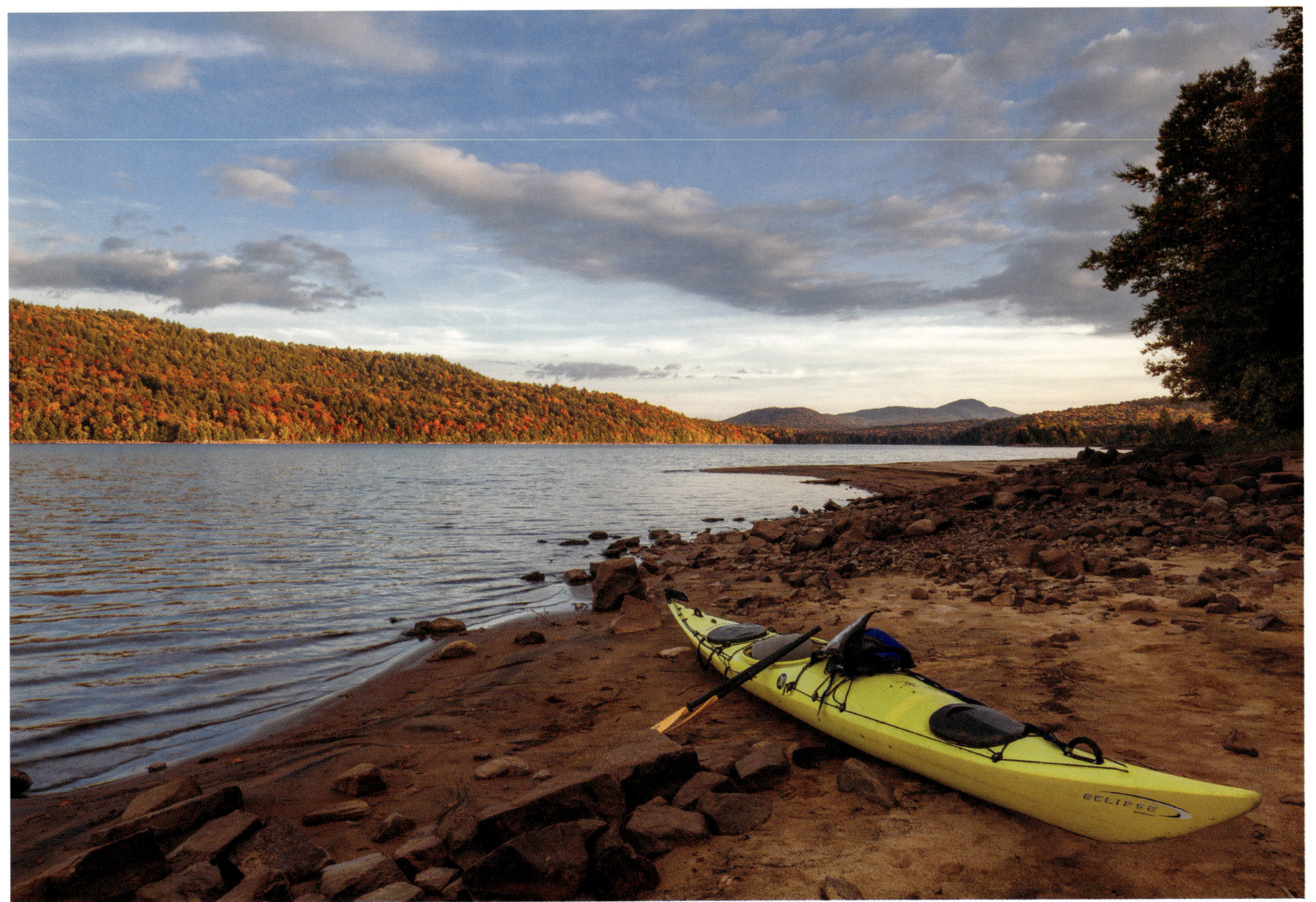

Kayak at a rocky wilderness beach on Indian Lake.

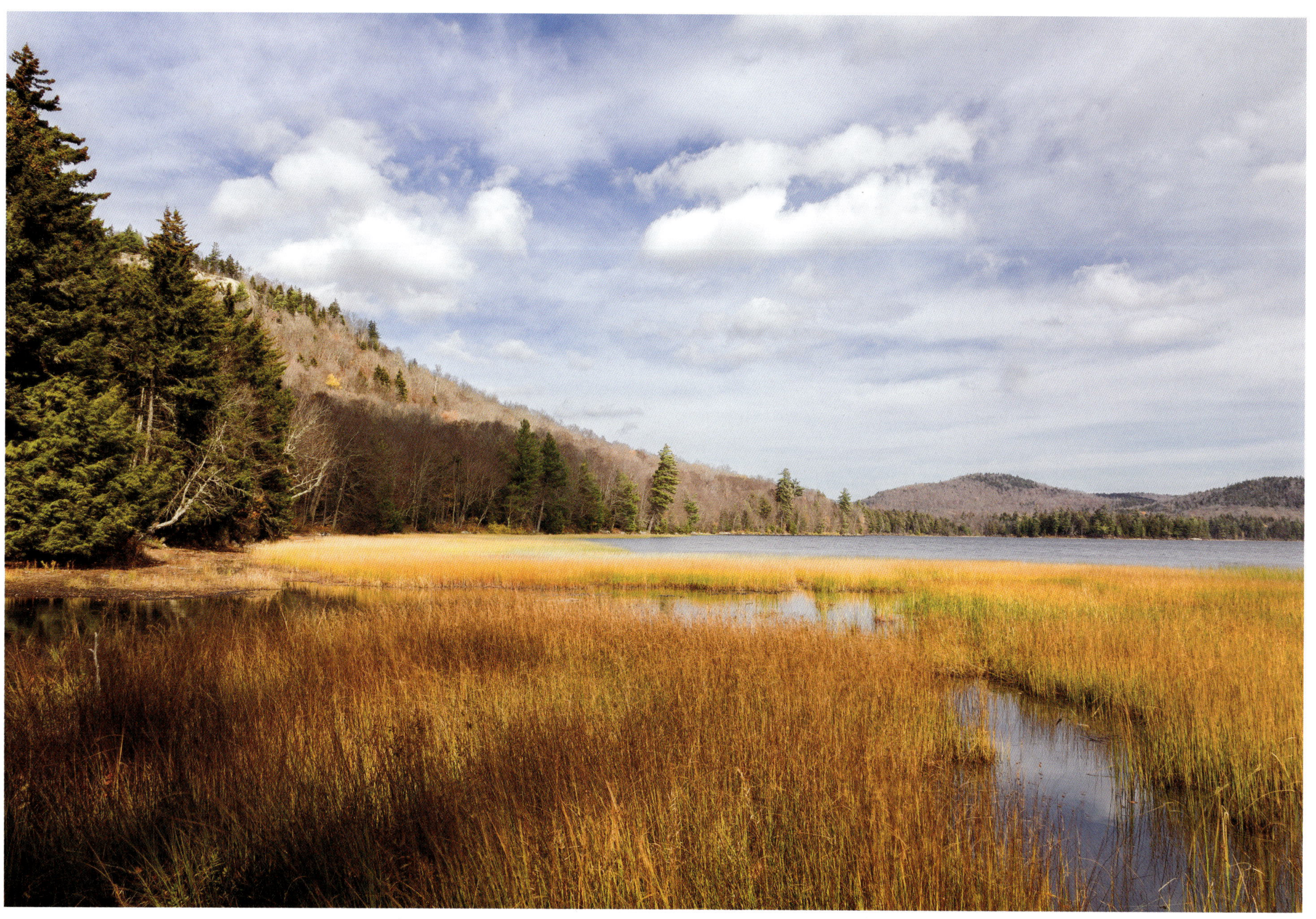

Luminous grasses on the shore of Lake Lila.

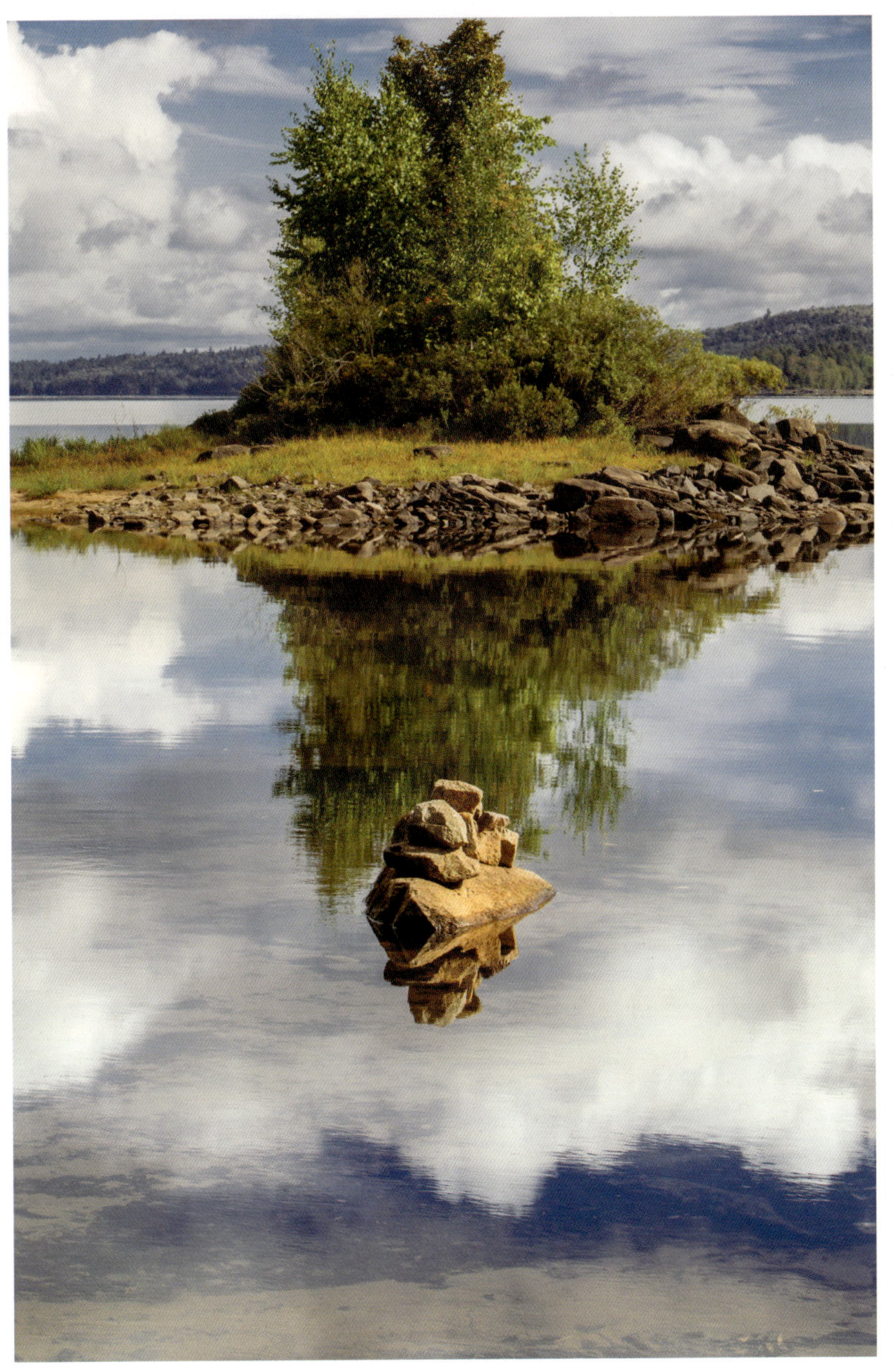

A Zen-like scene from our campsite on Indian Lake.

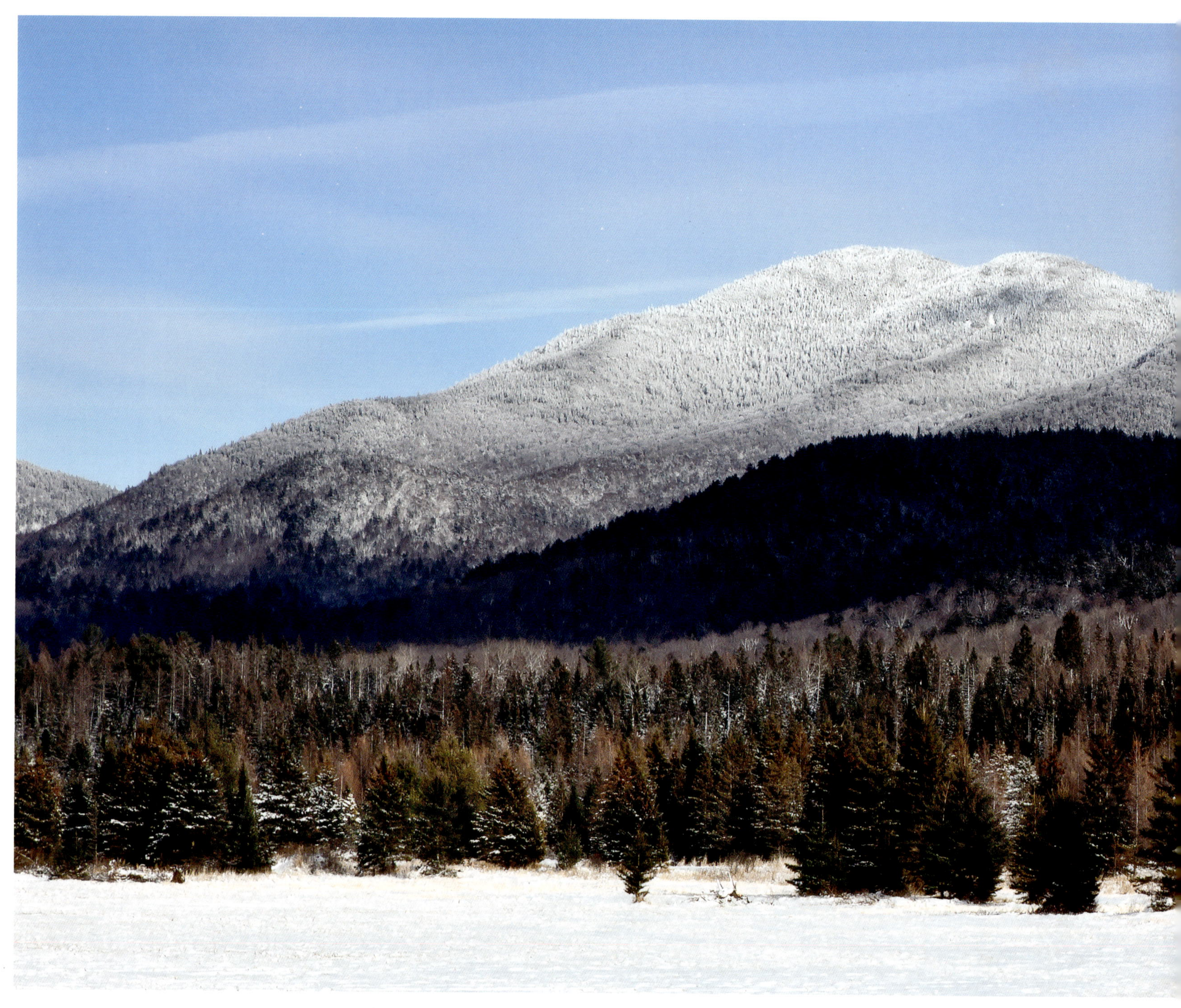

A clearing snowstorm sets off a view of the Sentinel Range near Lake Placid.

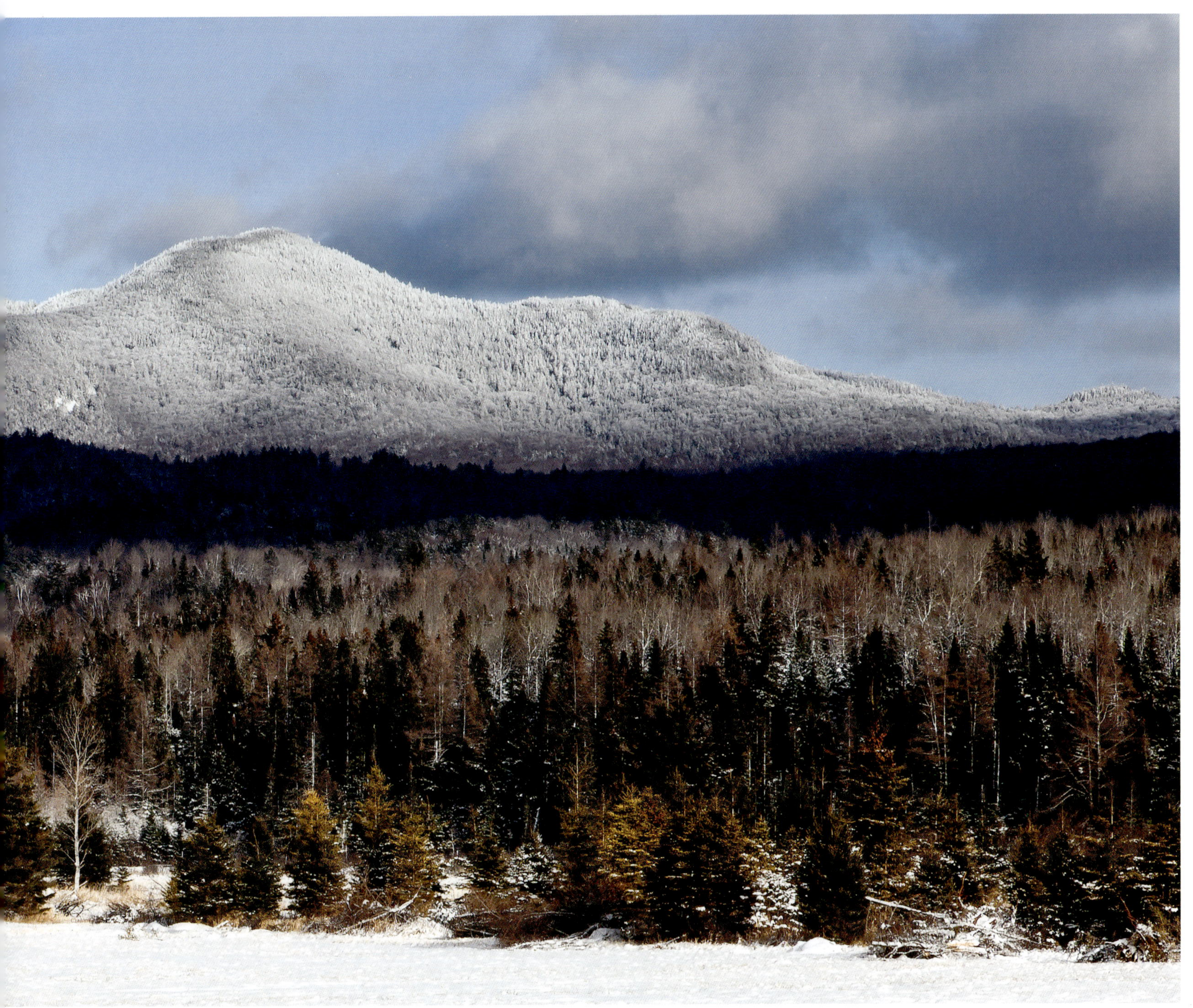

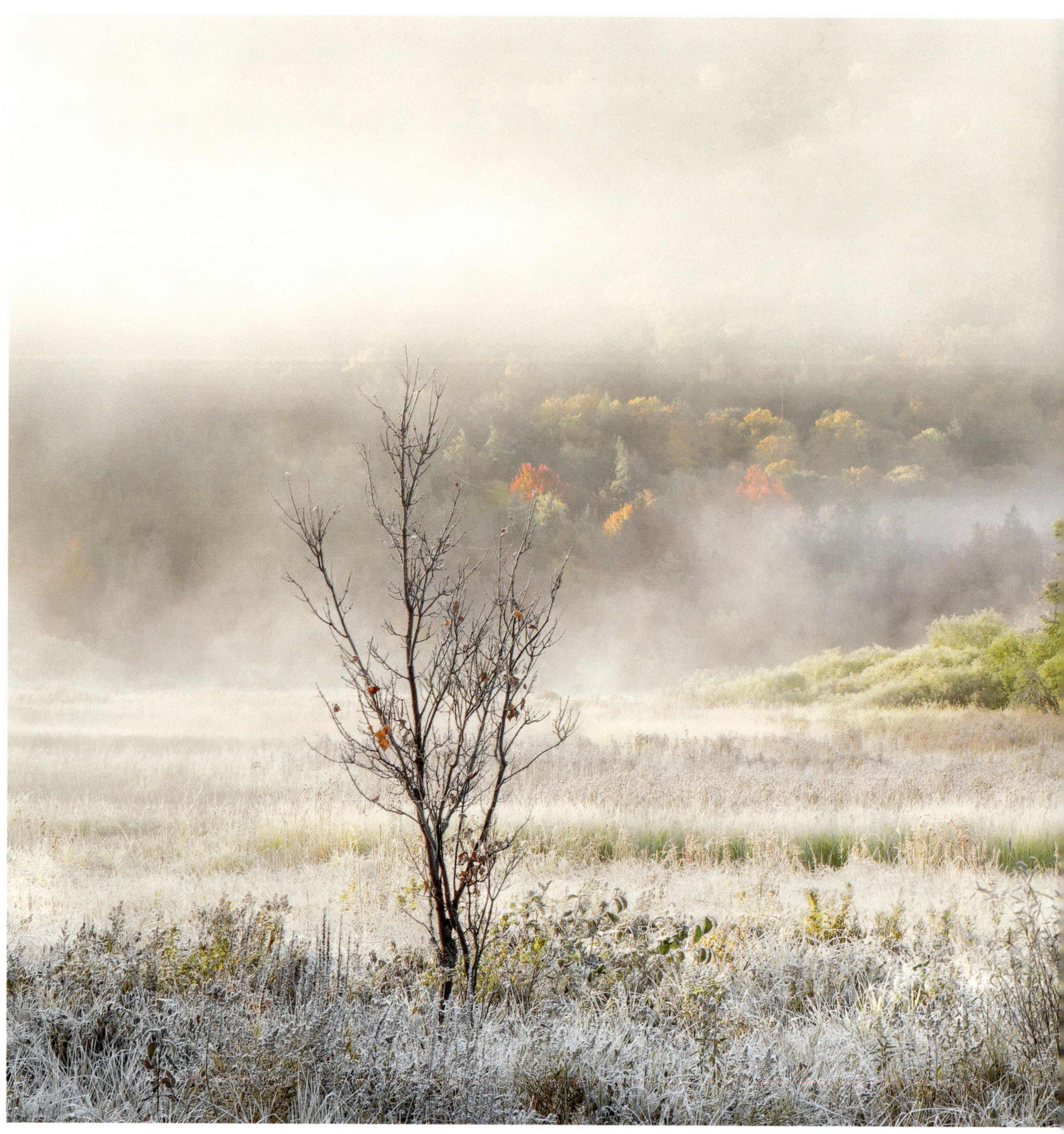

An early freeze frosted the wetlands near the Saranac River in the fall.

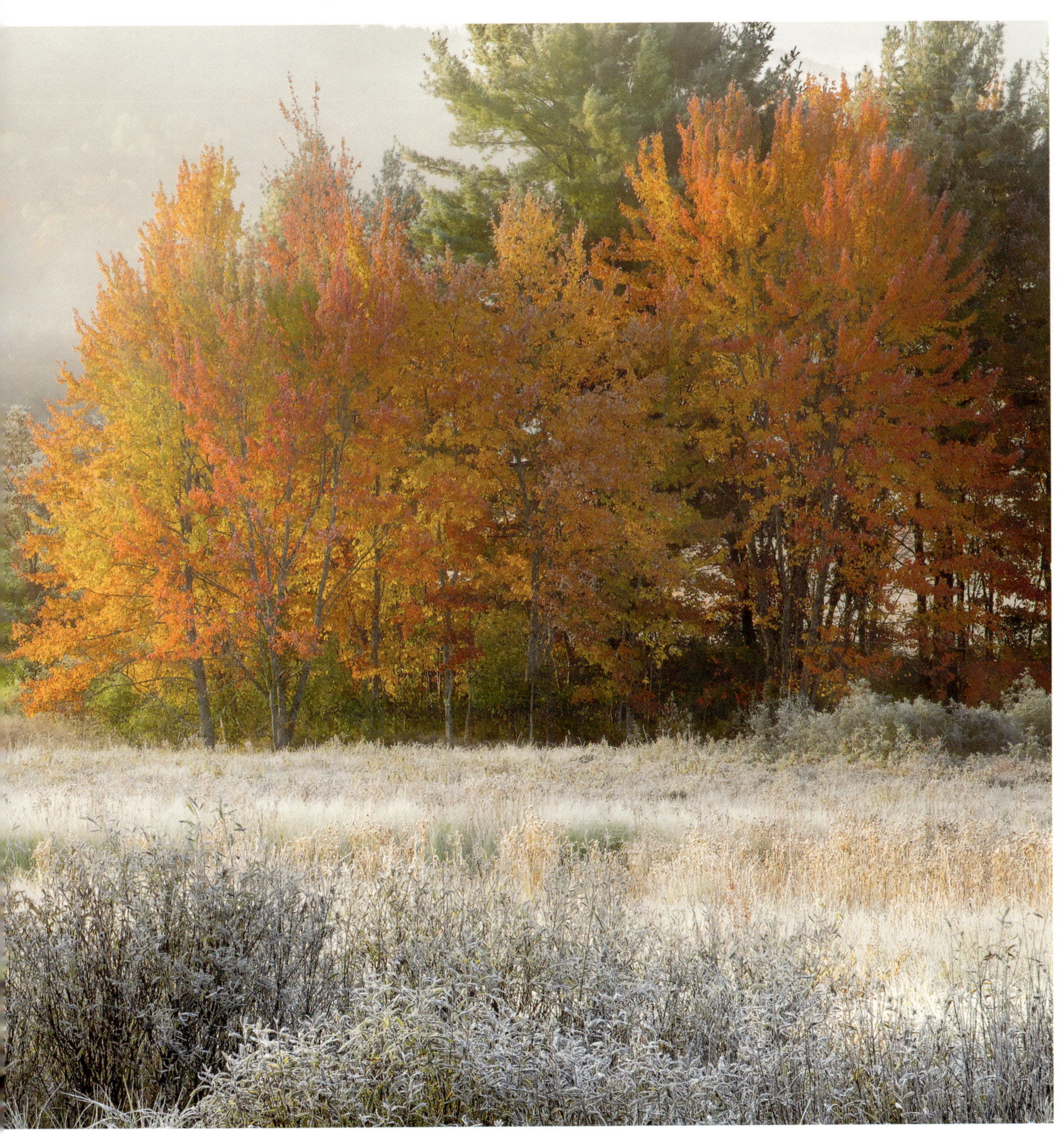

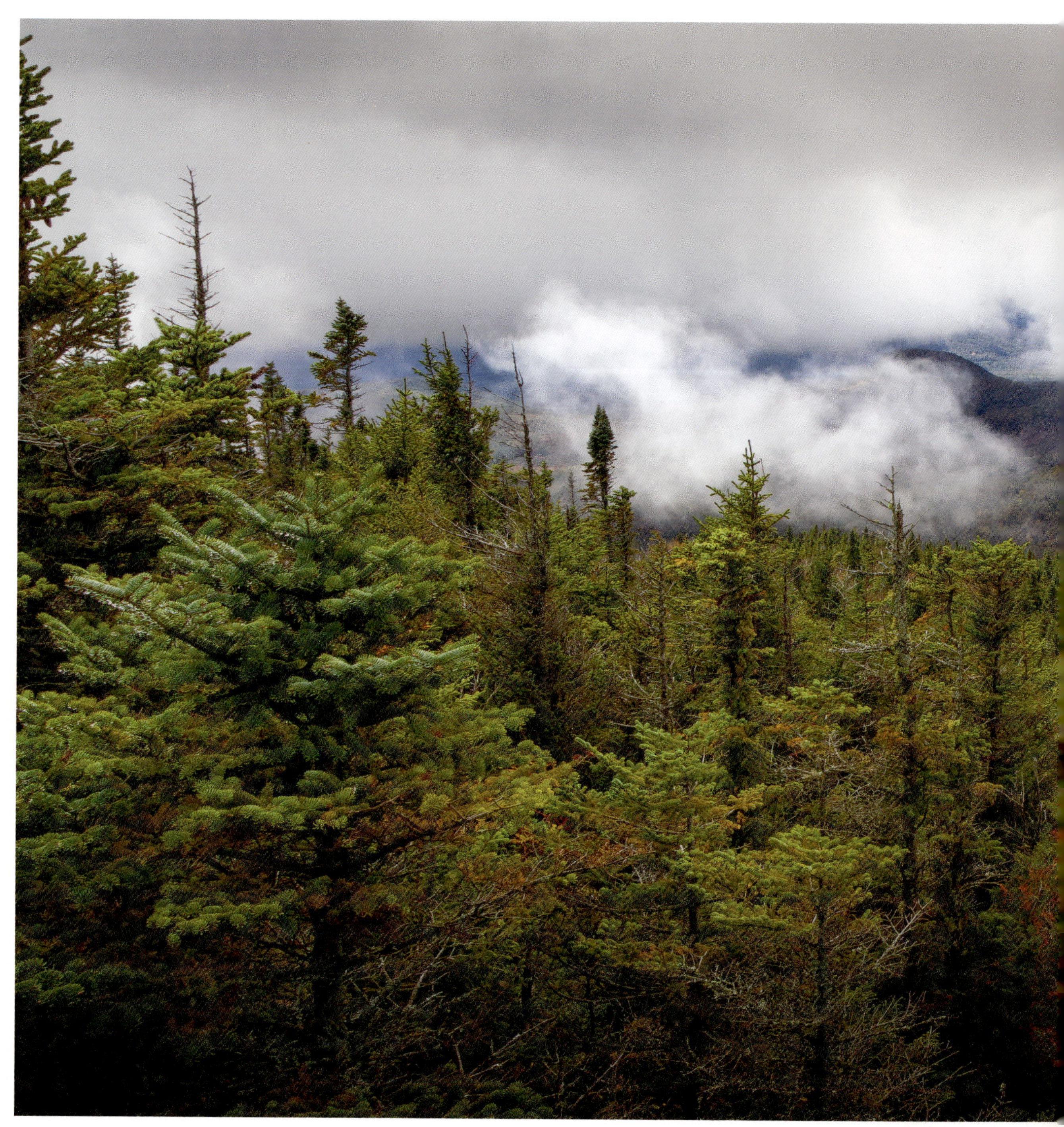

Clear Pond from the trails on the Elk Lake Lodge property.

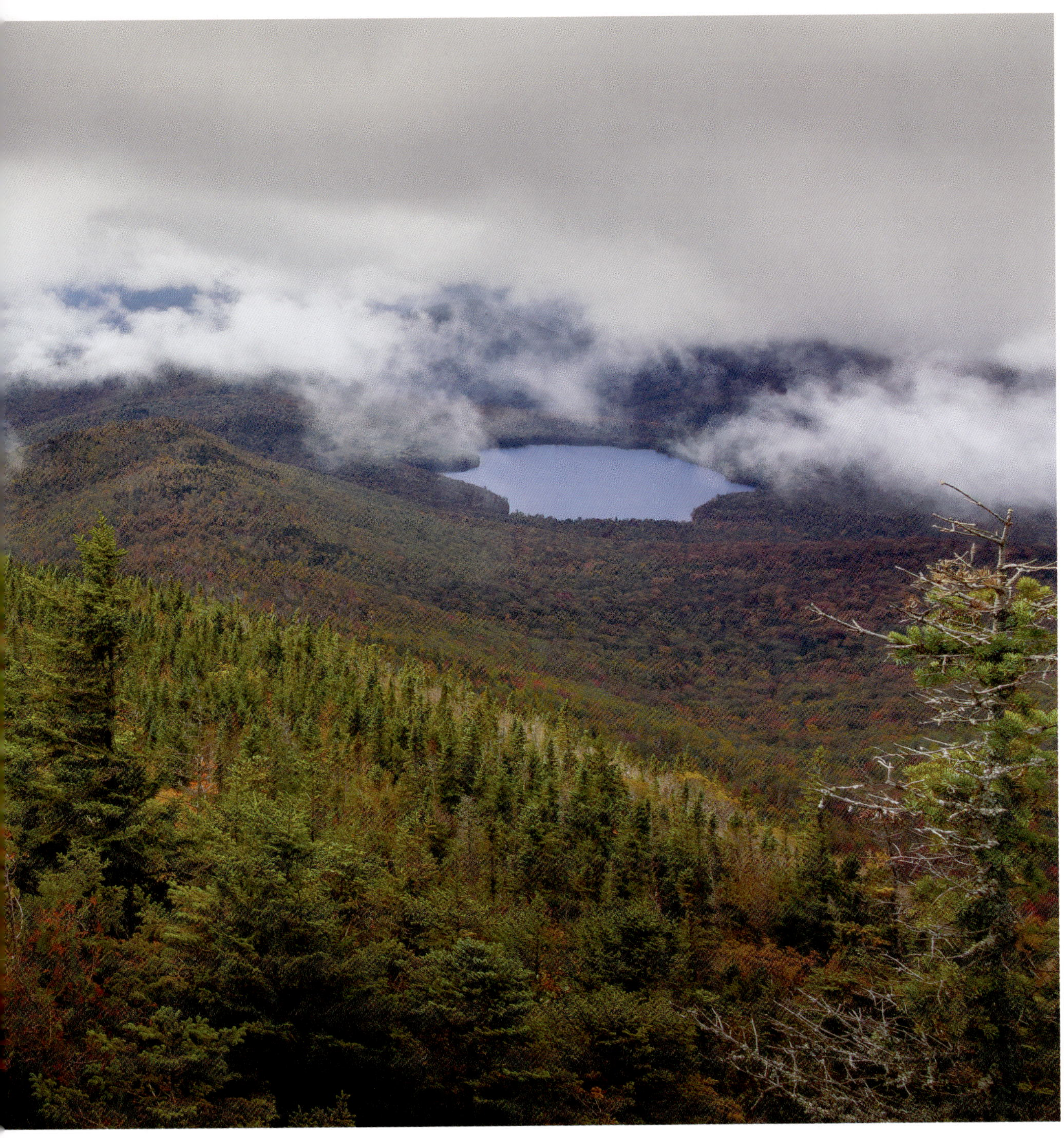

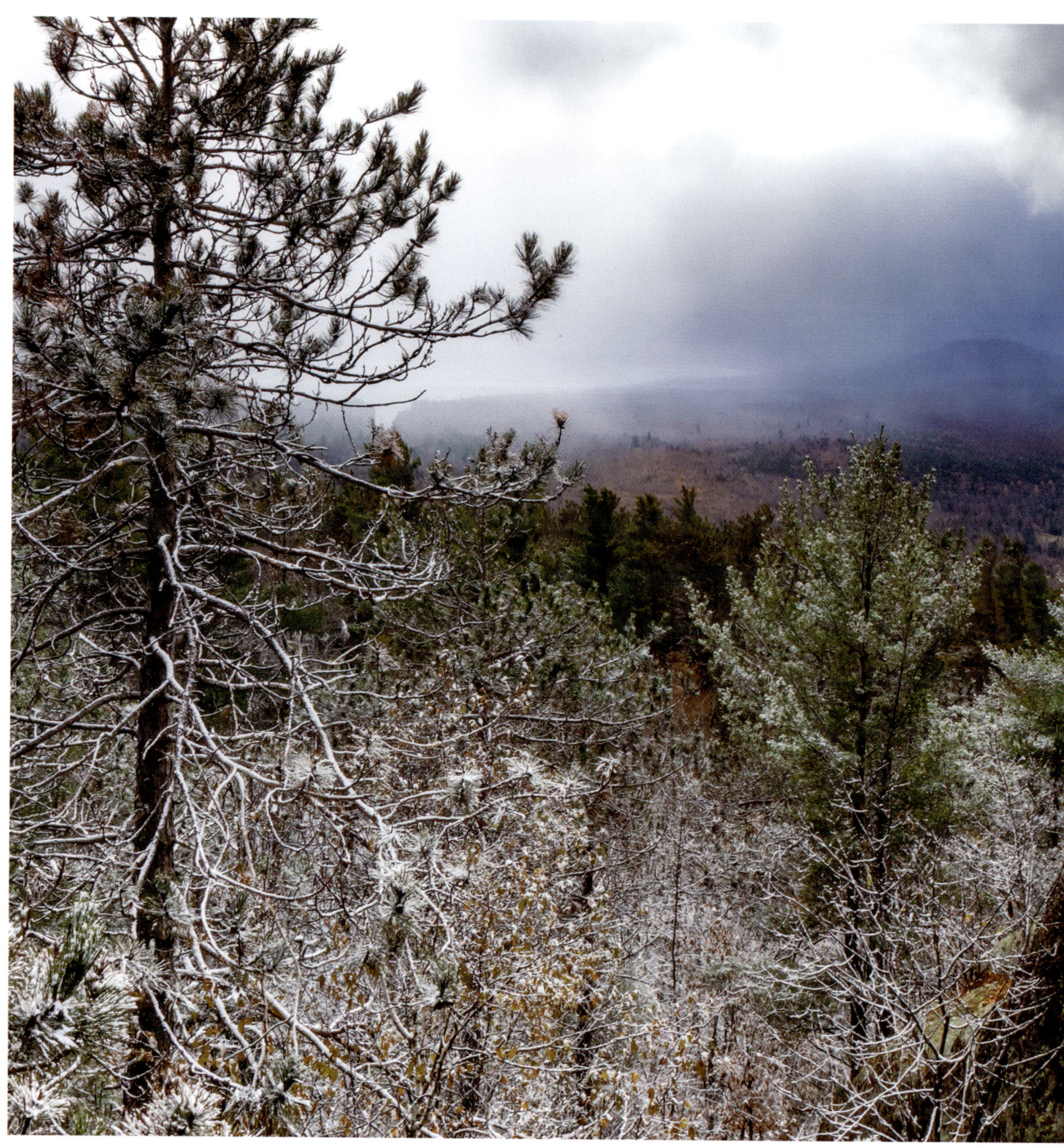

As we hiked up Silver Lake Mountain during peak fall foliage, a snowstorm passed through and dusted everything with fresh snow. When we got to the top, we could see the trailing edge of the storm moving off toward the lake.

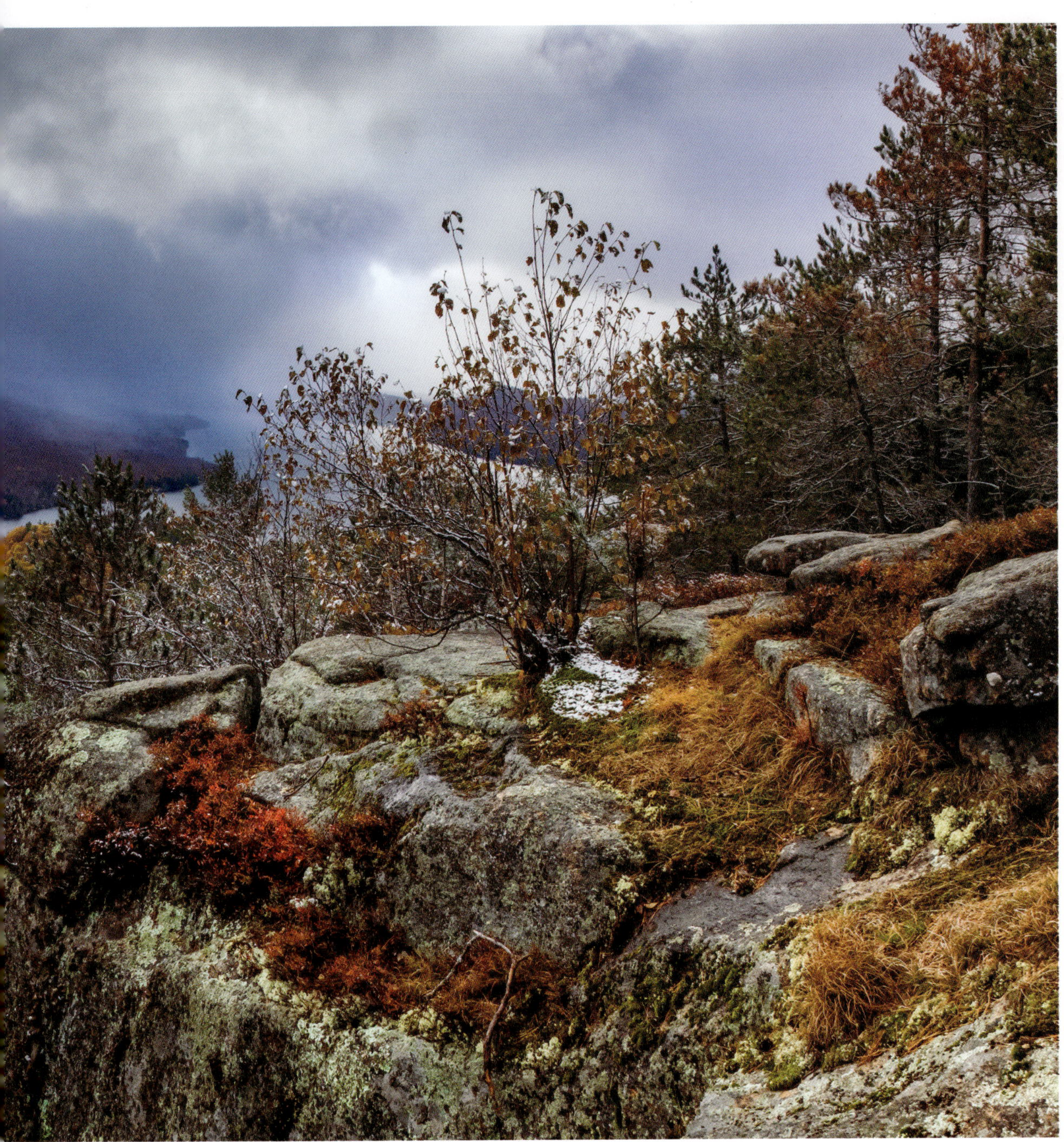

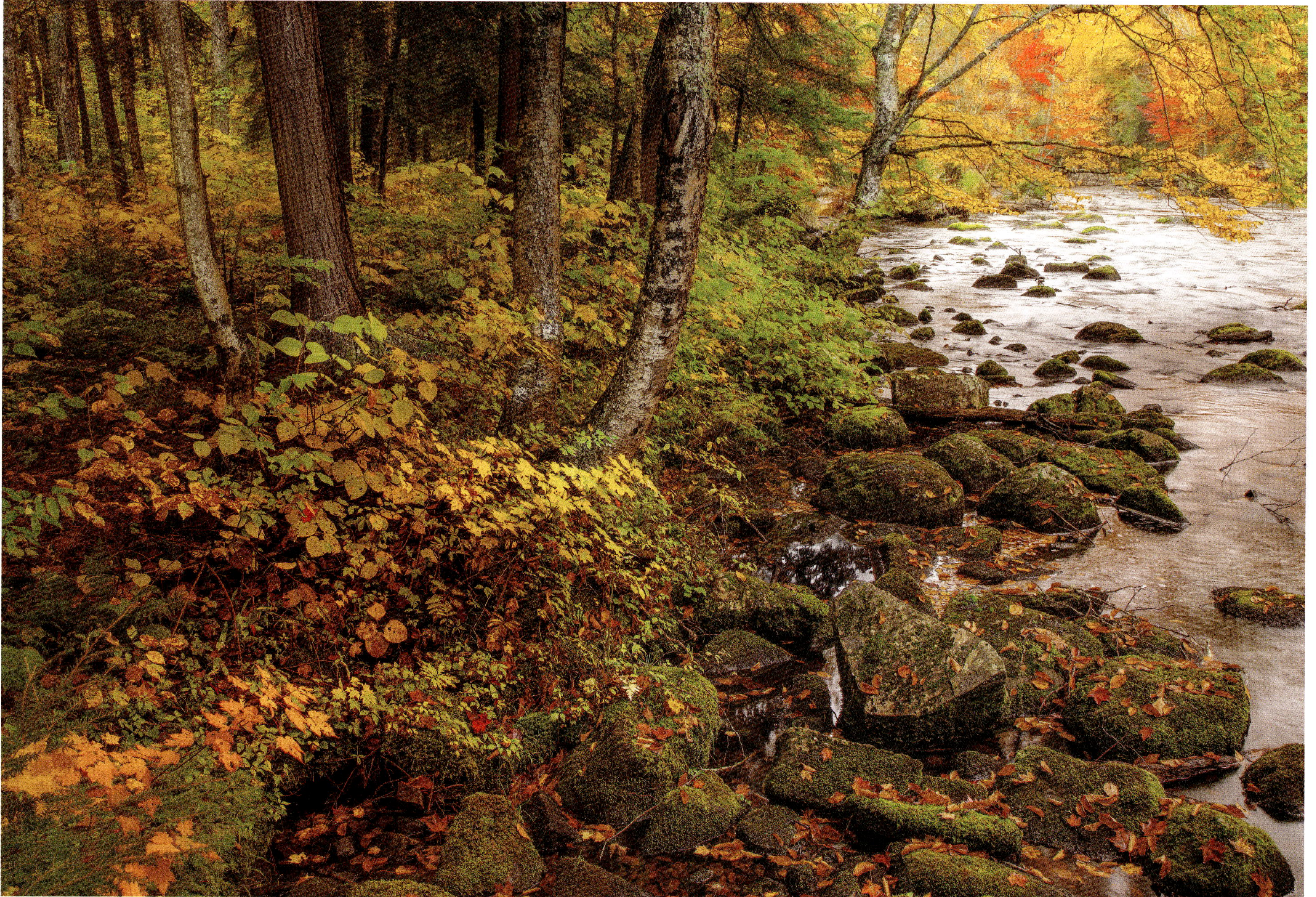

Fall scene along the shore of the Meacham Lake outflow.

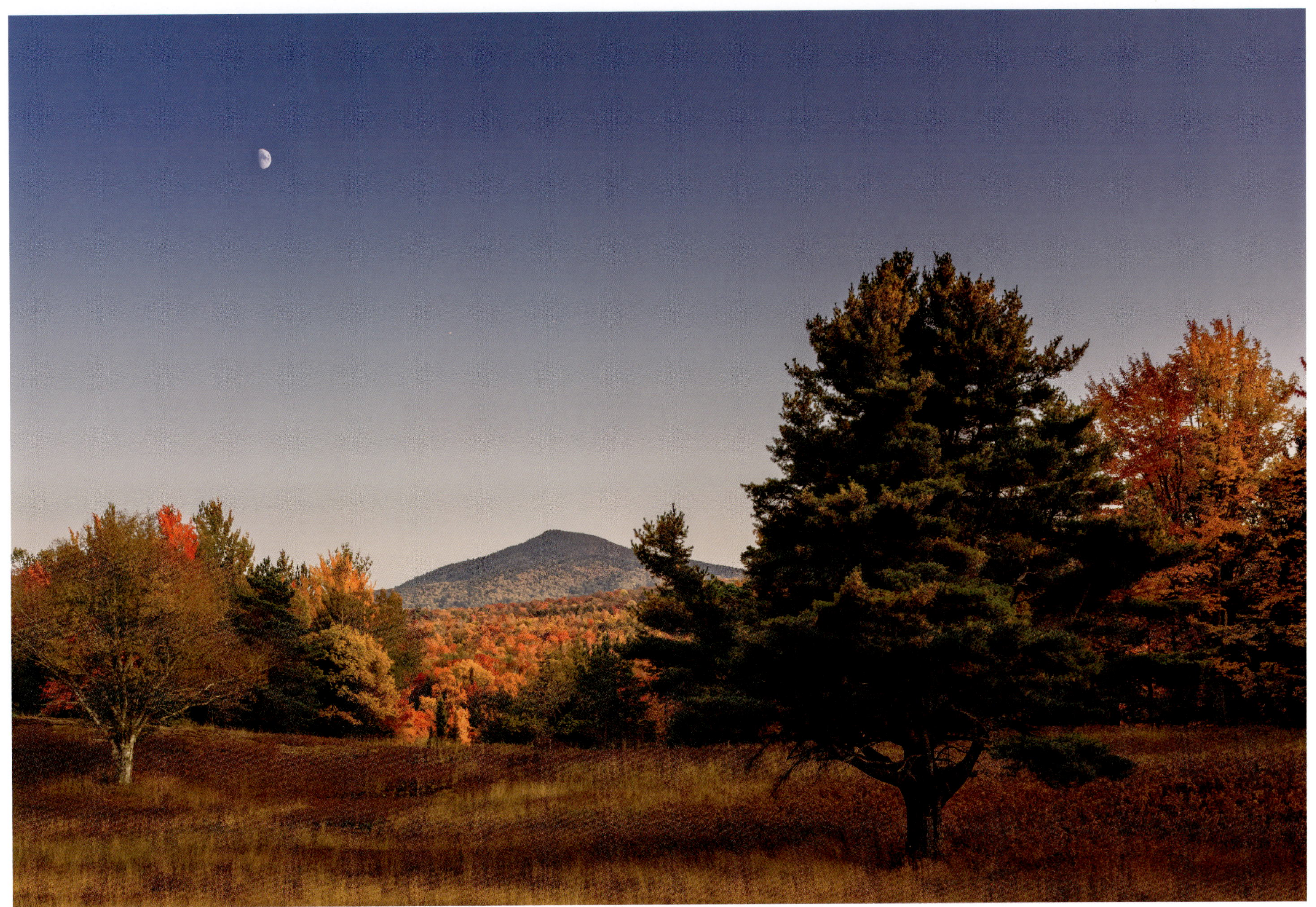

Evening half moon near the Cedar River Flow along the Northville-Placid Trail.

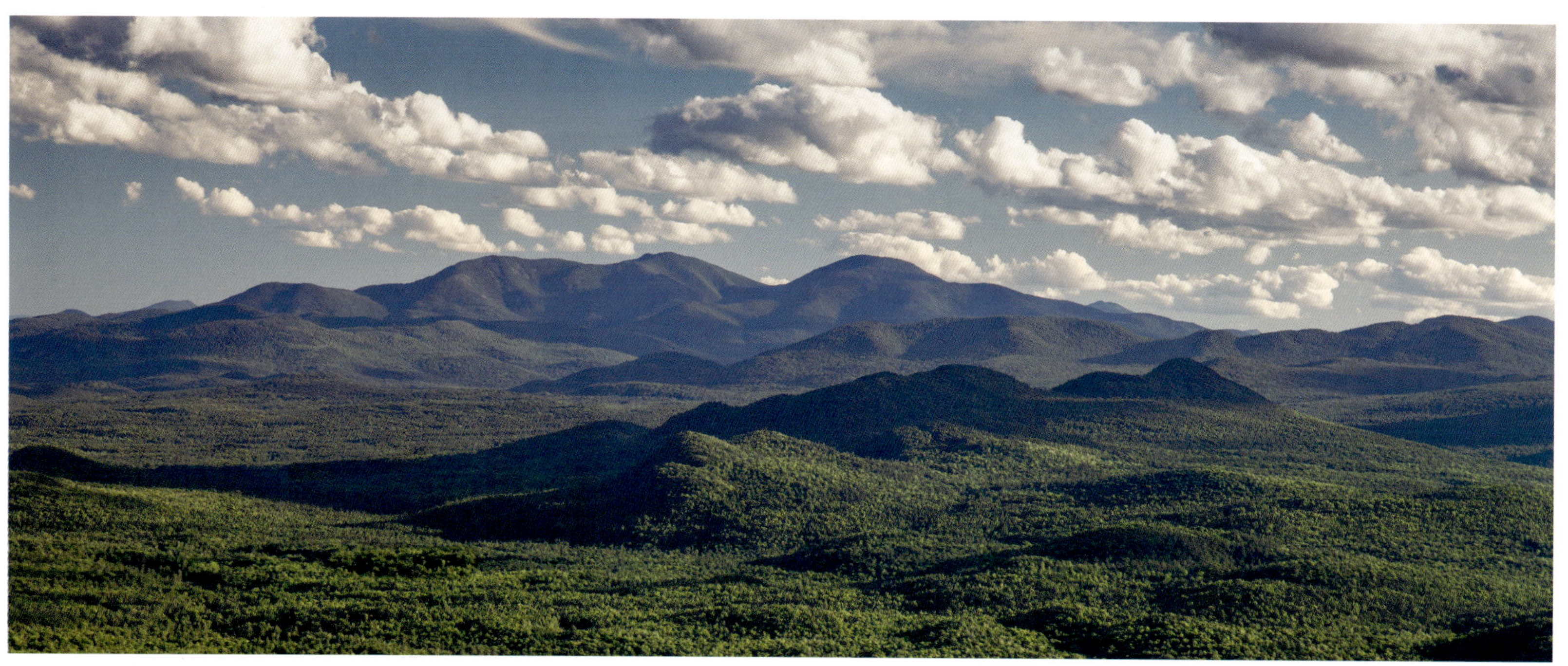

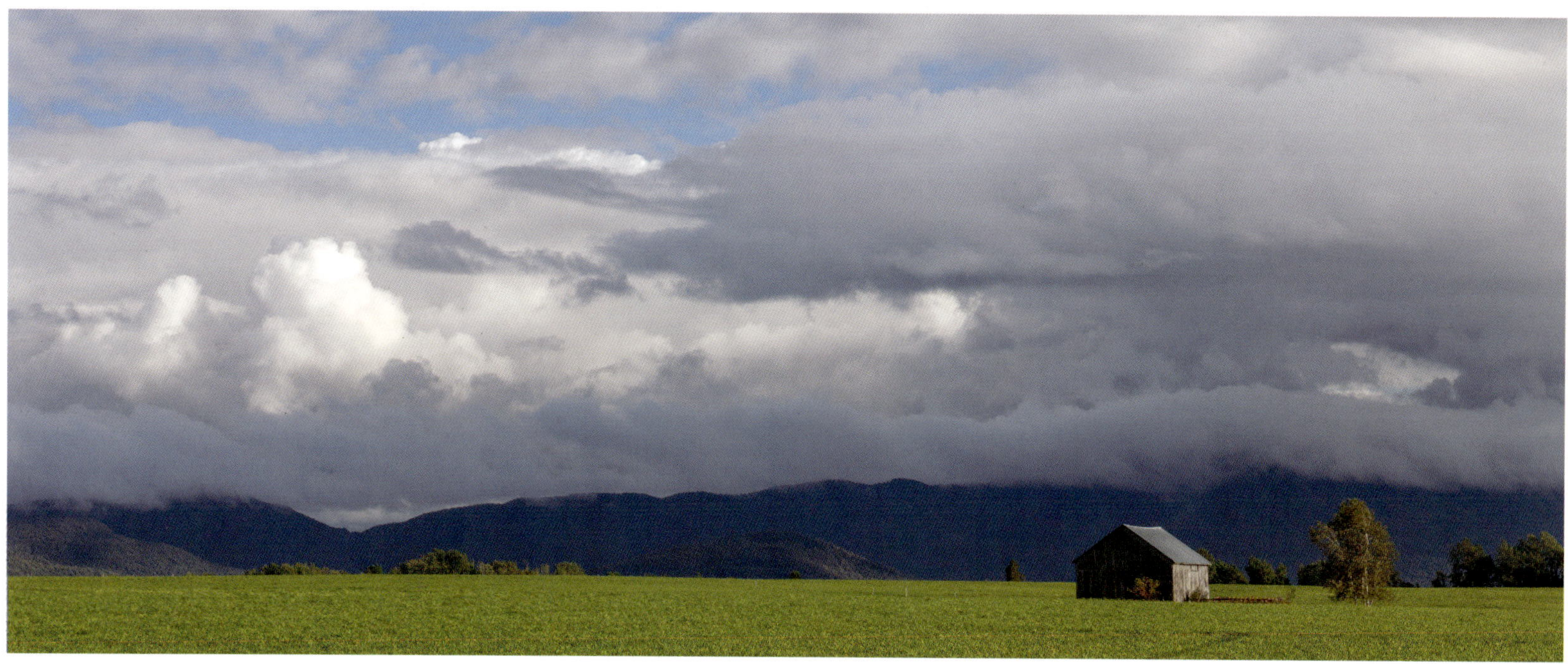

Top: Summer green on the High Peaks from Poke-O-Moonshine Mountain.
Bottom: Barn on a high plateau among the shrouded mountains.

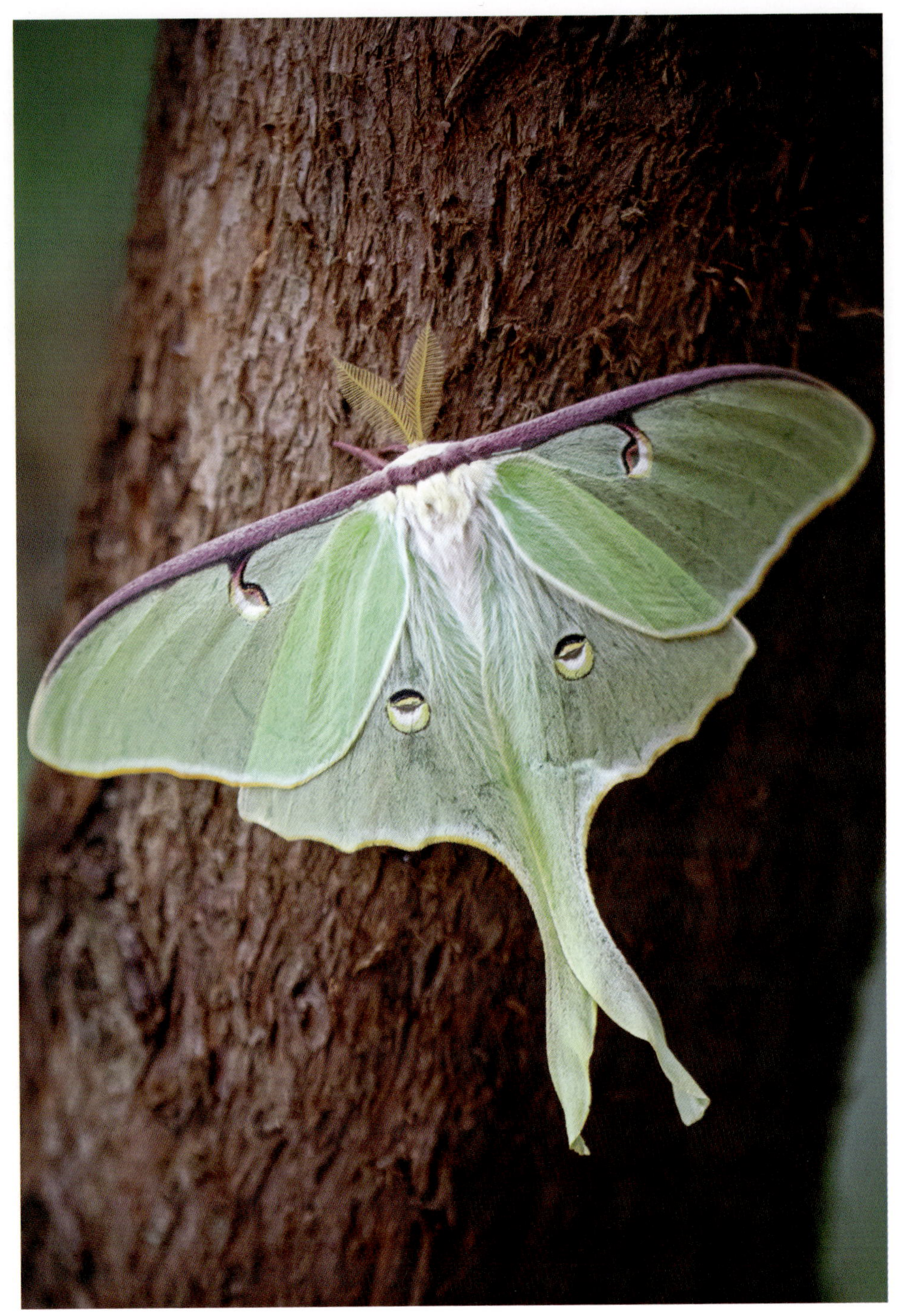

Luna moths can be larger than a grown man's hand with his fingers spread.

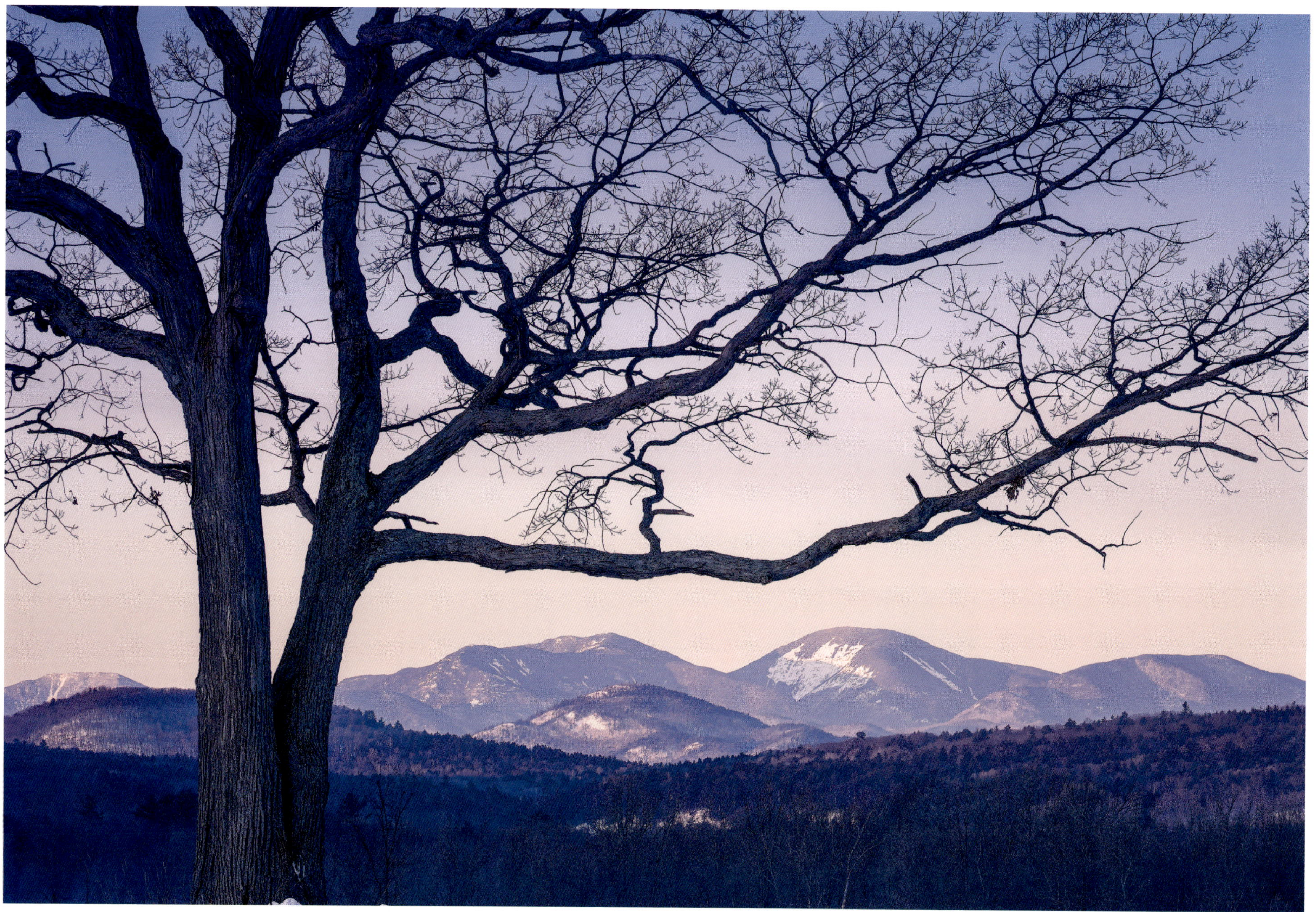

A lone tree frames the High Peaks from the east.

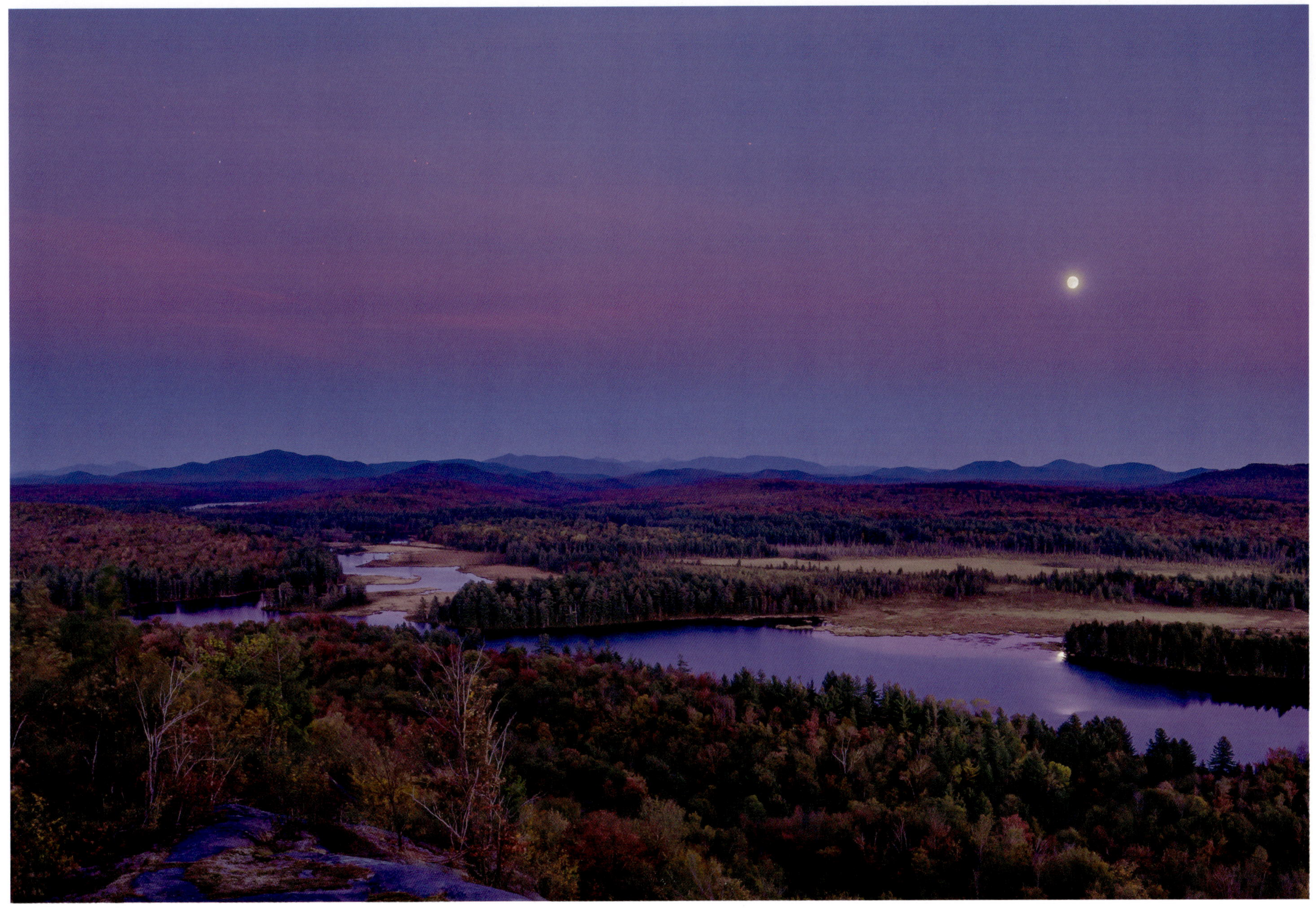

Moonrise from Low's Ridge.

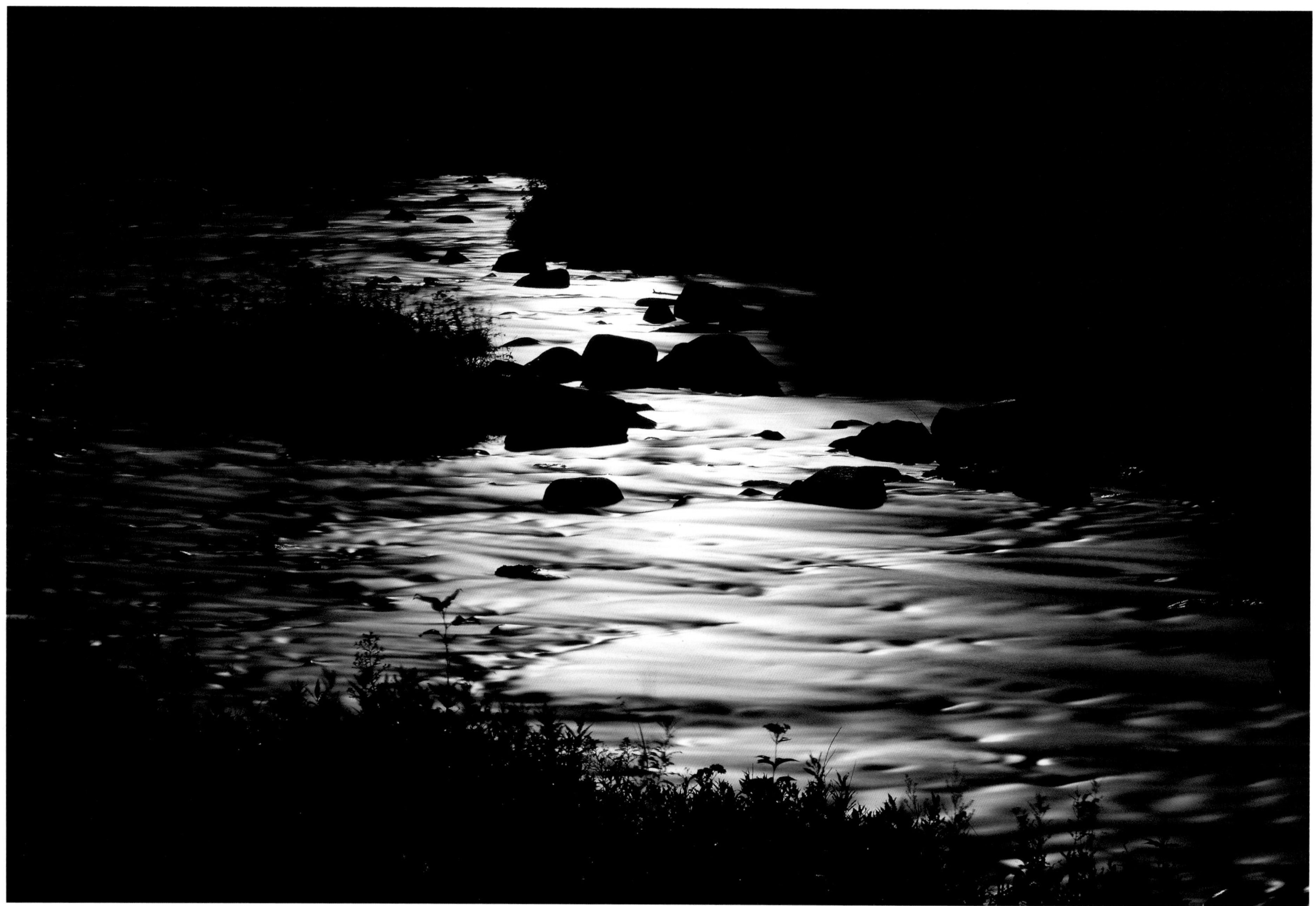

 Saranac River under the moonlight. A long, three-minute exposure made the rapids look like molten silver.

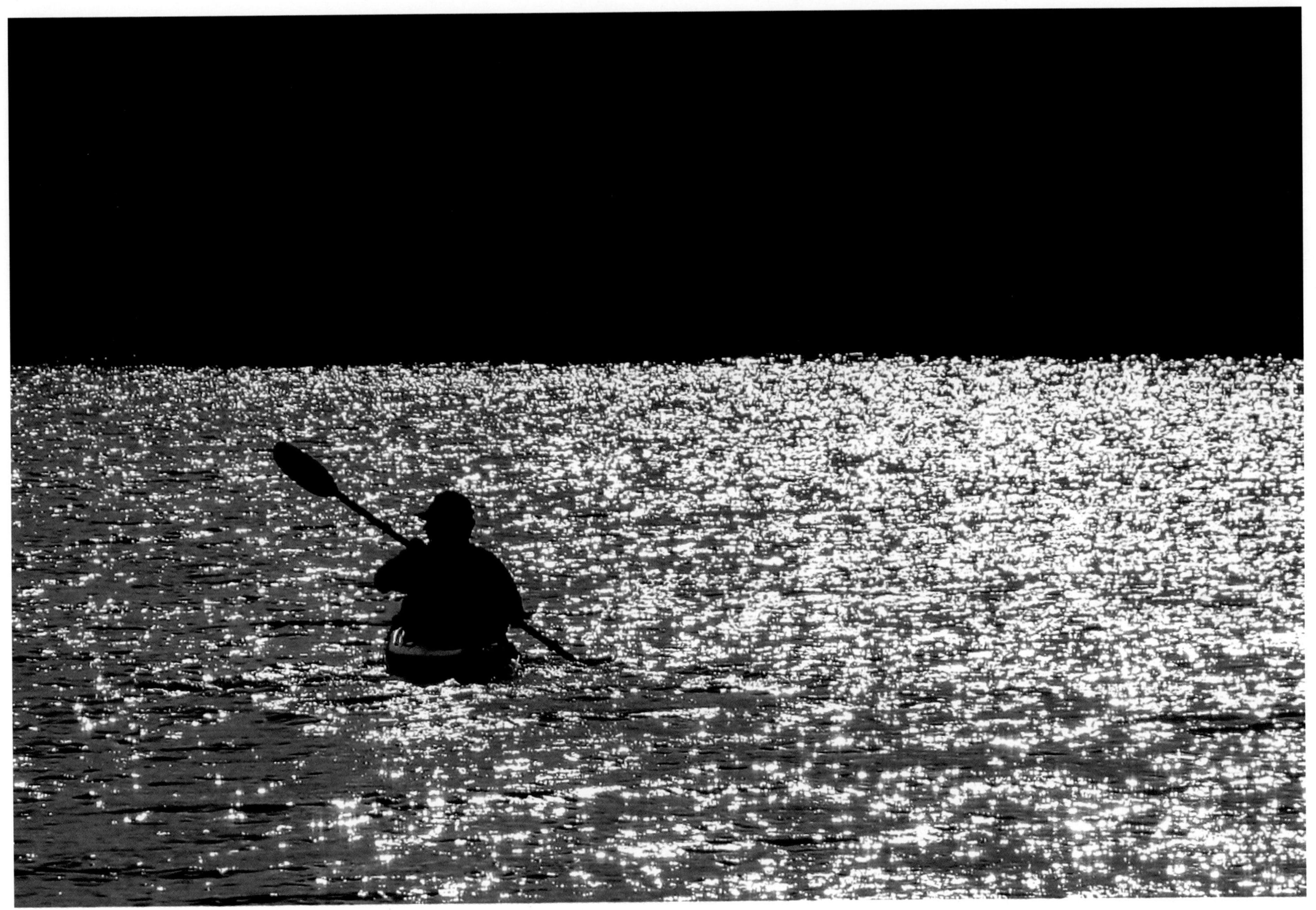

Heading back in the silvery, late light of evening after a day of paddling on Franklin Falls Pond.

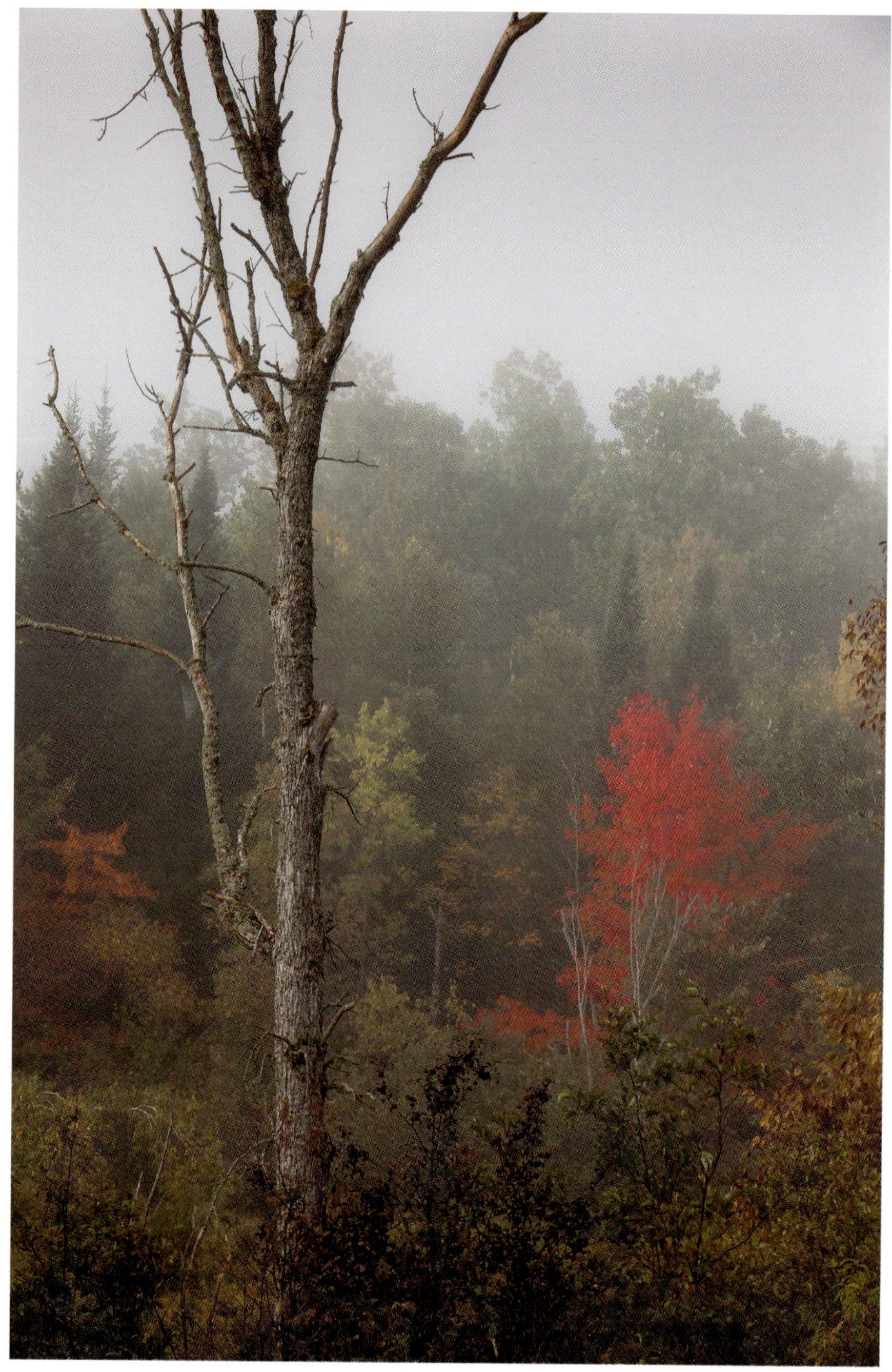

First fall colors emerge on a misty morning.

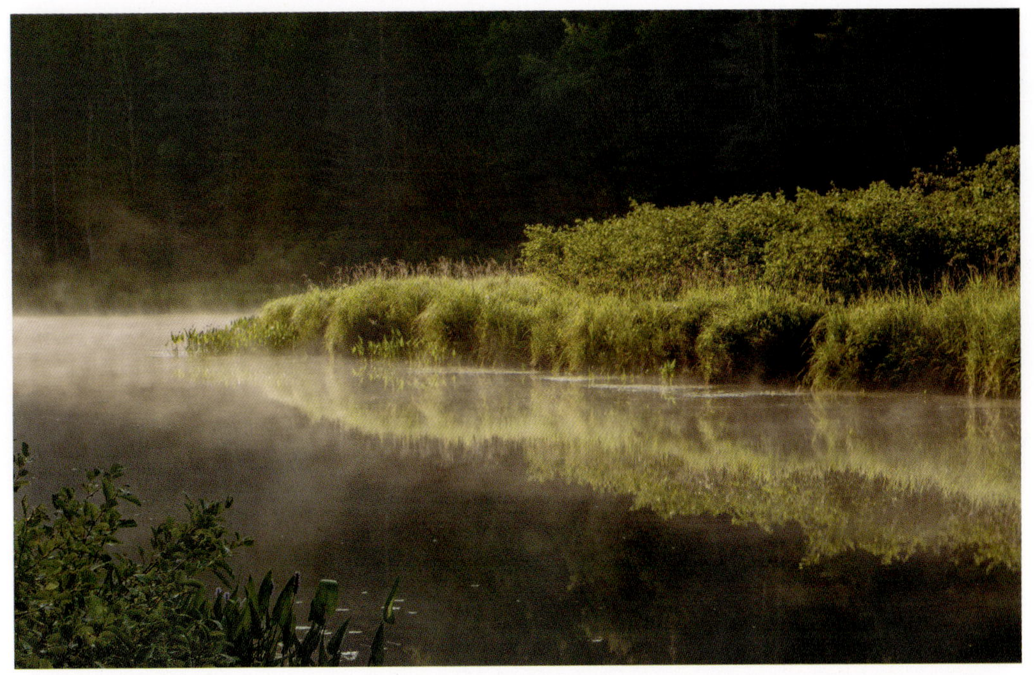

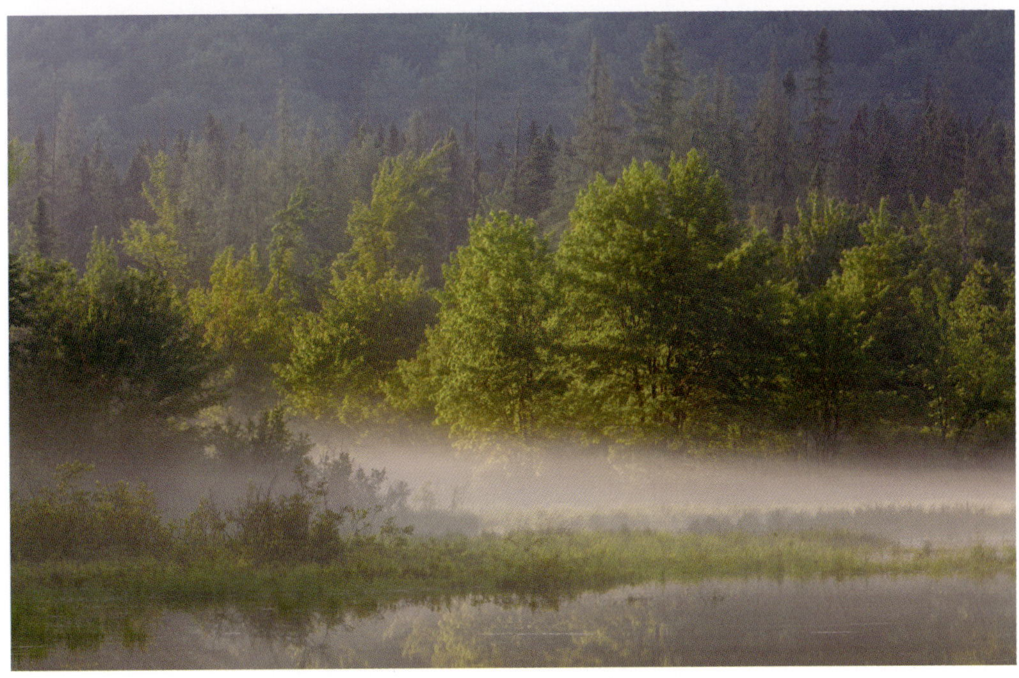

Top: First light along a stream near Speculator.
Bottom: Ground fog along the Saranac River near the town of Saranac Lake.

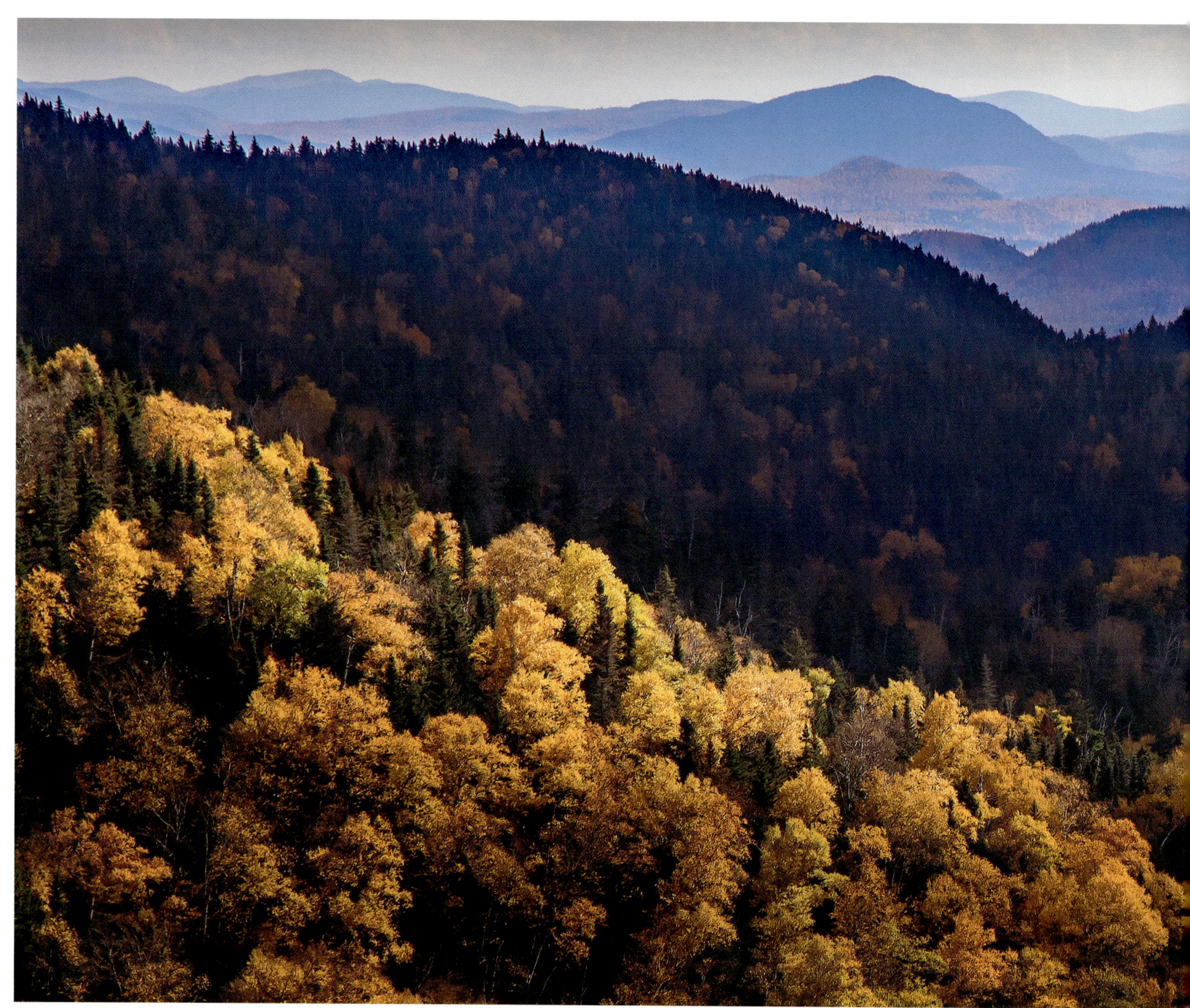

Yellow highlights and layered blue mountains from the top of Hopkins Mountain.

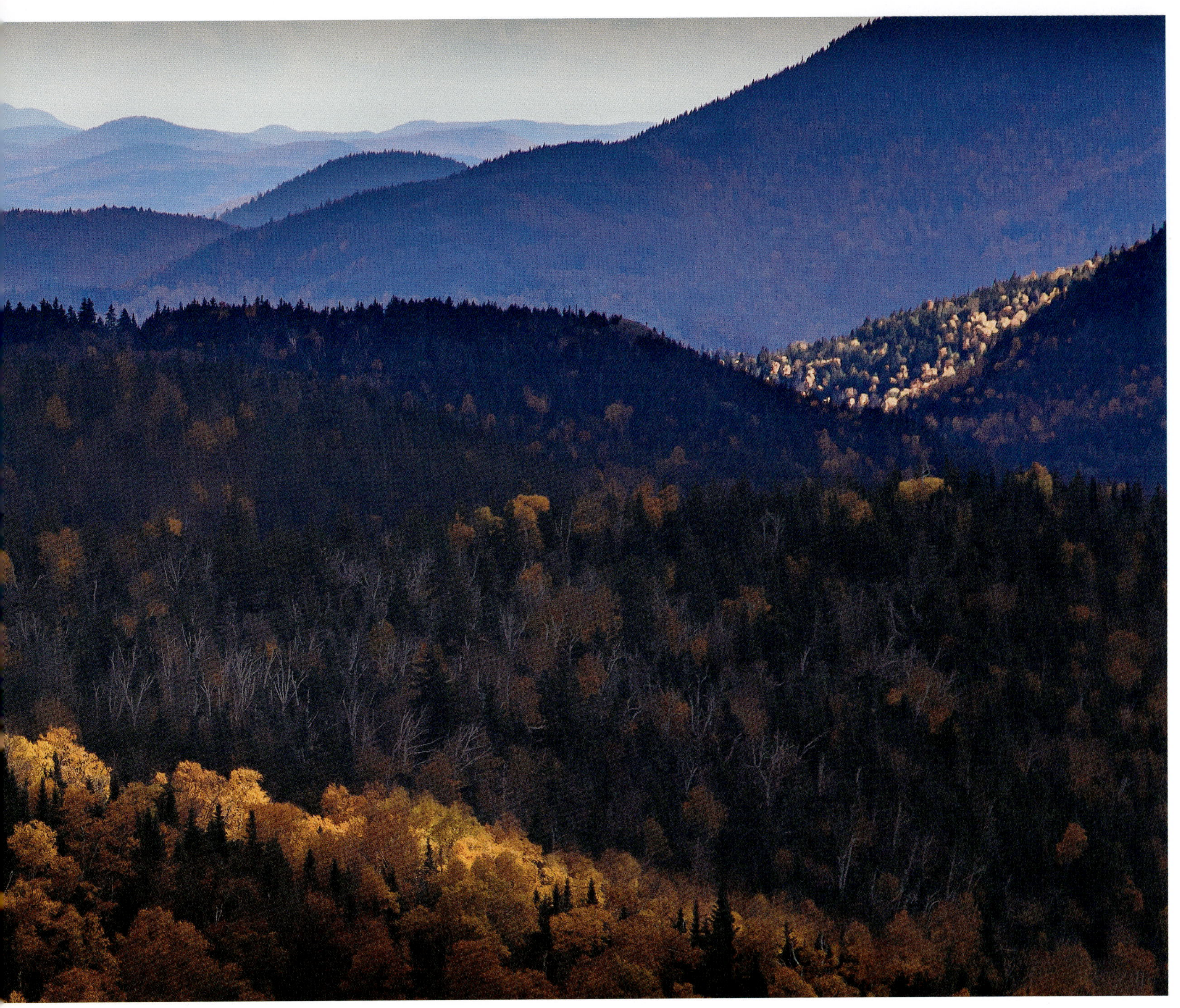

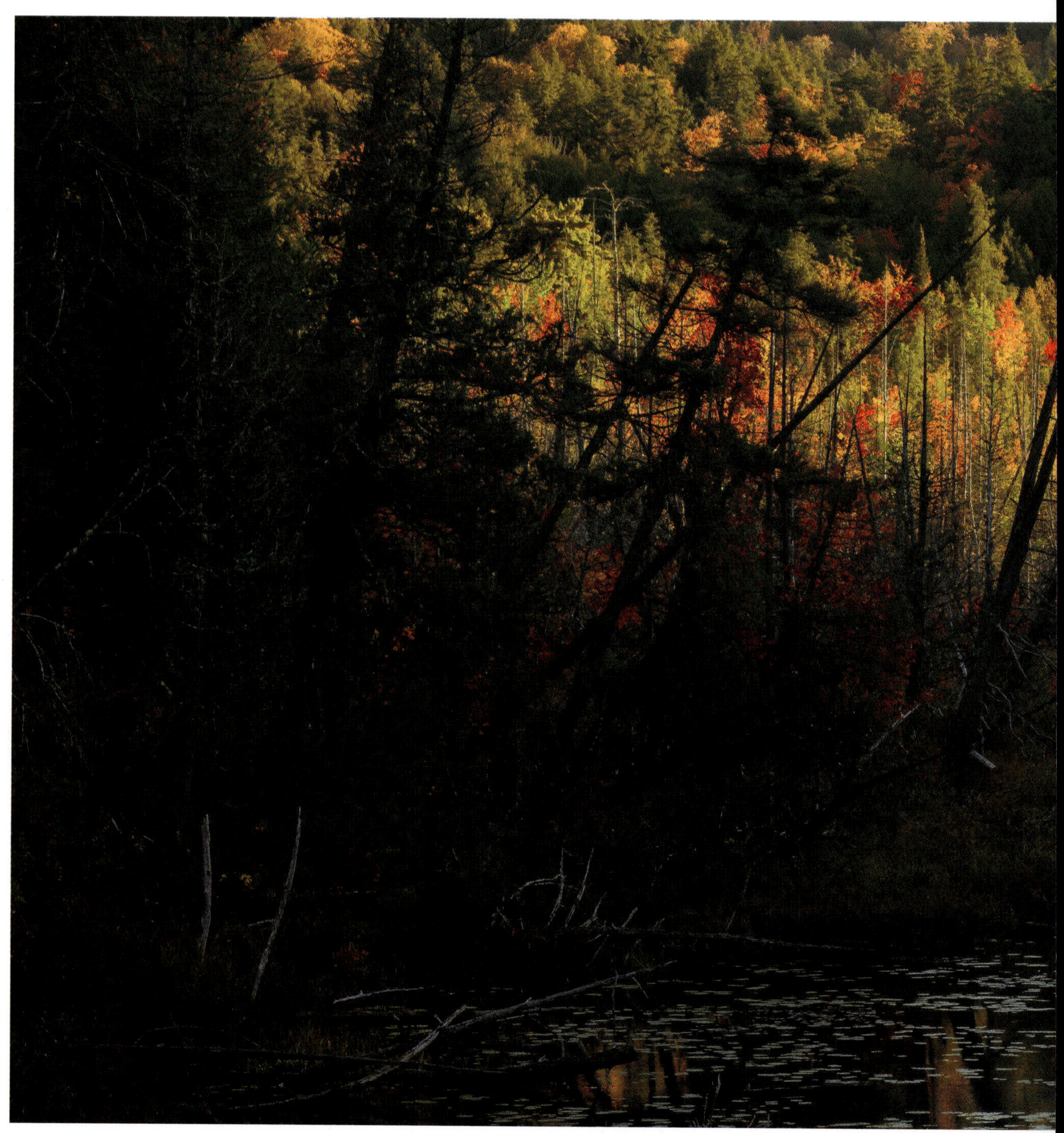

Late light highlights the colors at the inflow from Ampersand Mountain into Middle Saranac Lake.

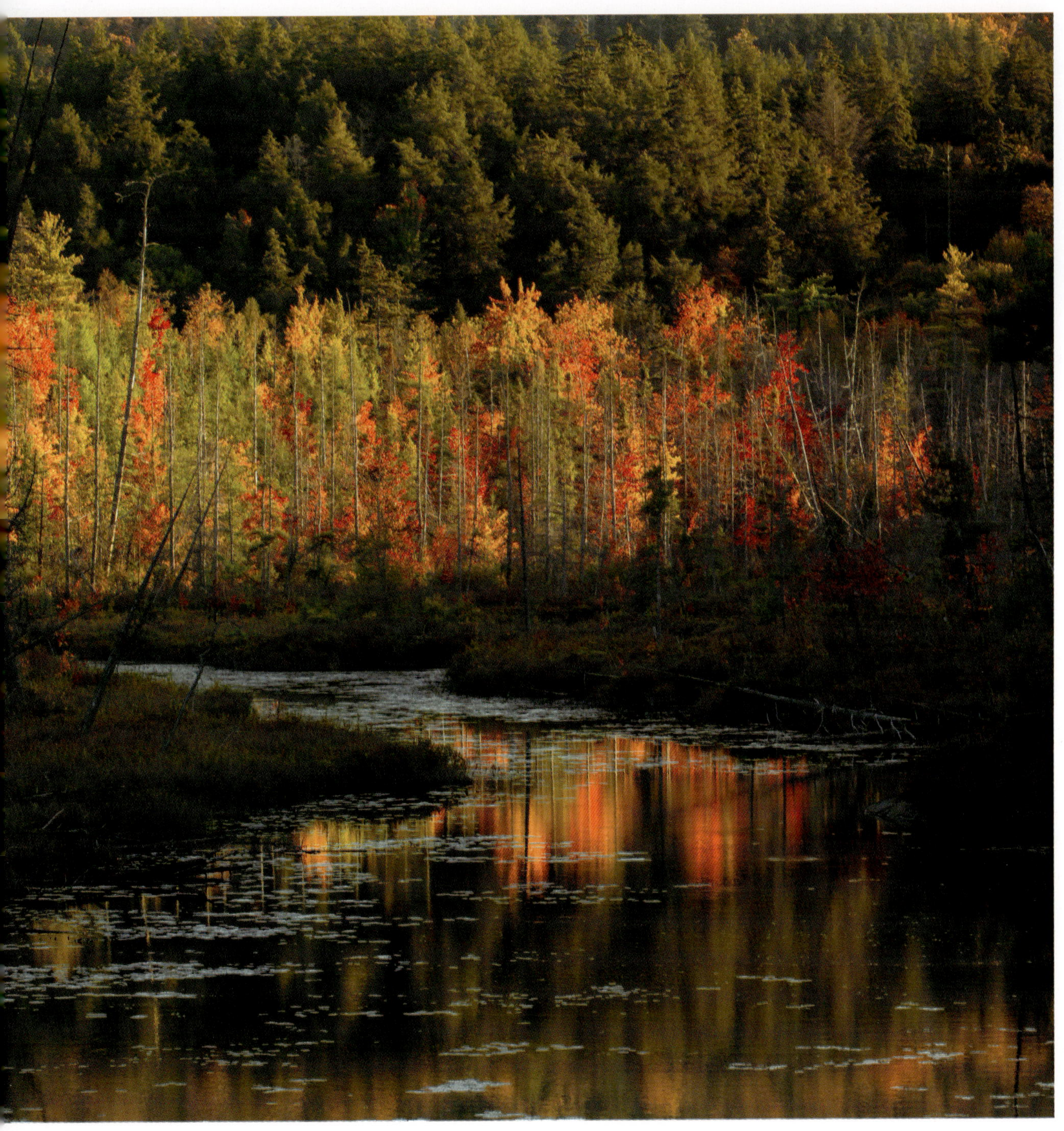

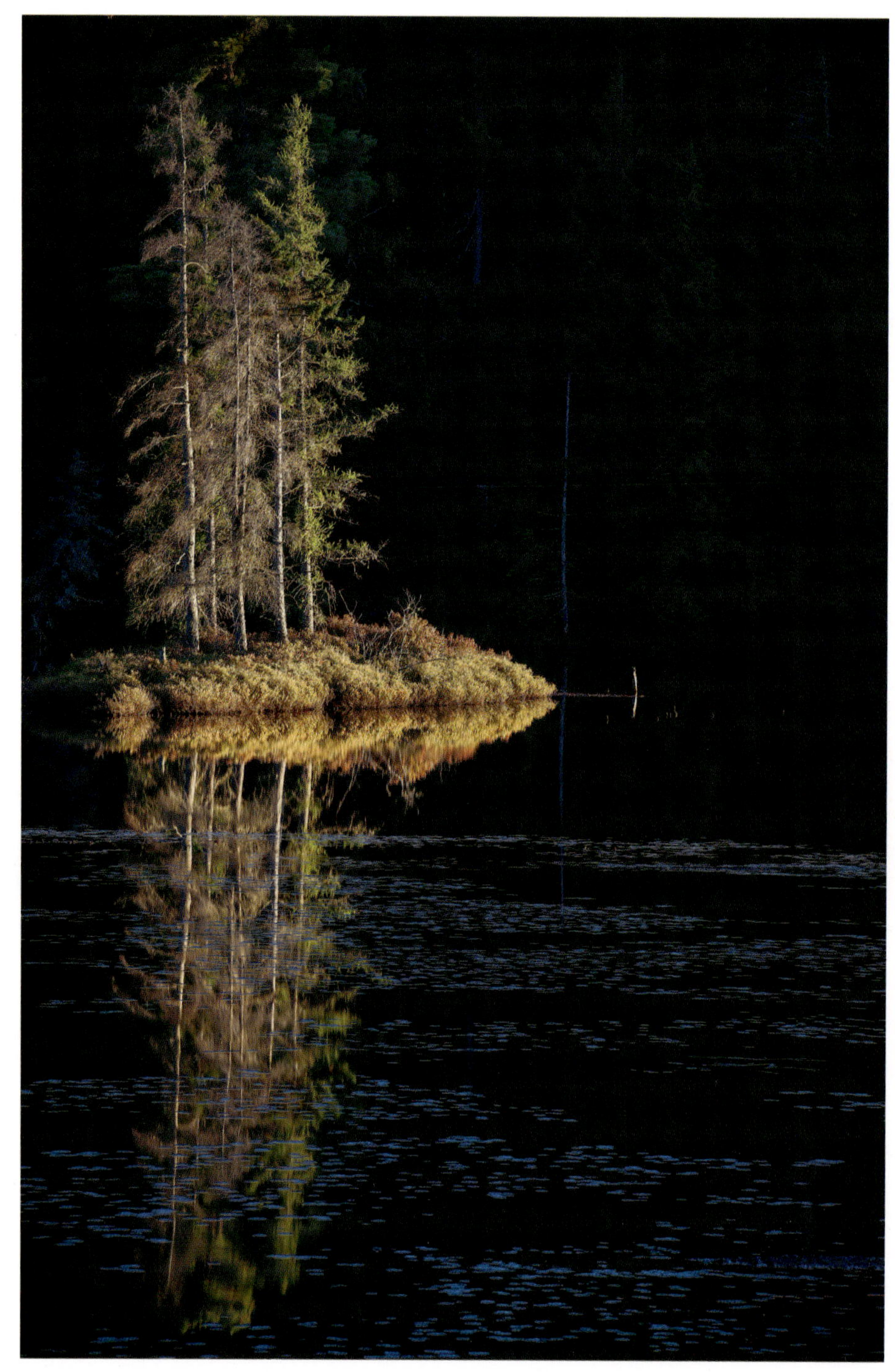

The last warm rays of the sun shine like a spotlight on a small island on Polliwog Pond.

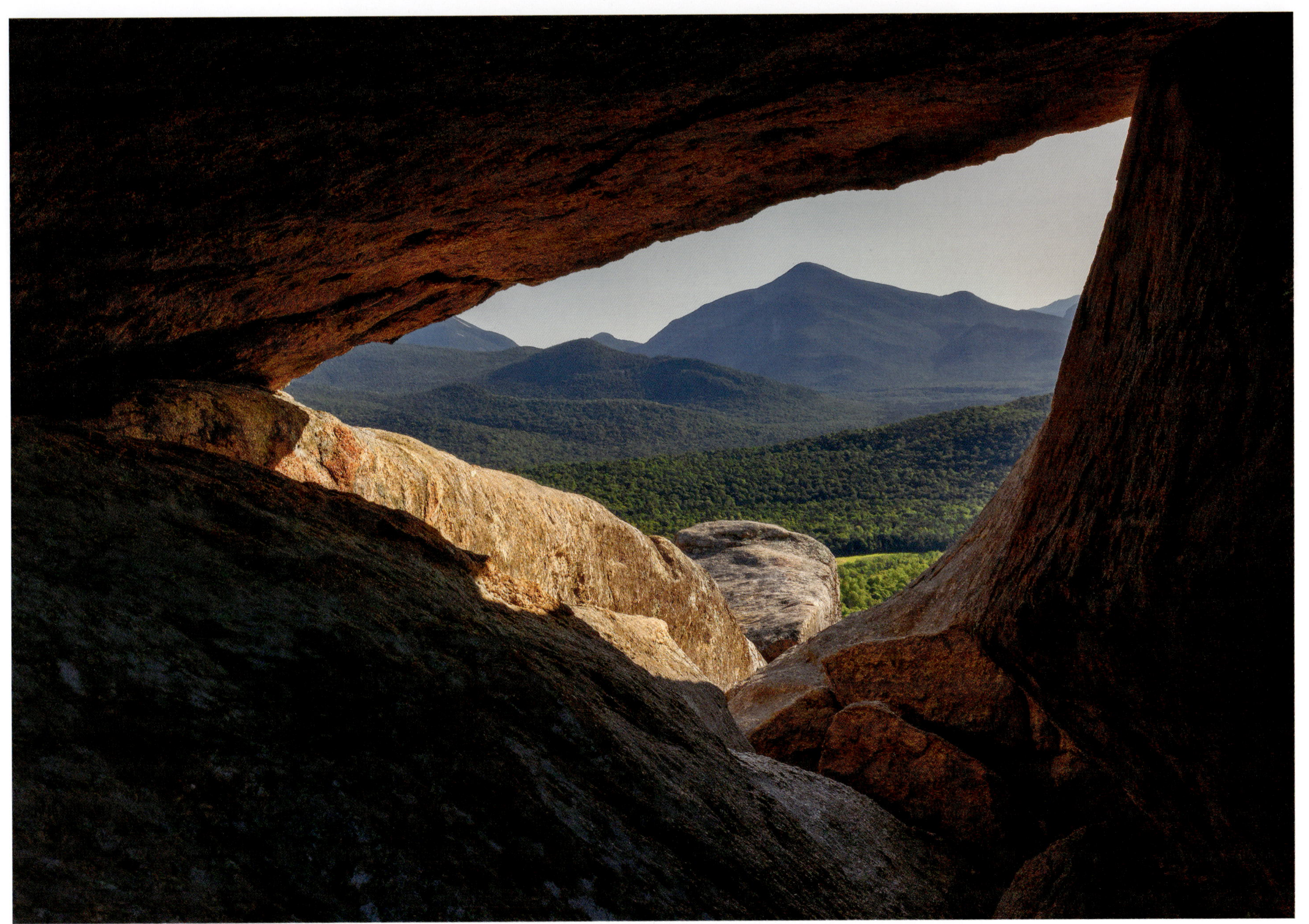

Algonquin Mountain framed by huge boulders in the High Peaks.

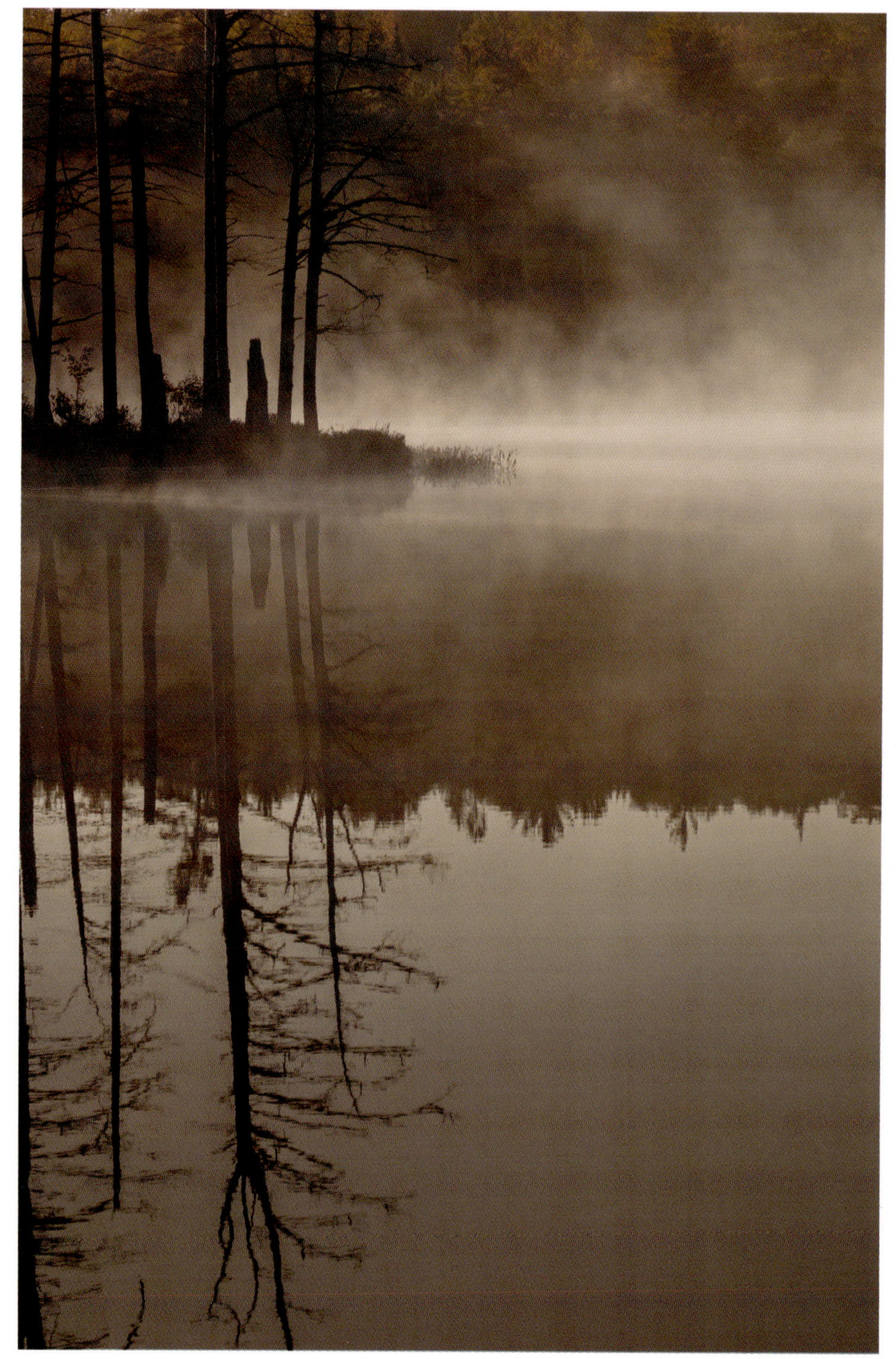

Early morning mist rising off the water at Massawepie Scout Camp.

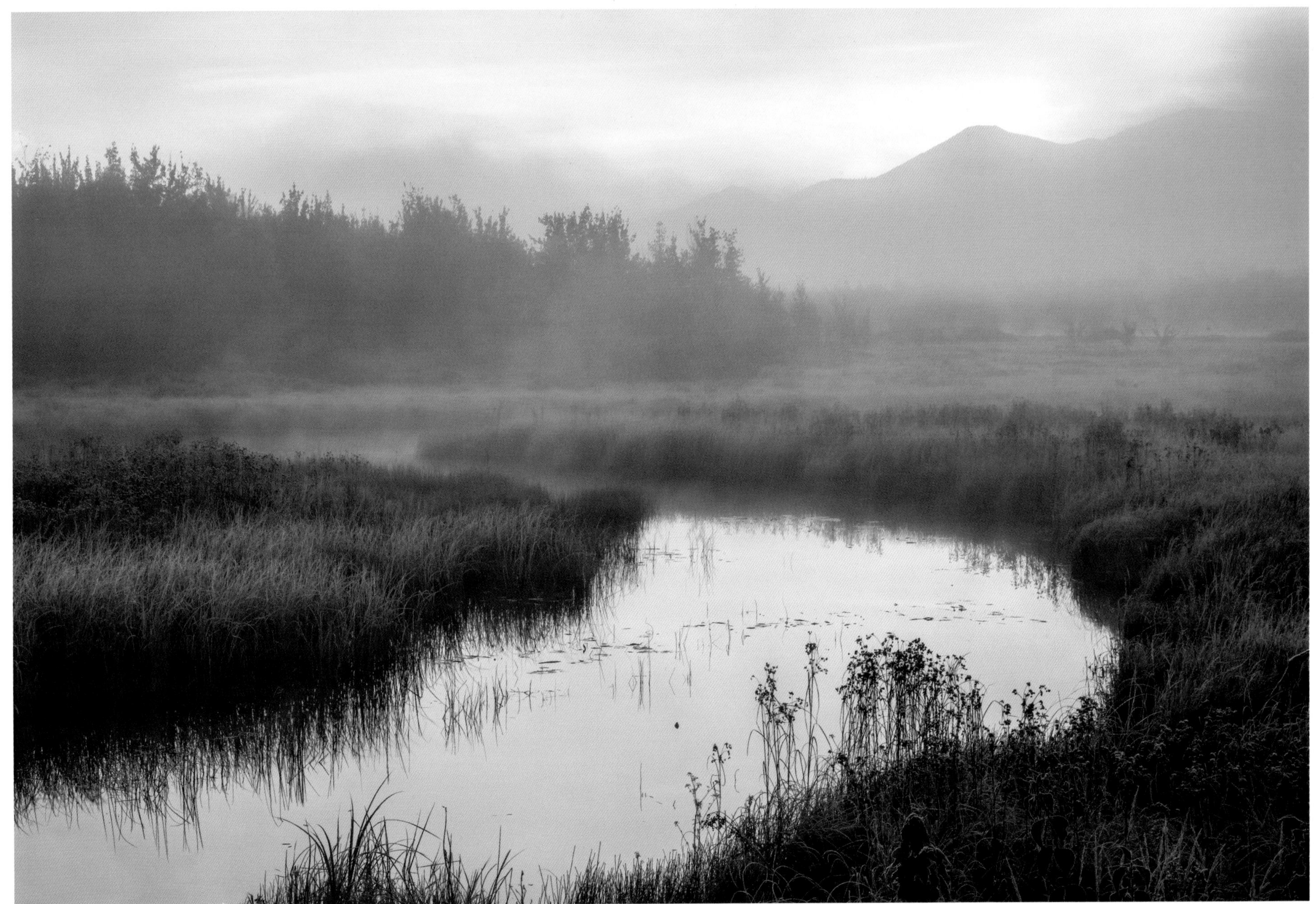

Seconds before the sun breaks over the mountains, the frosted shore is still in shade as the Saranac River snakes into the distance.

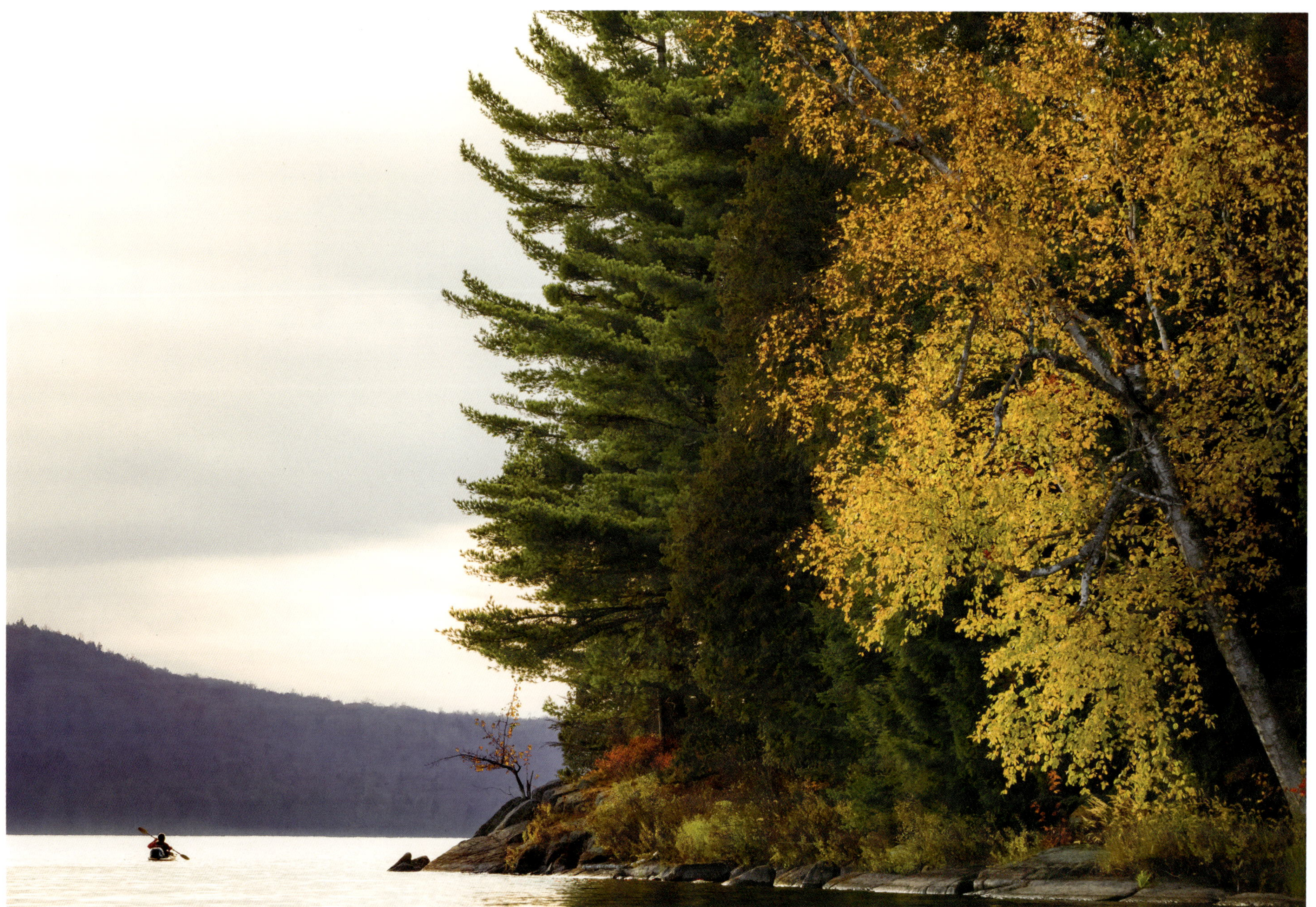

A lone kayaker is dwarfed by the surrounding landscape on Lake Lila.

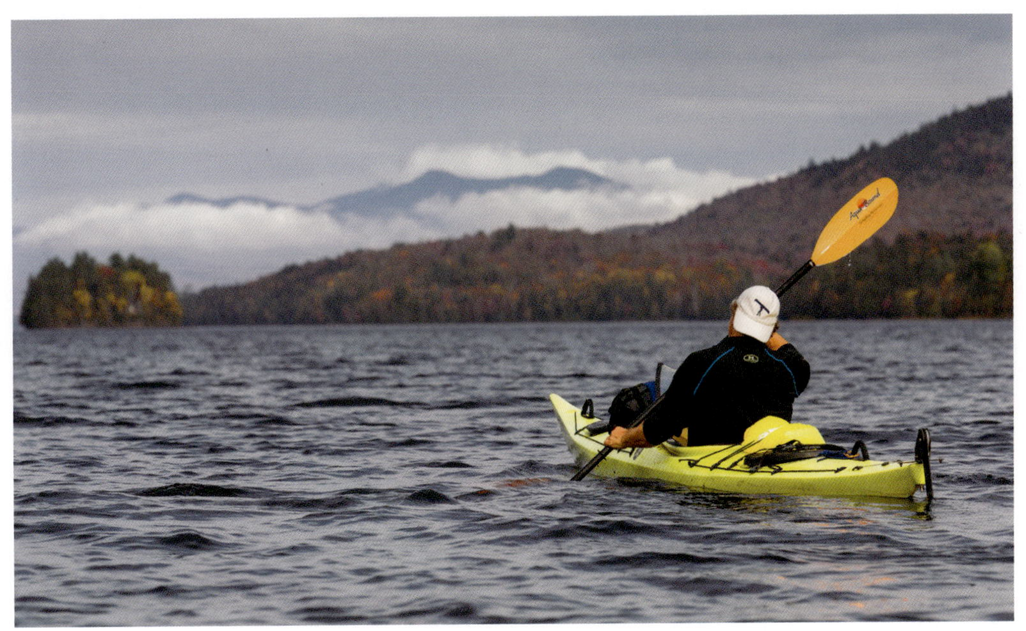

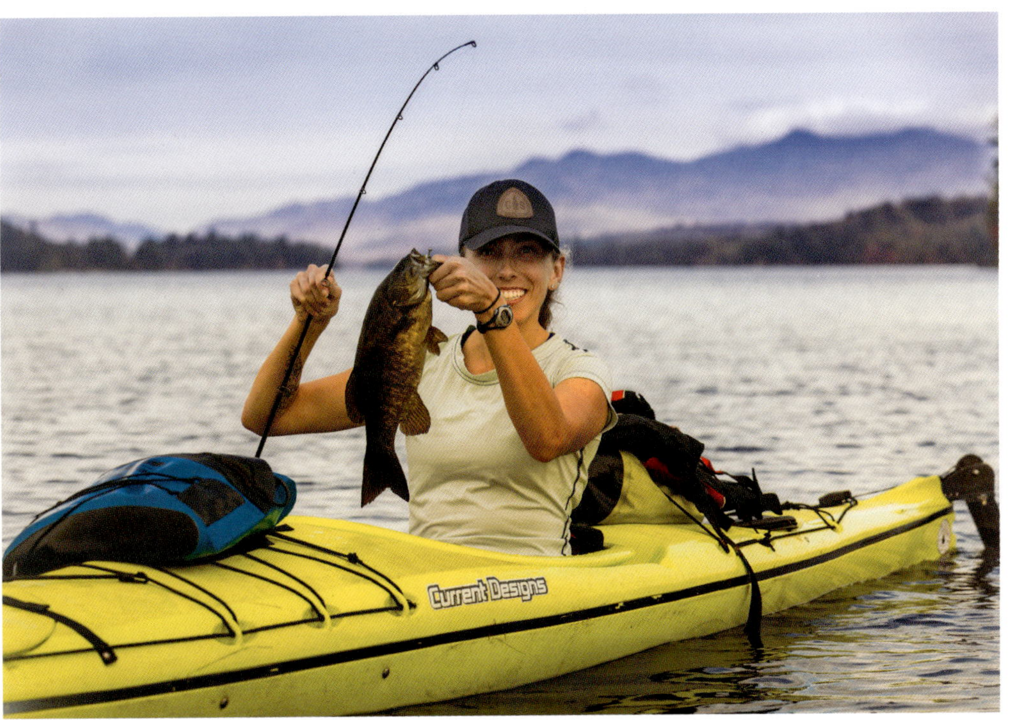

Top: Kayaking to the next campsite on Long Lake in early October.
Bottom: A happy fisherwoman grabs a good-sized bass while kayak trolling on Long Lake.

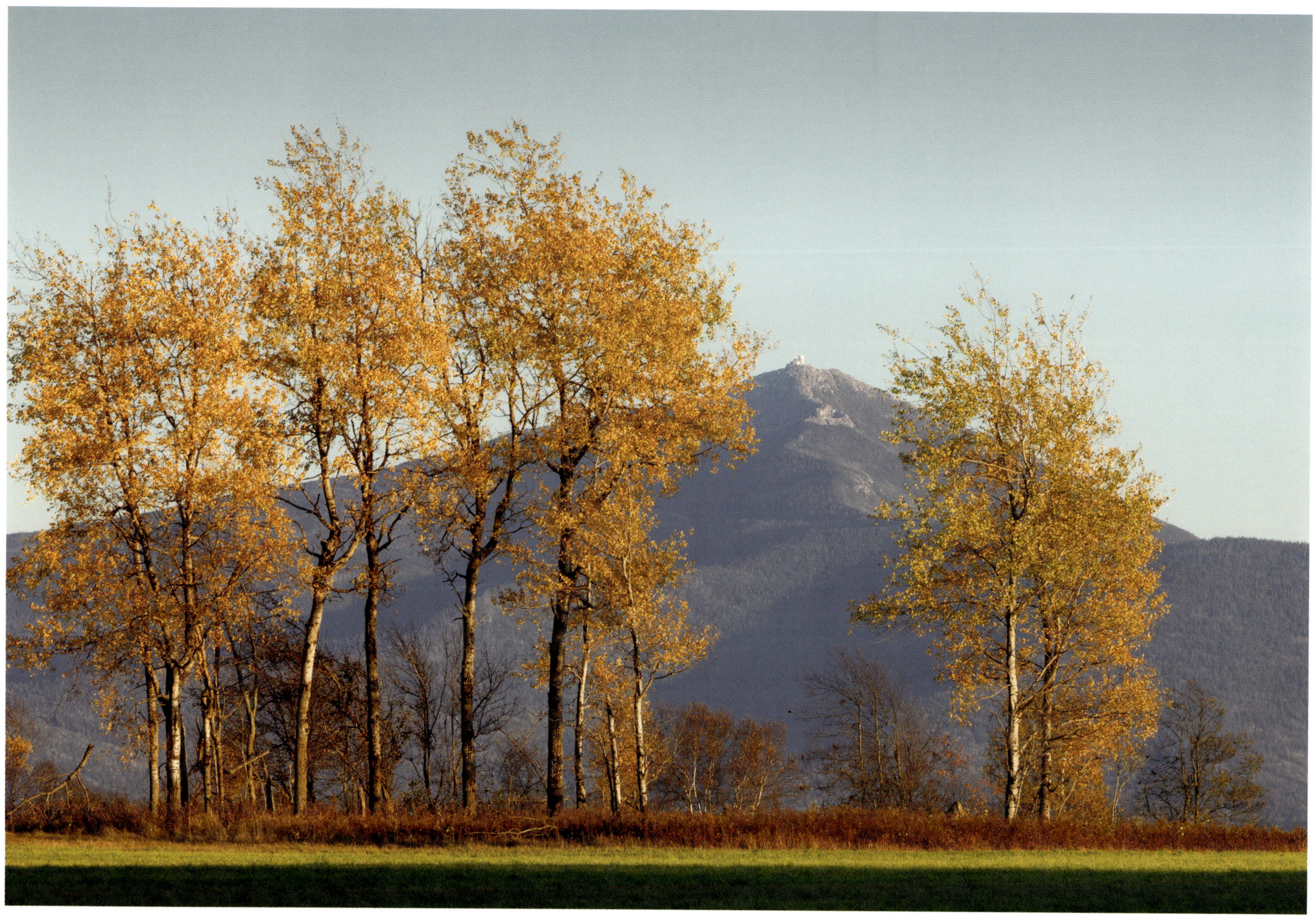

A stand of poplars sets the stage for a view of Whiteface with its Atmospheric Sciences Research Center.

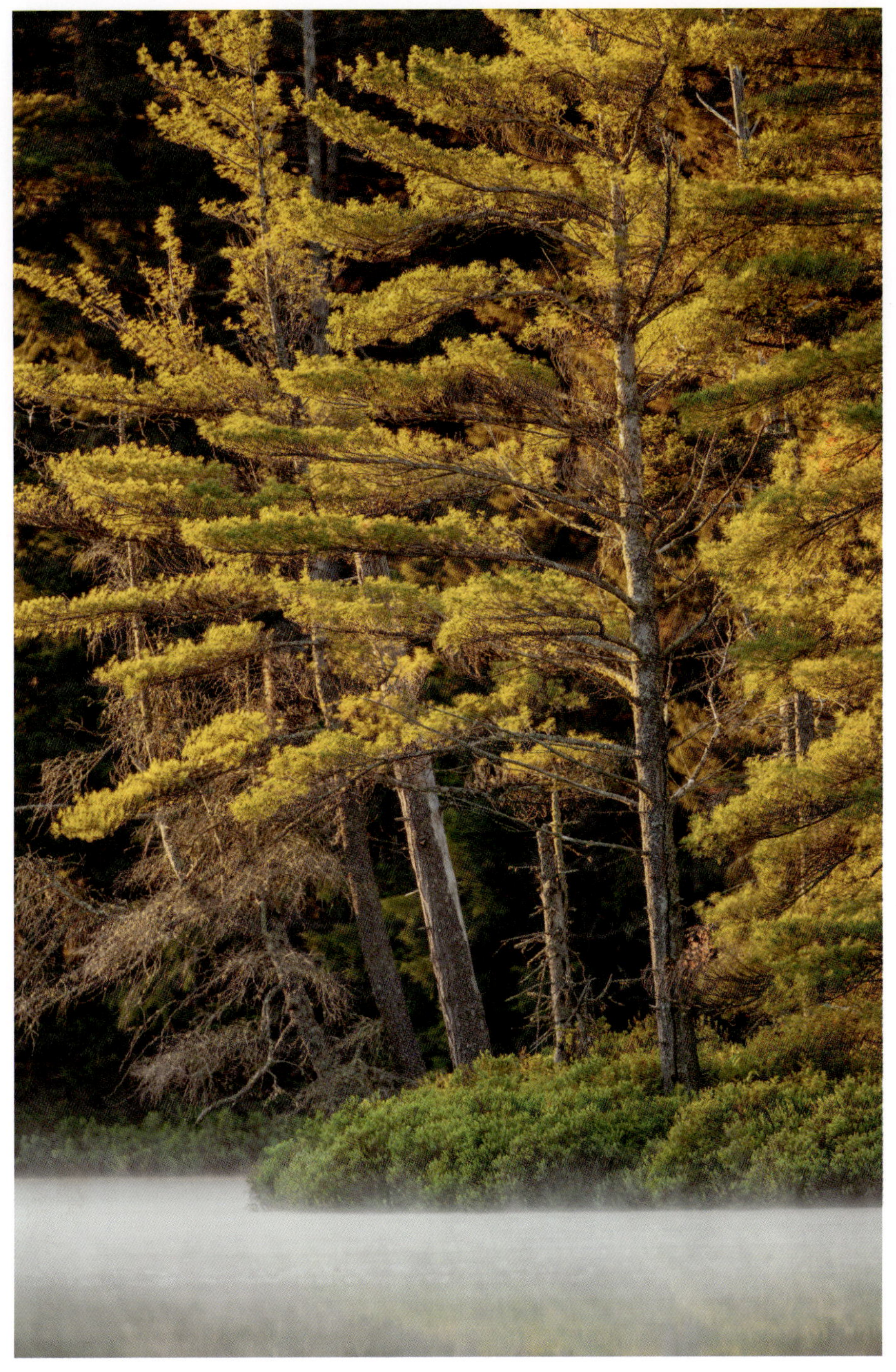

White pine across from my campsite in the Saint Regis Canoe Area.

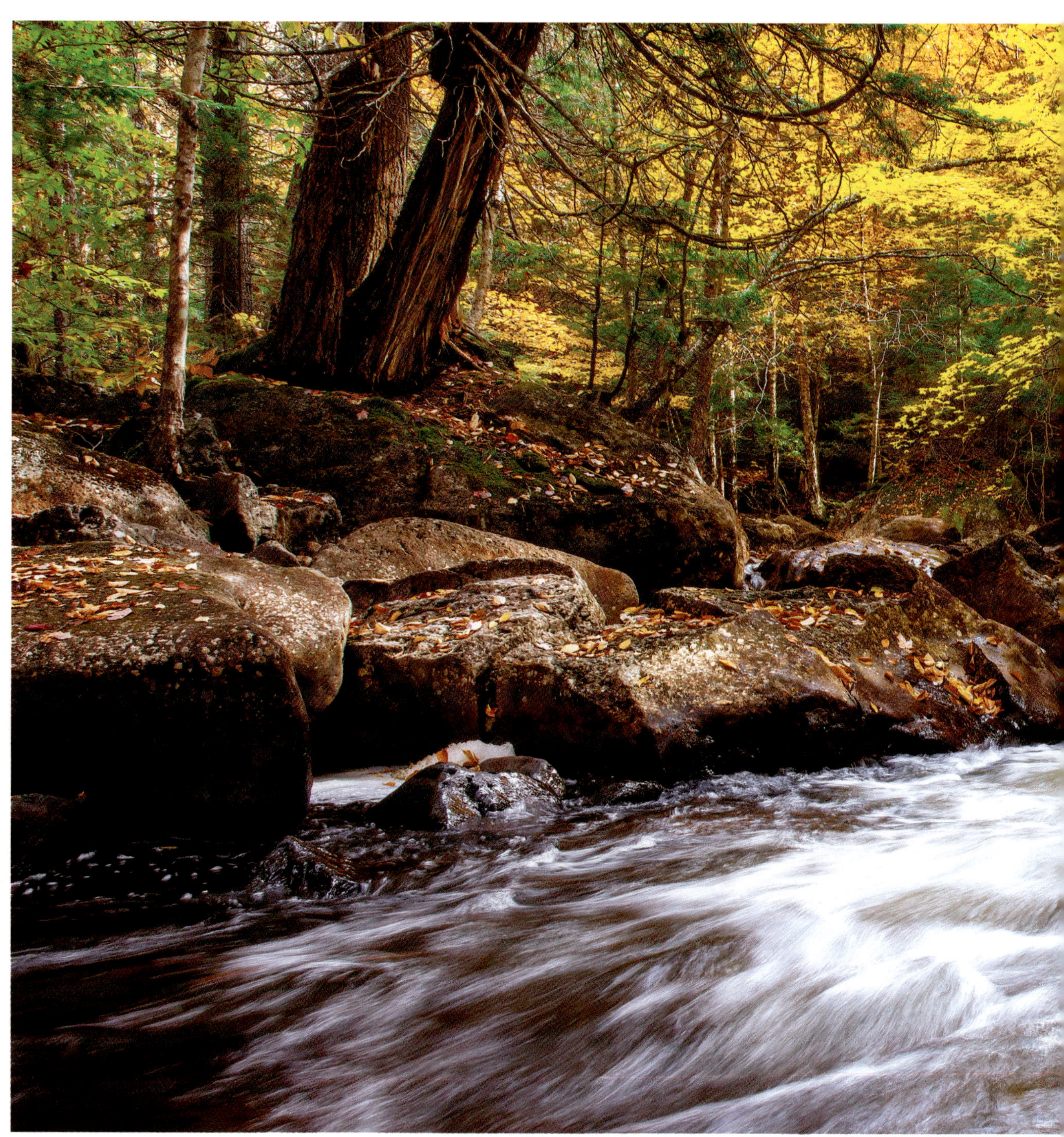

Cascading stream in the shadow of Ampersand Mountain.

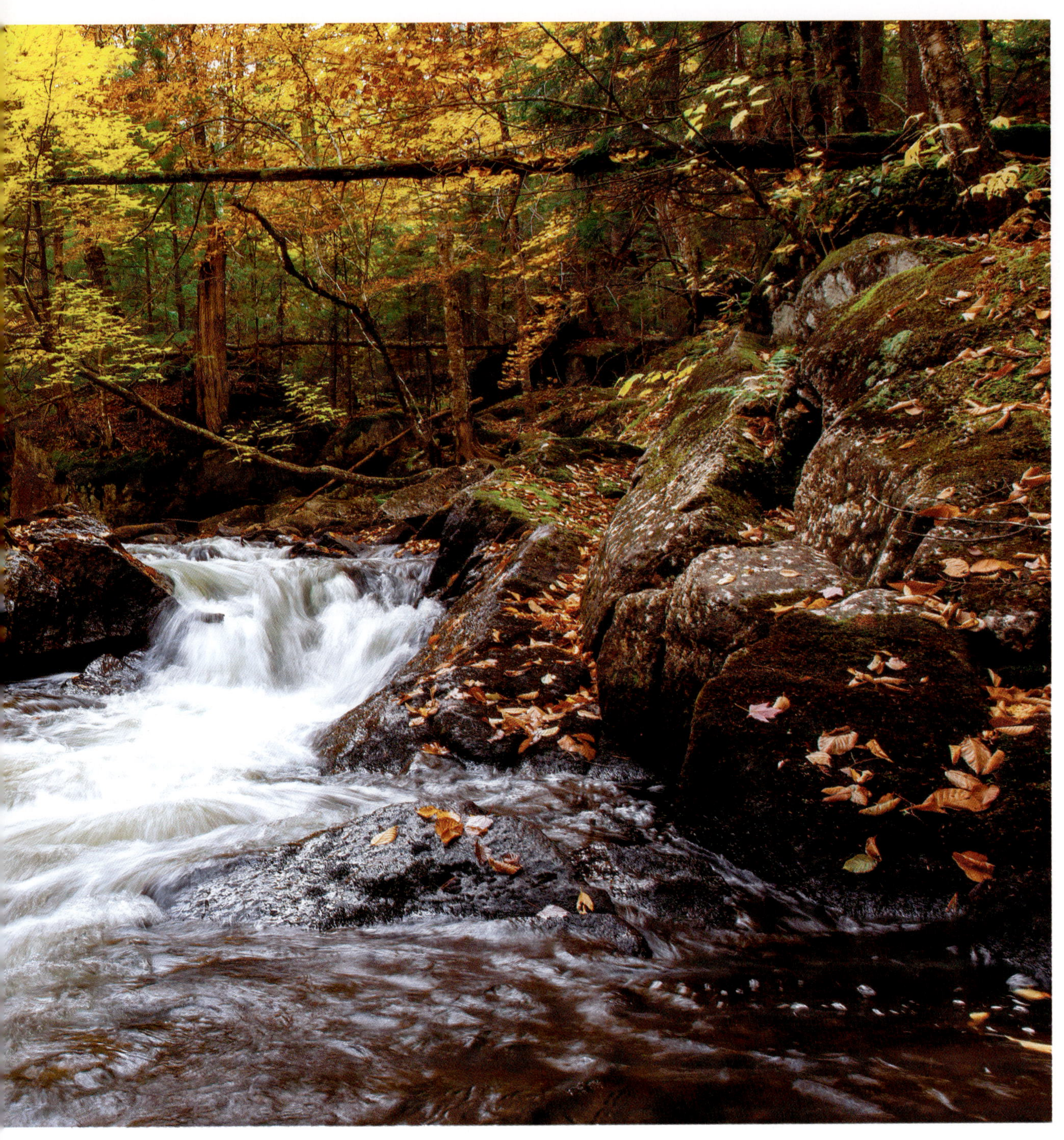

A stand of ice-covered trees in the farmlands east of the High Peaks.

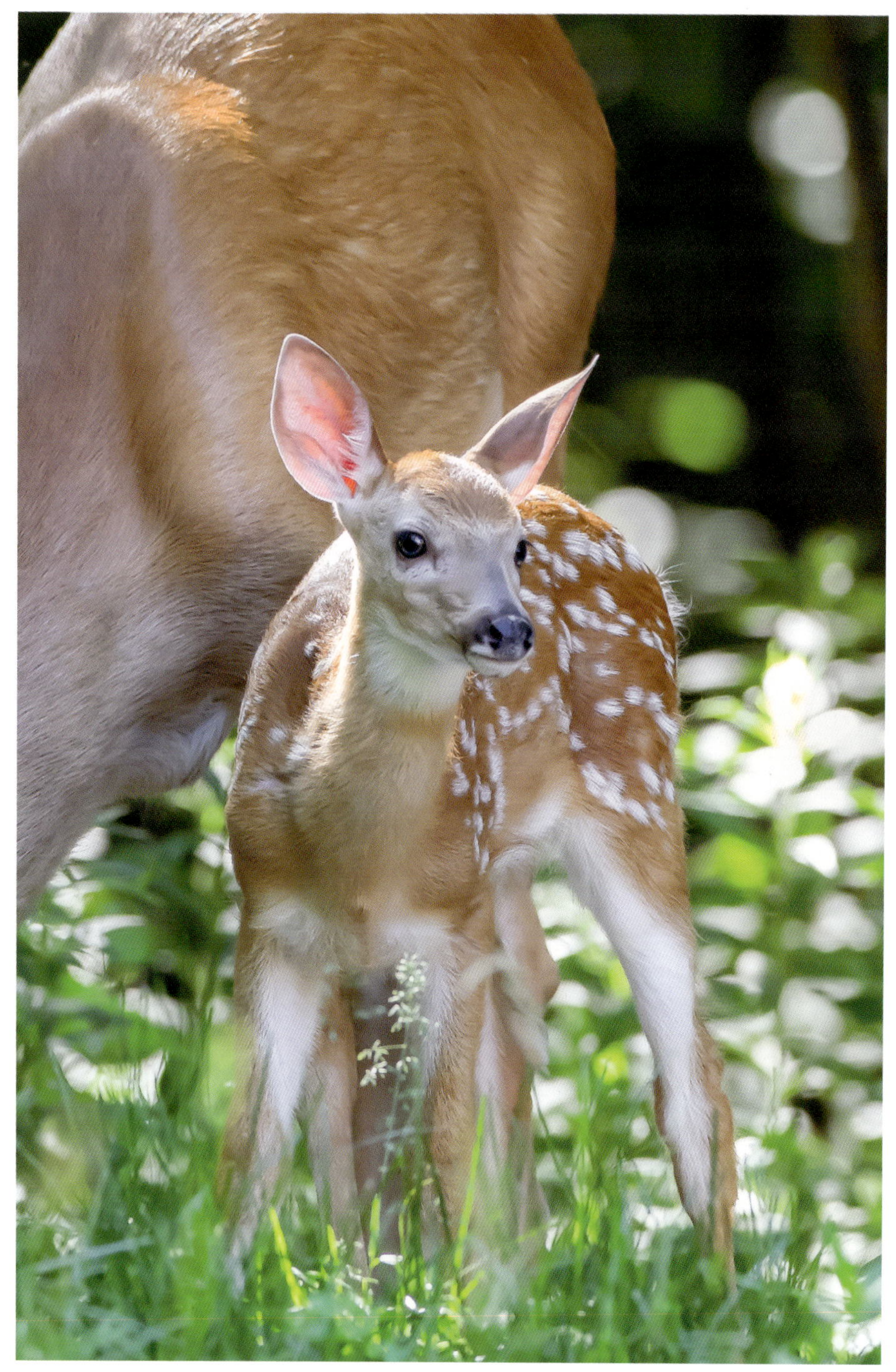

A young white-tailed deer fawn forages for breakfast with her mother.

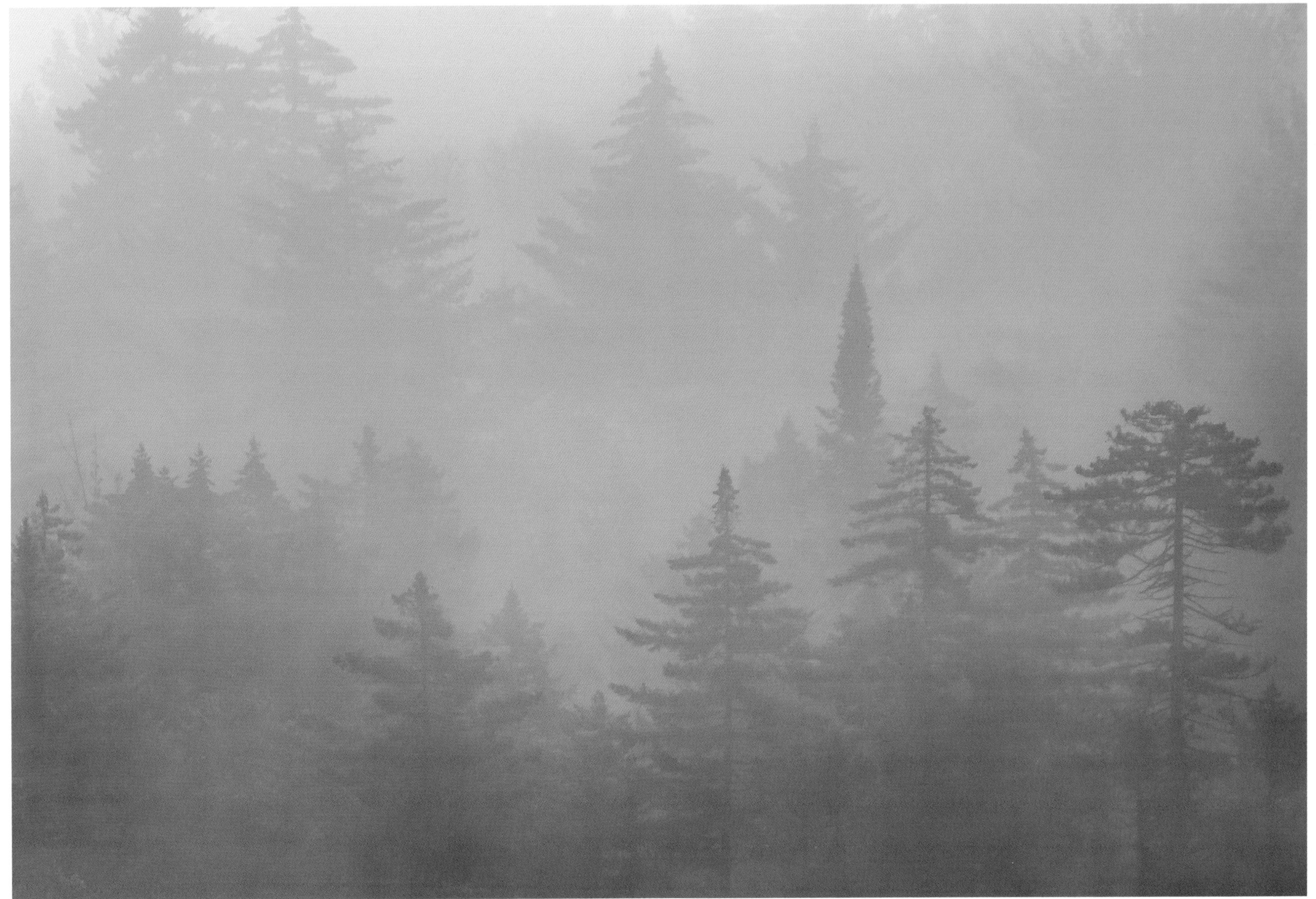

Misty morning on Helldiver Pond.

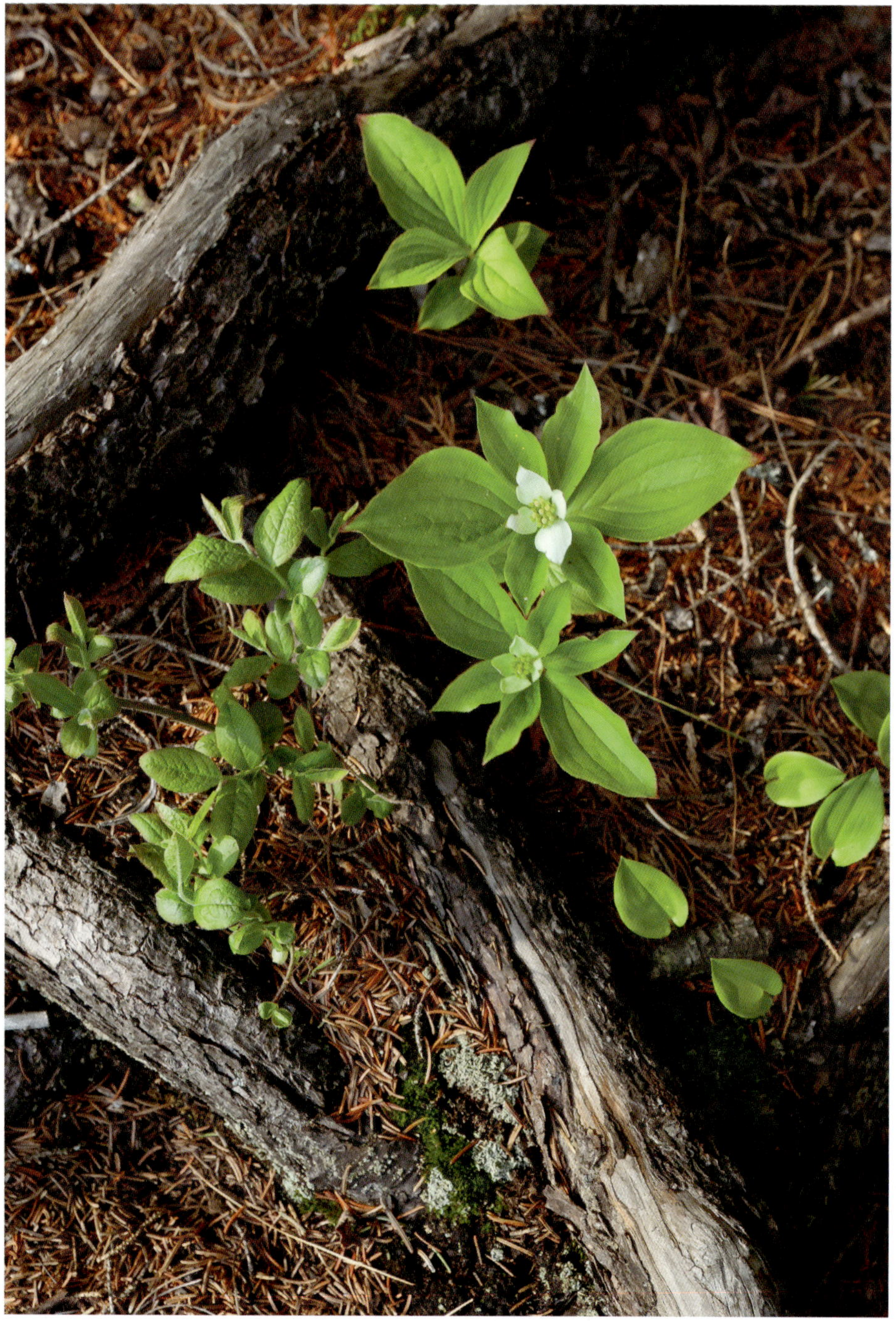

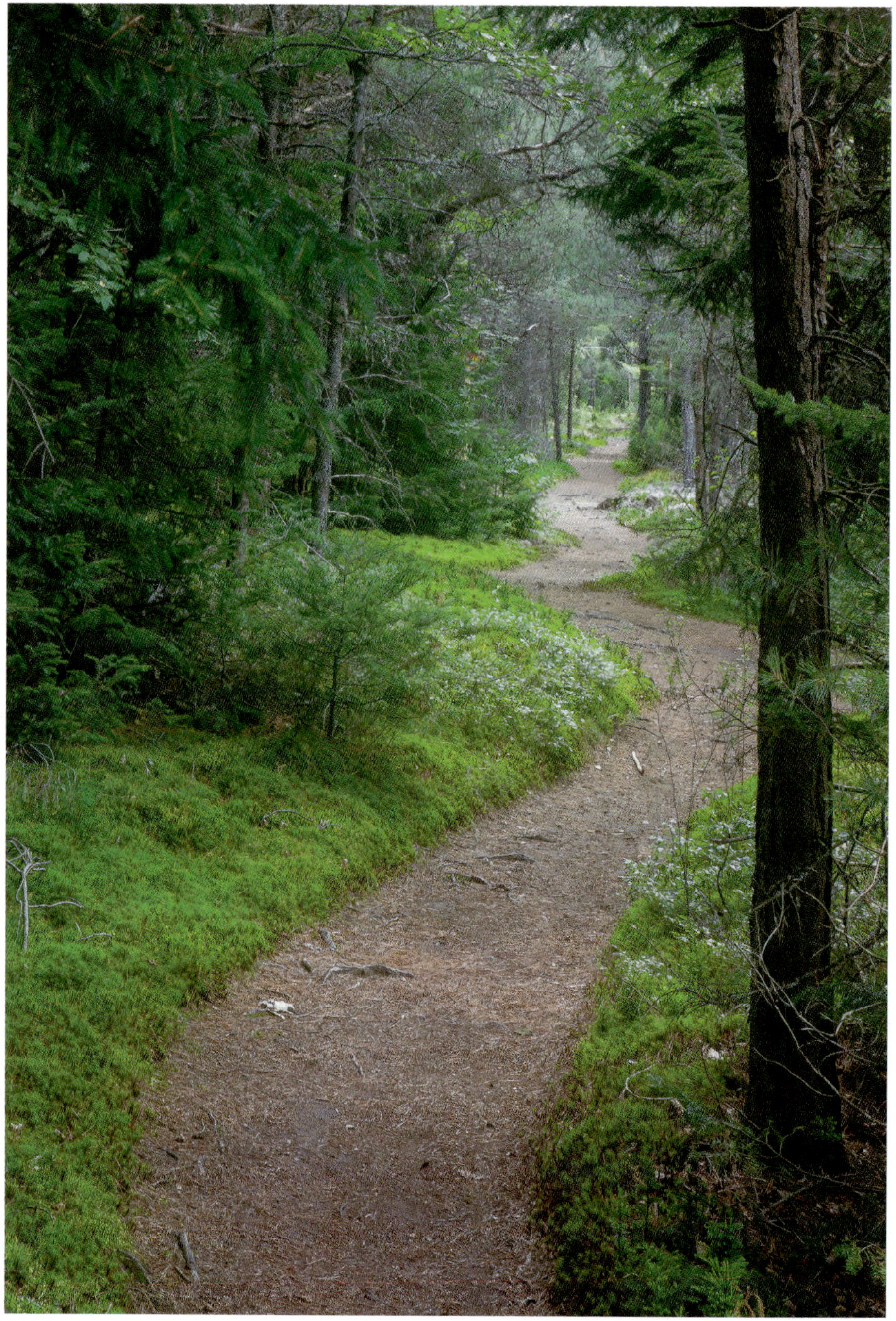

Bunchberry on the forest floor.

Old trail to Mount Van Hoevenberg.

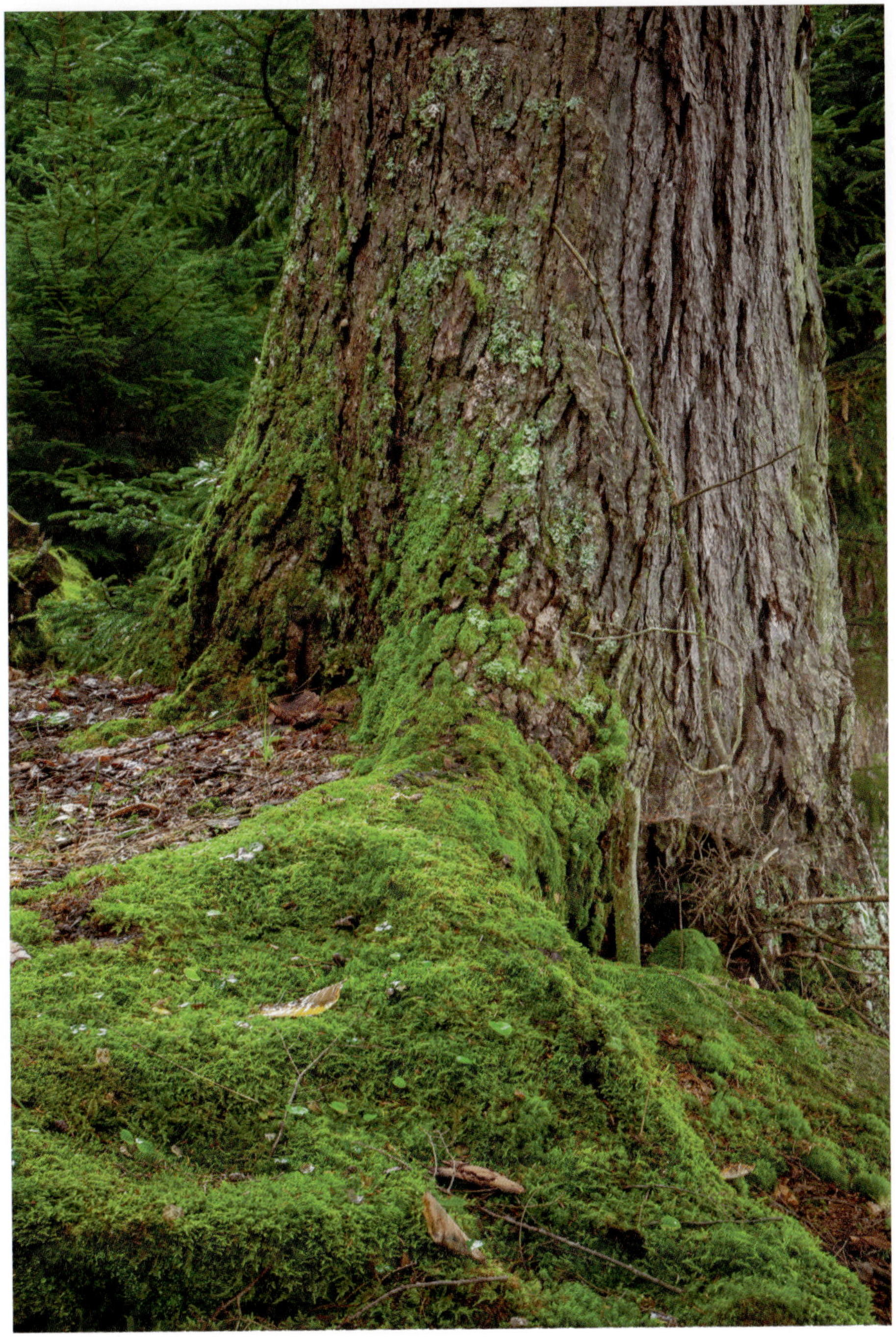

Moss covers tree roots on the shore of Lake Lila.

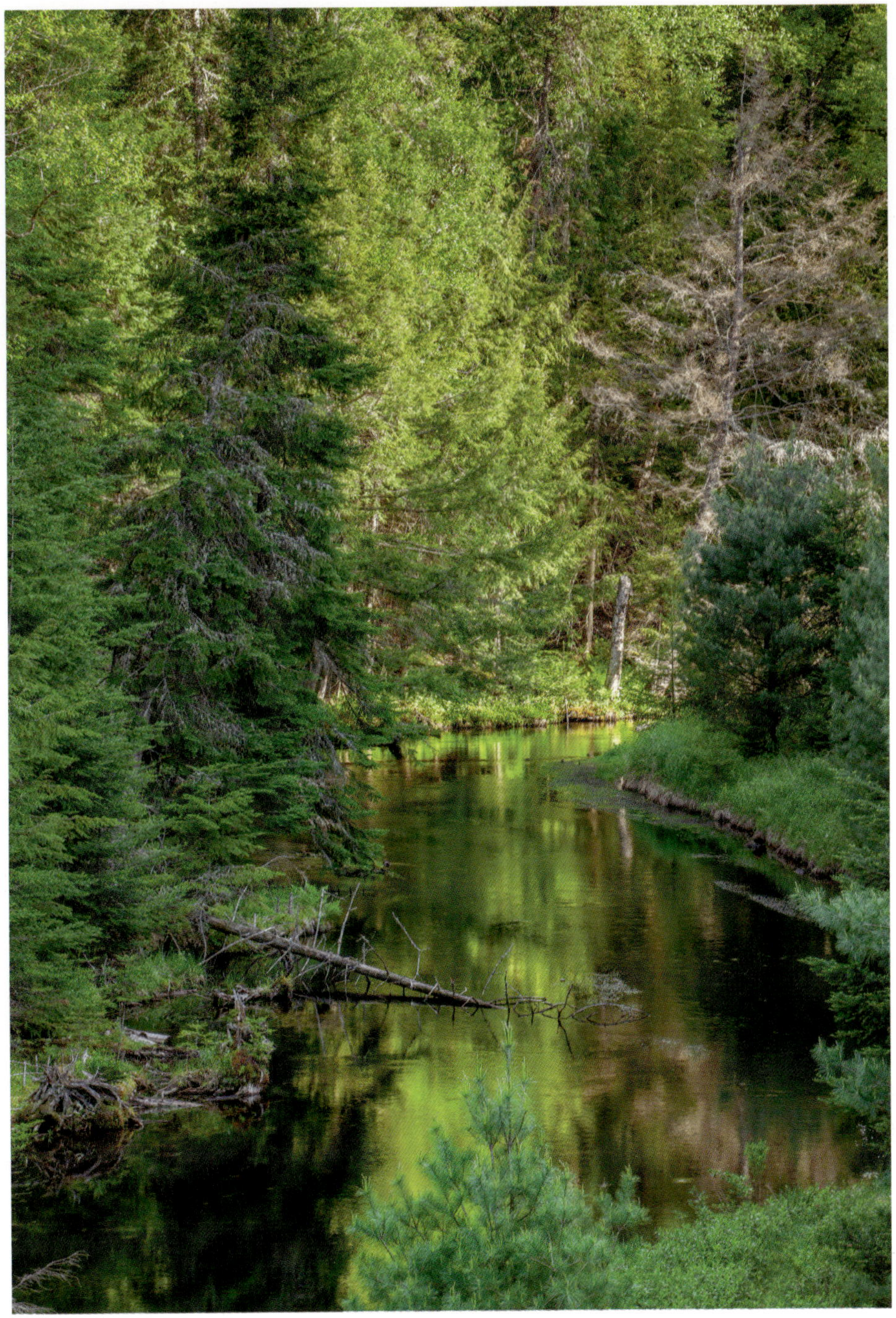

A winding stream near Lake Clear as the
early rays of the sun angle through the trees.

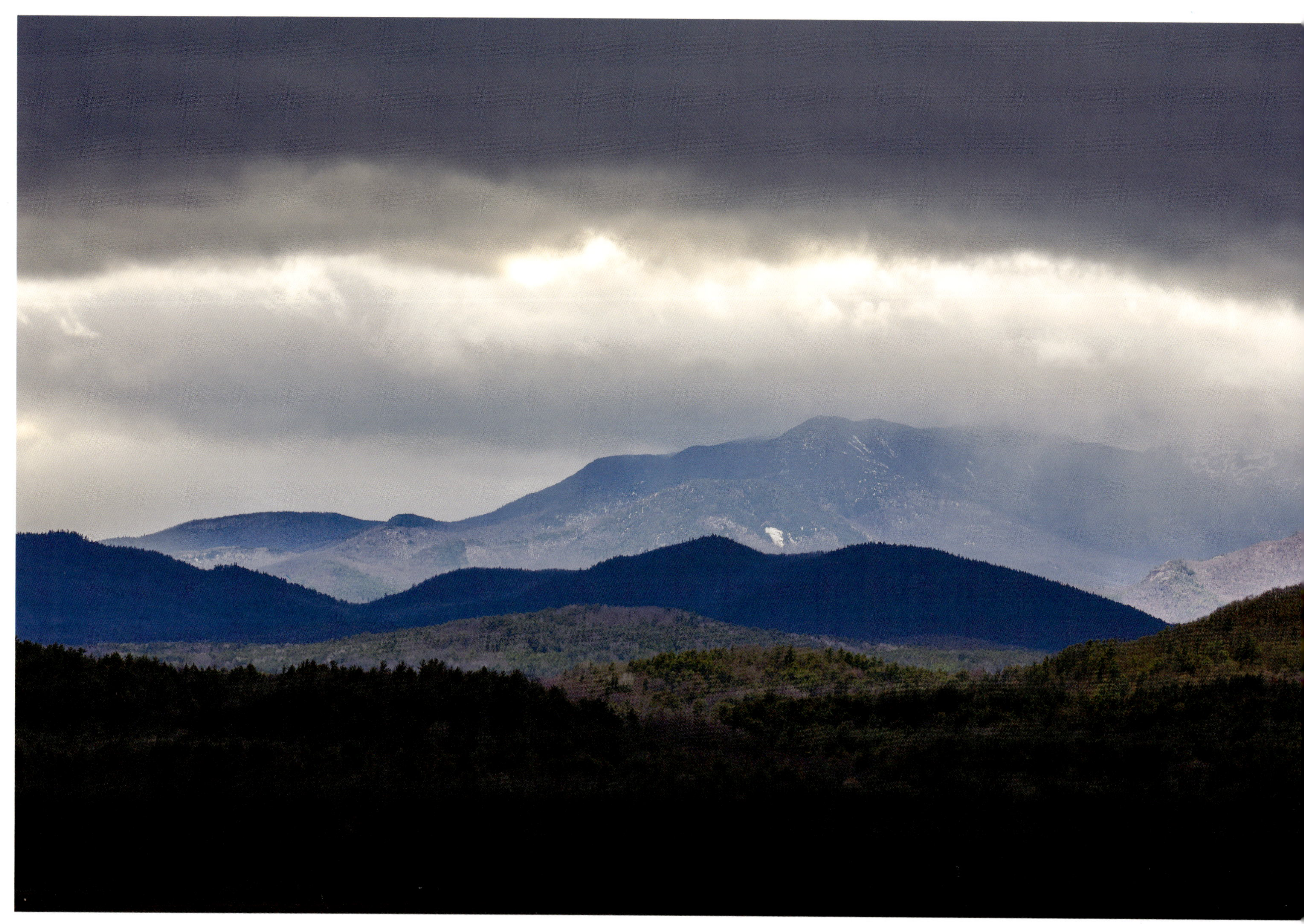

View of the High Peaks from the east as a storm passes through.

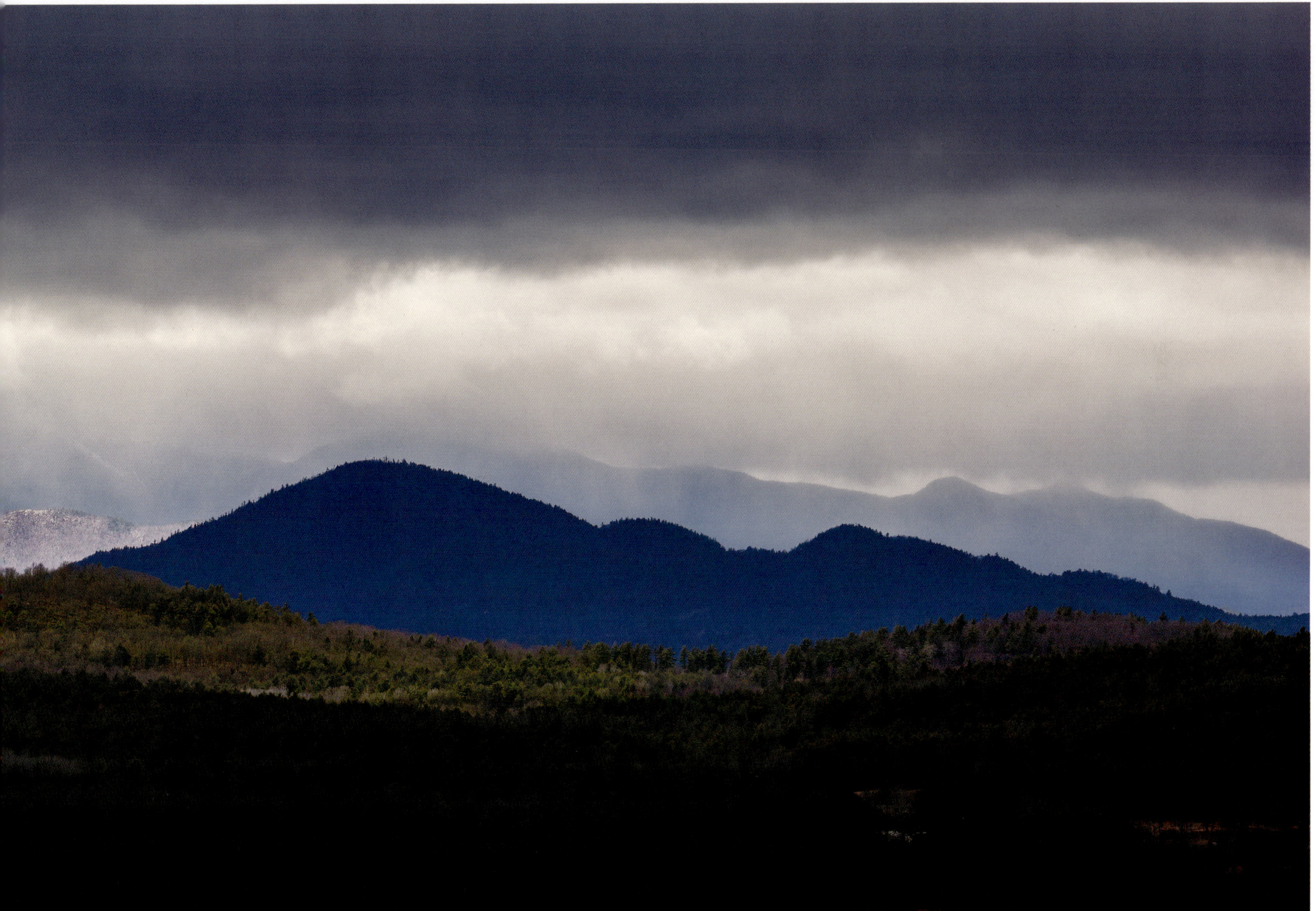

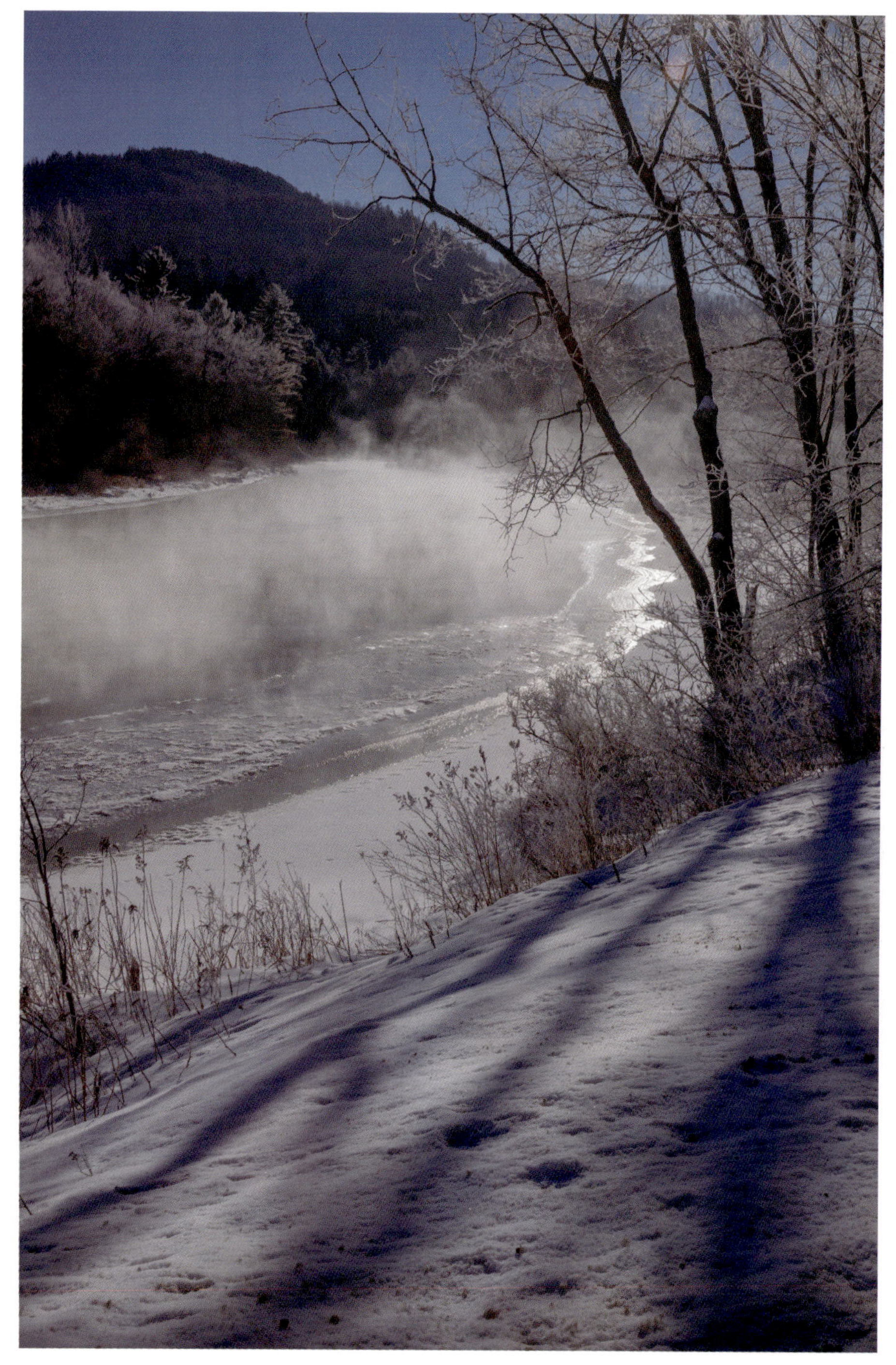

Cold morning along the shore of the Saranac River.

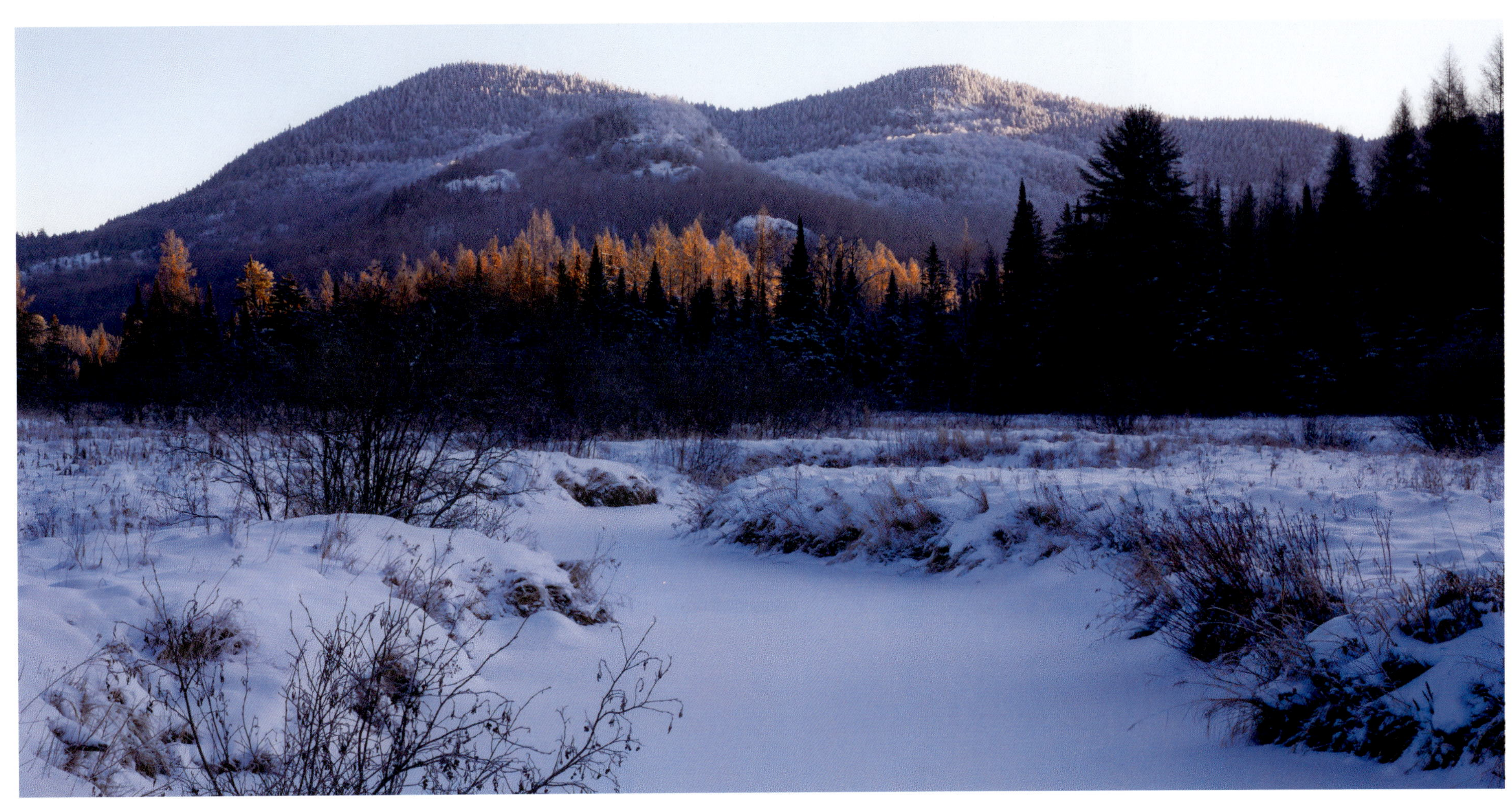

Sunrise highlights a stand of trees on a cold morning along Alder Brook.

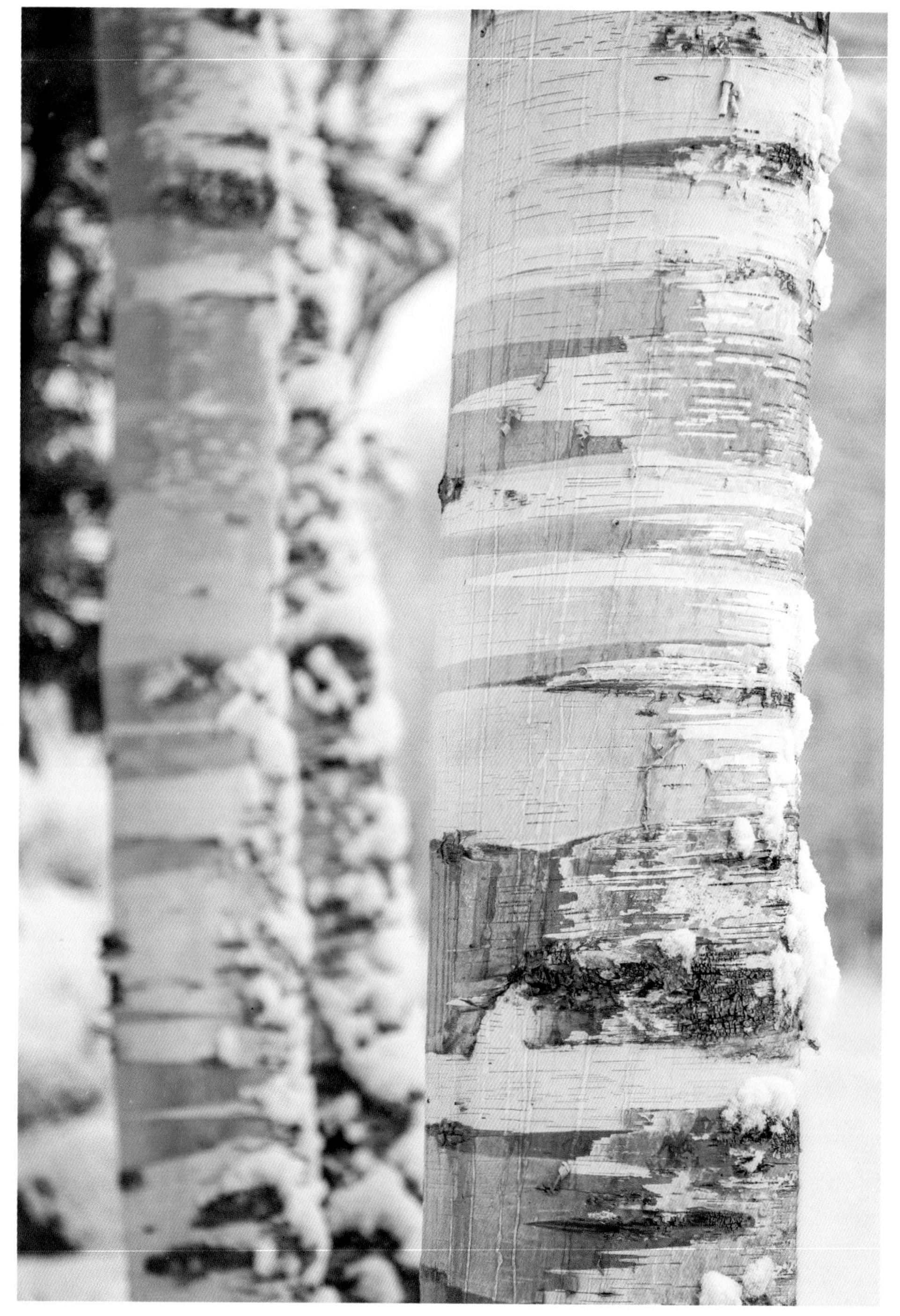

Paper birch in winter.

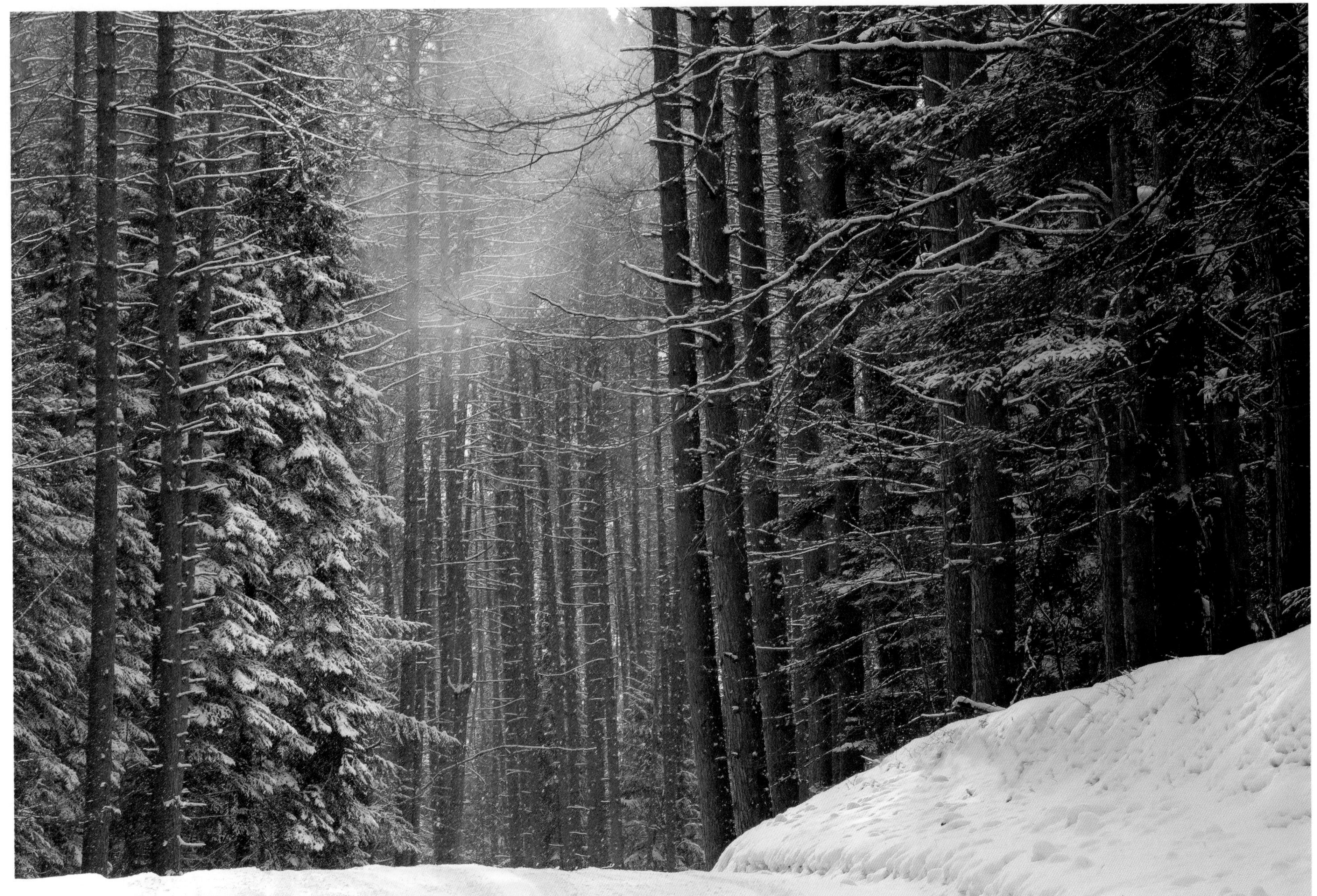

Snow blows off the tops of the trees on Coreys Road.

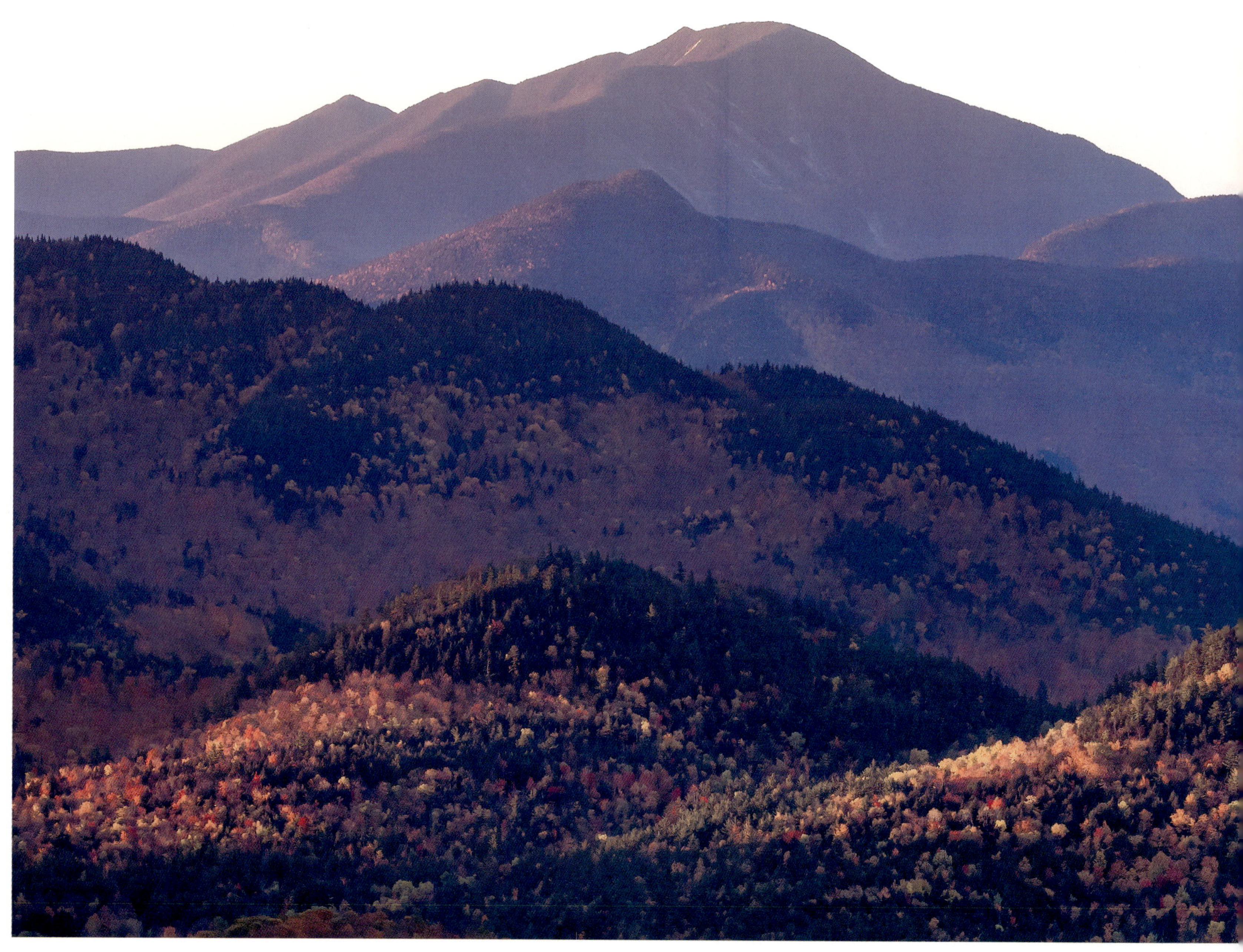

Telephoto view of the High Peaks from Big Crow Mountain.

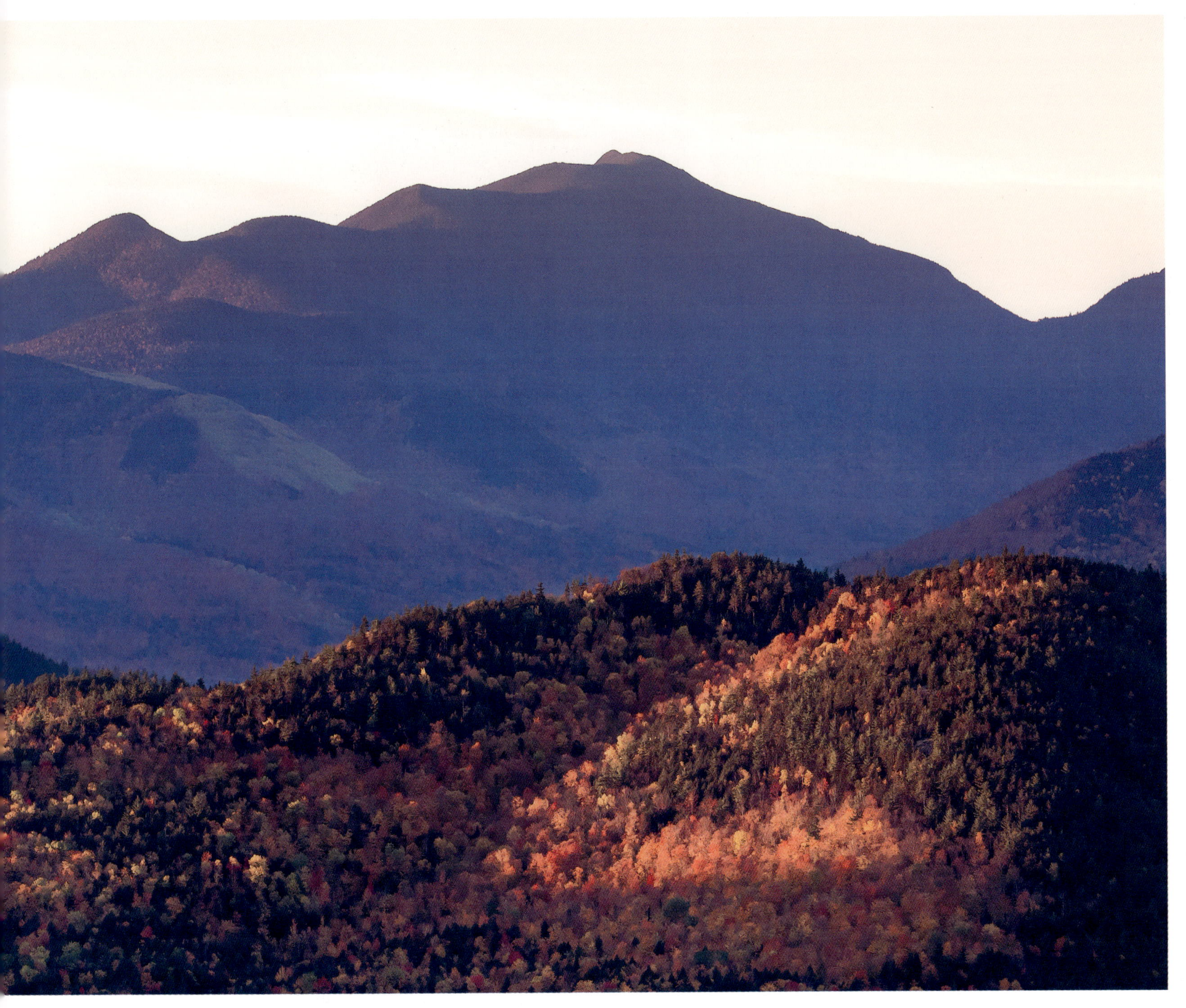

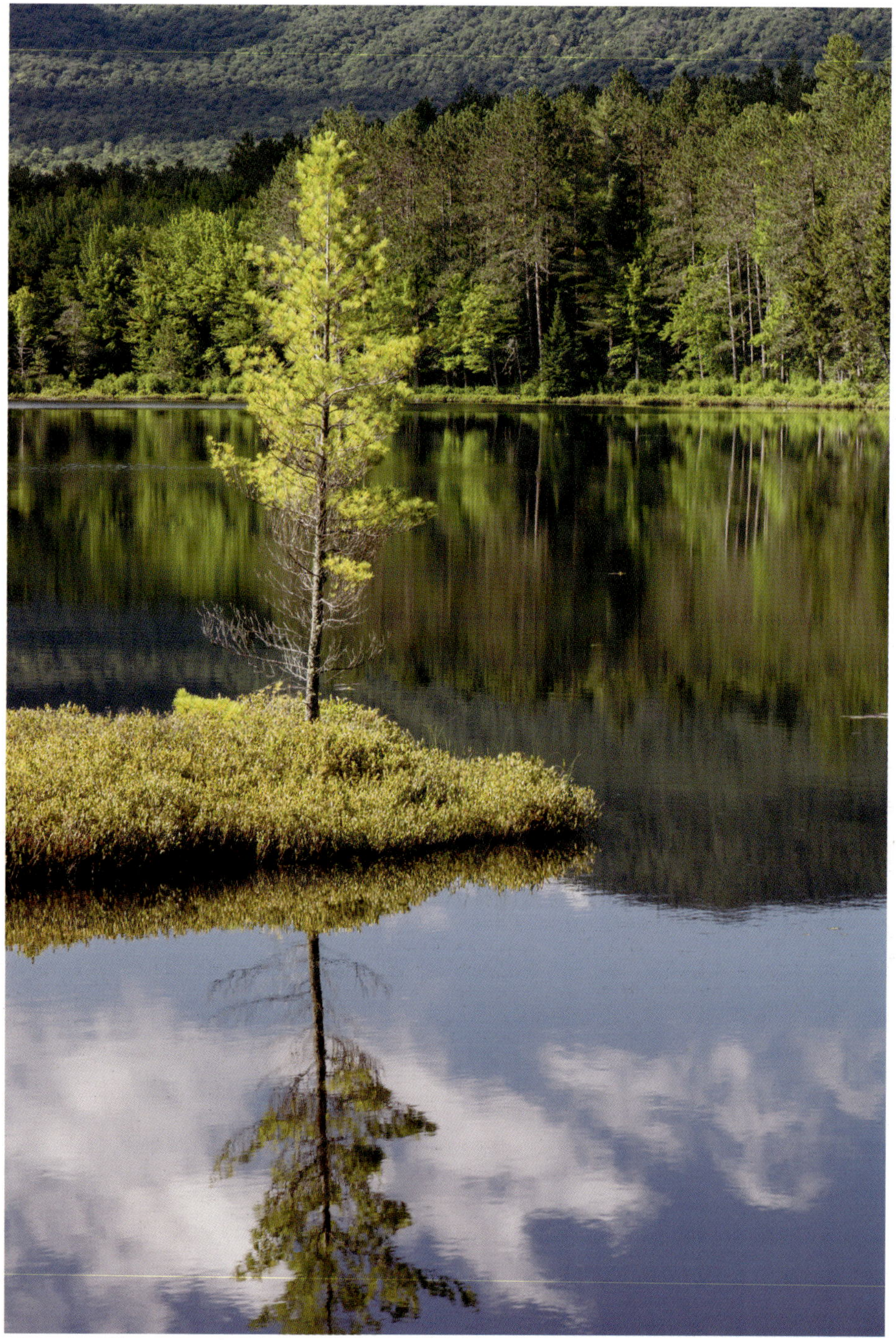

Solitary tree on an island at Duck Pond.

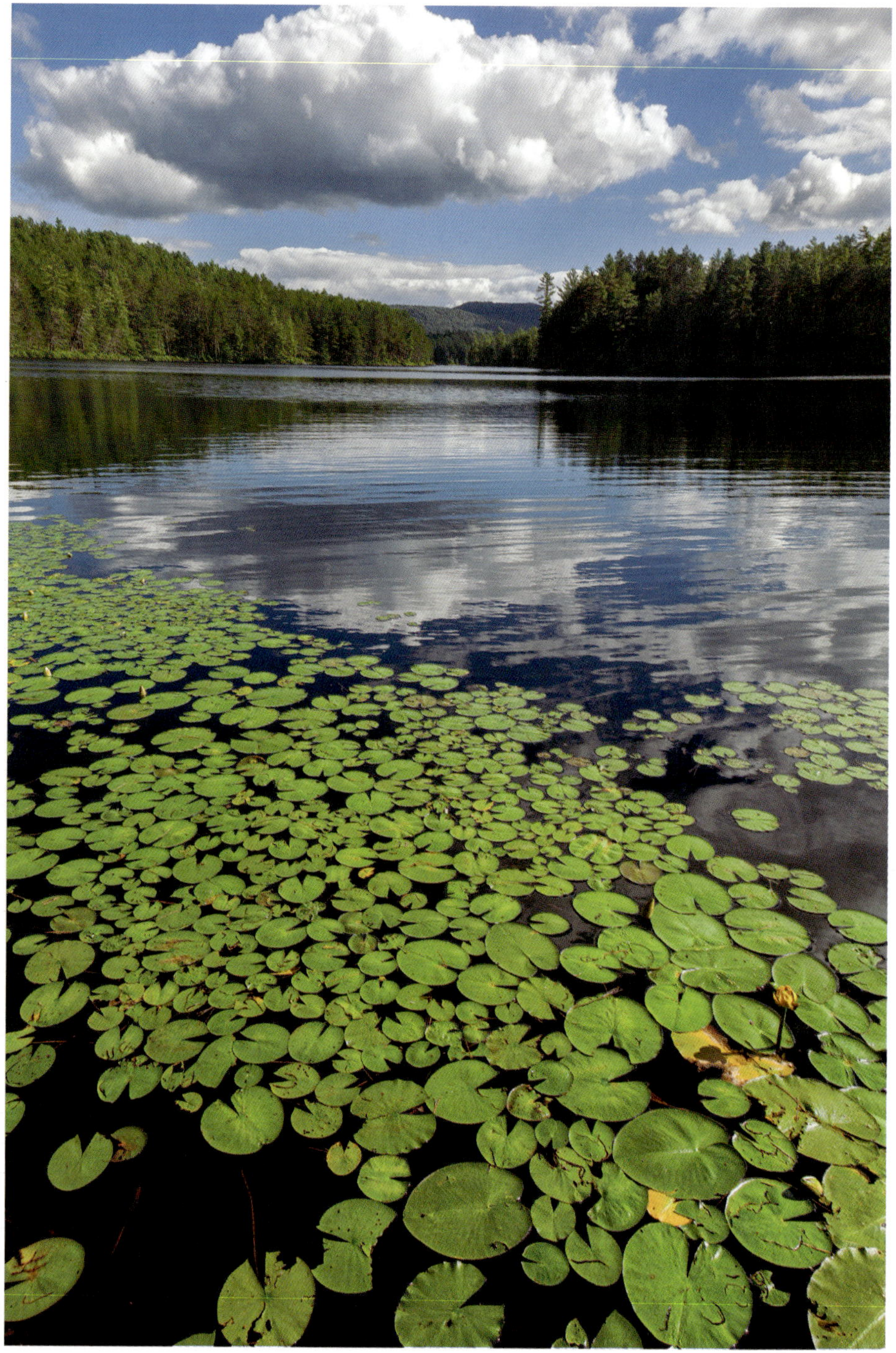

Water lilies and puffy clouds over an Adirondack lake near Malone.

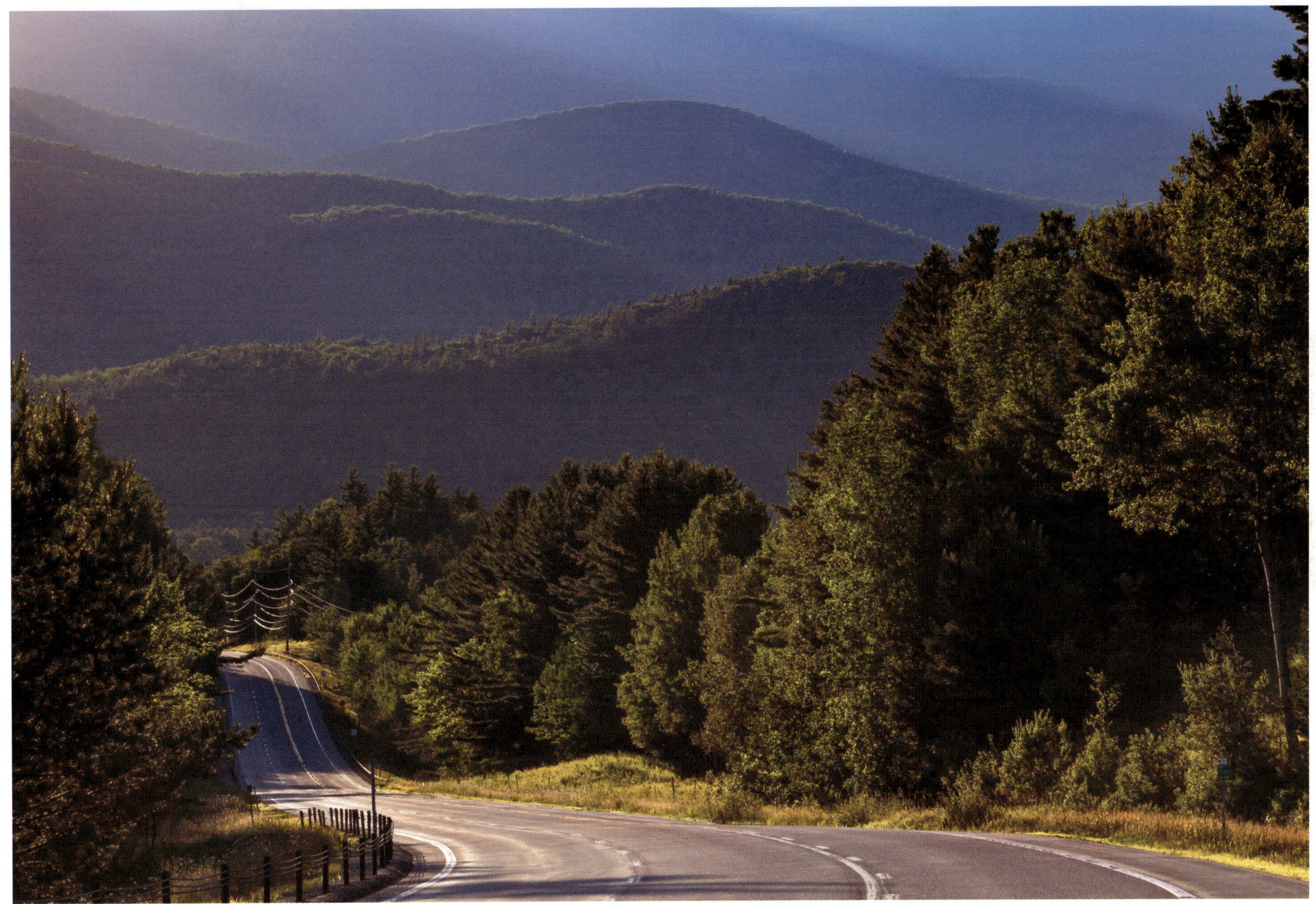

Route 9N as it winds down into the Keene Valley near Elizabethtown.

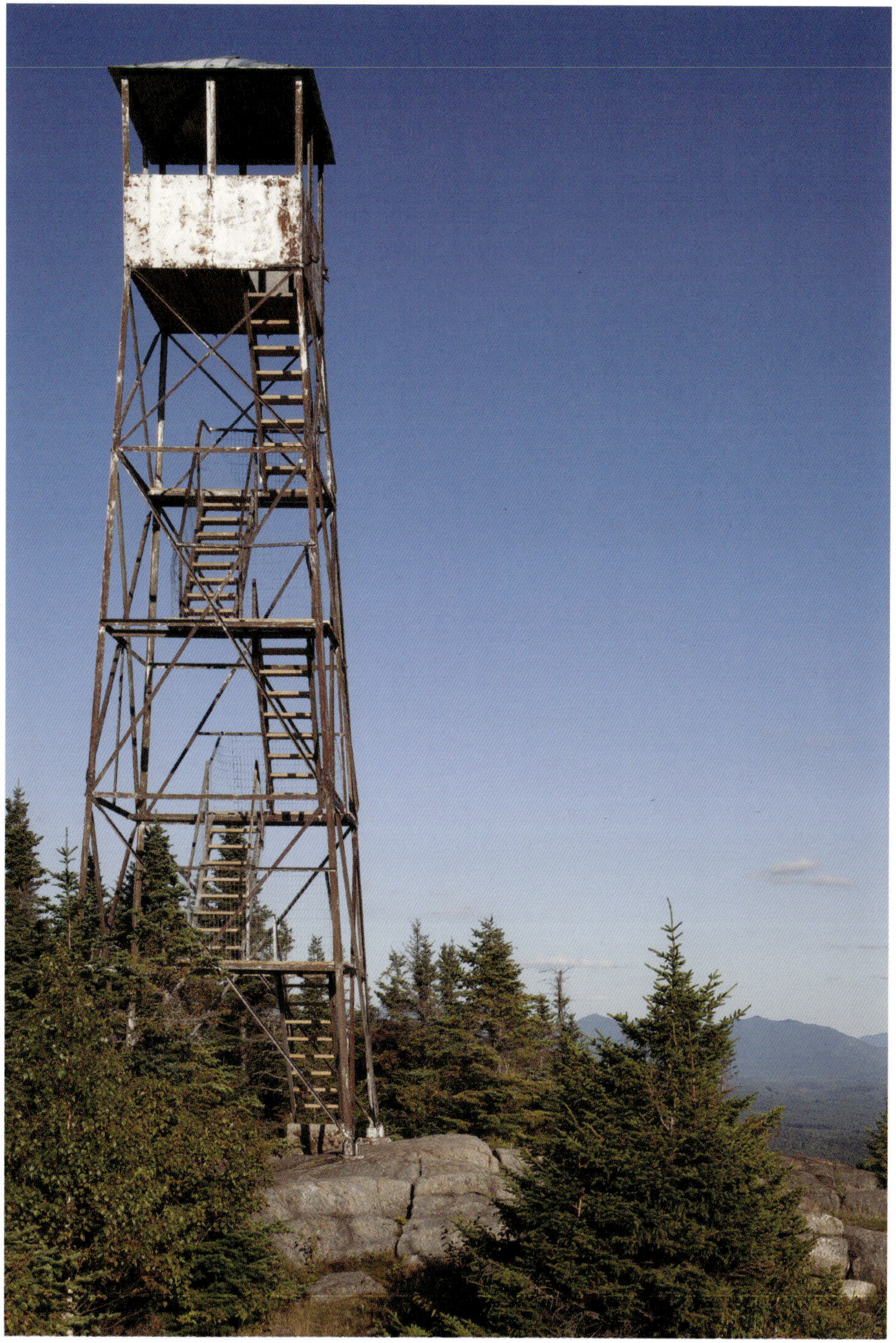

Fire tower on Hurricane Mountain.

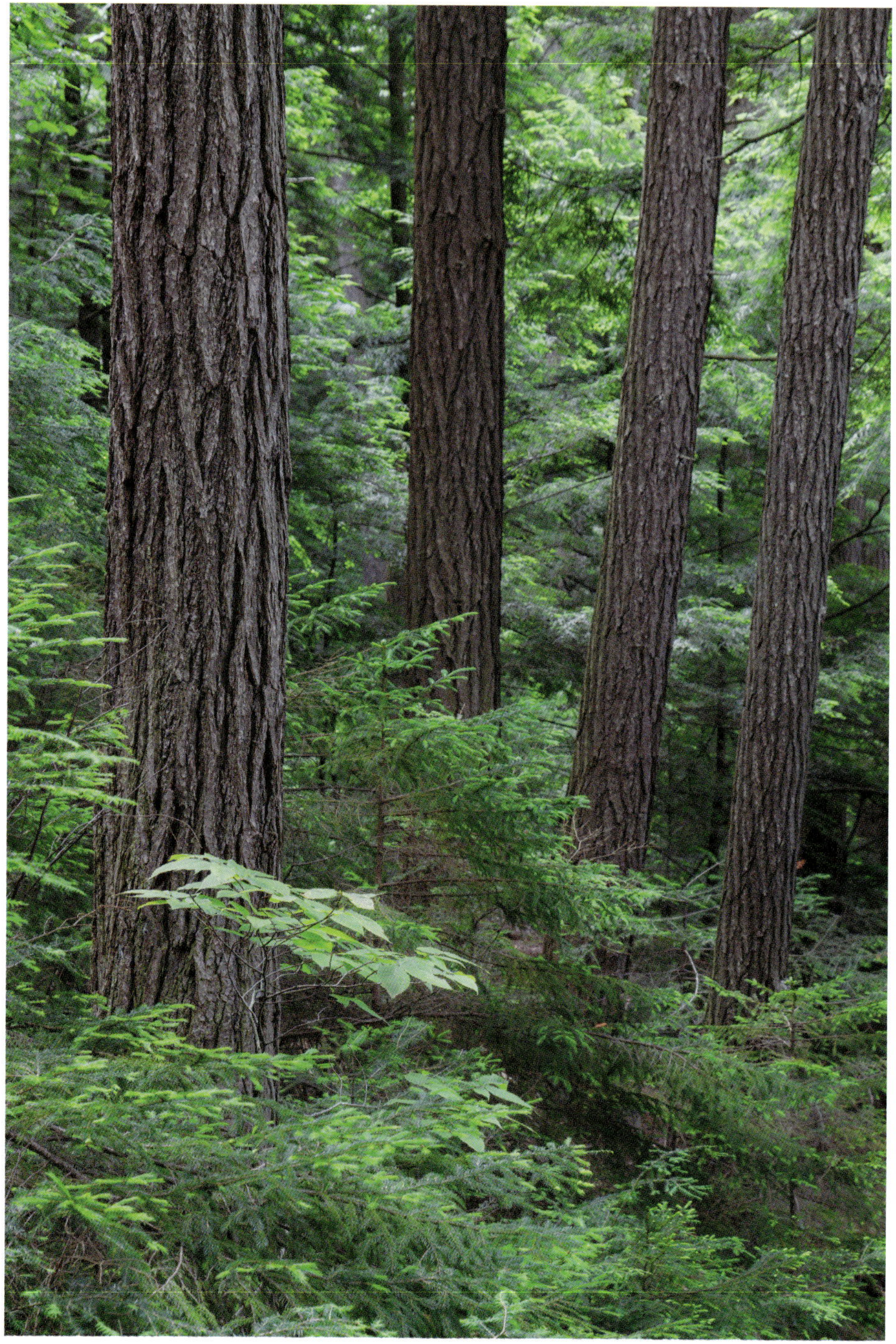

Four old friends near Upper Saranac Lake.

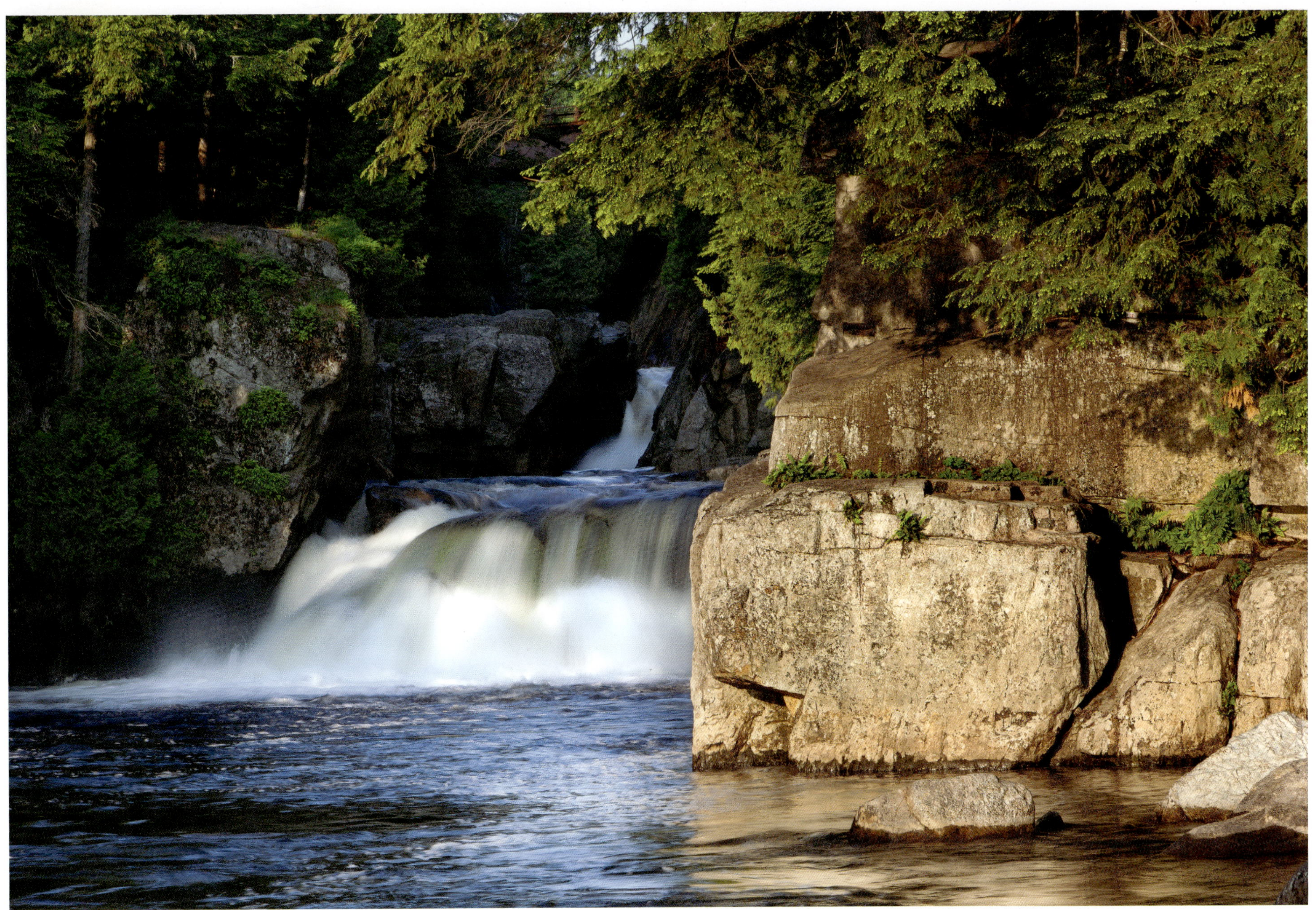

This section of the Ausable River, as it runs through a narrow gorge, is called "The Flume." During spring runoff the water flow is powerful.

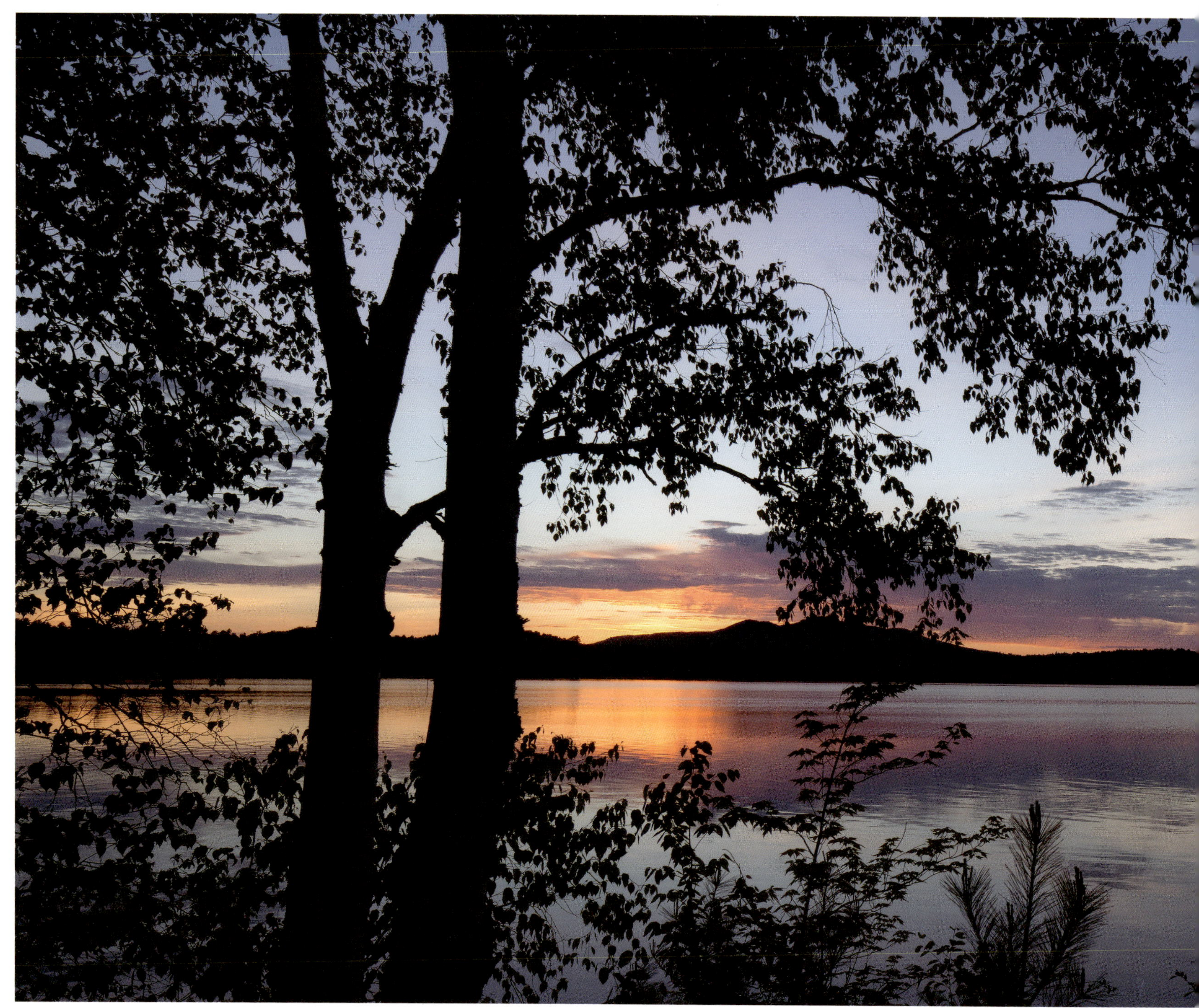

Saint Regis Mountain at sunset with Lake Clear in the foreground.

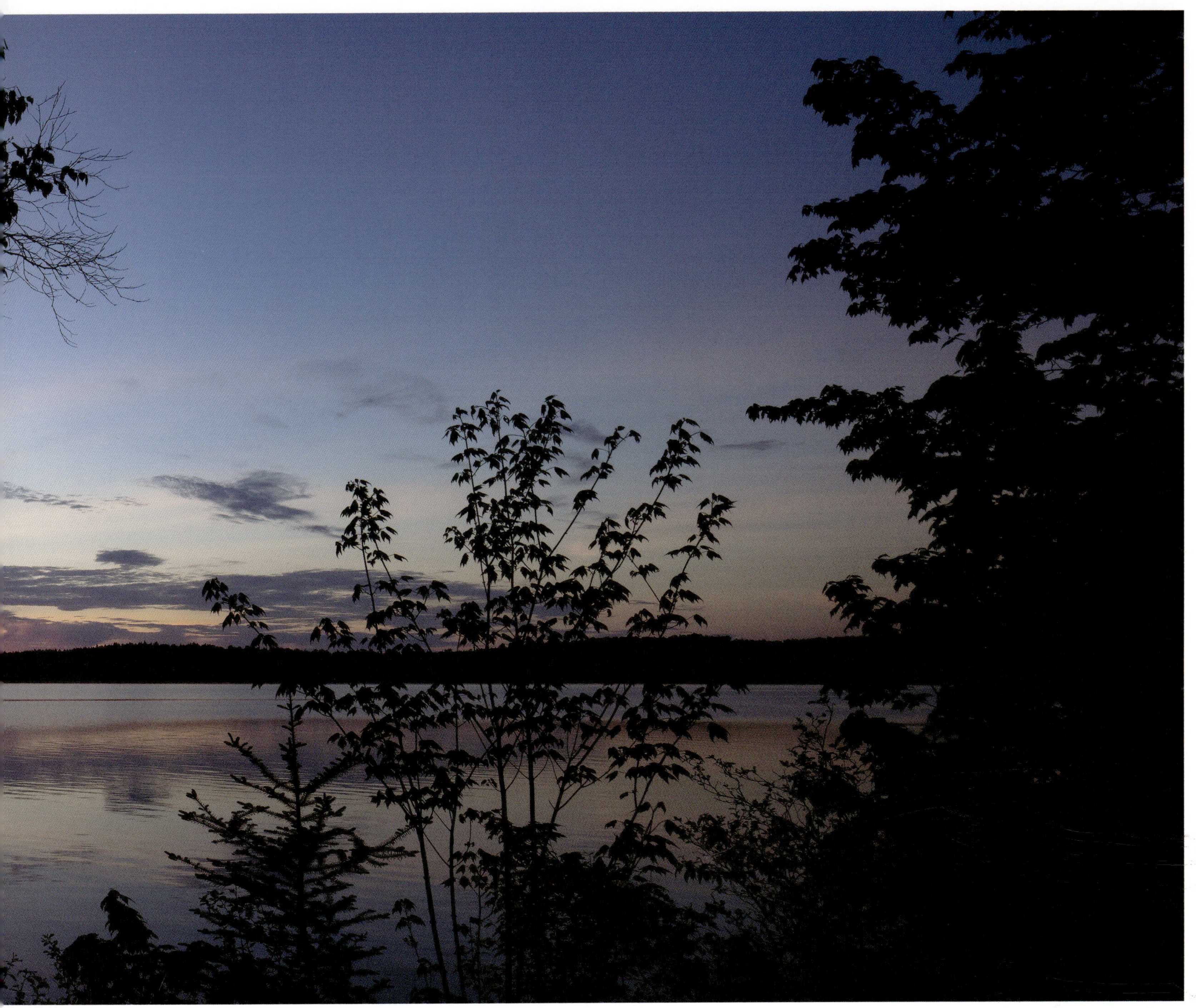

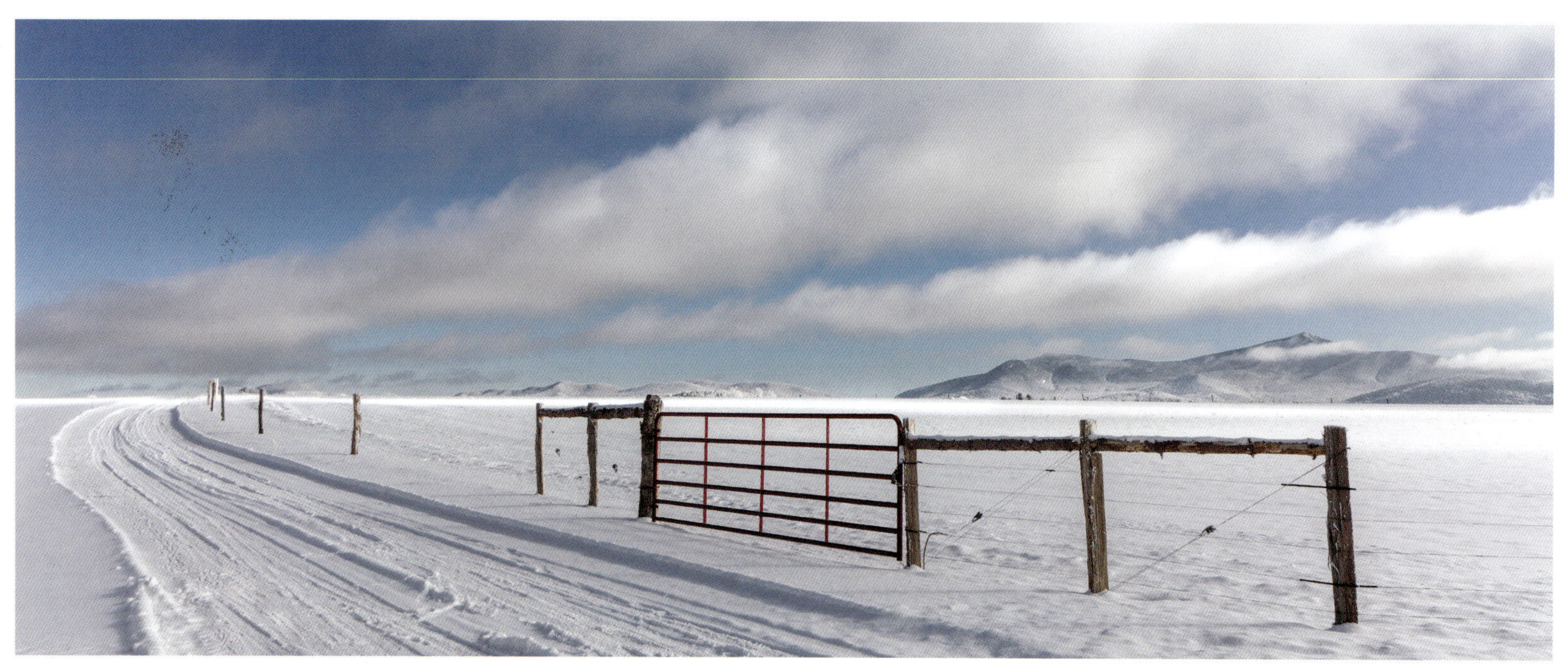

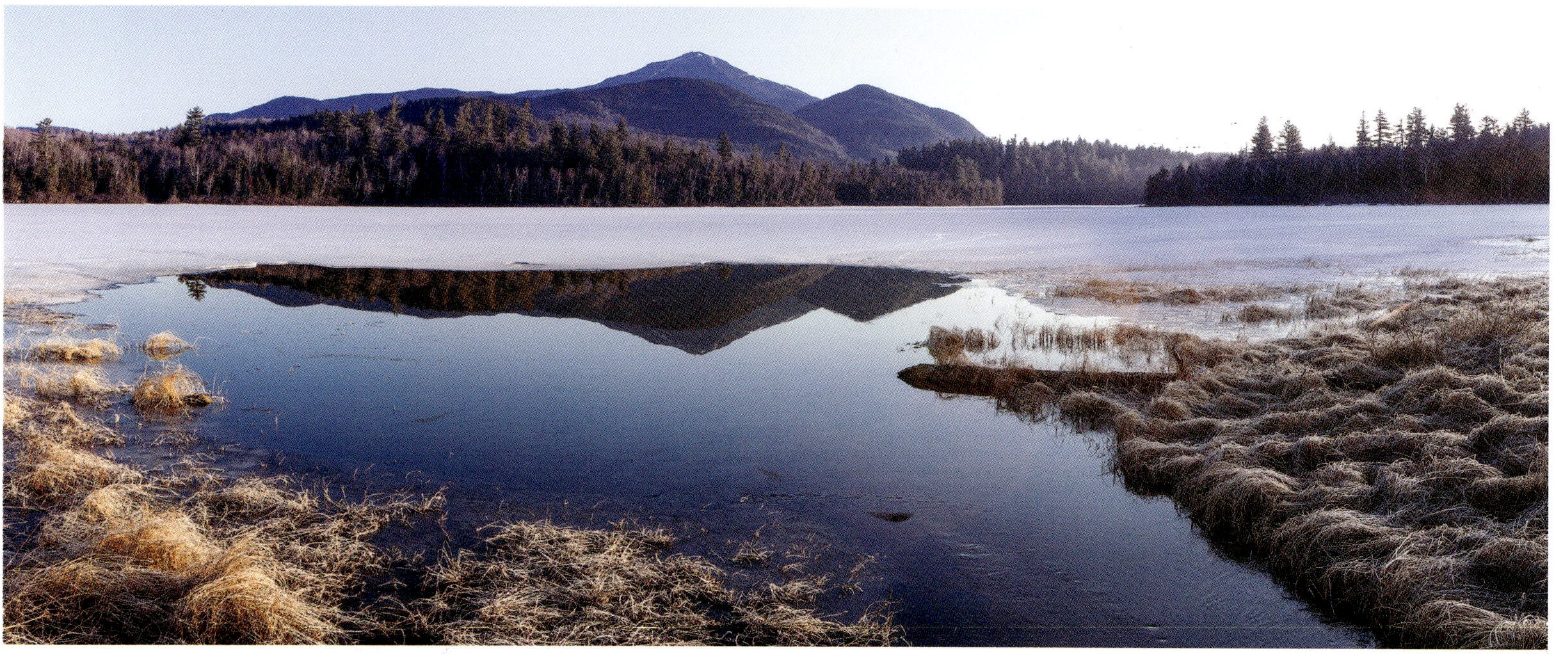

Top: A working farm on a high plateau with Whiteface Mountain on the horizon.
Bottom: Ice-out on Connery Pond.

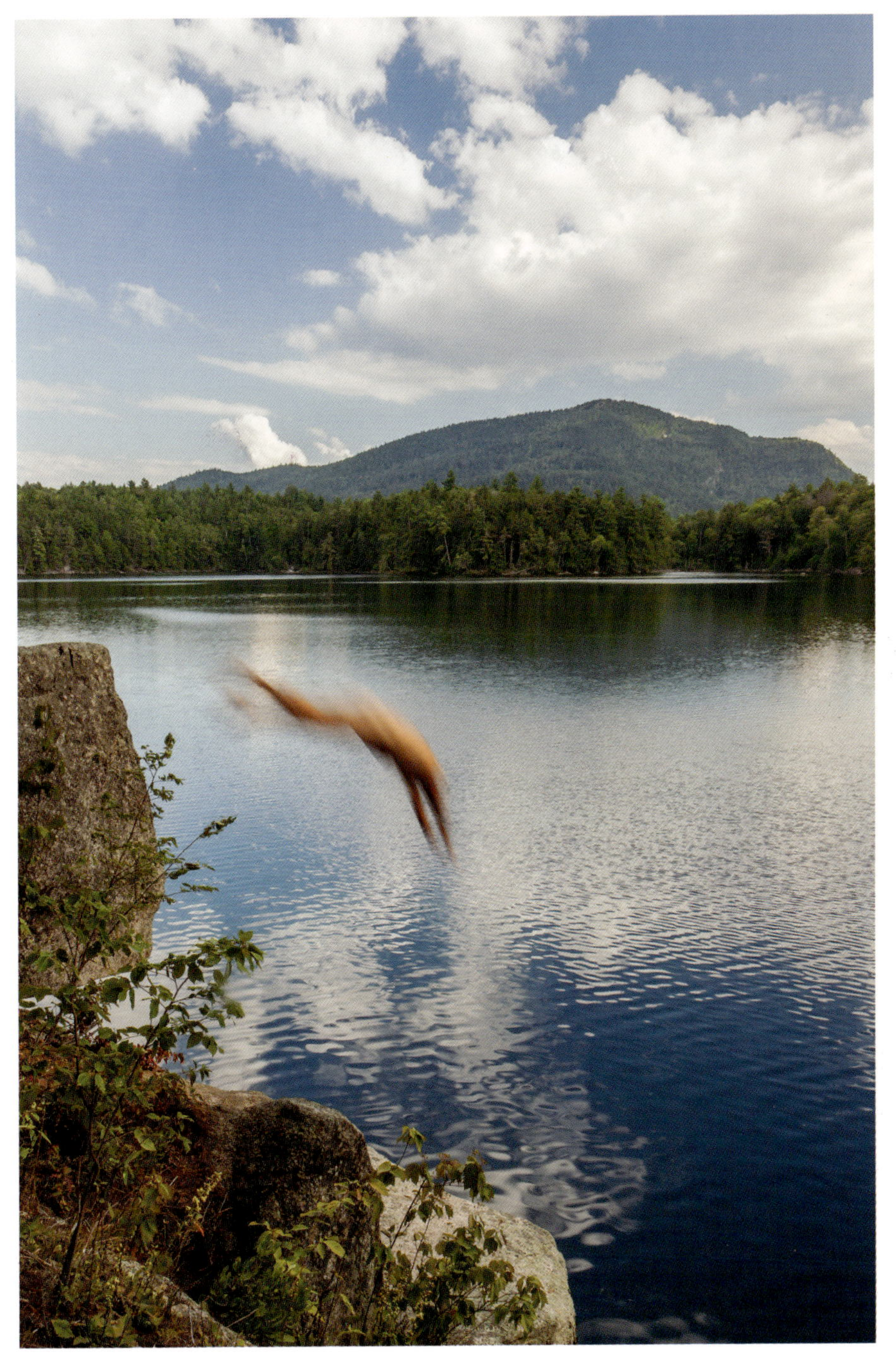

Skinny-dipping in the deep, clear waters of the Pharaoh Lake Wilderness.
There is nothing like an Adirondack lake on a hot summer day.

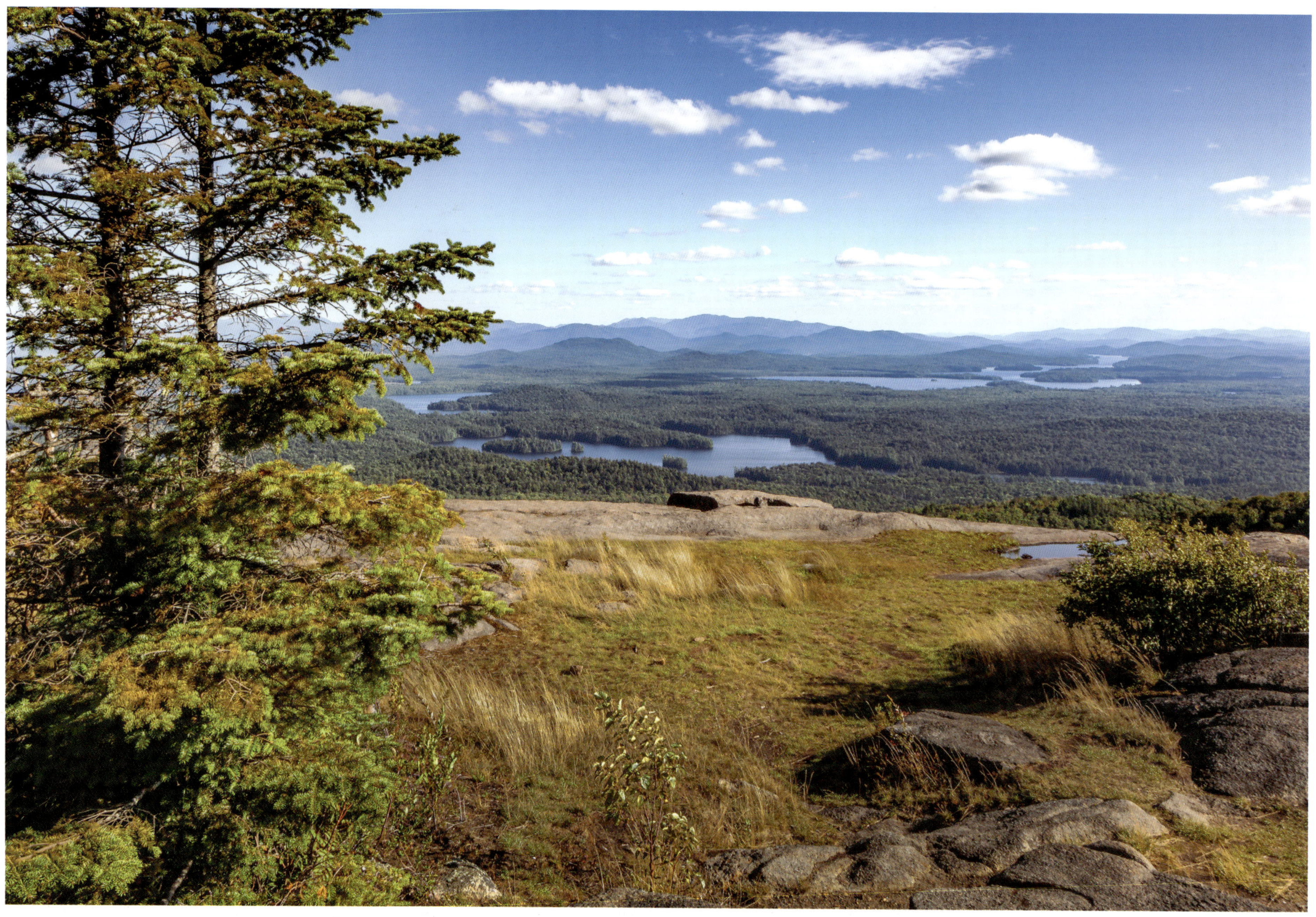

The Saint Regis Canoe Area as seen from Saint Regis Mountain.

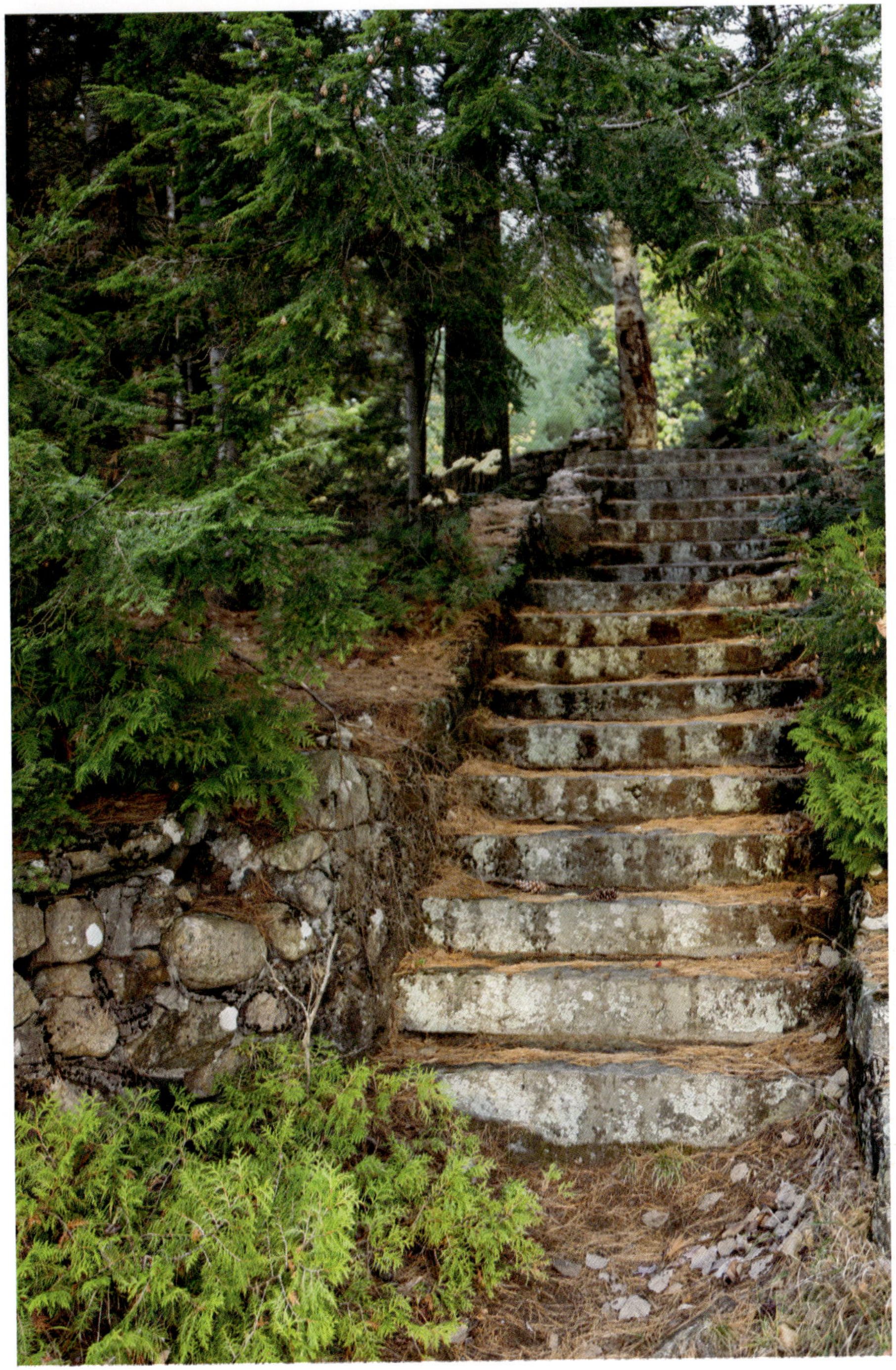

Old stone stairs to an abandoned foundation on Long Lake.

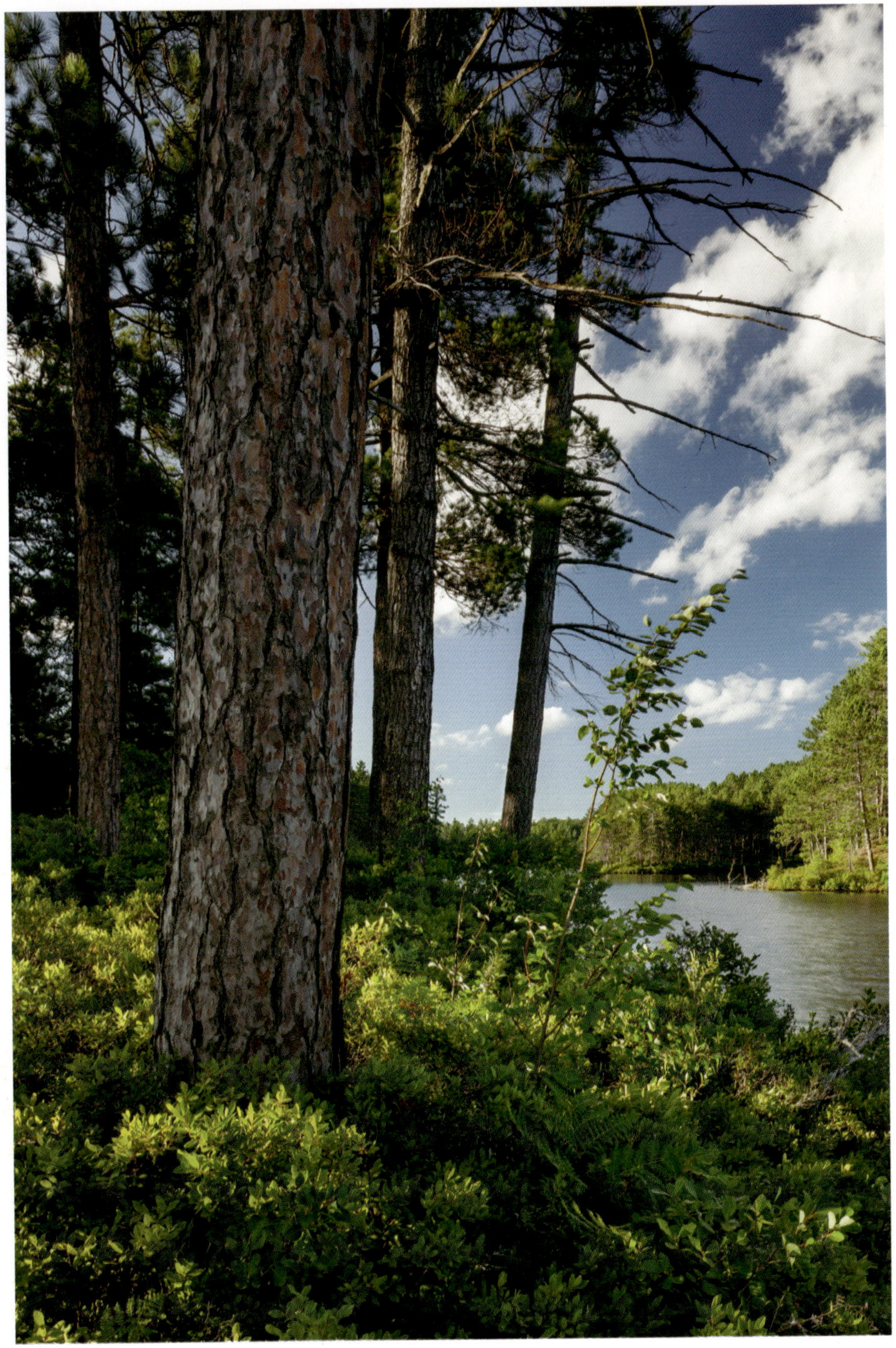

Looking back from a small point of land on a friend's property near Paul Smith's College. This property has been in the same family for five generations.

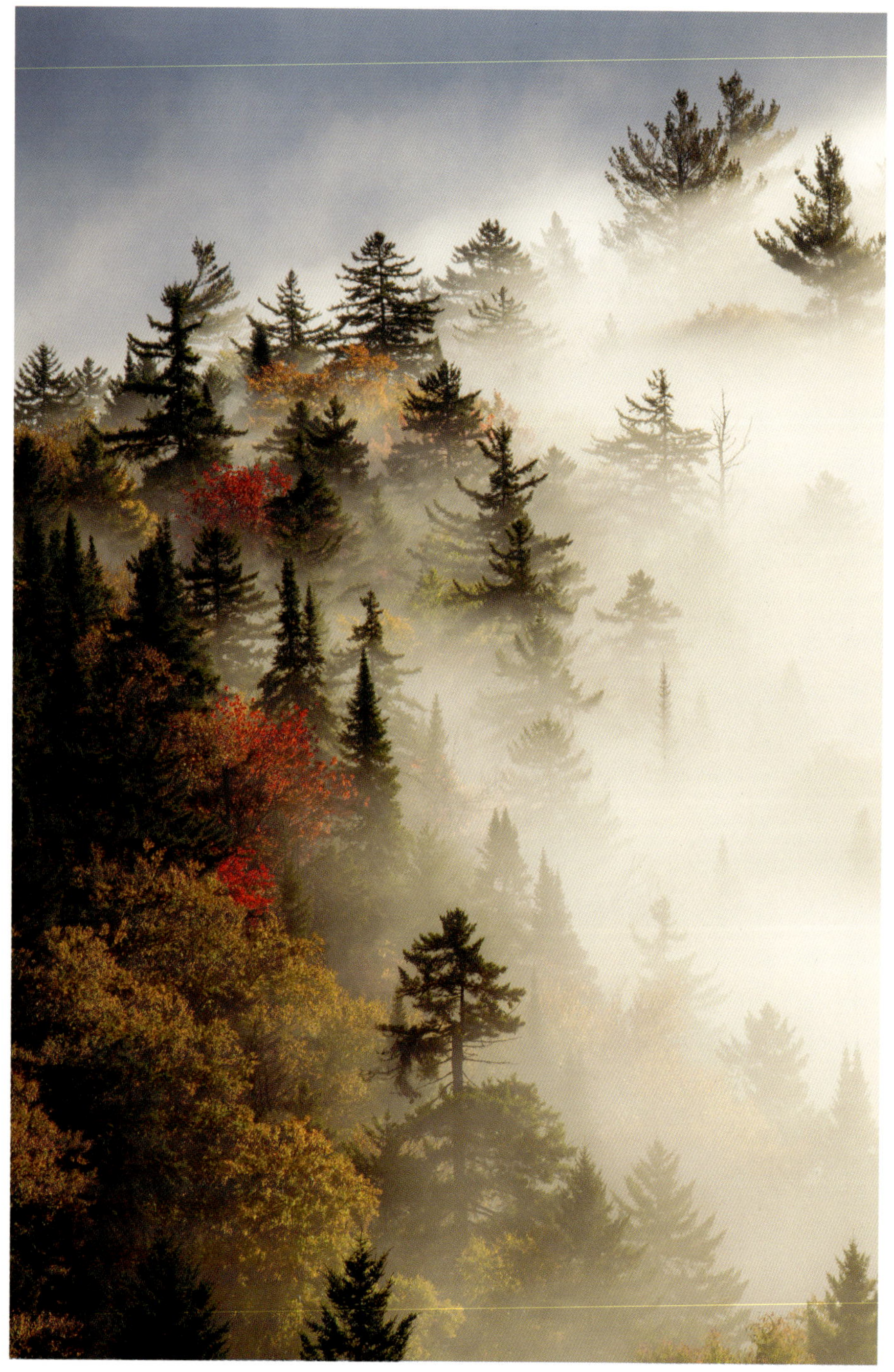

Trees in the fog on Goodnow Mountain.

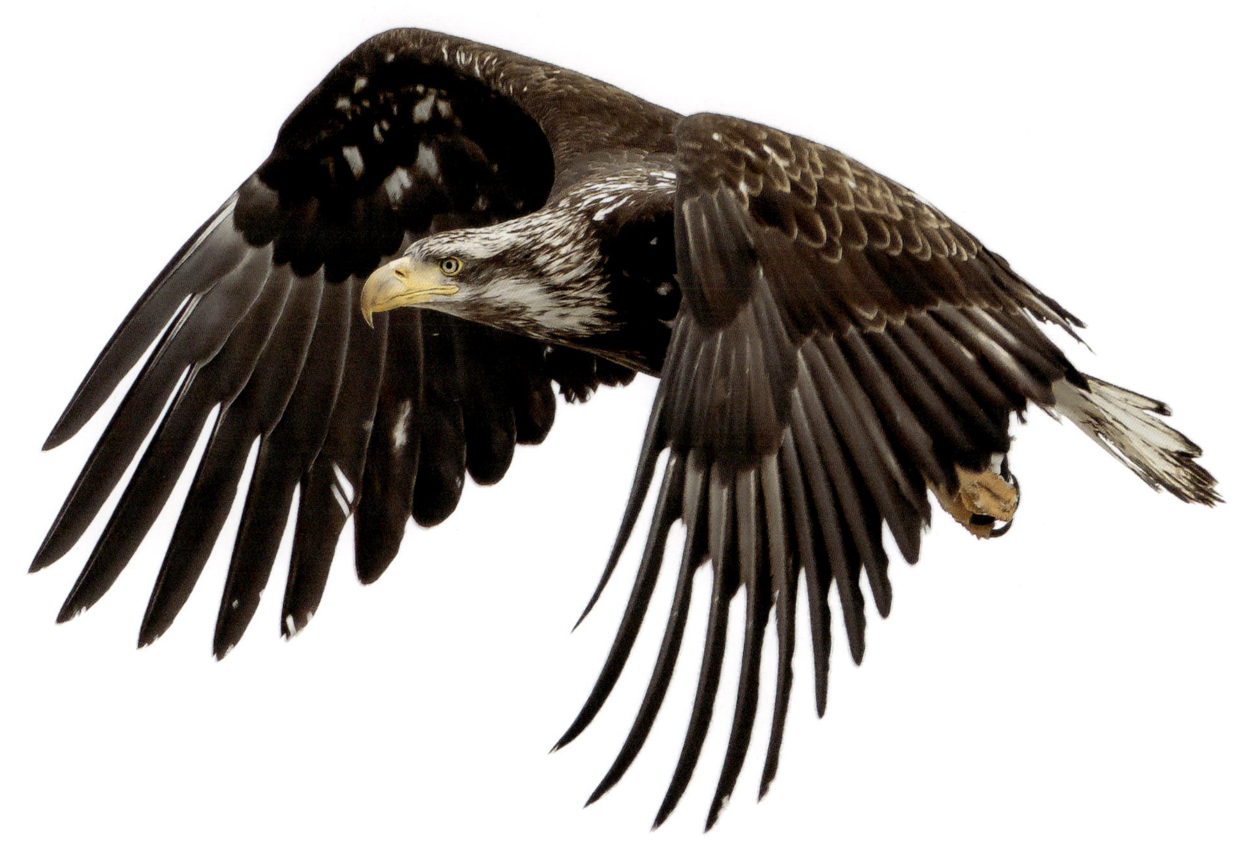

Juvenile bald eagle in flight at Ausable Point.

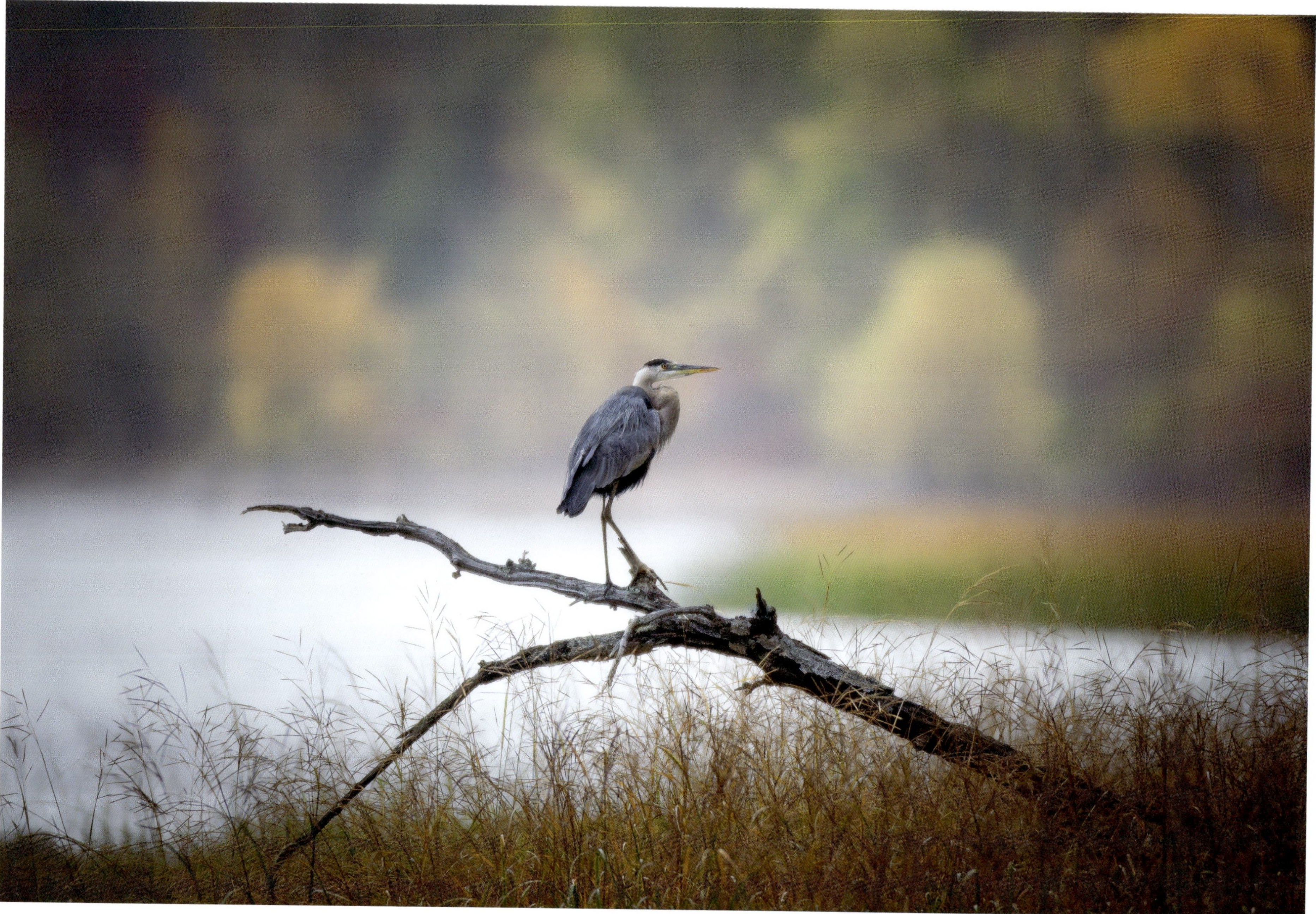

Great blue heron on a fallen tree at Ausable Point.

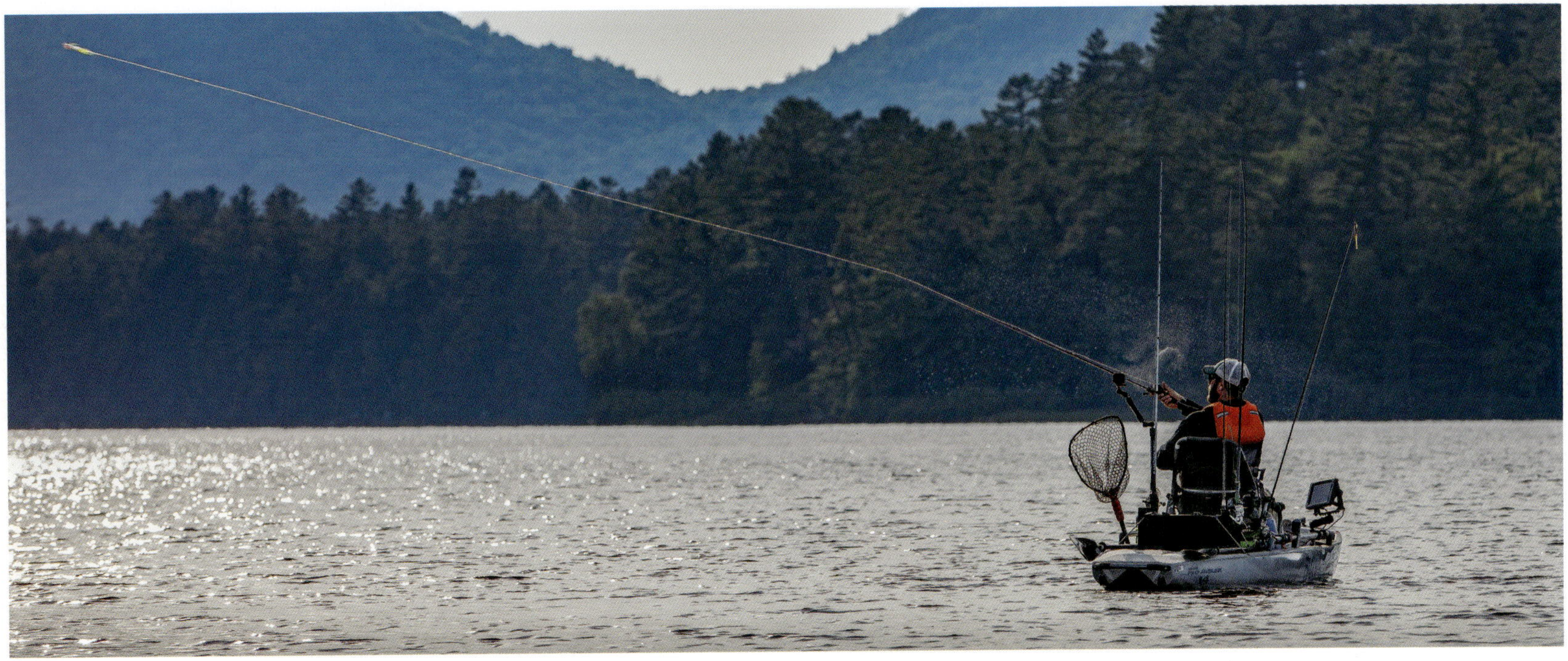

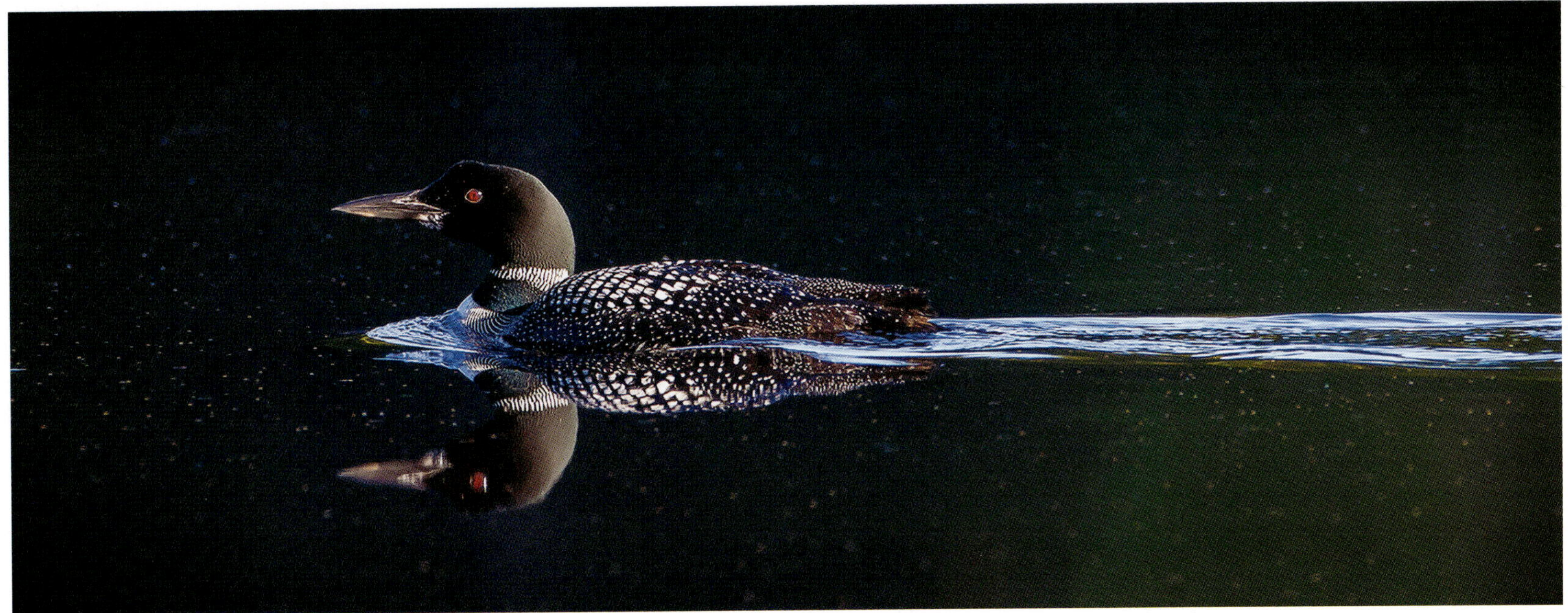

Top: Casting for bass on Osgood Pond near White Pine Camp.
Bottom: Loon cruising across an Adirondack lake.

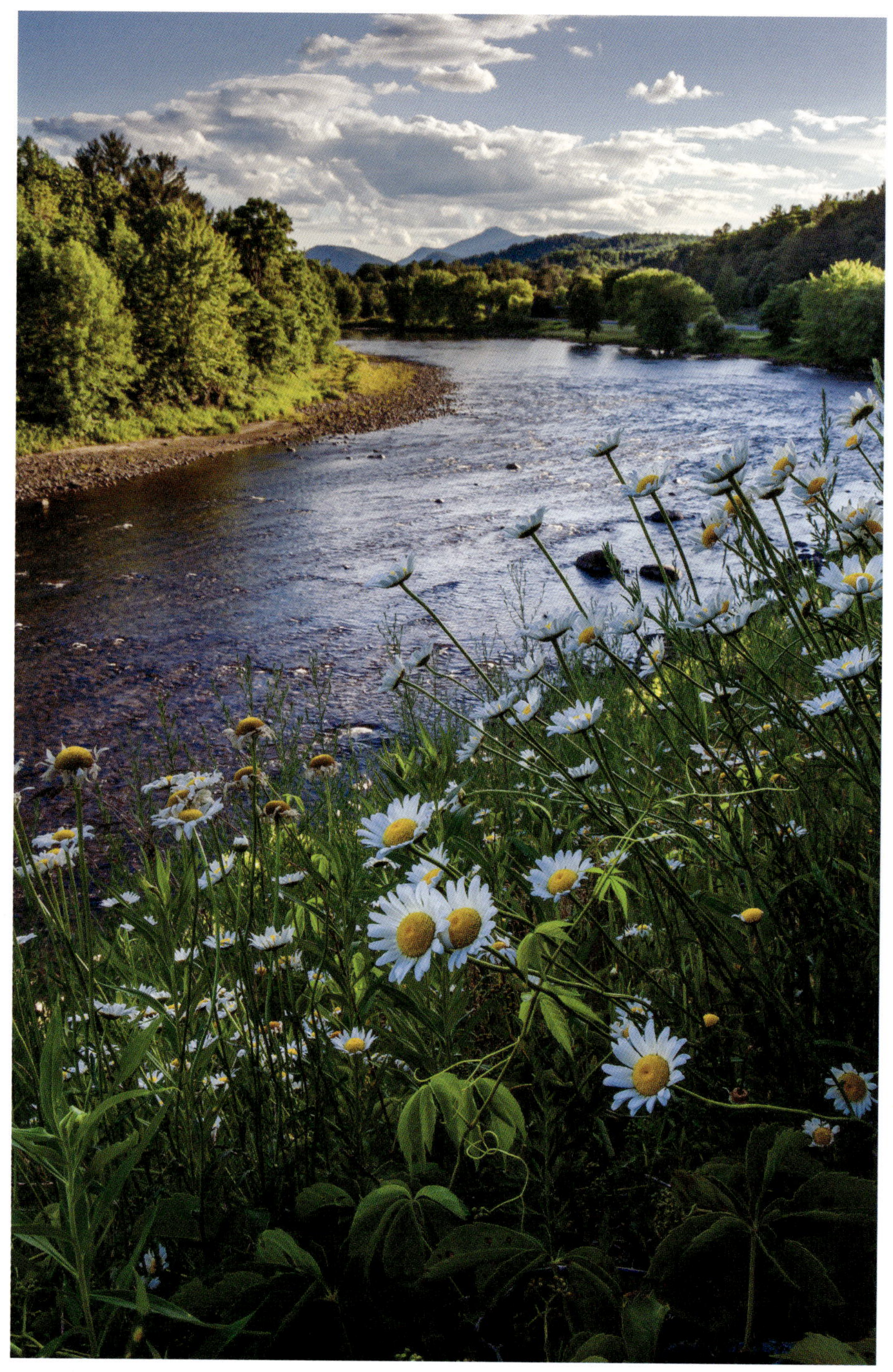

Daisies in bloom along the West Branch of the Ausable River near Ausable Forks.

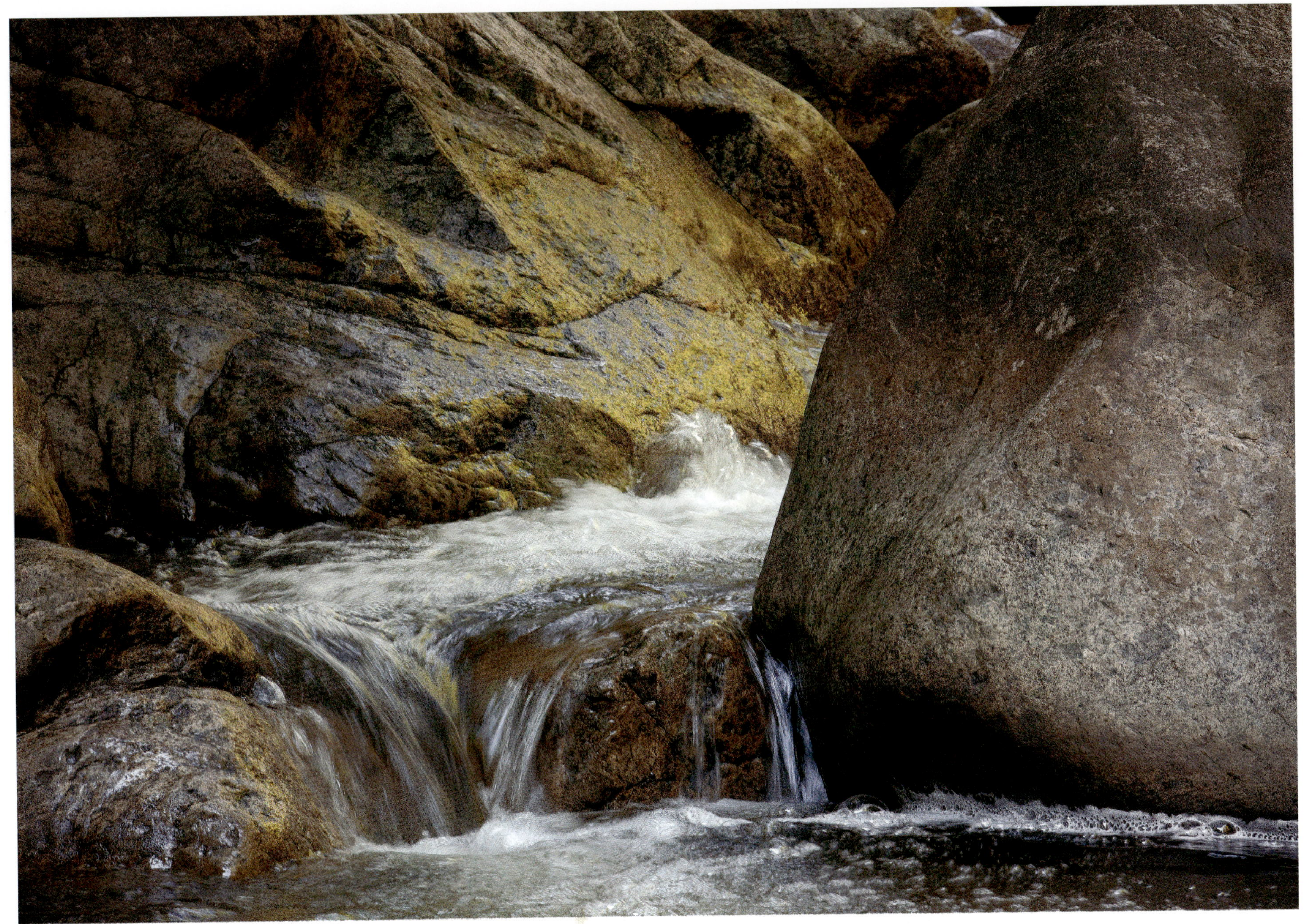

A stream babbles over glacial rocks to form a swimming hole on the trail to Little Porter Mountain.

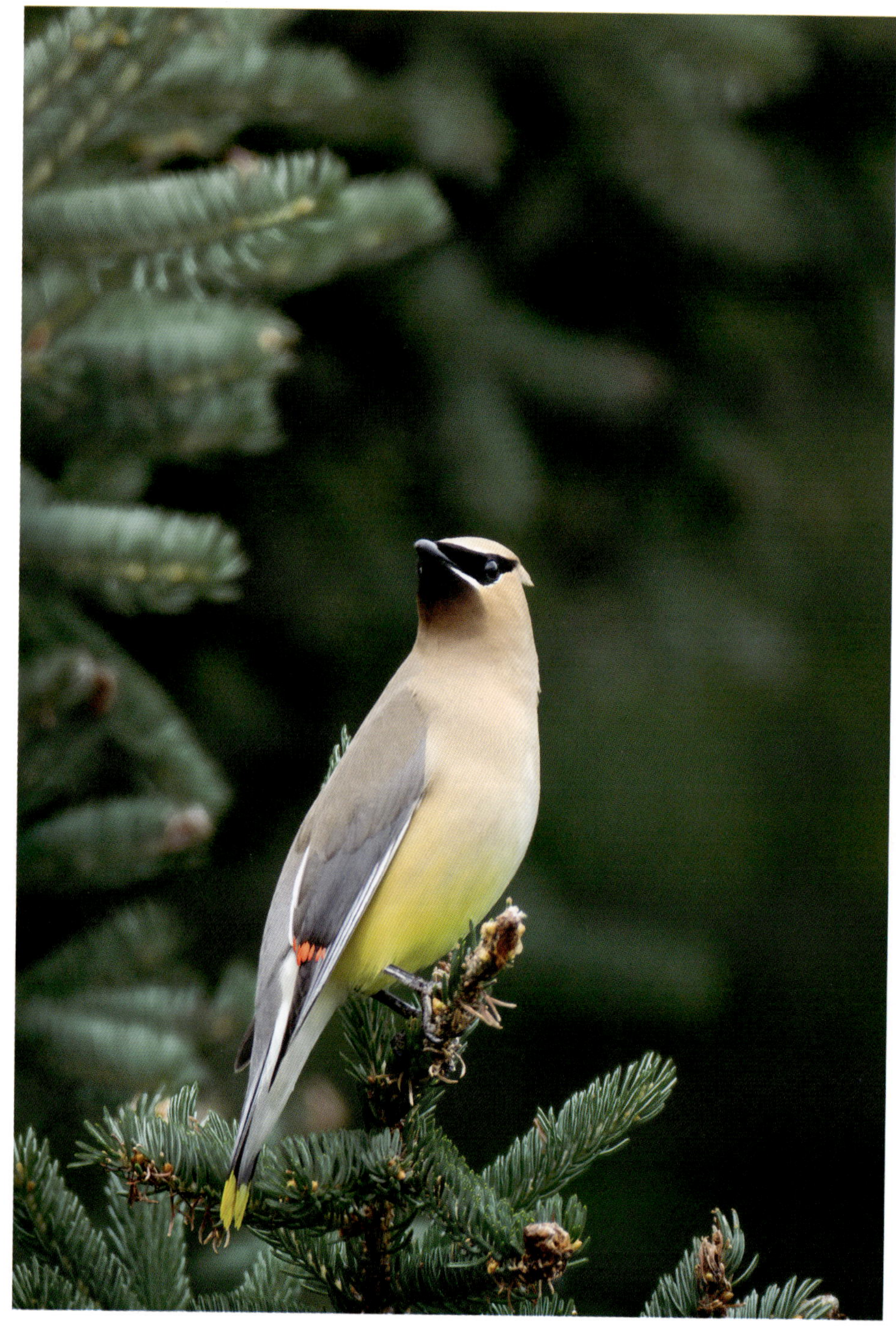

Cedar waxwing striking a pose.

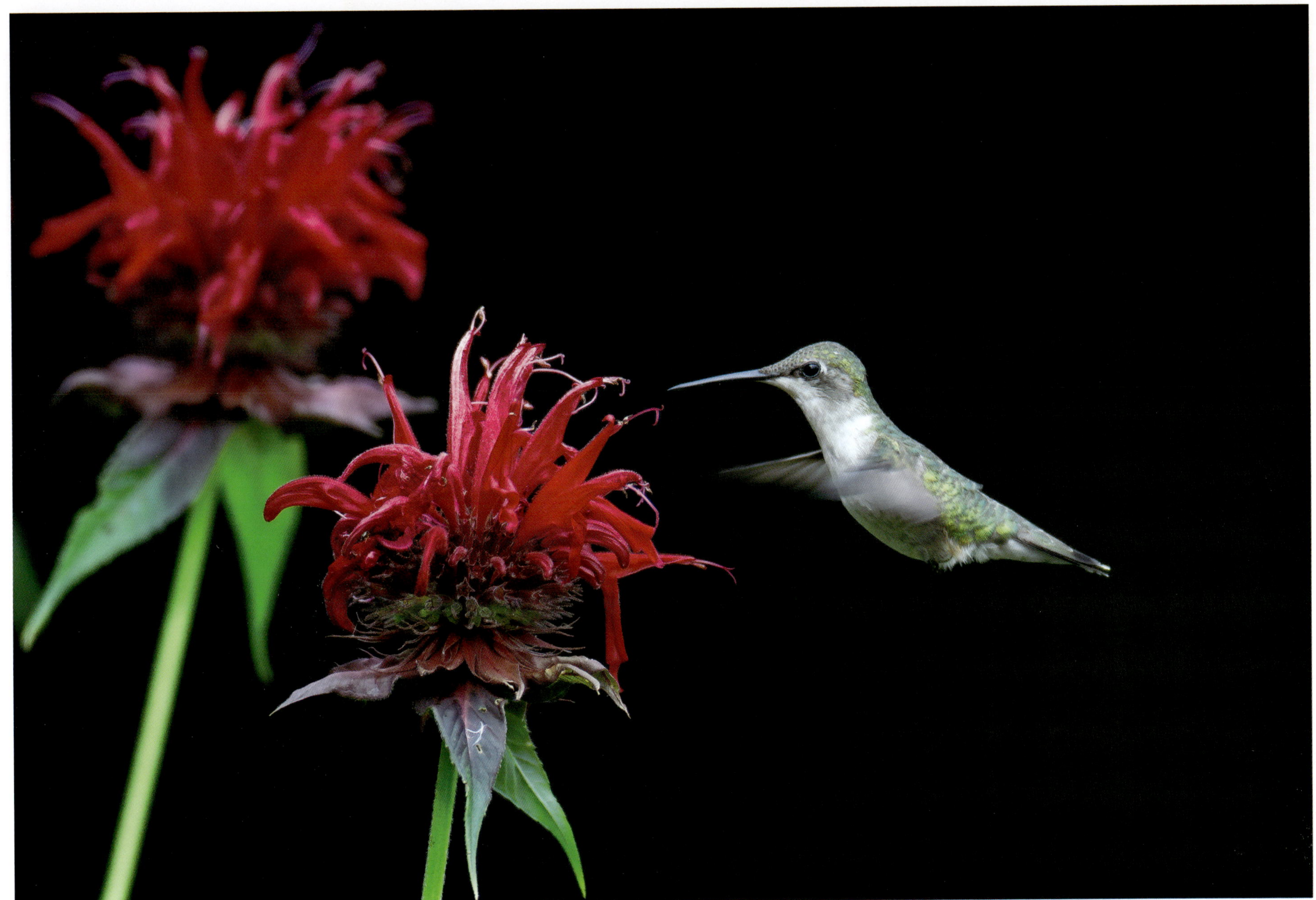

Female ruby-throated hummingbird and monarda.

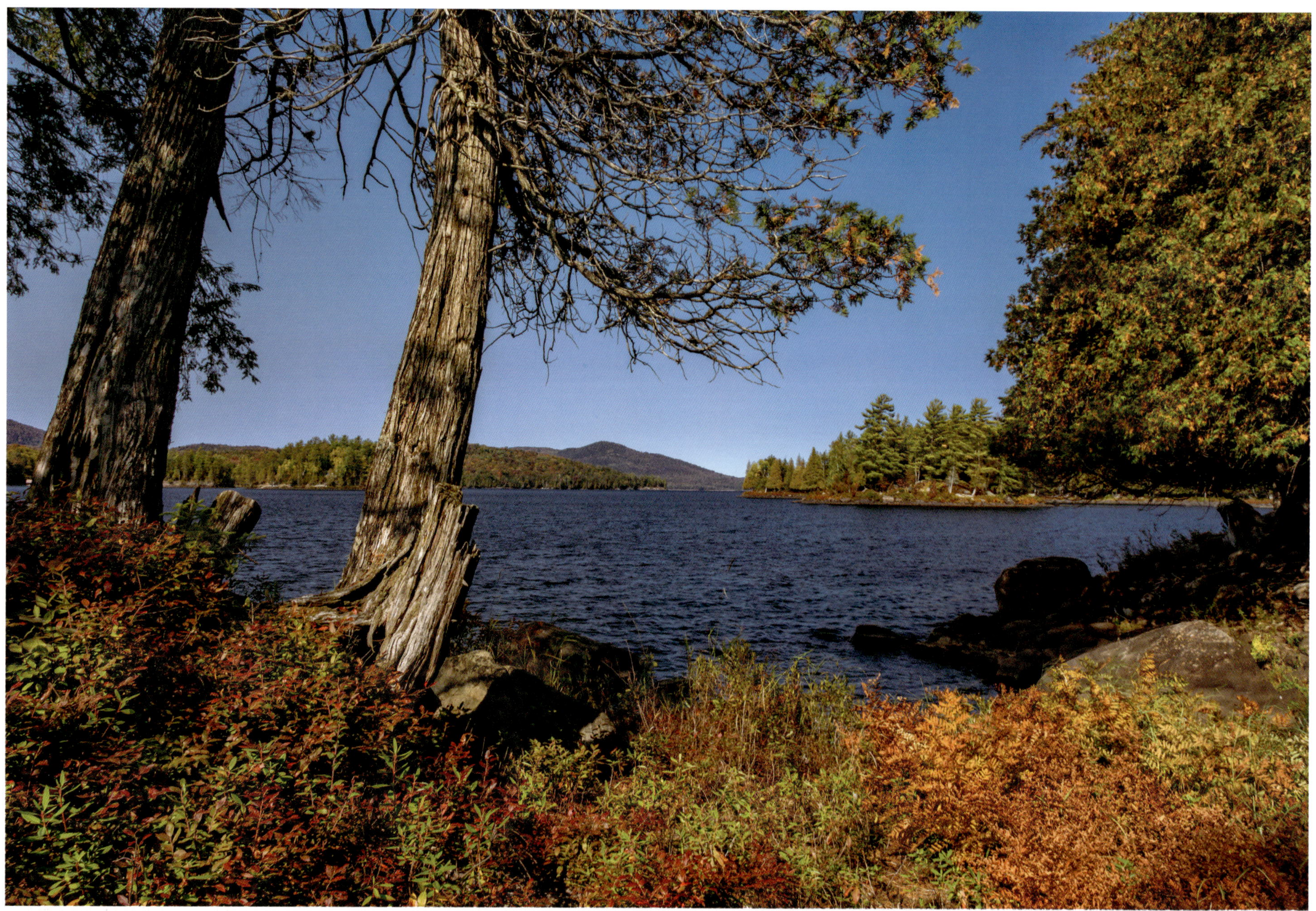

Shore scene along Long Lake.

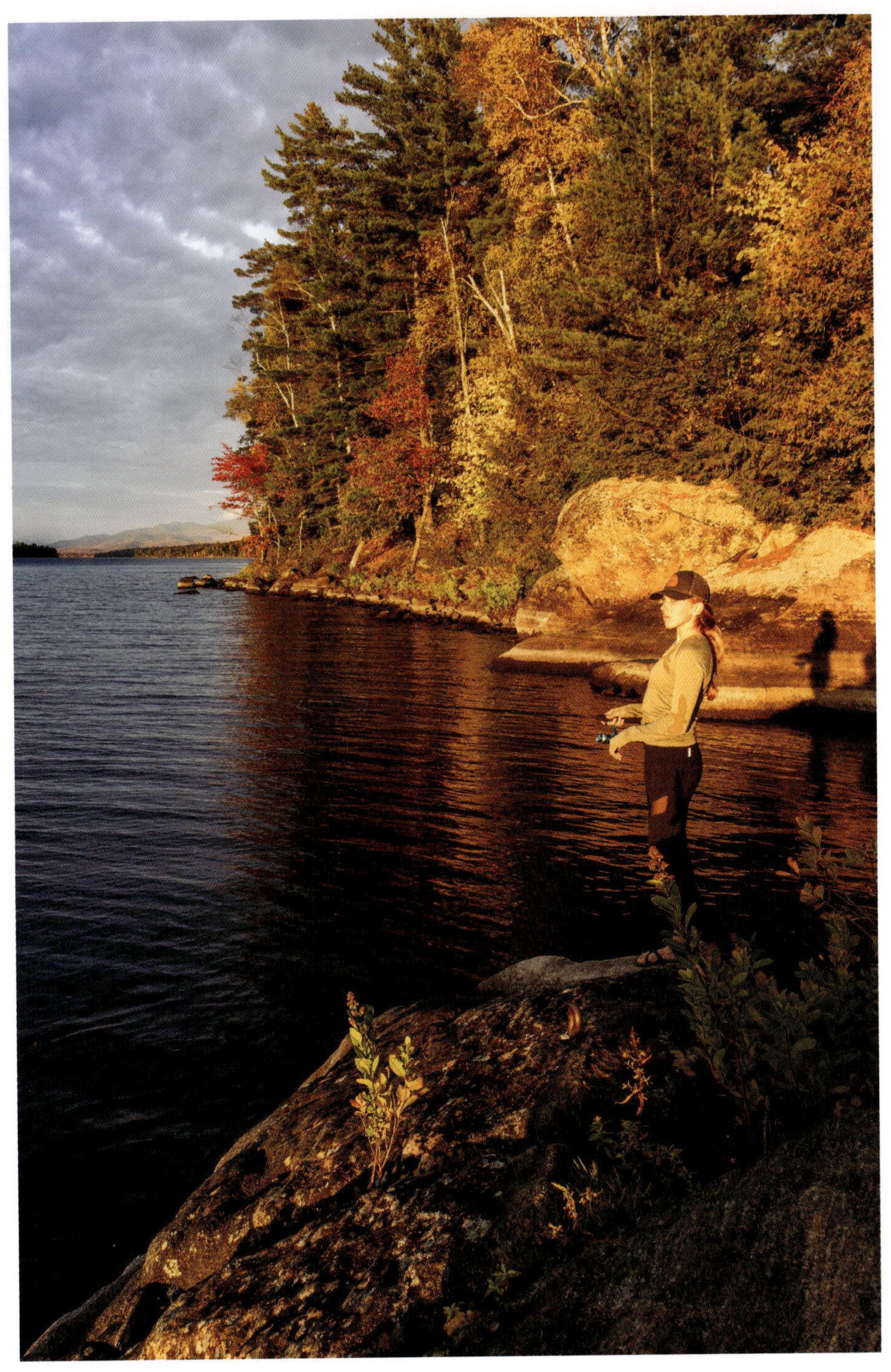
Fishing under the last golden rays before sunset on Long Lake.

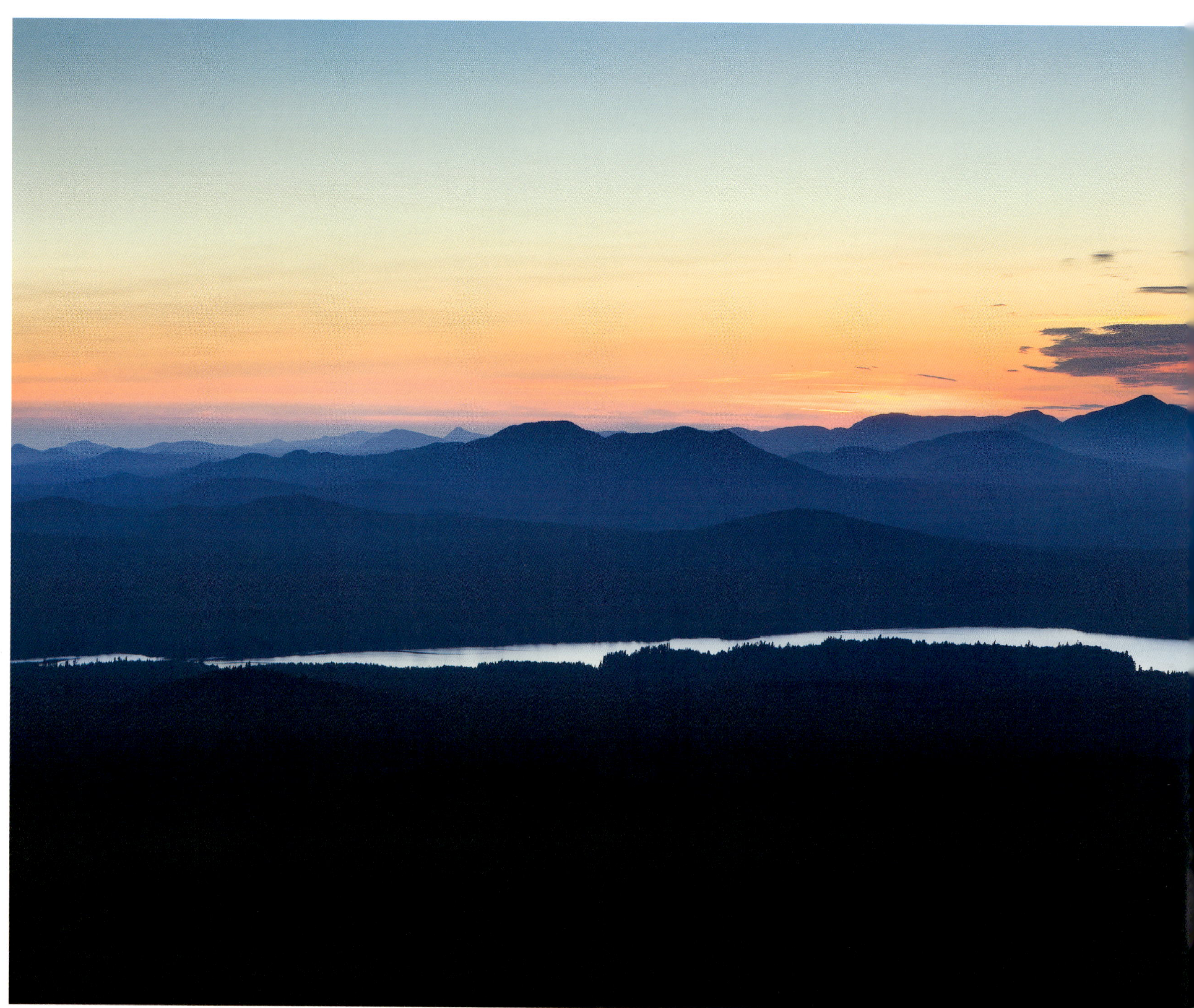

Sunrise from the top of Catamount Mountain looking west over Union Falls Pond.

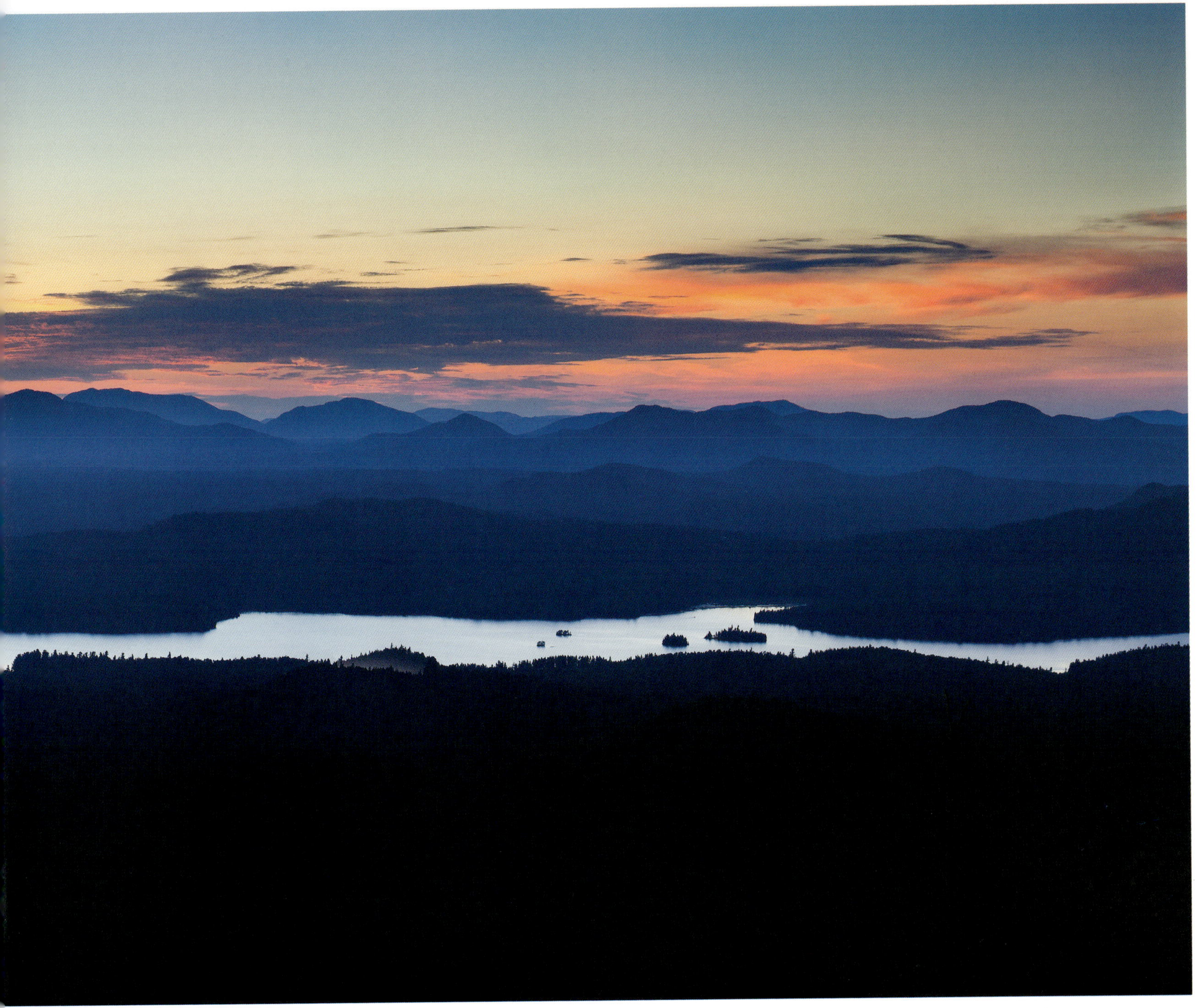